The Harlem Renaissance (1918–37) was the most influential single movement in African American literary history. Its key figures include W. E. B. Du Bois, Nella Larsen, Zora Neale Hurston, Claude McKay, and Langston Hughes. The movement laid the groundwork for all later African American literature, and had an enormous impact on later black literature worldwide. With chapters by a wide range of well-known scholars, this Companion is an authoritative and engaging guide to the movement. It first discusses the historical contexts of the Harlem Renaissance, both national and international; then presents original discussions of a wide array of authors and texts; and finally treats the reputation of the movement in later years. Giving full play to the disagreements and differences that energized the renaissance, this Companion presents the best of current wisdom as well as a set of new readings encouraging further exploration of this dynamic field.

GEORGE HUTCHINSON is Chairman of the Department of English and Booth Tarkington Professor of Literary Studies at Indiana University, Bloomington.

THE CAMBRIDGE COMPANION TO
THE HARLEM RENAISSANCE

EDITED BY
GEORGE HUTCHINSON
Indiana University

CAMBRIDGE
UNIVERSITY PRESS

CAMBRIDGE UNIVERSITY PRESS
Cambridge, New York, Melbourne, Madrid, Cape Town, Singapore, São Paulo

Cambridge University Press
The Edinburgh Building, Cambridge CB2 8RU, UK

Published in the United States of America by Cambridge University Press, New York

www.cambridge.org
Information on this title: www.cambridge.org/9780521673686

First published 2007

Printed in the United Kingdom at the University Press, Cambridge

A catalogue record for this publication is available from the British Library

Library of Congress Cataloguing in Publication data
The Cambridge companion to the Harlem Renaissance / edited by George Hutchinson.
p. cm.
Includes bibliographical references (p. 254) and index.
ISBN-13: 978-0-521-85699-7 (hardback)
ISBN-10: 0-521-85699-X (hardback)
ISBN-13: 978-0-521-67368-6 (pbk)
ISBN-10: 0-521-67368-2 (pbk)
1. American literature – African American authors – History and criticism. 2. American
literature – 20th century – History and criticism. 3. Harlem (New York, N.Y.) – Intellectual
life – 20th century. 4. Modernism (Literature) – United States. 5. African Americans in
literature. 6. African American aesthetics. 7. Harlem Renaissance. I. Hutchinson,
George, 1953 – II. Title: Companion to the Harlem Renaissance.
PS 153.N5C345 2007
810.9'896073–dc22   2006039244

ISBN 978-0-521-85699-7 hardback
ISBN 978-0-521-67368-6 paperback

CONTENTS

NOTES ON CONTRIBUTORS

EMILY BERNARD is Associate Professor of English and ALANA US Ethnic Studies at the University of Vermont. She has edited two books. *Remember Me to Harlem: The Letters of Langston Hughes and Carl Van Vechten* (Knopf, 2001) was a *New York Times* Notable Book of the Year. *Some of My Best Friends: Writers on Interracial Friendship* (Amistad, 2004) was chosen by the New York Public Library as a Book for the Teen Age, 2006. Her essays have been published in several anthologies and journals, such as *American Scholar, Modernism/Modernity*, and *Studies in American Fiction*. Bernard has received fellowships from the Ford Foundation and the National Endowment for the Humanities, and was a Resident Fellow at the W. E. B. Du Bois Institute at Harvard University. She is currently at work on a book about interracial dynamics during the Harlem Renaissance.

MICHAEL A. CHANEY is an Assistant Professor of English at Dartmouth College. He is the author of *Fugitive Vision: Between Image and Word in the Antebellum Slave Narrative*, forthcoming from Indiana University Press.

MARGO NATALIE CRAWFORD is an Assistant Professor of African American Literature and Culture in the Department of English at Indiana University-Bloomington. She is the coeditor, with Lisa Gail Collins, of *New Thoughts on the Black Arts Movement* (Rutgers University Press, 2006). She is the author of *Rewriting Blackness: Beyond Authenticity and Hybridity* (Ohio State University Press, forthcoming).

J. MARTIN FAVOR is Associate Professor of English and Chair of the African and African American Studies Program at Dartmouth College. He is the author of *Authentic Blackness: The Folk in the New Negro Renaissance* (Duke University Press, 1999).

GEORGE HUTCHINSON is Booth Tarkington Professor of Literary Studies and Chairman of the Department of English at Indiana University, Bloomington. He is the author of *The Ecstatic Whitman: Literary Shamanism and the Crisis of the Union* (Ohio State University Press, 1986), *The Harlem Renaissance in Black and White* (Belknap/Harvard University Press, 1995), and *In Search of Nella Larsen: A Biography of the Color Line* (Belknap/Harvard University Press, 2006).

LAWRENCE JACKSON is Associate Professor of English and African American Studies at Emory University. Professor Jackson earned his PhD at Stanford University and he has held fellowships from the National Humanities Center, the W. E. B. Du Bois Institute, the National Endowment for the Humanities, and the Ford Foundation. In 2002 he published a biography of Ralph Ellison called *Ralph Ellison: Emergence of Genius* (Wiley). His work has appeared in *American Literature*, *American Literary History*, *Southern Literature*, *African American Review*, and *Massachusetts Review*.

CARLA KAPLAN is the Davis Distinguished Professor of American Literature at Northeastern University. She has published five books, including, most recently, *Zora Neale Hurston: A Life in Letters* (Doubleday, 2002), which was a finalist for the NAACP Image Award and was listed as a notable book and best book of the year by *The New York Times* and *New York* magazine, and a Norton Critical edition of Nella Larsen's *Passing* which is forthcoming in 2007. Her next book, *Miss Anne in Harlem: The White Women of the Black Renaissance*, will be published by HarperCollins. Kaplan is the recipient of grants and fellowships from the NEH, the Schomburg Center for Research in Black Culture, the New York Public Library's Cullman Center for Scholars and Writers, the W. E. B. Du Bois Institute for African and African American Research, and the Guggenheim Foundation, among others.

DAVID KRASNER is the author of *American Drama 1945–2000* (Blackwell, 2006) and coeditor of *Staging Philosophy: New Approaches to Theater, Performance, and Philosophy* (University of Michigan Press, 2006). He is the editor of the forthcoming *Theatre in Theory 1900–2000: An Anthology* (Blackwell) and author of the forthcoming two-volume *A History of Modern Drama* (Blackwell). He co-edits the series "Theater: Theory/Text/Performance" from the University of Michigan Press; twice received the Errol Hill Award from the American Society for Theatre Research; and serves on numerous editorial boards. He teaches theater, drama, and performance at Yale University.

WILLIAM J. MAXWELL is Associate Professor of English and Interpretive Theory at the University of Illinois, Urbana-Champaign, where he teaches modern American and African American literature. He is the author of the award-winning book *New Negro, Old Left: African-American Writing and Communism between the Wars* (Columbia University Press, 1999) and the editor of Claude McKay's *Complete Poems* (University of Illinois Press, 2004). He is now at work on *FBEyes: How Hoover's Ghostreaders Framed African-American Modernism* for Princeton University Press.

CARL PEDERSEN is Associate Professor in the Department of English, Germanic, and Romance Studies, University of Copenhagen. He has contributed essays to many books and journals and has co-edited several books, including *Black Imagination and the Middle Passage* (Oxford University Press, 1999), *Mapping African America* (LIT, 1999), *Consumption and American Culture* (Free University of Amsterdam

Press, 1990), and *American Studies: A Source Book* (Akademisk Forlag, 1989, 1993). He has also been an editor of *American Studies in Scandinavia*.

MARK A. SANDERS is Associate Professor of African American Studies and English at Emory University. He is the author of *Afro-Modernist Aesthetics and the Poetry of Sterling A. Brown* (University of Georgia Press, 1999) and the editor of *A Son's Return: Selected Essays of Sterling A. Brown* (Northeastern University Press, 1996).

A. B. CHRISTA SCHWARZ was educated at Bonn University (Germany), at Queen Mary and Westfield College (University of London, England), and at the University of Sussex (England), where she completed her doctorate in 1999. She is an independent scholar, and author of *Gay Voices of the Harlem Renaissance* (Indiana University Press, 2003). Her research interests include African American literature and history – particularly the era of the Harlem Renaissance – the German youth movement culture, and detective fiction. She has taught at the University of Potsdam (Germany) and the Free University (Berlin, Germany) and currently lives in Berlin.

CHARLES SCRUGGS is a Professor of American Literature at the University of Arizona. He is the author of *The Sage in Harlem: H. L. Mencken and the Black Writers of the 1920s* (Johns Hopkins University Press, 1984) and *Sweet Home: Invisible Cities in the Afro-American Novel* (Johns Hopkins University Press, 1993), and the co-author of *Jean Toomer and the Terrors of American History* (University of Pennsylvania Press, 1998).

JAMES SMETHURST is an Associate Professor of Afro-American Studies at the University of Massachusetts-Amherst. He is the author of *The New Red Negro: The Literary Left and African American Poetry, 1930–1946* (Oxford University Press, 1999) and *The Black Arts Movement: Literary Nationalism in the 1960s and 1970s* (University of North Carolina Press, 2005). He is also the co-editor of *Left of the Color Line: Race, Radicalism and Twentieth-Century Literature of the United States* (University of North Carolina Press, 2003) and *Radicalism in the South since Reconstruction* (Palgrave Macmillan, 2006). He is currently working on a study of African American literature and culture from 1880 to 1918 and ideas of artistic modernity and modernism in the United States.

JEFFREY STEWART is Professor of History and Art History at George Mason University. Dr. Stewart, who earned a PhD in American Studies from Yale University in 1979, is the recipient of many academic honors and fellowships, the most recent a W. E. B. Du Bois Institute Fellowship at Harvard University in 2004–5, another a Fulbright Lectureship in American Intellectual History at the University of Rome III in 2003. He is the author of many papers, essays, articles, and books, including the popular history *1001 Things Everyone Should Know about African American History* (Doubleday, 1998) and the collection of Alain Locke's lectures, *Race Contacts and Inter-racial Relations*, for Howard University Press; he edited the exhibition catalogue *Paul Robeson: Artist and Citizen* (Rutgers University Press, 1998). Currently, he is finishing a biography of Alain Locke.

CHERYL A. WALL, Distinguished Professor of English at Rutgers University, is author of *Women of the Harlem Renaissance* (Indiana University Press, 1995) and *Worrying the Line: Black Women Writers, Lineage, and Literary Tradition* (University of North Carolina Press, 2005). She edited two volumes of writing by Zora Neale Hurston for the Library of America, as well as critical casebooks on *Their Eyes Were Watching God* and "Sweat." Her current scholarship focuses on the art and legacy of Toni Cade Bambara, Toni Morrison's career as editor, and the African American essay.

MARK WHALAN is a Lecturer in American Literature and Culture at the University of Exeter. He is the editor of *The Letters of Jean Toomer, 1919–1924* (University of Tennessee Press, 2006), and the author of *Race, Manhood and Modernism in America: The Short Story Cycles of Sherwood Anderson and Jean Toomer* (University of Tennessee Press, forthcoming) and *Soldiers of Democracy: The Great War and the Culture of the New Negro* (University Press of Florida, forthcoming).

CHRONOLOGY

A chronology of Harlem Renaissance artists and writers

William Edward Burghardt Du Bois (1868–1963)
James Weldon Johnson (1871–1938)
Alice Dunbar-Nelson (1875–1935)
Angelina W. Grimké (1880–1958)
Carl Van Vechten (1880–1964)
Jessie Redmon Fauset (1882–1961)
Anne Spencer (1882–1975)
Alain LeRoy Locke (1886–1954)
Marcus Garvey (1887–1940)
Zora Neale Hurston (1891–1960)
Nella Larsen (1891–1964)
Claude McKay (1891–1948)
Walter White (1893–1955)
Jean Toomer (1894–1967)
George Samuel Schuyler (1895–1977)
Marion Vera Cuthbert (1896–1989)
Florence Mills (1896 –1927)
Rudolph Fisher (1897–1934)
Marita Bonner (1898–1971)
Aaron Douglas (1898–1979)
Paul Robeson (1898–1976)
Eric Walrond (1898–1966)
Sterling Allen Brown (1901–89)
Gwendolyn B. Bennett (1902–81)
Arna Bontemps (1902–73)
Langston Hughes (1902–67)
Wallace Thurman (1902–34)
Countee Cullen (1903–46)
Josephine Baker (1906–75)
Richard Bruce Nugent (1906–87)
Dorothy West (1907–98)

A chronology of significant events and publications of the Harlem Renaissance

1919

- 369th Regiment, or the "Harlem Hellfighters," marches up Fifth Avenue to Harlem, February.
- W. E. B. Du Bois' First Pan-African Congress meets in Paris, February.
- Marcus Garvey founds the Black Star Shipping Line, June.
- Race riots erupt in various cities, including Charleston, Knoxville, Washington, DC, Chicago, and Omaha, June to September.
- Commission on Interracial Cooperation (CIC) founded, September.
- Oscar Micheaux releases his first film, *The Homesteader*, in Chicago.
- Publication of Benjamin Brawley's *The Negro in Literature and Art in the United States*.

1920

- The Negro National League, the first of baseball's "Negro leagues," is established, January.
- 18th Amendment (Prohibition) takes effect, January.
- Universal Negro Improvement Association (UNIA) convention held at Madison Square Garden, August.
- 19th Amendment (Women's Suffrage) passed.
- Actor Charles Gilpin stars in O'Neill's *The Emperor Jones*, opening at the Provincetown Playhouse, November.
- James Weldon Johnson becomes executive secretary of the NAACP and its first black officer, December.
- Publication of W. E. B. Du Bois' *Darkwater* and Claude McKay's *Spring in New Hampshire*.

1921

- Black Swan Phonograph Corporation founded by Harry Pace, March.
- *Shuffle Along*, the first musical written and performed by African Americans Eubie Blake and Noble Sissle, opens on Broadway at the David Belasco Theater, May.
- African American artists, including Henry Tanner and Meta Vaux Warrick Fuller, exhibit work at the 135th Street Branch of the New York Public Library.
- Race riots in Tulsa, June.

- Second Pan-African Congress meets in London, Brussels, and Paris, August and September.
- Marcus Garvey founds African Orthodox Church, September.
- Publication of Benjamin Brawley's *Social History of the American Negro*, Blaise Cendrars' *Anthologie nègre*, and René Maran, *Batouala*.

1922

- Bessie Coleman becomes the first African American woman to stage a public flight, September.
- House of Representatives, led by L. C. Dyer of Missouri, approves first Anti-Lynching bill, but it is defeated by Southern Senators who filibuster for twenty-one days, December.
- Meta Warrick Fuller exhibits her sculpture "Ethiopia Awakening" in New York.
- Publication of *The Book of American Negro Poetry* edited by James Weldon Johnson, Claude McKay's *Harlem Shadows* and Georgia Douglas Johnson's *Bronze: A Book of Verse*.

1923

- Third Pan-African Congress meets in London and Lisbon, January.
- National Urban League publishes *Opportunity: A Journal of Negro Life* with Charles S. Johnson as editor, January.
- National Ethiopian Art Players stage Willis Richardson's *The Chip Woman's Fortune*, the first serious play by a black writer on Broadway, May.
- Claude McKay delivers his "Report on the Negro Question" before the Fourth Congress of the Third International in Moscow, June.
- Marcus Garvey is sentenced to five years in prison for mail fraud, June.
- The Cotton Club opens, September.
- Publication of Marcus Garvey's two-volume *Philosophy and Opinion of Marcus Garvey* and Jean Toomer's *Cane*.

1924

- *Opportunity* magazine's Civic Club Dinner, March. Touted by literary historians as the inaugural event of the New Negro movement, the dinner symbolizes a merger of white publishers and black writers.
- Actor Paul Robeson appears in O'Neill's *All God's Chillun Got Wings*, May.
- "Dixie to Broadway," an all-black musical revue, premieres at the Broadhurst Theater in New York City, October.

- First prize in the Witter Bynner Poetry Competition goes to Countee Cullen.
- Publication of Jessie Fauset's *There Is Confusion,* Walter White's *The Fire in the Flint,* W. E. B. Du Bois' *The Gift of Black Folk,* and Marcus Garvey's *Aims and Objects for a Solution of the Negro Problem Outlined.*

1925

- Marcus Garvey is convicted of mail fraud and jailed in the Atlanta Penitentiary, February.
- Publication of Alain Locke and Charles Johnson's special issue of *Survey Graphic,* "Harlem: Mecca of the New Negro," featuring black writers, March.
- A. Philip Randolph organizes the Brotherhood of Sleeping Car Porters, May.
- Negro Literary and Historical Society opens at 135th Street Branch of the New York Public Library, May 7. The same day, W. E. B. Du Bois, Carl Van Vechten, James Weldon Johnson, Walter White, Ridgely Torrence, and Arthur Spingarn meet to discuss formation of the Krigwa Players, to be based at the library.
- The first literary awards sponsored by *Opportunity* go to Langston Hughes, Countee Cullen, and Zora Neale Hurston, May.
- Josephine Baker debuts on the Parisian stage in *La Revue Nègre,* July.
- At the first *Crisis* awards ceremony held at the Renaissance Casino (a mecca of upscale African American nightlife), Countee Cullen wins first prize, November.
- Zora Neale Hurston enters Barnard College.
- American Negro Labor Congress meets in Chicago, October.
- First full-length Broadway play by an African American, Garland Anderson's *Appearances,* opens at the Frolic Theatre on Broadway, October.
- Paul Robeson makes his feature film debut in Oscar Micheaux's *Body and Soul,* November.
- Wallace Thurman moves from Los Angeles to New York.
- Publication of Countee Cullen's *Color,* DuBose Heyward's *Porgy,* Alain Locke's *The New Negro,* and *The Book of American Negro Spirituals* edited by James Weldon Johnson and J. Rosamond Johnson.

1926

- Countee Cullen accepts position as Assistant Editor of *Opportunity* and writes a regular column entitled "The Dark Tower."

- First celebration of Negro History Week, February.
- Savoy Ballroom, where many of the period's jazz dance crazes originate, opens in Harlem, March.
- Carnegie Corporation purchases Arthur Schomburg's collection for the New York Public Library, October.
- Harmon Foundation sponsors its first annual African American art exhibition at the New York Public Library, awarding works by Palmer Hayden and Hale Woodruff.
- *Crisis* awards go to Arna Bontemps' poem "Nocturne at Bethesda," Countee Cullen's poem "Thoughts in a Zoo," Aaron Douglas's painting "African Chief," and a portrait by Hale Woodruff.
- Publication of Wallace Thurman's *Fire!!*, Langston Hughes' *The Weary Blues*, Carl Van Vechten's *Nigger Heaven*, Eric Walrond's *Tropic Death*, W. C. Handy's *Blues: An Anthology*, and Walter White's *Flight*.

1927

- Manager Abe Saperstein forms the Harlem Globetrotters basketball team, January.
- Paul Green's drama *In Abraham's Bosom*, which had an all-black cast, wins the Pulitzer Prize, May.
- Fourth Pan-African Congress held in New York.
- Ethel Waters first appears on Broadway in the all-black revue *Africana*, July.
- Dorothy and DuBose Heyward's play *Porgy* opens on Broadway, September.
- By order of President Calvin Coolidge, Marcus Garvey's sentence is commuted and he is deported to Jamaica, December.
- Duke Ellington begins playing at the Cotton Club, December.
- A'Lelia Walker, renowned as hostess and "joy goddess" of the Renaissance, designs a tearoom salon called "The Dark Tower" after Cullen's column in *Opportunity*, which opens officially in early 1928.
- Publication of Miguel Covarrubias' *Negro Drawings*, Countee Cullen's *Ballad of the Brown Girl, Copper Sun*, and *Caroling Dusk*, Arthur Fauset's *For Freedom: A Biographical Story of the American Negro*, Langston Hughes' *Fine Clothes to the Jew*, James Weldon Johnson's *God's Trombones: Seven Negro Sermons in Verse* and *The Autobiography of an Ex-Colored Man* (reprint of the 1912 edition), and *Plays of Negro Life*, edited by Alain Locke and Montgomery T. Gregory.

1928

- Archibald Motley exhibits paintings at the New Galleries in New York and becomes the first artist of any race to appear on the cover of the *New York Times*, February.
- On April 9, Countee Cullen marries Nina Yolande, daughter of W. E. B. Du Bois, in what is described as one of the most lavish weddings in New York history; they divorce in 1930.
- Wallace Thurman edits *Harlem: A Forum of Negro Life*, a short-lived, literary magazine like *Fire!!*, with illustrations by Aaron Douglas and Richard Bruce Nugent, November.
- Publication of W. E. B. Du Bois' *The Dark Princess*, Rudolph Fisher's *The Walls of Jericho*, Nella Larsen's *Quicksand*, and Claude McKay's *Home to Harlem*.

1929

- The Negro Experimental Theatre formed at 135th Street branch library, February, directed by Regina M. Anderson and Dorothy Peterson.
- Wallace Thurman's play *Harlem*, written with William Rapp, opens at the Apollo Theater on Broadway, February.
- "Paintings and Sculptures by American Negro Artists," an exhibition sponsored by the Harmon Foundation, is held at the National Gallery in Washington, DC, May.
- Negro Art Theatre founded, June.
- National Colored Players founded, September.
- Stock Exchange crashes on Black Thursday, October 29.
- Publication of Countee Cullen's *The Black Christ and Other Poems*, Jessie Fauset's *Plum Bun*, Claude McKay's *Banjo*, Nella Larsen's *Passing*, Wallace Thurman's *The Blacker the Berry*, and Walter White's *Rope and Faggot: The Biography of Judge Lynch*.

1930

- *The Green Pastures*, a musical with an all-black cast, opens on Broadway, February.
- NAACP successfully contests President Hoover's nomination of renowned racist John J. Parker to the Supreme Court, March.
- Sufi Abdul Hamid founds the Universal Holy Temple of Tranquillity in Harlem.
- Black Muslim founder Wallace Fard Muhammad opens the Islam Temple in Detroit, July.

- Agatha Scott, wife of Brigadier General Benjamin O. Davis, Jr., founds the Northeasterners, Inc., an elite black women's social club.
- Colored Merchants' Association (founded in Alabama, 1928) spreads to Harlem.
- *La Revue du Monde Noir* founded in Paris.
- Publication of Randolph Edmonds' *Shades and Shadows*, Charles S. Johnson's *The Negro in American Civilization: A Study of Negro Life and Race Relations*, James Weldon Johnson's *Black Manhattan*, and Langston Hughes' *Not Without Laughter*.

1931

- The Scottsboro trial runs from April through July.
- Publication of Arna Bontemps' *God Sends Sunday*, Jessie Fauset's *The Chinaberry Tree*, Langston Hughes' *Dear Lovely Death*, *The Negro Mother*, and *Scottsboro Limited*, Vernon Loggins' *The Negro Author: His Development in America to 1900*, George S. Schuyler's *Black No More*, and Jean Toomer's *Essentials*.

1932

- Twenty young black intellectuals, including Dorothy West, Langston Hughes, and group leader Louise Thompson, sail to Russia to make the film *Black and White*, June.
- Sculptor Augusta Savage opens her first Savage School of Arts and Crafts in Harlem.
- Blacks begin to desert the Republican Party in large numbers.
- Publication of Sterling Brown's *Southern Road*, Countee Cullen's *One Way to Heaven*, Rudolph Fisher's *The Conjure Man Dies*, Langston Hughes' *The Dream Keeper*, Claude McKay's *Gingertown*, George Schuyler's *Slaves Today*, and Wallace Thurman's *Infants of the Spring*.

1933

- Dudley Murphy releases the film *The Emperor Jones* starring Paul Robeson.
- NAACP launches a campaign against segregation with a suit against University of North Carolina School of Pharmacy, March.
- Future Congressman Adam Clayton Powell, Jr. leads a demonstration for better health care in Harlem, April.
- Publication of Jessie Fauset's *Comedy, American Style*, James Weldon Johnson's *Along This Way*, and Claude McKay's *Banana Bottom*.

1934

- W. E. B. Du Bois resigns from *The Crisis* and NAACP after disagreements with NAACP secretary Walter White and a marked shift toward separatism in Du Bois' editorials, January.
- *Challenge* magazine founded by Dorothy West and friends.
- No longer presenting burlesque shows, the Apollo Theater showcases African American musicians and accepts African American patrons for the first time, January.
- Led by Howard Law School Dean Charles Houston, the NAACP and the American Fund for Public Service campaign against segregation and discrimination, October.
- Oscar Micheaux releases the film *Harlem after Midnight*.
- Sponsored by the PWA, Aaron Douglas paints four murals for the New York Public Library entitled *Aspects of Negro Life*, completed by November.
- Rudolph Fisher and Wallace Thurman die, December.
- Publication of Arna Bontemps' *You Can't Pet a Possum*, Randolph Edmonds' *Six Plays for the Negro Theatre*, Langston Hughes' *The Ways of White Folks*, Zora Neale Hurston's *Jonah's Gourd Vine*, James Weldon Johnson's *Negro Americans: What Now?*, George Lee's *Beale Street: Where the Blues Began*, and *Negro: An Anthology*, edited by Nancy Cunard.

1935

- The Harlem Race Riot erupts over discriminatory employment policies of white-owned businesses, March.
- The Museum of Modern Art opens the landmark exhibition *African Negro Art*, March.
- *Porgy and Bess*, the opera with an all-black cast, opens on Broadway, October.
- Langston Hughes' *Mulatto* becomes the first full-length play by a black writer to open on Broadway, October.
- Fifty per cent of Harlem's families are reportedly unemployed.
- Carl Van Vechten holds his first exhibition of photographs in *The Leica Exhibition* at Bergdorf Goodman in New York.
- Publication of Countee Cullen's *The Medea and Other Poems*, Zora Neale Hurston's *Mules and Men*, George Wylie Henderson's *Ollie Miss*, and Willis Richardson and May Sullivan's *Negro History in Thirteen Plays*.

1936

- Oscar Micheaux releases his film *Temptation*.
- Aaron Douglas paints murals for the Hall of Negro Life at the Texas Centennial Exposition in Dallas, formal dedication in June.
- Jesse Owens wins four gold medals at the Olympics in Berlin, August.
- Paul Robeson and Hattie McDaniel appear in James Whale's film musical *Show Boat*.
- Publication of Arna Bontemps' *Black Thunder*.

1937

- Paul Robeson stars in the film *King Solomon's Mines*.
- Joe Louis defeats James J. Braddock to become heavyweight boxing champion of the world, June.
- Publication of Claude McKay's *Long Way from Home*, Zora Neale Hurston's *Their Eyes Were Watching God*, and Sterling A. Brown's *The Negro in American Fiction*.
- *Challenge* magazine revived as *New Challenge*, carrying Richard Wright's "Blueprint for Negro Writing."

1938

- Richmond Barthé completes his *Dance* reliefs for the Harlem River Housing Project in New York.
- Jacob Lawrence holds his first solo exhibition at the Harlem YMCA and completes his *Toussaint l'Ouverture* series, February.
- Langston Hughes' play "Don't You Want to be Free?" marks the opening of the Harlem Suitcase Theatre, April.
- James Weldon Johnson dies in an automobile accident.
- Publication of Zora Neale Hurston's *Tell My Horse*, an anthropological study of Jamaican and Haitian culture, and of Richard Wright's *Uncle Tom's Children*.

1939

- New York World's Fair features Augusta Savage's sculpture "The Harp," April.
- Publication of Zora Neale Hurston's *Moses: Man of the Mountain*.

1940

- Benjamin O. Davis, Sr., becomes the first black general in the United States Army, October.
- Publication of Langston Hughes' *The Big Sea*, Claude McKay's *Harlem: Negro Metropolis*, and Alain Locke's *The Negro in Art*.

(Information for the above chronology has been compiled from a number of sources, particularly Kellner's *Harlem Renaissance: A Historical Dictionary for the Era* and Watson's *The Harlem Renaissance.*)

GEORGE HUTCHINSON

Introduction

The Harlem Renaissance – what a complex and conflicted aura the term evokes! People can scarcely agree on what it means. A vogue. A blossoming. A failure. A foundation. A few stars. A movement of black self-assertion against white supremacy, connected with anticolonial movements world-wide, or a local phenomenon gradually co-opted and destroyed by white voyeurs, cultural colonialists taking advantage of black naifs, opportunists, or weak-kneed bourgeois artists. A post hoc invention of cultural historians, now abundantly exploited by publishers, New York tour guides, and even, of late, real estate investors.

What is commonly called the Harlem Renaissance today was known as the Negro Renaissance in its own time. "Negro": a word of pride, of strong vowels and a capital N. The thick diagonal strode forward and put its foot down. "Negro" no longer signifies to most people what it did in the early to mid-twentieth century. A Spanish derivative, it did not exactly mean "Black" in American English – it was *sui generis*, a word only used to indicate persons of the slightest (non-"white") sub-Saharan African descent, regardless of color, but it seized on the essential meaning of the metaphor of the one mighty "drop [of blood]" that made one "black." Racial segregation was racing toward its apogee. Race was the word of the hour. Race suicide. Race purity. Race man. Race woman. The Passing of the Great Race. "Arise, O Mighty Race!" Enter the New Negro.

The Harlem Renaissance in literature was never a cohesive movement. It was, rather, a product of overlapping social and intellectual circles, parallel developments, intersecting groups, and competing visions – yet all loosely bound together by a desire for racial self-assertion and self-definition in the face of white supremacy. The interplay between intense conflict and a sense of being part of a collective project identified by race energized the move-ment and helps account for our enduring fascination with it.

Scholarship on the movement has itself been conflicted, contradictory, and passionate, for the issues with which the "renaissance" authors struggled have remained. The field of Harlem Renaissance studies is all competing interpretations, from its inception to the present. What role should or did Marxism play in black political and intellectual culture? How important is the fact that many of the important writers were gay or bisexual? What are the political obligations of the black artist, and do they carry formal, thematic, or technical implications for the practice of art? How should or does or did African American culture articulate with American culture more generally? What should be made of the extensive involvement of black with white authors and patrons of the time, given the imbalances of power between them and the whites' inherited prejudices or blindnesses? How might one reconcile the "mixed" nature of African American (or Anglo-African, or Afro-Caribbean) cultural expression with the claims of racial solidarity and autonomy? What does it mean to be "Negro"? What is race? Harlem Renaissance writers, like many people today, disagreed with each other over the answers to these questions. A "companion" to the Harlem Renaissance must allow dissonance, overlap, and multiplicity to inform its very structure.

Some of the confusion and disagreement about what has come to be known as the "Harlem Renaissance" derives from a conflation of several overlapping phenomena. The term "Negro Renaissance" arose in the early to mid-1920s to signify a general cultural awakening and moment of recognition – both self-recognition (for it was a very self-conscious phenomenon) and recognition from "without." The Negro Renaissance, at this time, signified primarily a blossoming of literary arts.

Associated with the renaissance was a New Negro movement, which is more amorphous and difficult to define. It was not specifically identified with literature and the arts. The authors of the Harlem Renaissance were considered "New Negroes," but they were not the first or the only "New Negroes." The term "New Negro" in something like its twentieth-century meaning went back to the 1890s at least. (Indeed, it can be traced to the late eighteenth century.) Booker T. Washington was a "New Negro" in those years, author of *A New Negro for a New Century* (1900), and his followers thought of New Negroes as those who were building up all-black institutions without questioning the dominant western notions of "progress" and capitalist economics. By the 1920s, Booker T. Washington (who had died in 1915) seemed like an "Old Negro" to many because of his accommodation to white power. In the early twentieth century, and particularly in the immediate aftermath of World War I, the term New Negro tended to signify militant self-defense against white supremacy, intellectual aspiration, and quite often political radicalism. After 1925 and the publication of Alain Locke's anthology *The New Negro*, the term often carried less overt "political" reference, and signified more a cultural affirmation of Negro identity expressed in poetry, fiction, drama, and the fine arts. In the course of the 1930s, this "culturalist" emphasis was often criticized, but, as Jeffrey Stewart argues in the first chapter of this book, the New Negro movement could be said to have extended to the late 1940s and beyond, setting the groundwork for the Civil Rights Movement of the 1950s.

The notion of a "New Negro" suggested the need to disengage from and overcome an "Old Negro" stereotype; yet the renaissance included a reevaluation of and pride in black history and heritage. Negro History Week – later Black History Month – was born during the renaissance. Arthur Schomburg assembled his important collection of manuscripts and books concerning black culture worldwide and sold it to the New York Public Library (NYPL) during the peak of the renaissance. Even before acquiring Schomburg's collection, the 135th Street branch of the NYPL (a major incubator and forum for the renaissance) had already started a "Negro" department, and a Society for the Study of Negro History and Literature had been founded there by the likes of James Weldon Johnson, Schomburg, and W. E. B. Du Bois. Carter G. Woodson had earlier founded a similar organization in Washington, DC.

Alongside and often intertwined with the Negro renaissance was the phenomenon of Harlem, and the Harlem "Vogue" that Langston Hughes indelibly scripted into the historical imagination of later generations by way of his first autobiography, *The Big Sea* (1940). But Hughes did not collapse what he termed the "Black Renaissance" into the Harlem, or Negro, Vogue. There was a Harlem Vogue, and more broadly a Negro Vogue of international dimensions, but there was also a "Black Renaissance." The "Vogue" referred to the interest some whites took in black arts and culture, popular music, Broadway shows featuring black performers, and the nightlife entertainment during Prohibition, when Harlem became a popular nightlife destination. The end of this vogue (which had a Parisian analogue centered in Montmartre) coincided less with Black Monday in 1929 than with the end of Prohibition in 1933. For different reasons, the timing was approximately the same in Paris.

A critique of the "Vogue" was an essential aspect of the renaissance itself (as several chapters in this volume reveal) and infused much of its literature as well as popular performance. Similarly, left-wing radicalism was not a "post-renaissance" phenomenon but a significant aspect of the movement, which was always energized by the contestation between different schools of thought, different disciplinary perspectives, and different social circles. This fact is epitomized in the oft-forgotten subtitle of Alain Locke's famous anthology *The New Negro: An Interpretation* (1925). Locke overtly attempted to steer African American intellectual and artistic work in a certain direction – toward a cultural self-reconstruction and a New Negro aesthetic building on what he called "folk values." (It was a shift of emphasis not atypical of intellectual culture in the twenties generally.) But plenty of people refused to go along. Points of view waxed and waned in influence, but there was no single "New Negro" cultural politics.

The renaissance also overlapped with or was part of a much broader, international Negro movement expressed in Pan-African congresses, Marcus Garvey's United Negro Improvement Association, and black intellectual communities outside the United States.[1] Other anticolonial and cultural nationalist movements were also occurring at the time, of which black intellectuals were very aware – in Ireland especially, in India, in South America, in Mexico, in China. Seen from an international perspective the Harlem Renaissance was part of a global phenomenon in which cultural nationalisms (sometimes crossing the boundaries of nation-states) were mobilized against imperialisms economic, political, and cultural. Marxism also provided an intellectual matrix of international dimensions in which not a few "New Negroes" participated.[2]

Attention to the international dimensions of black intellectual culture between the World Wars has sometimes put in question the emphasis on Harlem and on American cultural politics in scholarship on the movement, which for many years ignored its international aspects. But these are and were overlapping (and sometimes competing) phenomena. Langston Hughes was a black internationalist, but much of his work was explicitly concerned with the struggle for black citizenship in the United States, as well as with articulating the meaning and power of black cultural expression in the context of "Americanism." He placed this struggle within an international frame (variously so in the course of his long career), but one viewed from an American point of view. Discovering in Africa that people there "would not believe that [he] was a Negro," Hughes did not assimilate the African notions of racial identity; instead he would continue to understand Africa through a black internationalist lens that was definitively "American."[3]

Indeed, alongside the diasporic aspect of the renaissance was an investment in some versions of American cultural nationalism through which the "Americanness" of African American culture seemed a central and potentially powerful resource. In the NAACP's *Crisis* magazine, for example, W. E. B. Du Bois and literary editor Jessie Fauset assailed the hypocrisy of white America while claiming, in the words of one of Fauset's fictional heroines, "There is nothing more supremely American than the colored American, nothing more made-in-America, so to speak." African Americans, the New Negroes often asserted, had given the United States its most distinctive cultural forms and were the truest believers in its democratic dreams. Links between American cultural nationalism and African American modernism were crucial features of the movement across other intellectual divides.

In the 1920s and 1930s, New York was the chief point of entry and exit for black culture between the United States and other parts of the world. The vast majority of publishers who took an interest in black writing were based in New York, and they were helping transform the face of modern and American literatures. The Garvey movement was headquartered in Harlem, not Lagos or Dakar or Paris, not in Kingston or Marseilles. Could one have seen, anywhere else in the world, the kind of spectacles Garvey was able to stage in Harlem? And would the words and images have gotten out to other places?

France was also a vibrant crossroads of black culture and intellect. Claude McKay's *Banjo*, set in Marseilles, gives one of the best accounts of the black diasporic cross-referencing that went on in France, and the novel deeply impressed Francophone black intellectuals associated with *nègritude*. Yet at the heart of that novel is an argument (by the Haitian stand-in for McKay himself) that working-class Negroes in the United States (but not exclusively American Negroes) are the most powerful and avant-garde of all black groups because they inhabit the most vital, rough-and-tumble, powerful capitalist and quasi-democratic nation in the world, while American-style racism helps bind them into a cohesive, racially conscious group. The transnational romance of race, for McKay, centers in the United States, and its most important material as well as intellectual and even cultural resources emanate from there, ineluctably shaped by the race-producing disciplines of America's one-drop rule.

Our very notion of who counts as a "Negro" in the world in the 1920s and 1930s privileges the racial discourse of the United States. Just as Africans did not take Langston Hughes to be a Negro when he visited there as a young sailor, neither did Mexicans when, before starting college, he stayed with his *"muy Americano"* (very American, in the Mexicans' view) father near Mexico City. His later friend and collaborator Nicolás Guillén in Cuba was proud to think of himself and Cuban culture as "mulatto." Had Nella Larsen been raised in the Danish West Indies, her father's birthplace, she would not have been a Negro. The mulatto elite of Claude McKay's Jamaica did not consider themselves "black," but he came to embrace the meaning of Negro as the United States institutionalized it. Even when we speak of "transnational" aspects of the Negro renaissance, we are speaking of something profoundly shaped by American racial culture and American power.

In the United States itself, the phenomenon had roots, and routes, outside New York City. Harlem, however, provided the movement with its symbolic capital and its institutional center of gravity, despite (and because of) the fact that very few of the "New Negro" writers were actually from Harlem. There one found a complex and culturally productive concentration of peoples of African descent: recent migrants from the rural South, immigrants from the Caribbean and Latin America (and even from Africa), native New Yorkers, and a burgeoning black professional class hailing from all sections of the United States. Moreover, black Harlem was a new community that seethed with energy, ensconced in the great communications as well as financial capital of the Western Hemisphere. The vast majority of important magazines and publishing houses for black writers were headquartered in New York.

Harlem was a kind of switchyard of black cultural "renaissancism" (to borrow a term from Houston Baker, Jr.).[4] If few of the artists and writers came from Harlem (or even New York), many of them first met each other there. At the height of the renaissance, many of the New York participants lived in other areas of the city. Even James P. Johnson, the "King of Harlem stride piano," lived in Queens. It is precisely the liminal, or betwixt-and-between, aspects of Harlem in the interwar period, combined with its concentrated "blackness," that made it so important to the renaissance. Harlem was too diverse, had too many new migrants and immigrants, too much intellectual dissensus, for any one group to establish cultural dominance. The 135th Street Branch of the New York Public Library became a major site for all sorts of intellectual and artistic cross-fertilization, in part because no one group could claim it as their own. That point holds more generally for Harlem in the 1920s and 1930s.

While scholars have debated the beginning and ending dates of the movement or its "phases," a general consensus remains that it took form after World War I and continued well into the 1930s. World War I was a serious blow to the prestige of "white" civilization and its discourse of rationality and progress. Black soldiers, experiencing relative freedom in Europe and battling to make the world "safe for democracy" returned to Jim Crow America ready to fight for their rights, buoyed by a growing black nationalist consciousness among the migrating masses. The Soviet Union, born of the Russian Revolution in the midst of the Great War, represented to many writers a more truly egalitarian social and political model than the capitalism of the western so-called "democracies," and it seemed more committed to ending racism.

The Great War also contributed to the Great Migration of blacks in the southern United States to northern cities and new opportunities for work and education. The American publishing industry exploded after World War I, and new firms (often founded by Jews) turned to new kinds of literature, including literature by African Americans. The Blues and Jazz took off as popular musical forms in the wake of the war and, aided by the new recording industry, appealed across lines of class, race, region, and nation. Conventions of gender and sexuality came under intense pressure. Prohibition provided the context for an enormous increase in illicit social activity, and the age of the nightclub bloomed. New black periodicals provided support and exposure for young authors, while the more liberal and radical "white" periodicals became interested in black talent as never before. Organizations like the NAACP and the National Urban League took advantage of the interest in black culture, featured literature and art in their "house" magazines, and staged literary banquets and great glittering balls with impressive floor shows for integrated crowds.

The Great Depression clamped down on the optimism of the late 1920s. The balls of the NAACP began losing money about 1931 and finally stopped. The nightclubs of Harlem were devastated by the end of Prohibition in 1933. David Levering Lewis has persuasively used the Harlem Riot of 1935 to mark the end of the movement from a social historian's perspective. From a literary point of view, Richard Wright's "Blueprint for Negro Writing" of 1937 and the publication of his novellas in *Uncle Tom's Children* (1938) seem to mark an emphatic turning point, while Zora Neale Hurston's *Their Eyes Were Watching God* (1937) – a novel Wright attacked – is generally considered one of the crowning achievements of the Harlem Renaissance. James Weldon Johnson, a key precursor, participant, and historian of the movement died in 1938, and soon thereafter Carl Van Vechten began accumulating manuscripts from "renaissance" participants for the James Weldon Johnson Memorial Collection housed at Yale, the most important archive of the movement. We therefore take the period 1918 to 1937 to reasonably encompass the Harlem Renaissance, while recognizing that periodization is always artificial and approximate.

By the early to mid-1930s, several writers were identifying the renaissance with tendencies they wished to put behind them. Thus began an attempt to identify the movement with a particular ideology or set of naive assumptions, a "school" of thought or a particular class bias. As Lawrence Jackson points out in this volume, the Negro Renaissance, increasingly identified specifically with Harlem and the "Negro Vogue" of the 1920s, became the "whipping boy" of later generations seeking to establish their own authority over what black literature could or should be and do. Yet their own visions, literary assumptions, affiliations, and techniques were rarely as distinct from various strains of the renaissance as they liked to believe.

One of the most tenacious myths about the Harlem Renaissance has been that interest in black literature and arts died in 1929 or 1930 because of the stock market crash. By almost any measure, as a literary and more broadly artistic phenomenon, one can find more happening in the arts and letters in the 1930s than in the 1920s. Considerably more black fiction was published in the 1930s than in the 1920s, by a broader range of publishers and magazines, despite a shrinkage in fiction publication overall. More Guggenheim Fellowships went to African Americans in the 1930s than in the 1920s. The Harmon Foundation became more active in supporting black arts in the 1930s than in the 1920s. Support provided by the Federal Writers Project, Federal Theater Project, and Federal Arts Project put to shame the piecemeal patronage of the late 1920s. Visual artists returning to Harlem in the 1930s opened up schools and workshops with a concentration of talent, experience, and youthful ambition far beyond anything known earlier, to the benefit of people like Romare Bearden, Jacob Lawrence, and Norman Lewis. Ethel Waters was one of the greatest stars on Broadway, and James Weldon Johnson was hired to teach creative writing at New York University. If the Vogue had ended, black "renaissancism" had endured.

Behind the negative use of the renaissance was a sense of the movement's "failure" aesthetically – it had, many felt, produced no weighty masterpieces – connected with disappointment that it had not done more to advance the black freedom movement. Certainly some renaissance participants had expected greater social efficacy for the movement than it was able to produce. Others never expected the arts to be able to transform the position of the mass of black people except through a long-term cumulative effect connected with other forms of endeavor. Literature had its place in the broad front of Negro advance, however. Speaking to an interviewer in 1929, at the very height of the Vogue, Nella Larsen stated, "Even if the fad for our writings passes presently, as it is bound to do I suppose, we will in the meantime have laid the foundation for our permanent contribution to American culture."[5] That judgment is now indisputable. But, of course, making a contribution to a culture is not the same as radically transforming an entrenched social structure.

Beginning in the 1980s, understandings and evaluations of the Harlem Renaissance began to shift. Black feminist interventions brought critical attention to the narrowing effects of prior criticism that tended to demote or screen out the contributions of black women to African American culture and their challenges to white women's feminism. Critics began questioning the assumptions behind narratives of the movement's "failure" and developed new methods of reading its authors' engagements with modernism and modernity. Reconsiderations of the meaning of "Modernism" – previously defined as a movement in which black writers played no part – coincided with a questioning of the segregation of "black" from "white" literature and growing dissatisfaction with prescriptive approaches to black writing that used racial "authenticity" as a standard of judgment. Post-structuralist theory also tended to undermine faith in notions of "authentic blackness" and brought increasing attention to the performative dimensions of "race" as well as its historical contingency. Postcolonial theory stressed the "hybridity" of expressions of formerly colonized peoples. Near the turn of the twenty-first century, growing interest in globalization and transnationalism helped inspire interest in those aspects of the renaissance that exceeded the ideological and geographical boundaries of the nation-state. New methods and theories of African American literature inevitably developed in relation to (while often challenging or transforming) such broad intellectual movements as second-wave feminism, post-structuralism, and psychoanalytic criticism. And in the rise of Queer Theory, as well as recuperation of the history of sexuality, the Harlem Renaissance became a site of intense critical interest.

As a result of these major shifts in the realm of literary scholarship the "canon" of the Harlem Renaissance has been under continuous contention and reconstruction since the late 1970s. Just as the movement's positioning at the intersection of wide-ranging and crucial historical developments has come to seem inarguable, today its literary achievement appears considerably more substantial than it did when Nathan Huggins published his path-breaking study, *Harlem Renaissance* (1971).

The middle section of this book provides an investigation of that canon as it appears to us today in relationship to the varied concerns and forms explored by the New Negro authors of the 1920s and 1930s. While we have tried to cover a broad range, we could hardly be comprehensive. While seeking clarity of analysis and expression, this book tries not to reduce key issues – the meaning of race, the relationship between race and writing, chronology, relations between white and black, sexuality, internationalism and nationalism – to a misleading consensus. We have attempted to put authors in conversation with each other in often new ways that both make sense historically and draw attention to major developments in form, theme, and technique, and that highlight key nodes of the network in which the literature emerged even as "Negro literature" developed into a semi-autonomous field. In keeping with the format of the Cambridge Companion series, this book (except in the Chronology) largely restricts its attention to the literary realm, but we encourage our readers to think beyond such boundaries, as the literary interacted profoundly with, and was shaped in relation to, other forms of expression that were also integral to the broader movement. Within our limitations, we have tried to present the best of current wisdom but also to offer a highly readable provocation to new formulations, new readings, and archival exploration.

NOTES

1. Brent Hayes Edwards, *The Practice of Diaspora: Literature, Translation, and the Rise of Black Internationalism* (Cambridge, MA: Harvard University Press, 2003).
2. See especially William J. Maxwell, *New Negro, Old Left: African American Writing and Communism between the Wars* (New York: Columbia University Press, 1999); and Barbara Foley, *Spectres of 1919: Class and Nation in the Making of the New Negro* (Urbana-Champaign: University of Illinois Press, 2003).
3. Langston Hughes, *The Big Sea* (1940; New York: Hill and Wang, 1993), p. 11.
4. See Houston A. Baker, Jr., *Modernism and the Harlem Renaissance* (Chicago: University of Chicago Press, 1987).
5. Marion L. Starkey, "Negro Writers Come Into Their Own," unpublished manuscript, in Alfred A. Knopf, Inc., Collection, Harry Ransom Humanities Research Center, University of Texas.

PART I

Foundations of the Harlem Renaissance

I

JEFFREY C. STEWART

The New Negro as citizen

In an America that prided itself on its exceptionalism, it was the Negro who was the most important exception to American citizenship. Unlike other Americans, with the exception of the Native Americans, African Americans had to wait until the passage of the Fourteenth Amendment in 1867, two hundred years after first arriving in North America, to become citizens, and wait another hundred years before they could exercise the rights of citizens everywhere in the nation. Because America has prided itself on its self-proclaimed pluralism, its justly lauded achievement of blending together so many diverse peoples into a common culture, some questions remained. What about the Negro? How could the Negro enter into an American notion of citizenship that was predicated on immigrants becoming "white" by defining themselves as "not black?" How could black people become citizens if black exclusion was the very ground of citizenship for others? Frederick Douglass perhaps put it best. Douglass asserted that Lincoln was a great man and the father of the new white nation that came into being with the Civil War. But the Negro was only Lincoln's stepchild, a fatherless child who had to find his or her own way into a citizenship alone. What was simply a passing anomaly to the rest of Americans marching to the drumbeat of celebratory democracy became, for the black citizen, what Henry James called a complex fate – for to forge a Negro into an American citizen would require that both America and the Negro be changed.[1]

By invoking James' metaphor, I intend to pursue here something more than the usual rehearsal of the American Negro's political citizenship woes. Those woes are real, of course. While the Constitution did not limit natural-born citizenship to whites, acts passed by Congress that followed, such as the Naturalization Act of 1793, suggested, as Judge Taney put it memorably in the Dred Scott decision of 1857, the Negro "had no rights that the white man was bound to respect." But blacks had exercised such rights to reward and punish their political friends and enemies during a series of elections in the early nineteenth century, as Negroes with property voted in such states as

Pennsylvania. Then, in the 1830s, during what is misnamed Jacksonian Democracy, the zero sum game of American citizenship began with poor whites obtaining the right to vote at the expense of all blacks losing their right to the franchise. Even after the Fourteenth Amendment's guarantee of citizenship rights to all regardless of race, women suffrage advocates would promise that black women would not receive the right to vote if white women got it. But such exclusion of black men and women from full citizenship rights was never complete, and being decentered politically had its advantages – it forced the Negro to invent new strategies, forge new identities, start over again with a new pitch, to pivot around American political structures to nevertheless affect the nation politically. In part through the adoption of a new name, the New Negro, black people at the beginning of the twentieth century announced a new political subject who had detoured around American electoral politics.[2]

Booker T. Washington in *A New Negro for a New Century* was the first modern black political philosopher to read the lessons of the industrial revolution of late nineteenth-century America and conclude that the problem of the black citizen was not a matter of democracy, but a question of power. If the black community possessed a thriving economy, with millions employed, and black Robber Barons dominating its polity, would the New Negro, Washington asks, really need integration? At Tuskegee Institute, which he founded and managed, Washington taught black students techniques of self-reinvention designed to turn black workers into twentieth-century capitalists. Through photographic self-portraits and portraits of Edwardian-looking students, Washington fashioned an image of the black business-minded man and woman who transcended plantation stereotypes. Here the essence of the New Negro mentality was displayed – the capacity to begin again and anew despite past tragedies. But Ida B. Wells critiqued Washington's re/construction of the New Negro as self-destructive on evidence that black businessmen and women in the South were being lynched precisely because they competed with white petit bourgeois interests. Even more important, the black masses ignored Washington's advice to "cast down your bucket" in the Jim Crow South and remain late capitalism's peasants by coming north and taking industrial jobs opened up by World War I. Black Nationalists eschewed Washington's accommodationist rhetoric to hail a different New Negro – the race conscious black masses who joined Marcus Garvey's anti-white Universal Negro Improvement Association. Black socialists saw another New Negro of black proletarianism, in the willingness of urban blacks to fight back against pogrom-like white riots in northern cities during 1919. The New Negro in the early twentieth century was an Exquisite Corpse, a work of art constantly added to by intellectuals who ignored or critiqued preceding portraits of the New Negro to create a composite image that was confusing if not confused.[3]

It helps to clarify the New Negro as an early twentieth-century trope of black radicalism if we focus on the Great Migration of the World War I years and its relationship to citizenship in the United States. For a key "right" of federal citizenship in the United States of America under the Constitution is the right to migrate from one state to another. But this was one of the first rights to be curtailed for free Negroes in the nineteenth century. The initial conflict that led to the Civil War – Missouri's barring of Negroes from the state while applying for admission to the Union – set a pattern of state exclusion of black citizens that continued after the war in white citizens excluding Negroes from cities and towns in the twentieth and twenty-first centuries. Citizenship, therefore, for the Negro has never been a given, but rather an unprotected right to be seized again and again. One citizenship outcome of the New Negro of the World War I years was that, by migrating north, blacks entered urban and industrial voting districts that would determine the nation's future. It is this "migrating peasant," as Alain Locke, the Harvard-educated author of the Harlem issue of *Survey Graphic* put it in 1925, who demands citizenship rights rather than waiting, like the Old Negro, to have them bestowed. And unlike other commentators, Locke minimized the sociological explanations of this migration, and emphasized its philosophical idealism, painting the black migrants as a visionary people who imagined that day when they would shape the American polity as agents of change. Here, then, is one of the crucial psychological elements of the post-World War I New Negro – a directness, forthrightness, and confrontational uprightness of men and women willing to demand rights, grab them by the throat if necessary, that Locke labeled the spirit of "self-determination" of the New Negro. While the fighting back character of recent migrants in 1919 is exemplary of this New Negro consciousness, it is really the migration prior to that "If We Must Die" attitude that is fundamentally revolutionary.[4]

Locke added his distinctive signature to the portrait of the New Negro by linking the younger generation of black writers to the Great Migration of hundreds of thousands of blacks leaving the South and coming to the North during World War I. For Locke, there were two New Negroes – the poor black masses changing the geography of American citizenship, and the young black writers reflecting that energy in literature. What brought the educated writers and the uneducated migrant together was their sequestration in segregated crucibles like Harlem, where the sense that they were all in the same place for the same reason – race – lowered the inherent class conflict in the Negro community. "A railroad ticket and a suitcase, like a Baghdad carpet, transport the Negro peasant from the cotton-field and farm to the heart of the most complex urban civilization ... Meanwhile the Negro poet, student, artist, thinker, by the very move that normally would take him off at a tangent from the masses, finds himself in their midst, in a situation concentrating the racial side of his experience and heightening his race-consciousness." By linking middle-class black writers to the agency of the black working class, Locke defined the New Negro as a metaphor that structured a set of oppositions and allowed a mixture if not a synthesis of divergent perspectives as well as personalities. "In a real sense it is the rank and file who are leading, and the leaders who are following. A transformed and transforming psychology permeates the masses."[5] The black artist was important, therefore, not as an isolated member of the "Lost Generation" of Gertrude Stein and F. Scott Fitzgerald, but as a cultural translator, who absorbed the social reality of black life in segregated America, and turned it into a unique American art. Turning years of elite American cultural ideology and assimilationist sociology on its head, Locke announced that race was the creative space in American culture.

Of course, race is *not* supposed to be a creative space if one consults most narratives of American culture. For the dominant metaphor of America was that of the "melting pot," a concept that has persisted in American thought far beyond its birth in early twentieth-century America. From that perspective, the trajectory of success laid out for the black educated was along a path of absorption into the mainstream, and barring that, as was the reality under Jim Crow segregation, lobbying against exclusion and for inclusion from the position of the outsider. This approach was also a part of the 1920s New Negro literature, epitomized in Claude McKay's poems "Mulatto" and "White House," poetry that protested against racism and the exclusion of blacks from the family and the "House" of America. Locke has been criticized for excluding "Mulatto" from the Harlem issue of the *Survey Graphic* and changing the title of "White House" to "White Houses" in an attempt to excise the protest element out of the New Negro and to "aestheticize" the "movement." But Locke rejected what he believed was McKay's excessive infatuation with protest in part because it suggested that the Negro could only be whole by being allowed in to a form of Americanism that the Negro knew already was corrupt. Locke sought a deeper politics than demanding redress from withholding whites. What was revolutionary about the politics of the migrating black masses was that they had stopped trying to force their way into a South that did not want them. Instead, they had gone within themselves, and found within the black experience a folk culture, a sense of self-respect, and an independent vision of what they should do. Rather than essentialist and based on the biology of the Negro, such a consciousness emerged from a distinctive culture, formed out of the particular historically bounded experience of a people, whose emergence as subjects in twentieth-century America was tied to an ability to thrive on one's own in American culture. Moreover, black migrants from the South, other parts of New York, other parts of the world, had founded in Harlem a northern urban community that nurtured a new modernist culture, folk and individualistic, naive and sophisticated, that other Americans, especially educated whites, wanted to assimilate, copy, and market as the New American Culture of the twentieth century.[6]

Because political citizenship had failed African Americans, Locke and other New Negro intellectuals invented a cultural citizenship that promised a new kind of American identity defined by culture instead of politics. Locke followed in the footsteps of Ralph Waldo Emerson, who, in "The American Scholar," rejected the Founding Fathers and their political notion of American identity as originating in the Declaration of Independence and the Constitution. For Emerson, America needed a cultural declaration of independence to fulfill its destiny; for the scholar, the artist, the poet, who rejected Europe and looked into him/herself and the common people of America, could find not only America's soul, but also the beginnings of a new more inclusive notion of what was American. Locke captured some of the idealism of nineteenth-century visionaries in his notion that the migrants, as well as the black artists of the 1920s, were motivated primarily by idealism; that the soul of the African American was in the "folk culture" of the common people; and that in rejecting aggressive assimilation of Anglo-American culture, the African American artist, like Emerson's "Poet," could imagine a higher sense of nationality for both whites and blacks in twentieth-century America. While Locke is often described as an aesthete, in part because he was a lover of art of all kinds, and gay black intellectual, the truth is that his ambitions for the New Negro movement were broader and larger, more akin to the aspirations of early nineteenth-century Boston to create an urban world committed to the production of great Americans, not simply great politicians.[7]

New Negro cultural citizenship was always, however, a dialectical engagement with whiteness and blackness in the formation of an alternative cultural ideal to the reigning nineteenth-century Anglo-American notion that all who were citizens had to worship England as their cultural forebear. Negro cultural citizenship had roots in another nineteenth-century argument, that of Anglo-African gentility, the pre-Jacksonian era concept epitomized by James Forten and Frederick Douglass, that to become a citizen the Negro had to imbibe the attributes of education, property ownership, personal refinement, and taste. But that gentility was itself overthrown by another cultural demand of the Jackson Presidency, the demand that the citizen must be white, an ideology even Irish, Italian, and Jewish immigrants had to embrace in order to become American citizens. New Negro writers in the 1920s rejected that demand by incorporating the folk culture of the black and funky masses newly arrived from the South in their black modernism. The unassimilated proletarian became the authentic, the uncompromised man and woman in Jean Toomer's *Cane*, Langston Hughes' *The Weary Blues* and *Fine Clothes for the Jew*, Rudolph Fisher's *City of Refuge*, and Claude McKay's *Home to Harlem*. In *Home to Harlem*, for example, Ray, the educated black intellectual, sees Jake, the working-class deserter, as the more authentic person who carries within him a technology of survival that Ray needs to give meaning to his life. But while foregrounding the black poor as American culture bearers, these works of fiction and poetry also announced a new kind of educated American subject, someone who had mastered both the culture of the masses and the culture of international modernism. The New Negro was, in reality, an on-going complex transaction between a black sense of self and a sense of self as urban, industrialized, and also white – a balancing act of constantly referring backwards and forwards, from lessons and loyalties of the past to creative immersions in an unruly present, all of which shaped not only the New Negro, but the urban space that emerged in the twentieth century North. As a result, a profoundly dialectical cultural citizenship emerged in black urban modernism whereby the American soul would be tested and melded anew with the cultures and the dangers that lurked therein – in a Harlem more advanced and modern than any other chocolate city of the Black Atlantic.[8]

New Negroes were never simply racial identities, but new, more complex personalities, black individuals, sparkling in their multifarious talents, inclinations, and aspirations, modern black people who appeared even more so when they traveled to other, less sophisticated, more provincial black towns. The New Negroes were far more complex personalities than even educated nineteenth-century Negroes they replaced as the intellectual leaders of the race. They were comfortable discussing European and white American thinkers, fluent in several languages, multitalented as writers, social scientists, dramatists, and, above all, provocative, outstanding conversationalists. More sophisticated than their racial forefathers when discussing race, being influenced by the new anthropological theories of Franz Boas, these New Negroes were also peers of the whites who sought to influence them. Alain Locke, a philosopher, aesthetician, and journalist penned several articles on the anthropological theory of race and influenced Boas's prodigy, Melville Herskovits, to revamp his entire theory of African survivals in the United States, which resulted in his groundbreaking work, *The Myth of the Negro Past*. Langston Hughes altered Carl Van Vechten's understanding of the spirituals, while at the same time being the most successful writer – poet, playwright, short story writer, lyricist, and novelist – of the group. One can hardly imagine a more interesting person to talk to at a party than Zora Neale Hurston, whose humor, brilliance, and recall made her the finest folklorist of the 1920s. Rudolph Fisher worked as a doctor by day, but wrote short stories at night, except when he could be found at Harlem parties trading witticisms with Alain Locke. Here was an outstanding group of intellectuals as well as artists, men and women as comfortable in the white intellectual world as the black, yet grounded by a commitment to try and find in the black experience a new voice of America. A new kind of enlightened American citizen had emerged – the race cosmopolitan, who was able to discuss the national literary and intellectual heritage in black and white, exhibit a worldliness and breadth of influences less evident in black nationalisms of the 1960s, yet remain committed to the race and the transformation of America through the culture of the black community.[9]

Despite the legitimate criticisms of the New Negro as largely a male and heterosexist cultural icon, it should be remembered that many talented women, gay, and lesbian intellectuals and artists found themselves in the New Negro movement. Richard Bruce Nugent was as flamboyant a gay man as one can imagine in the Harlem of the 1920s and seemed not to suffer greatly because of it. Many women writers were blocked or simply not promoted by the male oligarchy of the New Negro; but others spoke of how thrilled they were to get to New York, such as Louise Thompson, who found she could be free, associate with brilliant men and women of the race, have intellectual discussions with interested whites at mixed race parties, and grow into a radical woman intellectual in the 1930s. Georgia Douglas Johnson, Gwendolyn Bennett, and Anne Spencer crafted a new poetry of love, intimacy, and maternal sacrifice that knitted together sentiments and metaphors from American women's poetry and the black experience. Even though most of these innovators would go unrecognized until rediscovered at the end of the century, the volumes of unpublished writings posthumously discovered testify to the fact that being ignored by the white mainstream press did not stop them from writing from the heart. To be New Negro meant to live in the present with the echoes of past crimes and silenced communities echoing in one's head, regardless of what the rest of the nation thought of it. And it meant dreaming in the 1920s of a new kind of citizenship, of at-homeness, grounded in a capacious black urban community that was far more advanced in its foregrounding of feminist and homosexual identities than the rest of the nation. It meant the courage to resist not only 100 percent Americanism, but also gender bias and homophobia within a black community in transition.[10]

The creativity of this New Negro in its second phase – the 1920s – reflected a pivotal, transitional moment in American history when the old rural agricultural world was disappearing and a new, alien, yet still communal, northern, industrial world was taking its place. In that process, black identities, like white ones, were freed from the old constraints on individualism and group consciousness that the old "medieval America," as Locke put it, had imposed on southern Americans, black and white. That transition brought a great deal of nostalgia, but also a greater idealism that anything was possible for the culturally self-conscious black personality.

But in the 1930s a new half generation of young people emerged who rejected the cultural citizenship argument of Alain Locke. They argued for a New Negro activism in the face of widespread employment discrimination and segregation in commercial establishments in Washington, DC. Claiming that the earlier artistic approach to gaining citizenship rights had failed, John P. Davis and other young black intellectuals adopted a Direct Action approach to the persistent segregation and discrimination in employment in the nation's capital. Although privately encouraged by Locke and others at Howard University, these young black intellectuals redefined the New Negro as an activist, willing to picket, boycott, and even be arrested to compel A and P Grocery Stores, the ironically titled Peoples Drug Stores, and other businesses operating in the black community to hire black workers as clerks or managers. By the late 1930s, the New Negro Alliance had scored a series of stunning victories against establishments fighting for their economic survival in the Great Depression. Unlike earlier, Booker T. Washington-like petty bourgeois black nationalist campaigns to patronize black-owned businesses, the "Don't Buy Where You Can't Work" campaign of the New Negro Alliance recognized the profound economic reality of black life in the urban North (and even Upper South) ghetto – that black communities were served principally by white corporations and businesses dependent on black consumers to survive in the Fordist stage of American industrial capitalism.[11]

Indeed, elements of the earlier New Negro movements resurfaced in the ideology of the New Negro Alliance. For it had been Henry Ford and other industrial capitalists who had opened their factories to black workers in the 1910s and set in motion the process by which hundreds of thousands of southern blacks would migrate into the North during the Great Migration. Beyond breaking the color bar in automobile industry employment, Ford had also recognized that every worker was a consumer, and by giving workers a living wage he increased the pool of potential consumers of his cars. The recognition that consumption, rather than production, drove the American economy in the twentieth century structured economic policy in the New Deal, and perhaps explains, in part, why the Supreme Court in 1938 ruled in favor of the New Negro Alliance's case demanding the right of consumers to protest hiring practices of businesses under the Norris-La Guardia Anti-Injunction Act, a law originally passed by Congress to protect the right to strike of workers. But what made this Alliance *New Negro* was its recognition that the consumer economy was *racialized* and that the shift to a Fordist, consumer-based economy empowered those segregated consumer markets to pressure local and national businesses for concessions around workers' rights, especially the potential worker's right to be employed. The New Negro Alliance defined a new interest in American politics in the twentieth century – that the historically segregated citizen was entitled to rights in a racialized democracy. Otherwise, that citizen could disrupt the economic peace the New Deal sought to craft between the capitalist and the worker in the Great Depression. The New Negro Alliance embodied the Lockean sense of cultural citizenship, since Davis' political strategy reflected the 1920s' demand for public *representation* – in art or politics. But in the heady success of its late 1930s victories, the New Negro Alliance, like earlier new beginnings in black history, gained energy from repudiating its antecedents.[12]

Perhaps Paul Robeson in the 1930s best embodied the two sides of the New Negro as cultural citizen and political rebel. Robeson was the 1920s New Negro artist in his singing of the spirituals and secular black folk music, his performance of black self-conscious roles in the drama of Eugene O'Neill, and his identification with Africa in his films and friendships with African leaders such as Nkrumah and Azikiwe. He was the race cosmopolitan, who, though proud of his race and cultural history, was not restricted in the range of his tastes, friendships, and influences. But Robeson became most effective as a New Negro ambassador to the world in the 1930s by using his cultural efficacy to open up a unique space in global politics. Robeson's gifts as a singer and an actor took him to Europe, where, as an expatriate in the 1930s, he transformed himself from being simply a New Negro artist to being an international New Negro political rebel. After starring in a London production of Shakespeare's *Othello*, Robeson read voraciously in the literature of socialism, became an outspoken critic of racism and international fascism, and issued his famous declaration – "the artist must elect to fight for freedom or for slavery. I have made my choice. I had no alternative." In concerts in European capitals, Robeson began to include the songs of native peoples in his program of spirituals, thereby knitting together the strivings for self-determination of blacks and Europeans. By doing so he avoided the trap of falling into the American alternative to racialized subjectivity – the assimilationist narrative, by which individuals and groups sacrifice their cultural and historical particularity for inclusion into white bread universality. Instead, Robeson crafted a position that the universality of the spirituals, for example, resided in their particularity to the black American struggle for freedom, an aspiration that linked them to other peoples fighting to gain their voice and sense of agency in the 1930s. Robeson began to speak to and about the aboriginal peoples whose culture and freedom were suppressed in nationalist identities, such as the fate of aboriginal peoples in the nationalist praxis of the Australian. He also included songs of workers, unions, and anticolonialist freedom fighters, broadening the New Negro from a black nationalist to a class and anticolonialist consciousness only hinted at in Locke's *The New Negro*. Interestingly, it was only while abroad that Robeson was able to transform himself from the New Negro as racialized subject to the New Negro as a global citizen.[13]

Back in the United States in the 1940s, Robeson was an even more active American citizen than before his sojourn in Europe. But a sea change in the New Negro was also occurring even as he became a very public cheerleader for the US–Soviet alliance in World War II. With the death of Franklin Delano Roosevelt, Harry Truman took over the White House and crafted a post-World War II foreign policy that led the nation into the Cold War. Robeson was appalled, because during his sojourns in the Soviet Union he had witnessed a progressive policy toward minorities, and formed a close bond with the Russian people. Robeson became an enemy of the Truman administration, and led the Presidential campaign of Henry Wallace, the Progressive Party candidate, to win the Presidency, and if not that, to spoil Truman's chance for reelection. That reelection seemed a long shot, because Truman was a weakened President by 1948, not only because of opposition to the Cold War, but because he had issued a number of executive orders and proposed a number of bills that positioned him as the most "progressive" President on Civil Rights so far in the nation's history. Why?[14]

A Second Great Migration out of the South and into such northern states as Pennsylvania, Ohio, and Illinois, but also into California, where the aircraft and shipbuilding industries employed thousands of blacks, had occurred during World War II mobilization. This second wave of migrants added to those who had come during World War I and had continued to come during the interwar period. Now, in some northern cities especially, the forming black ghettos constituted sizeable and pivotal voting majorities. In addition, many more African Americans than in World War I were drawn into the armed forces during World War II, experiencing first hand the cruelties of segregated American military service, both within the Army and Navy, but also in the southern towns where training camps were often located. The World War II experience of mobilization, interstate migration, and government-sanctioned discrimination produced a second-generation New Negro consciousness, heightened even more by the well-publicized postwar violence toward returning black servicemen in the South. Unlike the earlier New Negro of the 1910s and 1920s that avoided a frontal assault on segregation and built race pride and racial institutions within its structure, this post-World War II New Negro citizen demanded America dismantle institutional segregation as the first step to Negro freedom in the United States. When Truman saw the southern wing of the Democratic Party bolt and form a separate party to run candidates against him because of the modest Rooseveltian Civil Rights initiatives that he sought to extend into postwar America, he decided his Presidency was lost unless he secured the support of these New Negro citizens in the northern and western states. Accordingly, he issued Executive Order 9981 to begin desegregating the Armed Forces, extended the life of a Presidential Committee on Civil Rights, and pressured Congress to pass an anti-lynching law, among other things. A sea change had certainly occurred. For in the 1920s the NAACP had been an isolated voluntary organization proposing anti-lynching legislation; but now, in 1948, it was the President himself who was pressuring Congress to pass the anti-lynching bill.[15]

The Great Migrations of millions of blacks out of the non-voting South and into the political efficacy of life in the North and West over the first half of the twentieth century had brought a revolution to American politics and American citizenship. For this voting block threw its support to Truman in the 1948 election, one of the closest in American history, and made the difference in allowing Truman to remain in the White House. While some blacks voted for Wallace, the black masses knew that he had little chance of winning the White House, and to vote for him would be at best a symbolic vote against the Cold War. But a vote for Truman would be a vote against the South and for desegregation, which Truman had stimulated in his executive order and his progressive position on Civil Rights with Congress. A race-based political consciousness among the black masses had made the practical political choice to use the franchise to change the racial dynamic politically in America rather than advance the global partnership with the Soviet Union that Robeson advocated from above. As Locke had said several decades earlier, "in a real sense it is the rank and file who are leading, and the leaders who are following." In the post-World War II political world, an even newer "transformed and transforming psychology permeates the masses." It is perhaps heartening to realize that that psychology had produced a Copernican revolution in the Democratic Party in 1948, creating a new party that revolved around the Negro citizen and not simply the southern white man.[16]

Of course, the influence of Robeson and other first-generation New Negro intellectuals had been critical to the emergence of this new consciousness.

Robeson's stinging critique of Truman's earlier reluctance to make Civil Rights a domestic priority, combined with the political reality of the black masses voting in the 1948 election, forced Truman to embrace a more aggressive posture on the issue of desegregation if he wanted national support of blacks for the Cold War. And Robeson had taken the lead in pressuring, among other things, the Baseball Association to integrate black players into the national pastime. Robeson was more able than other first-generation New Negroes to play a role in the post-World War II New Negro world because of having remade his political consciousness while living abroad. But while he had been abroad important changes had occurred in the composition of the New Negro consciousness in the United States, especially among the young men who had served in the military or reached maturity in the urban North and the urban South during that war. They had adopted the earlier New Negro innovation that power was dispersed in America not to individuals but to groups in the service of a new idea – that dismantling segregation was the first and most important item on the New Negro agenda.[17]

But at the same time, something crucial was lost: the message of cultural citizenship, a sense that even if one dismantled the apparatus of de jure segregation, for example in the army, and left the rest of the system intact, that did not fundamentally eradicate the ideology of white supremacy or alter the larger system of economic manipulation that fueled it. One may have cut off the legs of segregation in the law; but in doing so, only set the stage for the reproduction of segregation as a de facto practice later, as has occurred in the post-Civil Rights era. In marching into the light of political citizenship, the New Negro of the third phase – who wished to become a citizen like the rest of Americans – became just that and no more: a political entity with perhaps a bit less efficacy than the white citizen in America. In a sense, the black became a citizen like all of the Americans who had been on the inside. But in doing so, s/he lost the advantage of being an outsider who could invoke a critique of the entire system of political representation that had been co-opted by corporations and economic elites. In an irony, the New Negro had become the American, for the American was also, whether white or Latino or Italian, increasingly a powerless entity in American politics.

Perhaps skepticism about the long-term healing effects of desegregation helps explain why another New Negro spokesperson, Zora Neale Hurston, lashed out so vociferously when the Brown vs. Board of Education decision was handed down by the Supreme Court in 1954. While her remarks have been generally understood as reactionary, there is another sense in which her criticism of the Brown decision can be understood. She argued that the decision was a slight on the kind of life and education and experiences black people had developed under segregation, by portraying that life as pathological because of the existence of segregation. For her, the Negro had been a cultural citizen before desegregation and would remain so afterwards. Of course, her remarks were also defensive, since she also understood that desegregation had the potential to dismantle the cultural formation called the New Negro and the autonomous black folk she had spent her life documenting. But what she feared and others later witnessed was the demise of the social base of the New Negro – which had been formed by accepting the possible permanence of segregation and creating subversive structures within its crevices. Now, with its dismantling, the New Negro concept, indeed the very use of the term Negro, lapsed, to be replaced in the middle 1960s by a new identity, of Blackness, formed in response to the reality of the persistence of white supremacy and white power even after the demise of de jure segregation. In a sense, both Hurston and Robeson, race cosmopolitans from different ideological perspectives, saw the necessity for an independent cultural citizenship grounded in the Negro, or now black, community that transcended even the post-World War II successes of expanded Negro political citizenship.[18]

Interestingly, after the major victories of the Civil Rights Movement of the mid-1960s, another intellectual and cultural rebellion surfaced, sometimes called the Black Power Movement, other times the Black Arts Movement, which looked back to the Harlem Renaissance for inspiration to reinvigorate a New Negro in the 1960s. While the Black Arts Movement tended to cleave off the interracial cosmopolitanism of the earlier movement, the later movement rediscovered and republished such canonical New Negro texts as Alain Locke's *The New Negro: An Interpretation*, the book version of the Harlem issue of *Survey Graphic*, in the 1960s.[19] That interest reflected, I want to argue, a desire to reconstruct American identity through the pluralistic cultural notion of citizenship explored in 1920s Harlem. The latter half of the twentieth century witnessed successive waves of other marginalized citizens – women, Native Americans, Chicanos/as, gays and lesbians – who, unwittingly or not, followed the path pioneered by the New Negro. For that earlier movement was a nursery for self-conscious minorities longing for the more spiritually capacious notion of citizenship America promised but seldom delivered.

NOTES

1. See Jeffrey C. Stewart, *1001 Things Everyone Should Know about African American History* (New York: Doubleday, 1998), pp. 110–72 for information on the Fourteenth Amendment and the struggle for citizenship. Frederick

Douglass, "Oration by Frederick Douglass Delivered on the Occasion of the Unveiling of the Freedmen's Monument in Memory of Abraham Lincoln," The Frederick Douglass Papers at the Library of Congress, Washington, DC. I would like to thank Faith Davis Ruffins, Curmie Price, and Prudence Cumberbatch for comments on earlier drafts of this chapter.

2. For text of opinion of the Supreme Court in the Dred Scott Case (1857) written by Chief Justice Taney, see http://www.let.rug.nl/usa/D/1851-1875/dredscott/dred3.htm. For information on Jacksonian "democracy" and black citizenship, see Emma Jones Lapsansky, "Since They Got Those Separate Churches: Afro-Americans and Racism in Jacksonian Philadelphia," *American Quarterly* 32 (Spring 1980), 54–78.

3. Booker T. Washington et al., *A New Negro for a New Century: An Accurate and Up-to-Date Record of the Upward Struggles of the Negro Race* (Chicago: American Publishing House [1900]). Ida B. Wells Barnett, *On Lynchings: Southern Horrors, A Red Record, Mob Rule in New Orleans* (New York: Arno Press, 1969). Henry Louis Gates, Jr., "The Trope of the New Negro and the Reconstruction of the Image of the Black," *Representations* 24 (1988), 135–49. See Deborah Willis, "Towards a New Identity: Reading the Photographs of the New Negro," PhD dissertation, George Mason University, 2003, for analysis of photographs of Washington and Tuskegee students. See William J. Maxwell, *New Negro, Old Left* (New York: Columbia University Press, 1999) for trenchant discussion of black radicalism in the 1920s. For information on the exquisite corpse in surrealist art, see Andrei Codrescu, ed., *The Stiffest of the Corpse: An Exquisite Corpse Reader* (San Francisco: City Lights Books, 1989).

4. Alain Locke, "Harlem," *Survey Graphic*, 1 March 1925, p. 630.

5. Ibid. Also, "Youth Speaks," *Survey Graphic*, 1 March 1925, pp. 659–60.

6. William J. Maxwell, ed., *Complete Poems of Claude McKay* (Urbana: University of Illinois Press, 2004). See also Winston James, *A Fierce Hatred of Injustice: Claude McKay's Jamaican Poetry of Rebellion* (London: Verso, 2001).

7. Ralph Waldo Emerson, *The Essential Writings of Ralph Waldo Emerson* (New York: Modern Library, 2000). David S. Reynolds, *Beneath the American Renaissance* (Cambridge, MA: Harvard University Press, 1989). Henry Mayer, *All On Fire: William Lloyd Garrison and the Abolition of Slavery* (New York: St. Martin's Griffin, 2000).

8. Claude McKay, *Home to Harlem* (1928; Boston: Northeastern University Press, 1987).

9. Walter Jackson, "Melville Herskovits and the Search for Afro-American Culture," *History of Anthropology* 4 (1986), 73–103. Arnold Rampersad, *The Life of Langston Hughes*, vol. 1: *1902–1941: I, Too, Sing America*, 2nd edn (New York: Oxford University Press, 2002), p. 111. For more on the personalities of the Harlem Renaissance writers, see David Levering Lewis, *When Harlem Was in Vogue* (New York: Penguin, 1997).

10. For criticism of the gender bias and misogamy of the Harlem Renaissance, see Gloria T. Hull, *Color, Sex and Poetry: Three Women Writers of the Harlem Renaissance* (Bloomington: Indiana University Press, 1987), Thadious M. Davis, *Nella Larsen, Novelist of the Harlem Renaissance* (Baton Rouge: Louisiana State University Press, 1996), and Cheryl Wall, *Women of the Harlem Renaissance* (Bloomington: Indiana University Press, 1995). On gay writers of the Harlem

Renaissance, see A. B. Christa Schwartz, *Gay Voices of the Harlem Renaissance* (Bloomington: Indiana University Press, 2003) and Bruce Nugent and Thomas Wirth, *Gay Rebel of the Harlem Renaissance* (Durham, NC: Duke University Press, 2002). Author's interview with Louise Patterson, 8 September 1990.

11. Michelle F. Pacifico, "'Don't Buy Where You Can't Work': the New Negro Alliance of Washington," *Washington History* 6 (Spring/Summer 1994), 66–88.

12. Ibid. For information on the Supreme Court decision *New Negro Alliance v. Sanitary Grocery Co., 303 U.S. 552 (1938)*, see http://www.justia.us/us/303/552/case.html.

13. Quote from Paul Robeson, *Here I Stand* (Boston: Beacon Press, 1998), p. 52. See Jeffrey C. Stewart, ed., *Paul Robeson: Artist and Citizen* (New Brunswick, NJ: Rutgers University Press, 1998), pp. 135–63, 253–300.

14. Ibid. pp. xxix–xxxi, 179–233.

15. See Mary L. Dudziak, *Cold War Civil Rights* (Princeton: Princeton University Press, 2002).

16. Ibid.

17. Stewart, *Paul Robeson*, pp. 54, 205.

18. On Hurston's criticism of the Brown decision, see Zora Neale Hurston, "Court Order Can't Make Races Mix," *Orlando Sentinel*, 11 August 1955. See also Valerie Boyd, *Wrapped in Rainbows: The Life of Zora Neale Hurston* (New York: Scribner, 2003), pp. 423–5.

19. *The New Negro: An Interpretation* (New York: Arno Press, 1968).

2

EMILY BERNARD

The Renaissance and the Vogue

"It was the period when the Negro was in vogue."[1] These words introduce readers of *The Big Sea*, a 1940 autobiography by Langston Hughes, to the era known today as the Harlem Renaissance, which commenced in 1924, and was the first significant literary and cultural movement in African American history. This sentence by Hughes captures what was at once transcendent and dispiriting about the era. The Harlem Renaissance was a moment when blackness was celebrated; but to be in vogue is to be in fashion, and fashions always die. As an era concerned with the vitalization as well as with the demise of African American identity, the Harlem Renaissance was an era best characterized by its contradictions: every point of celebration was also a source of contention. This chapter begins with a discussion of the contradictions at the root of the ideological issues that occasioned what was both glorious and grim about Harlem in the 1920s. But before we can get to the achievements of the Harlem Renaissance, we must confront the problems inherent in the term "Harlem Renaissance" itself.

Was the Harlem Renaissance an actual renaissance? Scholarship on this period supports competing points of view. *Webster's New World Dictionary* defines a "renaissance" as a "rebirth" or "revival." Some historians and critics believe that what took place during the Harlem Renaissance years was not a rebirth, as such, but only another stage in the evolution of African and African American art that had begun with the inception of African presence in America. While it is true that African and African American art forms never died – new ones were created and evolved even during slavery – a particular black American identity was born after Emancipation, and that was the "New Negro." The Harlem Renaissance is also known as the New Negro Movement.

The term "New Negro" was not invented during the Harlem Renaissance, but had, in fact, been circulating in American public discourse since the 1700s. The New Negro was more than a persona; he was an idea, an ideological construction. The New Negro was invented, in part, by blacks attempting to correct the negative stereotypes about them that were already in play by the time they arrived in the New World. As Henry Louis Gates explains in his essay "The Trope of a New Negro and the Reconstruction of the Image of the Black," "Almost as soon as blacks could write, it seems, they set out to redefine – against already received racist stereotypes – who and what a black person was, and how unlike the racist stereotype the black original indeed actually could be."[2] Black people created the "New Negro" as an attempt to convert popular stereotypes about blacks from those based upon absence (of morality, intelligence, and other basic features of humanity) to presence. A preoccupation with this term, and the hope of liberation it represented, became a near-obsession for Harlem Renaissance intellectuals. In fact, Gates suggests that the Harlem Renaissance was finally not much more than a vehicle created to contain the "culturally willed myth of the New Negro" (132).

What is a "New Negro," exactly? An accurate definition of the New Negro is impossible without an appreciation of its counterpart, the Old Negro. The philosopher and Harlem Renaissance power broker Alain Locke describes the Old Negro in "The New Negro," an introduction to his anthology, *The New Negro*, the definitive anthology of the Harlem Renaissance. "The Old Negro, we must remember," Locke writes, "was a creature of moral debate and historical controversy. His had been a stock figure perpetuated as an historical fiction partly in innocent sentimentalism, partly in deliberate reactionism."[3] If you have seen D. W. Griffith's *Birth of a Nation*, you have seen the Old Negro. Picture the antics of the nameless black extras that populate that 1915 film, and you will comprehend immediately the kinds of associations that the phrase "Old Negro" conjured for black Americans of the early twentieth century; conversely, these same images also suggest the kind of corrective ideological labor that the "New Negro" was meant to perform.

It is important to note that Locke's essay "The New Negro" begins with, and in some sense relies upon, a discussion of the Old Negro. In many ways, the term "New Negro" does not even make sense without its counterpart, "Old Negro." Ultimately, in fact, the terms are hardly in opposition at all. Instead, they are in dialectical harmony and fundamentally necessary to each other. It is not implausible to say that a definition of one term is only really possible in light of the other. In other words, the New Negro is finally everything the Old Negro is not, and vice versa.

"Negro life is not only establishing new contacts and founding new centers, it is finding a new soul," Alain Locke proclaimed in the opening pages of *The New Negro* (xxvii). The world of African American arts of the 1920s was intoxicated with the idea that it had invented itself, not only in terms of its creative ambitions, but also as a locus of a new black identity, namely the New Negro. Black intellectuals of the Harlem Renaissance invested in the ideology of the New Negro all of their ambitions to liberate black people – psychologically, socially, and even politically – from the denigration of the slave past.

In "Racial Doubt and Racial Shame in the Harlem Renaissance,"[4] African American Studies scholar Arnold Rampersad writes: "a modern renaissance (English, Irish, American, what-have-you) seems to me to depend in a fundamental way on the presence of strong feelings of inferiority, cultural and otherwise, at the very moment – paradoxically – of the repudiation or transcendence of those feelings of inferiority in the name of progress, emancipation, and independence" (32). The paradox that Rampersad speaks of is embedded in the term "New Negro" itself. The inextricability of the terms "Old Negro" and "New Negro" presented a problem for black intellectuals of the 1920s intent upon severing the relationship between the two types, embracing the latter while turning the collective racial back on the former, thereby obliterating forever the ugly history of shame and servility that the Old Negro represented. But the progress promised by the New Negro Movement, or Harlem Renaissance, could be evident only in relation to the agonizing history that the term "New Negro" was meant to obscure. Continuous comparisons between Old Negro and New Negro were necessary to maintain distinctions between the two types. That meant that the figure of the Old Negro had to be kept alive and in the center of discussions about racial progress. So, it was finally impossible for Harlem Renaissance intellectuals to leave the Old Negro behind. They needed him; he reminded them of exactly what they were shedding as well as what precisely they were trying to become. The necessity of keeping close at hand the very image they were trying so desperately to cast off created an intellectual anxiety among Harlem Renaissance intellectuals, an anxiety that served as the primary fuel of the New Negro Movement.

The acute self-consciousness of the New Negro Movement had led scholars to question its legitimacy. But even if the Harlem Renaissance was a "culturally willed myth," as Gates has argued, or "a forced phenomenon," as David Levering Lewis asserts, its importance in African American cultural history is undeniable.[5] Even the term "New Negro," with its contradictory assertions of inferiority and triumph, represents accurately the tug of war that lay at the root of black consciousness throughout this period. The Harlem Renaissance was the first cohesive cultural movement in African American history. Never before had African Americans had an opportunity to take on the project of national identity with such intensity. The Harlem Renaissance, then, became almost literally a way for African Americans to write themselves into the narrative of American identity. The debates that took place during this period about how best to represent the significance of African American achievement on the national stage are debates that continue to resonate in African American intellectual circles to this day.

Ideological complexities aside, the Harlem Renaissance was also spectacular as a material phenomenon. Harlem itself was a bustle of activity; inside cabarets, buffet flats, speakeasies, and ballrooms, each dancer, singer, and musician seemed more ingenious than the one who came before her. In "Spectacles in Color," a chapter in *The Big Sea*, Hughes captures the particular social alchemy of Harlem during the 1920s in his descriptions of a Harlem drag ball, lodge parties, funerals, weddings, and the enterprising ways of Reverend Dr. Becton, a popular Harlem preacher (273–8). "Harlem likes spectacles of one kind or another – but then so does all the world," Hughes writes (274). For a time, the world came to see the spectacle that was Harlem, which was, for a time, like no other spectacle anywhere.

The cultural activity that has come to characterize the Harlem Renaissance was by no means limited to Harlem, whose geography, in spatial terms, consists of only two square miles at the northern tip of Manhattan. African American art, music, literature, and politics also thrived during the New Negro Movement in cities like Chicago, Detroit, Philadelphia, and Washington, DC, where more than quarter of a million blacks settled after fleeing southern poverty and racial violence during the Great Migration. Importantly, there was meaningful creative interplay between African American, Caribbean, and African writers during the Harlem Renaissance years. African American artists were concerned with what was being produced in other parts of the Diaspora as much as they were with the artistic flowering within their own borders. Most recently, a 2003 study by Brent Edwards, *The Practice of Diaspora: Literature, Translation, and the Rise of Black Internationalism*, makes evident the crucial feature of black internationalism that was actually embedded within the framework of the Harlem Renaissance itself.[6]

Still, despite its inherent limitations, Harlem, New York, was unique as a city that spoke to black hopes and dreams. "I was in love with Harlem long before I got there," Langston Hughes wrote in a 1963 retrospective essay, "My Early Days in Harlem."[7] During the Harlem Renaissance years, Hughes spent more time away from Harlem than in it. In his autobiography, *The Big Sea*, and his correspondence to friends like Arna Bontemps, Carl Van Vechten, and others, Hughes keeps a faithful catalog of the numerous journeys he took within and without the borders of the United States during the years Harlem was in vogue. And yet when he writes of Harlem itself, he describes the singular romantic spell the neighborhood cast over him. As a teenager in Mexico with his father, Hughes "had an overwhelming desire to see Harlem," he wrote in *The Big Sea*. "More than Paris, or the Shakespeare country, or Berlin, or the Alps, I wanted to see Harlem, the greatest Negro city in the world" (62). He describes his first subway trip to Harlem: "I went up the steps and out into the bright September sunlight. Harlem! I stood there, dropped my bags, took a deep breath and felt happy again" (81).

Hughes was not alone. "I'd rather be a lamppost in Harlem than Governor of Georgia," went a popular saying of the day. No city in the North captured the imagination of the black migrant more fiercely than Harlem, which was first a Dutch settlement before it became German, then Irish, then Jewish, then black, after a considerable real estate war and subsequent white flight out of Harlem neighborhoods. The neighborhoods that comprised Harlem, known as the "black mecca," were not only famously elegant, they became home to some of the most diverse black populations in the country. Laborers fresh from the South rubbed elbows with African Americans who had know wealth, independence, and social prestige for generations. Immigrants from the West Indies and Africa encountered black people with entirely different sensibilities and customs. Some of these subcultures blended harmoniously while others did so grudgingly, but all of this mixing provided excellent fodder for African American artists determined to translate the cultural upheaval they saw around them into their art. In 1928, Harlem alone claimed 200,000 black residents.

Black migrants mingled with African American natives of New York across culture and class lines, both outdoors – along the elegant avenues and broad sidewalks that characterized Harlem – and indoors – inside cabarets, buffet flats, speakeasies and ballrooms that dominated nightlife in the city. The Harlem Renaissance flourished alongside the Jazz Age, an era that recalls the institutions that made it famous, nightclubs like the Cotton Club, Connie's Inn, and Small's Paradise. It was nightlife that brought Langston Hughes to Harlem. There were plenty of practical reasons for Hughes, as an aspiring young writer, to set his sights on Harlem in the 1920s. Most prominently, New York had recently supplanted Boston as the center of American publishing. But the spectacle of Harlem nightlife was what enchanted Hughes and got him to Manhattan. "To see *Shuffle Along* was the main reason I wanted to go to Columbia," Hughes confesses in *The Big Sea* about his college choice. Hughes lasted at Columbia only a year, but he would have a relationship to Harlem and its culture for the rest of his life. In the portion of *The Big Sea* devoted to the Harlem Renaissance, Hughes credits shows like *Shuffle Along* (1921) and *Runnin' Wild* (1923), and the Charleston, with launching the Harlem Renaissance: "But certainly it was the musical revue, *Shuffle Along*, that gave a scintillating send-off to that Negro vogue in Manhattan, which reached its peak just before the crash of 1929, the crash that sent Negroes, white folks, and all rolling down the hill toward the Works Progress Administration" (223). Hughes saw other shows that year, he writes, "but I remember *Shuffle Along* best of all. It gave just the proper push – a pre-Charleston kick – to that Negro vogue of the 20's, that spread to books, African sculpture, music, and dancing" (224).

Shows like *Shuffle Along* lent dimension to the vogue of the Negro, bringing white people to Harlem "in droves," Hughes recalls. White interest in Harlem created the central paradox of the New Negro Movement. White financial support was essential to the success of the Harlem Renaissance, but it also forced restraints on black creative expression. In the case of Harlem nightlife, for instance, while white interest meant increased revenue in Harlem neighborhoods, it also meant that black patrons had to sit in segregated, "Jim Crow," sections in order to accommodate its downtown clientele, who came to Harlem to look at black people but not experience them as equals. Hughes describes the phenomenon in *The Big Sea*: "So Harlem Negroes did not like the Cotton Club and never appreciated its Jim Crow policy in the very heart of their dark community. Nor did ordinary Negroes like the growing influx of whites toward Harlem after sundown, flooding the little cabarets and bars where formerly only colored people laughed and sang, and where now the strangers were given the best ringside tables to sit and stare at the Negro customers – like amusing animals in a zoo" (224–5). There was a substantial and meaningful disharmony between white and black experiences in Harlem. Hughes explains it well: "So thousands of whites came to Harlem night after night, thinking the Negroes loved to have them there, and firmly believing that all Harlemites left their homes at sundown to sing and dance in cabarets, because most of the whites saw nothing but the cabarets, not the houses" (225). The thrill of Harlem nightlife brought to the fore the intractable nature of American racism that made real black progress – the kind hoped for in *The New Negro* – impossible.

"Rent parties," thrown ostensibly to raise rent money for the host, became important avenues for African Americans to congregate privately, away from the curious gazes of white people. However successful these parties were at giving blacks in Harlem sanctuary from inquiring white eyes, they could not resolve the larger conundrum of white influence on the Harlem Renaissance, a conundrum to which this chapter will return.

If at night New York and Harlem roared, then during the day it thrived, too, as home to the most important social and political institutions of the Harlem Renaissance period: the National Association for the Advancement of Colored People (NAACP), the National Urban League, and the Universal Negro Improvement Association (UNIA). Each of these institutions had distinct personalities embodied by the individuals most closely associated with them as well as by the magazines and newspapers they produced. The NAACP had its most visible spokesperson in the scholar, activist, and novelist W. E. B. Du Bois, who edited *The Crisis*, the house organ of the NAACP. The National Urban League had educator and writer Charles S. Johnson, who edited its magazine, *Opportunity*. The UNIA was founded and led by Marcus Garvey, who also edited the organization's weekly newspaper, *Negro World*. These organizations and magazines were among several that were crucial during the Harlem Renaissance because of their dedication to social and political progress for black people. In addition, *The Crisis* and *Opportunity* in particular were critical because of their commitment to the identification and development of African American literature and art. For most African American writers, getting a book published may have been the ultimate goal, but newspapers and magazines reached the broadest audiences, and, because of this, constituted significant vehicles for cultural expression during the Harlem Renaissance.

The question of which years mark the Harlem Renaissance generates as much debate as many other aspects of the cultural movement, but this chapter identifies 1924 as the initial year of the Harlem Renaissance period because of a party given in March of this year by *Opportunity* editor Charles S. Johnson. Johnson originally intended to throw this party as a way of honoring Jessie Fauset, literary editor of *The Crisis*, on the publication of her first novel, *There Is Confusion* (1924). In the end, 110 members of the New York literati, black and white, attended the dinner, which was held at the Civic Club, the only elite club in Manhattan that welcomed both black people and white women. Black and white editors, writers, and publishers addressed the crowd and referred to their common belief that a new era had begun for black creativity.

After the dinner, Paul Kellogg, editor of the sociological periodical *Survey Graphic*, suggested to Charles S. Johnson that his magazine devote an entire issue to African American culture, and that Johnson serve as editor of the volume. Johnson enlisted the philosopher Alain Locke to help him assemble the issue. In March 1925, a special edition of *Survey Graphic*, entitled "Harlem: Mecca of the New Negro," was released. It was the most widely read issue in the magazine's history, selling 42,000 copies – more than twice its regular circulation. Months later, Alain Locke expanded this special edition into an arts anthology, *The New Negro* (1925), widely recognized as the first manifesto produced by the Harlem Renaissance. *The New Negro*, which featured portrait drawings as well as essays, poetry, and fiction, includes the work of most of the key figures of this movement.

Inspired by the success of his 1924 dinner, Charles S. Johnson decided that *Opportunity* would host a literary contest; prizes would be awarded in

May 1925. The first announcement for the contest appeared in the August 1924 issue of *Opportunity*. Johnson titillated his readers by adding new names of influential whites who would serve as judges for each issue. Ultimately, twenty-four respected white and black editors, publishers and artists served as contest judges in five categories: essays, short stories, poetry, drama, and personal experiences. The wife of Henry Goddard Leach, editor of *Forum* magazine, contributed the prize money, which totaled $470.

The awards ceremony, held in May 1925, was a resounding success: 316 people attended to witness future luminaries like Sterling Brown, Roland Hayes, E. Franklin Frazier, Zora Neale Hurston, Eric Walrond, Countee Cullen, and Langston Hughes accept their awards. Cullen and Hughes, who would always be rivals for the hearts of Harlem Renaissance poetry lovers, dominated the poetry category. One of Hughes' signature poems, "The Weary Blues" (1925), took the first prize. At the end of the evening, Johnson announced that Casper Holstein, king of the Harlem numbers racket, would fund the second annual *Opportunity* contest.

Charles S. Johnson and *Opportunity* provided an impetus for the literary flowering of the Harlem Renaissance, but no magazine and no single figure meant more to this period than *The Crisis* and its editor, W. E. B. Du Bois. *The Crisis* also held literary contests, and Du Bois presided over the first, which was held in November 1925. *The Crisis* had an enormous circulation – 95,000 at its peak in 1919 – so to be published there was a sign of success, at least among the black middle class. Nothing was published in *The Crisis* that did not meet Du Bois' exacting standards. Between 1919 and 1924, when he became deeply involved in the Pan-African Congress movement, Du Bois relied upon his literary editor at *The Crisis*, Jessie Redmon Fauset, to uphold his standards. These years were rich for African American writing, and Jessie Fauset's understanding of the literary contours of the Harlem Renaissance was reflected in the foresight she demonstrated by publishing writers like Langston Hughes and Jean Toomer before other gatekeepers did so. Fauset left *The Crisis* in 1926. By that time she had made a substantial impact on the magazine and, by extension, the Harlem Renaissance. She would go on to write three more novels of her own.

Du Bois had seen the coming of a Negro renaissance as early as 1920, when he had announced in the pages of *The Crisis* his belief in the importance of black writers asserting authority over their own experience. For too long, he believed, blacks had endured the ridicule of white artists who had risen to success by reducing African Americans to their most debased elements (here, think again of *Birth of a Nation*). Because art had the potential to liberate black people from social bondage, Du Bois believed, it should be approached with gravity. In 1926, he wrote, famously, in *The Crisis* that he did not "care a damn" for any art that did not do the work of racial uplift. As editor of *The Crisis*, his words carried weight.

The passion in Du Bois' words signals a larger tension that was at work in the Harlem Renaissance literary community by 1926. On one side were intellectuals like Du Bois, who believed that black art should always serve as good propaganda for the race. On the other side were writers like Langston Hughes and Wallace Thurman, who defended their right to represent the Negro as they pleased, in both positive and negative lights. Hughes wrote a 1926 essay for *The Nation*, "The Negro Artist and the Racial Mountain," which represented not only his personal philosophies about artistic freedom, but also the philosophies of the "younger generation of Negro Artists," as Hughes christened them. Explicitly, "The Negro Artist" was a response to "The Negro-Art Hokum," a caustic essay by satirist George S. Schuyler, also published in *The Nation* in 1926, who used his essay to lampoon the idea that an authentic black art actually existed. In "The Negro Artist," Hughes staked his own position in the continuous debate about the meaning and purpose of Negro art.

These disparate aesthetic philosophies found concrete purpose in the scandal surrounding a single book, *Nigger Heaven*, and its singular author, Carl Van Vechten. When *Nigger Heaven* was published in 1926, Van Vechten, a novelist, cultural critic, and Negro arts enthusiast, had been a presence in the Harlem Renaissance since its inception. At the 1925 *Opportunity* awards dinner, he made a point of introducing himself to the evening's brightest star, Langston Hughes. Within three weeks of this meeting, Van Vechten had secured for Hughes a contract with Alfred A. Knopf, Inc. for his first book of poetry, *The Weary Blues* (1926), and suggested the title for the volume, as well. Van Vechten would serve as a mentor to Hughes for the rest of his life. He would also come to serve as a champion of the work of Nella Larsen, whom he would also guide to publication at Knopf, as well as Zora Neale Hurston, who deemed him a "Negrotarian." Van Vechten also rescued from obscurity the anonymously published *Autobiography of an Ex-Colored Man* (1912), and reissued it in 1927 as a novel by James Weldon Johnson, the well-known African American political and cultural figure, and his close friend. Van Vechten was far from the only white person who championed the cause of black arts during the Harlem Renaissance. Charlotte Mason, for instance, patron to Langston Hughes and Zora Neale Hurston, exercised power over the movement, albeit in her private, individual relationships with Hughes, Hurston, and Alain Locke, who introduced Mason to Hughes and Hurston, among others. There were other powerful white figures in the New Negro Movement, but none outdistanced Carl Van Vechten in his commitment to and impact on black arts and letters.

Van Vechten called *Nigger Heaven* his most serious novel, and it was the only novel he would publish about African American life and culture. When the book came out, he was already the author of four novels that had, collectively, made him a bestseller and a celebrity. In addition, he had published numerous articles in popular, mainstream publications, like *Vanity Fair*, extolling the virtues of spirituals and the blues, arguing for their recognition as authentic American art forms. Still, Van Vechten had concerns about how African Americans, not his primary readership heretofore, would react to his representation of Harlem life. In order to address these concerns, he anonymously composed a questionnaire for *The Crisis*, "The Negro in Art: How Shall He Be Portrayed?" in 1926. Answers to this questionnaire were solicited from a racially diverse group of literary figures from all corners of the American literary world, and then published in *The Crisis* over a period of several months. Six months later, *Nigger Heaven* was published.

Du Bois hated *Nigger Heaven*, and published a scathing review of it in *The Crisis*, advising readers to "drop the book gently into the grate." Hughes defended the book in newspapers articles and even in his 1940 autobiography, *The Big Sea*. The opposing viewpoints held by these two were matched by reviews by others that were equally extreme. Both loved and hated, *Nigger Heaven* went through nine printings in its first four months, selling more copies than any other Harlem Renaissance novel.

In 1926, Carl Van Vechten and his novel *Nigger Heaven* had become handy symbolic means for some black writers to announce their desire to break away from literary conventions that had, according to these writers, traditionally constrained the black writer. A 1926 journal *Fire!!* became the clearest articulation of the aesthetic goals of this younger generation, which included Langston Hughes, Zora Neale Hurston, Richard Bruce Nugent, and Wallace Thurman. In *Fire!!*, conceived and edited by Wallace Thurman, these writers and their peers wrote about sex and Carl Van Vechten, among other topics, as a way of critiquing censorship and racial parochialism in literature. As much as the editors of *Fire!!* dreamt that their magazine would operate free of white support, such a goal proved unrealistic. An actual fire put an end to the journal, which lasted for only one issue.

The threat that Van Vechten seemed to pose to black culture was bigger than his novel. Van Vechten was unambivalent and unapologetic about his own feelings about the "vogue" of the Negro: he was all for it. He felt black people should be for it, too. He described his beliefs in his own response to *The Crisis* questionnaire he had anonymously composed: "The squalor of Negro life, the vice of Negro life, offer a wealth of novel, exotic, picturesque material to the artist," he wrote. "Are Negro writers going to write about this exotic material while it is still fresh," he questioned, "or will they continue to make a free gift of it to white authors who will exploit it until not a drop of vitality remains?" Six months after he published these statements in *The Crisis*, *Nigger Heaven* was released.

Like W. E. B. Du Bois, many black readers felt betrayed by *Nigger Heaven*. "Anyone who would call a book Nigger Heaven would call a Negro a Nigger," a *New York News* reviewer put it succinctly. Van Vechten would always claim the title was meant to be ironic. He explained that "nigger heaven" was a common term used in Harlem to refer to the balcony section in segregated theaters usually reserved for black patrons. He insisted that he had employed it as a metaphor to comment more generally upon the cruelties and absurdities of segregation and racism. But Van Vechten also believed that his status as an "honorary Negro" somehow absolved him of racism; or at least, it lent him an authority to use "nigger," a term sometimes used privately between blacks but traditionally forbidden whites. Finally, a combination of naiveté and arrogance led him to believe he was unique, a white man who had transcended his whiteness.

The book had its black defenders, however. Among them was Langston Hughes. "No book could possibly be as bad as *Nigger Heaven* has been painted," Hughes wrote in the *Pittsburgh Courier* in 1927; in his review, he sidestepped the question of whether the novel had literary merit. Even when he returned to the controversy nearly fifteen years later in *The Big Sea*, he never claimed that the book should be appreciated as an exceptional work of literature. Instead he sympathized with those who felt alienated by the racial epithet that was the title, but insisted that readers put the issue in perspective. "The critics of the left, like the Negroes of the right, proceeded to light on Mr. Van Vechten, and he was accused of ruining, distorting, polluting, and corrupting every Negro writer from then on," Hughes recounted.

Of all his black associates, Van Vechten was most often accused of corrupting Langston Hughes, particularly when *Fine Clothes to the Jew*, Hughes' second book of poetry, was published in 1927. *Fine Clothes* drew as much fire for its title and sensual content as did *Nigger Heaven*. Critics who associated *Fine Clothes* with Van Vechten's influence on Hughes either did not know or did not care that Hughes had composed most of the poems before he met Van Vechten. When Hughes defended Van Vechten, then, he was essentially defending his own artistic decisions.

Hughes was also motivated to defend *Nigger Heaven* because he shared a similar aesthetic sensibility with its author. In his 1926 essay, "The Negro Artist and the Racial Mountain," Hughes proclaimed: "Let the blare of Negro jazz bands and the bellowing voice of Bessie Smith singing Blues penetrate the closed ears of the colored near-intellectual until they listen and perhaps understand." Hughes found the social anxieties of the "smug Negro middle class," as he called them, boring. He was inspired by the way the black majority lived: "These common people are not afraid of spirituals, as for a long time their more intellectual brethren were, and jazz is their child."

Langston Hughes loved the "low-down folks," which is how he referred to the black working class. His passion was matched in intensity by that of Carl Van Vechten. When in the March 1926 issue of *The Crisis*, Van Vechten champions "the squalor of Negro life, the vice of Negro life," he sounds unmistakably like Langston Hughes when he celebrates "the so-called common element" who are fond of "their nip of gin on Saturday nights" in "The Negro Artist and the Racial Mountain." Both Hughes and Van Vechten defended the black artist's right to paint the world and its citizens as he saw them, but Van Vechten's position contained a decidedly pragmatic element, as is evident in this excerpt from "Moanin' Wid a Sword in Mah Han," a 1926 essay by Van Vechten about Negro spirituals:

> It is a foregone conclusion that with the craving to hear these songs that is known to exist on the part of the public, it will not be long before white singers have taken them over and made them enough their own so that the public will be surfeited sooner or later with opportunities to enjoy them, and – when the Negro tardily offers to sing them in public – it will perhaps be too late to stir the interest which now lies latent in the breast of every music lover.[8]

In other words, African Americans should heed the call of the market – and fast. Van Vechten's argument is premised upon the inevitability of white fascination with the fiction of black primitivism. If the white gaze is here to stay, then black people should manipulate it in their own interests. We may bristle at Van Vechten's brutal cynicism and essentialist language, but the outcome he describes above is a veritable cliché in the annals of African American culture. White spectatorship – and appropriation – is, finally, a central facet of African American cultural history.

The urgency in Van Vechten's language foreshadows, unhappily, the outcome of the Harlem Renaissance. A black movement that was necessarily dependent on white support, the New Negro Movement was diminished by the Wall Street Crash of 1929, and then effectively terminated by the Great Depression. Just as dramatically as the Negro found himself in vogue in 1924, he found himself out of fashion a few years later. Economic realities notwithstanding, "How could a large and enthusiastic number of people be crazy about Negroes forever?" Hughes asks rhetorically in *The Big Sea* (228). But even though vogues die, they are reborn, and with that rebirth are often transformed into something greater. Black communities were devastated by the Crash, and yet African American art thrived and evolved to negotiate the realities of new economic, social, and political conditions, including new forms of white institutional support. Some scholars continue to isolate the Harlem Renaissance as having been uniquely tied to white influence for its existence. But the inextricability of white investment in black culture has been a constant feature of African American life. If the New Negro Movement is unique, it is so because it remains unmatched as the most serious collective attempt on the part of black writers and artists to grapple with the complexity of African American identity in the modern world.

NOTES

1. Langston Hughes, *The Big Sea* (New York: Hill and Wang, 1940), p. 228.
2. Henry Louis Gates Jr., "The Trope of a New Negro and the Reconstruction of the Image of the Black," *Representations* 24 (Fall 1988), 131.
3. Alain Locke, ed., *The New Negro* (New York: Touchstone, 1997), p. 5.
4. Arnold Rampersad, "Racial Doubt and Racial Shame in the Harlem Renaissance," in Genevieve Fabre and Michel Feith, eds., *Temples for Tomorrow: Looking Back at the Harlem Renaissance* (Bloomington: Indiana University Press, 2001).
5. David Levering Lewis, *When Harlem Was in Vogue* (New York: Oxford University Press, 1989).
6. Brent Hayes Edwards, *The Practice of Diaspora: Literature, Translation, and the Rise of Black Internationalism* (Cambridge, MA: Harvard University Press, 2003).
7. Langston Hughes, "My Early Days in Harlem," *Freedomways* 3 (1963), 312–14.
8. Carl Van Vechten, "Moanin' Wid a Sword in Mah Han'," *Vanity Fair* 1926. Reprinted in Bruce Kellner, ed., *"Keep A-Inchin' Along": Selected Writings of Carl Van Vechten about Black Art and Letters* (Westport, CT: Greenwood Press, 1979), p. 55.

3

MICHAEL A. CHANEY

International contexts of the Negro Renaissance

The exceptional character of the Harlem Renaissance as a watershed of self-directed "Negro" arts and letters and the popular view of its centralization in Harlem have led to an unfortunate occlusion of its international dimensions. The "New Negro Movement" bloomed within a global network of epiphenomenal cultural nationalisms and folk revivals. In the first two decades of the twentieth century, pulses of decolonization rippled throughout Asia, the Caribbean, and Ireland, catalyzed by China's 1901 Boxer Rebellion, the Russian Revolution of 1917, and postwar efforts to accommodate European ethnic minorities in their struggles for self-determination. Much of the scholarship surrounding the Harlem Renaissance, however, has approached it at the expense of the global as a phenomenon of primarily national significance despite the persistent emphasis on internationalism in the works and life experiences of the movement's leading figures. Even when this emphasis is noted, as with the much-studied Negro vogues of Paris and Berlin, the international scope of the movement's influence and impact has been conceptualized according to an American context rooted in slavery, reconstruction, migration, and segregation. Nevertheless, a few scholars, such as Robert Stepto, Michel Fabre, and Melvin Dixon, have outlined the global contours of the Harlem Renaissance currently being reexamined and theorized anew by Brent Hayes Edwards, George Hutchinson, and others, so that the transnational shape of the movement and the disparate worldviews of its writers may come more fully into view.

Before twentieth-century Atlantic crossings, the international mobility of African American creativity and thought depended upon crossings of the Mason-Dixon Line. Indeed, the peculiar institution of slavery and the vicissitudes of its relation to transatlantic abolitionism thrust many African Americans into an international spotlight, touring Europe with lectures and speeches in recruit of antislavery support. From European vantage points, prominent ex-fugitives such as William Wells Brown, Frederick Douglass, Henry "Box" Brown, Sarah Parker Remond, and William Craft wrote letters and editorials displaying comparative insights into American racism that would echo later in the works of black expatriates from W. E. B. Du Bois, who pursued two years of graduate study in Germany, to James Weldon Johnson, who wrote *Autobiography of an Ex-Colored Man* (1912) during a three-year stint as United States consul in Puerto Cabello, Venezuela; and from Langston Hughes, who taught English in Mexico before traveling widely, to subsequent writers like Richard Wright and James Baldwin, who both sought refuge in France from the oppressions of Jim Crow segregation. Just as European travel enlarged the race consciousness of black writers, the presence of African American abolitionists in England had a profound effect on the emerging nationalism of English citizens, consolidating Victorian notions of class and difference.[1] By the end of the nineteenth century, only a few black antislavery exponents held official diplomatic posts serving Latin American and African countries, but innumerable other African American sailors, musicians, soldiers, and missionaries spanned the globe, sustaining the unofficial circuits of transatlantic exchange and cultural syncretism that Paul Gilroy convincingly discovers operating throughout the nineteenth and early twentieth centuries.

On a grander scale, the First World War ushered in an upsurge of nationalist propaganda that was on the surface congruent with the broadest aims of the Harlem movement. But rallying cries for the enfranchisement of hitherto oppressed European ethnic groups resonated ironically for many African Americans, whose exclusion from the domestic agenda of cultural pluralism reinforced postwar disillusion among leading black intellectuals. And yet, as George Hutchinson has argued, crucial links still existed between optimists of America's unique postwar position to make good on a dream of integration, including figures like Waldo Frank and Jean Toomer.[2]

The war thus became a stage both real and imagined on which black artists and activists dramatized possibilities for a purgative union of entrenched social conflicts, not just between blacks and whites as with Du Bois' eventual capitulation to support the war effort despite the prejudicial treatment of African American soldiers, but also between blacks divided by class. The war interlude of Jessie Fauset's *There Is Confusion* (1924) sets the intraracial reconciliation of the educated Philip and the working-class Maggie in Europe, as though the barrier that separates bourgeois and folk is made porous by the backdrop of international crisis. The liberatory promise of an imagined Europe to unravel America's stultifying racial proscriptions of identity became a trope in Fauset's later novels as well: the ending of *Plum Bun* (1929) takes place in Paris while the last third of *Comedy: American Style* (1933) is set in the south of France. As Cheryl Wall and Brent Edwards have shown, Fauset's Du Bois-inspired anti-imperialism and devotion to

Allied rhetoric of self-determination were crystallized in experiences abroad. Living in France during the summer of 1914 upon the outbreak of war and attending the second Pan-African Conference with Du Bois in Paris in 1921 forged in her a sophisticated historical sensitivity to international crises and social justice that she articulated, for some readers, more cogently in her essays than in her novels. Although once roundly criticized for endorsing bourgeois elitism, Fauset's novels have been reassessed in light of their often subtle critique of gendered double standards, subtleties no doubt finely tuned by her experiences overseas. Like Larsen's *Quicksand* (1928), Fauset's *Comedy: American Style* rejects the easy myth of expatriate escapism found in Johnson's *Autobiography of an Ex-Colored Man*. In stranding her heroine alone in France with a miserly racist for a husband, Fauset emphasized how "sexism, European exoticism, [and] class barriers" reveal the masculine bias in fantasies of European escape that ignore such antagonisms.[3]

Although African American writers held diverse views of the war and subsequent efforts to maintain international as well as interethnic accord in the League of Nations, Fauset's investments in European locales make clear how deeply intertwined the war and what it variously symbolized became for artists of this period. International campaigns to uphold the sovereignty of dispossessed and displaced peoples became a legacy of the peace process, influencing the Harlem Renaissance as well as other global outpourings of cultural nationalism.[4] As with nineteenth-century abolitionism, the war drove American blacks onto European stages, this time as cultural diplomats performing jazz music for international audiences and to enormous acclaim. The vogues surrounding jazz performances in Paris and elsewhere returned home to Harlem with the famous "Hell Fighters," who offered celebrated concerts of the same music in Harlem which had won them so much applause overseas. But even as home-grown African American culture circulated through Europe, Harlem movement visionaries were equally inspired by popular European forms of folk art.

A precursor of the Harlem Renaissance typically cited as an influence by researchers of the period is the Irish Renaissance. Driven by such late nineteenth- and early twentieth-century figures as J. M. Synge, W. B. Yeats, Sean O'Casey, and Lady Gregory, the Irish Renaissance's revival of Celtic folklore and language played cultural partner to a politics of Irish independence and became known to Americans after a successful tour by the Abbey Theatre in 1911. Similarities enabling affiliation between the Irish and African Americans included a history of oppression and colonization, the degradation of ancestral language and religion, and a marginal position as creators of national cultures despite being longstanding stereotypes within them.

Moreover, luminaries of the Harlem Renaissance invoked the Irish Renaissance directly as a model for an efflorescence of art that would aid programs for racial justice and spread knowledge of African American culture. Playwright Willis Richardson exhorted African American artists to emulate the Irish theater movement as "an excellent model" in a 1919 *Crisis* essay.[5] Poetry too was championed by James Weldon Johnson as a productive forum from which the Negro poet could reclaim the dignity of vernacular language. In the 1922 preface to his anthology *The Book of American Negro Poetry*, Johnson urged "the colored poet" to do "something like what Synge did for the Irish; he needs to find a form that will express the racial spirit by symbols from within rather than by symbols from without."[6] Likewise, Alain Locke in his 1925 introduction to the *New Negro* anthology compared Harlem to other "nascent centers of folk-expression and self-determination" and noted that it "has the same rôle to play for the New Negro as Dublin had for the New Ireland or Prague for the New Czechoslovakia."[7] Influenced by cultural revolutions in Russia, Hungary, and Italy, the Harlem and Irish Renaissances both emphasized the ambassadorial task of the arts in facilitating self-governance and liberation from colonial power.

But African American interest in the Irish Renaissance was not limited to paradigms for politicized art. A stronger political connection was drawn between the fight for Irish sovereignty and that of African Americans in Marcus Garvey's 1920 speech to his Universal Negro Improvement Association. Before thousands assembled in Madison Square Garden, Garvey read aloud a telegram he was sending to the president of the newly instated Irish Parliament: "We believe Ireland should be free even as Africa shall be free for the Negroes of the world."[8] In "Keep[ing] up the fight for a free Ireland," Garvey was expressing a belief in the interrelation and mutual dependency of international movements for ethnic self-determination based on a shared relationship to domination and social minoritization rather than a narrower concept of racial affiliation.

In addition to the Irish model of insurgent aesthetics, the evolving political climate of the Caribbean had an enormous impact on the Harlem movement, since so many of the immigrants who doubled America's population of foreign-born blacks between 1900 and 1910, like Claude McKay and Marcus Garvey, hailed from there. Other distinguished Afro-Caribbeans associated with the Harlem Renaissance included writers such as Nella Larsen (though identified more with her maternal Danishness than with her paternal West Indian heritage), Eric Walrond (Guyana/Barbados), W. A. Domingo (Jamaica), and Cyril Briggs (Nevis); as well as political leaders Richard Moore (Barbados) and Hubert Harrison (St. Croix), minister

Ethelred Brown (Jamaica), bibliophile Arthur Schomburg (Puerto Rico/St. Thomas), and photographer Austin Hansen (St. Thomas). The conflicting histories, dialects, and sensibilities of class, gender, and race that these figures brought with them to the black metropolis were unified by shared experiences of colonial struggle against American expansion and contributed to the movement's growing but in no way univocal expression of black internationalism.

By the 1920s the United States had established itself through military and economic measures as an imperial authority in the Caribbean. At the turn of the century, the USA had imposed severe limitations upon the sovereignty of Cuba and Panama as wars over Cuban independence and the Panama Canal culminated in sanctions privileging American political and financial control. As a result of various treaties as well as the Platt Amendment (1903), which would become a political paradigm for American dominance in the Caribbean and Latin America, political enfranchisement within the weaker nations was restricted to whites as opposed to majorities of African descent. This racial elitism was enforced by constant threat of American military action and sustained by the establishment of American constabularies. Continuing policies of military intervention instated by Teddy Roosevelt, the avowed anti-imperialist Woodrow Wilson occupied Haiti and the Dominican Republic in 1915 and 1916. Although opposition to the relatively small numbers involved in US troop activity remained limited throughout the Caribbean and Central America (particularly when compared to the 65,000 troops sent to stifle guerrilla uprisings in the Philippines between 1899 and 1902), significant uprisings occurred in Nicaragua in 1912 and in Haiti in 1919 and 1920. According to US reports, more than 3000 Haitians died in anti-American insurrections in Haiti during these years.[9] A chief cause of the Haiti rebellions was the reinstitution by American gendarmerie of the corvée system in road building, a formerly abolished method of forced labor whose reestablishment brought with it renewed social divisions based on racial classifications. Resuscitating forms of racial hierarchy rooted in the slave trade ensured that even though strict military control over these regions diminished in the ensuing years, which saw growing domestic opposition to American involvement in Caribbean and Latin American countries, the impact of a cultural and economic occupation would linger in ways not lost on Langston Hughes during his visits to the region in the 1920s and 30s.

Championing Caribbean decolonization, Hughes introduced the Cuban and Haitian writers he had met during his travels there to American audiences through seminal translations. With Mercer Cook he translated *Masters of the Dew* (1947), a novel by Jacques Romain of Haiti, and with Ben Frederic Carruthers he translated the poetry of Nicolás Guillén, who had earlier translated Hughes' "I, Too, Sing America" into Spanish and whom Hughes in turn had inspired to incorporate the Afro-Cuban rhythms of the *son* into his first collection, *Motivos de Son* (1930), as Hughes had done with the blues in his own poetry. But excursions to the Caribbean were not only occasions for the replenishment of Hughes' anti-imperialism. He often went with a desire for physical and spiritual replenishment, finding a salubrious "temporary erasure of identity" in tropical environments peopled by those who shared his skin tone as well as his outrage for Yankee exploitation.[10] Indeed, in a land that Hughes associated with the heroics of L'Ouverture, he found that the "Haitian people live today under a sort of military dictatorship backed by American guns."[11] Sensitive, perceptive, and critically reflective of his own national and racial identity, Hughes developed insights into the complexity of racial subjection during his international ventures. "It was in Haiti," he noted, "that I first realized how class lines may cut across color lines within a race, and how dark people of the same nationality may scorn those below them."[12]

In the USA the influx of what is now considered the "first wave" of "Caribbeaners" reached an apex in the mid-1920s, coinciding with the height of renaissance activity and affecting the social milieu of black Harlem dramatically. Presenting vast differences in national affiliation, religious customs, dialect, education, and ideologies of class from one another and African Americans, Caribbeans exposed the absurdity of US systems of racialization which blindly homogenized blacks in static opposition to whites and forced a sometimes ominous recognition of the obstacles facing black coalitions of culture and politics for even the most utopian leaders of the Renaissance.

To address some of these obstacles of miscommunication or – as Brent Hayes Edwards insightfully theorizes them – problems of "translation," a special issue of *Opportunity* in November of 1926 sought to ease tensions between native and immigrant black communities by providing a "wider and deeper acquaintance ... with the large group of Negroes who have come to these shores" in the hopes of achieving editor Charles Johnson's vision of an "essential friendship" between the two groups.[13] For Johnson, the select assemblage of Caribbean newcomers to American metropolises could offer the New Negro "an invaluable stimulation" in cultivating new perspectives on "North American race situations." Thwarting this stimulation, however, were reciprocal hostilities between and among these groups, diagnosed by Johnson as "snobbishness and jealousies, resentment and group selfishness," which he intended the issue's contributors to dispel. To that end, an indirect contribution appeared in the form of Waldo Frank's review of *Opportunity* business manager Eric Walrond's *Tropic Death* (1926), a collection of short stories recounting the migratory experiences of Caribbean laborers and their novel encounters with racist forms of US labor discrimination administered in the Panama Canal zone. Walrond's protagonists suffer as a result of their clashes with systems of demotion based entirely on a stark colorism so alien to their native conceptualizations of a worker identity that is contingent upon class, regional affiliation, and skill level.

Three poems by Claude McKay supplemented the special edition's creative reflection on the immigrant experience of dislocation. His "Desolate," "My House," and "America in Retrospect" may be read alongside the rest of the issue as lyrical comments on the contradictions inherent to the Caribbean condition in the USA. The speaker of "My House" bewails feeling "peculiar in an alien atmosphere" and knowing "the dark delight of being strange" (6) though surrounded by others who "wear a kindred hue" (3). Even so, the introspective "penalty of difference in the crowd" (7) characterizing McKay's migrant consciousness also comes with an advantage: a romantic independence that engenders – as in "America in Retrospect" – the "freedom and peace" (12) that permits creative expression. The same America that McKay accuses of making him "a stoic introvert" (8), therefore, also facilitates his role as a poet. The trade-off between empowerment and self-imprisoning insularity available to *Opportunity* readers of these two poems – readers who may have been encouraged to find in them poetic coordinates for the Caribbean and America – is rendered problematic by the consistently dour mood of "Desolate." Here the phantasmal tropical scenes mourned as "forever gone" continue to haunt the speaker, predicating life in the new country on a thoroughly homeless condition.

The presence of so many Caribbean migrants in New York also helped to radicalize Renaissance politics as Caribbean-born organizers drew upon a "long and distinguished tradition of resistance" to promulgate socialism to the Harlem masses.[14] In an essay reprinted in *The New Negro* from a special issue of *Survey Graphic*, the Jamaica-born Wilfred Adolphus Domingo struck a nearly vainglorious tone when describing the particular "Gift" of radicalism given by Caribbean immigrants to African Americans: "without them [Caribbean immigrants] the genuinely radical movement among New York Negroes would be unworthy of attention."[15] Though Domingo would go on to briefly edit Garvey's newspaper, *The Negro World*, his ethnic partisanship and commitment to the particularity of his Caribbean identity would later lead him to found the Jamaican Progressive League in New York City in 1936. Similarly, Cyril V. Briggs, who was born in Nevis, established the African Blood Brotherhood for African Liberation and Redemption in 1919, an international organization of revolutionary socialism, one year after launching *The Crusader*, a journal that aimed to cultivate in African

Americans a tactical awareness of their position within a global racial dynamic that would ideally culminate in nation-building collaboration with West Indian republics.

Aside from their contributions as journalists and founders of radical newspapers, Caribbean activists fomented an atmosphere of grassroots militancy in Harlem, bringing current events and cutting-edge intellectualism to street corner speeches, or the "stepladder forum" – so called because of the use of these perches to improvise unofficial symposia whenever and wherever speakers could summon an audience. In one contemporary description of such a talk by famed speaker Hubert Harrison, the *New York News* of August 28, 1926 marveled at the rhetorical finesse with which Harrison outlined similarities between Darwinian evolution and the Marxist theory of the "development from capitalism to a state of communism."[16]

Yet even if they used similar tactics to get their messages across, Caribbean activists did not always have the same message. They agreed, for the most part, on federal action against lynching, improvements of working conditions for black laborers, and increased education, particularly with respect to the effects of Diaspora, colonialism, and racism. At the same time, fractious argument erupted over such questions as whether political platforms should privilege race or ideology, if they should endorse trade unions, and to what extent individuals inadequately protected by government should defend themselves against racist attacks.[17]

That Caribbean leadership coincided with the influx of communism in Harlem was not overlooked by those critics wary of the ideological conflict Marxism posed to the Harlem community's fidelity to religious traditions or to the vision of racial nationalism espoused by many in the movement. Nevertheless, aftershocks of the Russian Revolution reverberated throughout African America, stirring many renowned members of the movement to become party members as well. Richard Wright, Claude McKay, Countee Cullen, and Langston Hughes supported the Communist Party, the latter even toured Moscow, as did McKay, Dorothy West, and Paul Robeson, while countless others took part in party-sponsored lectures and discussion circles.

According to Mark Naison accusations of "manipulation, disillusionment, and betrayal" typify scholarly interpretations of the relationship between Soviet leaders and black American communists.[18] Yet William J. Maxwell cogently exposes the injudiciousness of earlier critics, such as Harold Cruse and David Levering Lewis, who treat Bolshevism as the alien influence that heralded the demise of the rebirth along with the Depression.[19] Instead of being "intellectually sidetracked" and implicitly controlled by communist influences, as Cruse maintains, Maxwell unearths the mutual influence of the

Comintern and Harlem radicalism.[20] McKay's "Report on the Negro Question," for example, was delivered to the Fourth Congress of the Comintern and thereafter commissioned by the Soviet State Publishing House to be expanded into the book that would become *The Negroes in America* (1923). Rejecting long-held critical assumptions regarding the impotence of blacks in American communism, Maxwell notes that despite McKay's thrilling reception in Moscow as an exotic, he was also able through his report to transfigure official Soviet policy, resulting in the Black Belt Nation thesis on the crucial role of African American workers in securing communist footholds in the USA.[21] Of course, by 1940 widespread apostasy to communism on the part of once zealous black writers like McKay would be associated, however erroneously, with the decline of the Harlem Renaissance.

Still, at the height of the renaissance new socialist philosophies spread through Harlem via the same conduits that disseminated the cultural products of a self-consciously "New Negro" – radical newspapers. The primary organ of black communism was *The Crusader*, founded in 1918 by Cyril Briggs. Propelled by the general atmosphere of radicalism following World War I, *The Crusader* sought to educate the masses on African history and culture, and combined the goals of literary enrichment familiar to other journals of the time with an unmitigated militancy inspired by Soviet Russia. One article from 1921 enjoined "thoughtful Negroes" to observe that only Soviet Russia exercised that vaunted "principle of 'self-determination' in its dealings with weaker peoples ... regardless of the color of the people with whom she is dealing."[22] As part of *The Crusader*'s campaign to internationalize Harlemites, fierce disagreements launched in editorials and emblazoned in its aims defined its brand of Bolshevism against the more socialist *Messenger*. And in relationship to other radical papers, Briggs departed from Garveyism, even while sharing *The Negro World*'s global vision, in advocating proletarian militancy of both black and white workers over and above Garvey's more restrictive racial concerns.

Notwithstanding the masculinist rhetoric of Brigg's radicalism, communism also influenced the emergence of black women's writing of the time. A proletarian aesthetic infused the work of Zora Neale Hurston and Dorothy West, most demonstrably in West's editorship of the progressive journals *Challenge* and *New Challenge* (1934–37), which consistently published clarion calls for African Americans to resolve the crippling effects of class fracture in the vein of earlier established journals such as *New Masses*, an organ of communism to which Hughes and others frequently contributed. Some of Hughes' notions about communism may have even been sharpened in repartee with his sometime typist and longtime friend, Louise Patterson.

Often behind the scenes, Patterson functioned as intellectual liaison to communism for many black writers, assisting Hughes and Hurston in their unfinished play "Mule Bone," hosting the Vanguard, a leftist salon, from her Convent Avenue apartment, founding the Friends of the Soviet Union, and leading the oft-noted culmination of Harlem's connection to communism in the film excursion to Moscow of 1932. Funded by literary grandees Malcolm Cowley, Waldo Frank, and others, the group included Patterson, Hughes, West, and nineteen other bohemians enthused by the promise of a color-blind system of social justice. The film *Black and White* was intended to dramatize this promise and to cement Soviet ties to the plight of "Negro life" in its depiction of an alliance between white and black workers. But whereas the project began with the troupe's reception, akin to McKay's in Russia, of ebullient celebration, it ended some months later with discord and disappointment. With her communist idealism intact, Patterson acquired the sobriquet of "Madame Moscow" by disagreeing with the opinion of some members of the company who felt the Soviets sabotaged the film's success in order to gain official US favor. After the dissolution of the film project, Patterson remained a committed Communist Party leader as well as a staunch defender of civil rights, taking the lead in protesting the Scottsboro affair, and producing the 1934 *Crisis* article "Southern Terror," which, according to Maxwell, evinces a style of "radical reportage in opposition to a triangular-homosocial rhetoric of working-class interracialism."[23] The majority of the Moscow film troupe also returned to the USA, while others, inspired by the racial tolerance they met with in Russia, continued to travel throughout Asia. Three members of the group even settled in Russia permanently. Hughes, on the other hand, aroused by yet another opportunity for international experience – he had already been to Mexico, Africa, Europe, and the Caribbean – deferred immediate return, choosing instead to spend a year touring Russia, China, and Japan, translating poetry, as in Cuba and Haiti, of leading writers and contributing blistering poetic attacks on America's military control of Columbia, that "dear girl" who has "slept with all the big powers/In military uniforms." Although rebuffed by Van Vechten as too sensational and lacking in lyricism, Hughes submitted such poems as well as essays on his personal experiences abroad ("Moscow and Me" and "Negroes in Moscow") to the *International Journal*.[24]

Itinerant impulses may have been particularly strong in Hughes and McKay, but many literary figures of the Harlem movement traveled widely and for various reasons, shoring up experiences as creative and intellectual fodder and honing a much-needed critical distance from American systems of racialization. In 1924 Jean Toomer spent time in France to study a brand of spiritual and physical enlightenment under Gurdjieff at the Institute for the

Harmonious Development of Man at Fountainebleau. Fashioning himself as a sort of guru of the Gurdjieff system, Toomer set up shop the following year in Harlem, performing magnetic lectures and attracting the likes of Langston Hughes, Zora Neale Hurston, Wallace Thurman, Nella Larsen, Rudolph Fisher, and Dorothy West. Toomer's zest for Eastern mysticism would result in several return trips to Gurdjieff's institute and a visit to India in 1939. Guggenheim Fellowships drew a number of writers abroad: Cullen to Paris in 1928, Larsen (the first African American woman to win the award for creative writing) to Spain and France in 1930, and Hurston to Jamaica and Haiti from 1936 to 1938 to investigate the Caribbean voodoo practices described in her travelogue *Tell My Horse* (1938).

More than any other region of the world, however, Africa became a galvanizing but also much disputed center of intellectual and political interest for the movement. As perhaps the most outspoken and prolific activist in the cause of African and African American coalition, W. E. B. Du Bois' interest in the liberation of Africa grew out of timely international concerns which he broadcasted to black America in *The Crisis* in 1919. The June issue of that year became the best-selling issue in the history of the journal, as it, like other issues of that year, extolled the promises of European ethnic liberation fostered by the Paris Peace Conference. After attending the conference, Du Bois used *The Crisis* to vehemently assert the need for such liberation to be extended to Africa and to lament the dearth of educational and employment opportunities for returning black soldiers who had helped to make the peace in Europe possible. Articles from that year also drummed up hope for what would become a life-long commitment for Du Bois: the establishment of the Pan-African Congress.

Although officially mantled as the secretary of the second Pan-African Congress, Du Bois was in reality its driving force, organizing meetings in 1919, 1921, 1923, and 1927 and canvassing for support through repeated *Crisis* essays that provided updates on the evolving mission of Pan-Africanism. Among its premier objectives was the creation of an Africa for Africans freed from the grasp of colonialism though aided by a heterogeneous confederation of international activists. And, as Cheryl Wall notes, Jessie Fauset's record of the alliance registers the "false simplicity" inherent to parallels between African and African American delegates who, to Fauset, seemed to possess a more militant ardor for the goals of the movement.[25] Like other writers of the period, Fauset's concerns would eventually lead her to visit the continent. In 1923, Du Bois had made his first visit there touring Liberia as Hughes was touring Senegal, Nigeria, the Cameroons, the Belgian Congo, and other coastal regions. Two years later, Fauset compiled her cinematic impressions of Algiers in an essay for *The Crisis*, maintaining an air of respectful appreciation for North African diversity that at times drifts toward exoticization.[26]

Some of these problems of translation were the result of twin exaggerations regarding Africa that were pervasive both in the New Negro movement and in American society at large. On the one hand, Africa was the exotic "dark continent," a land awash in a primitive culture that some elite artists and white philanthropists opposed to the desiccated exhaustion of western modernity. On the other hand, that same primal culture was to many African Americans a mark of shame, supposedly both anterior and inferior to European traditions. For many writers of the movement, these mixed attitudes resulted in a conflicted sense of Africanicity formed out of the simultaneous disavowal of white exoticization or idealization of Africa and affirmations for a sense of diasporic connectedness to African history, politics, and culture. An example of this conflicted predicament resounds in Countee Cullen's poem "Heritage," with its evocation of the "double part" the black American plays with respect to an African heritage he rejects consciously and aesthetically, but never completely nor without acknowledging the significance of that heritage, if only as a mystery. As "great drums" beat and "dark blood dammed within" is ready to burst, he disclaims Africa and asserts unconcern for the past or "Last year's anything?" Africa, therefore, is associated with an image assembled by whites of the sensual and exotic, the dark past steeped in primitivity, an image which must be rejected or at minimum renegotiated to be of use to the more conventional poet Cullen aspires to be.

Appealing more to the sensibilities of the black urban masses, Marcus Garvey redirected the growing hold that western visions of Africa imparted to blacks by spreading a triumphantly Afrocentric message. "A renascent mother Africa" was a theme of his earliest performances on Harlem street corners in the spring of 1916, and would remain so when his words attracted thousands by the end of 1918. By then, the message would be carried by more than words as Garvey adorned his celebrity and his organization (UNIA) with sensational uniforms, titles, and pageantry. With sights set on one of the few African independent nations, Liberia, Garvey amplified the entrepreneurial spirit that characterized many Caribbean immigrants, starting the Black Star Line Steamship Corporation and its successor shipping line, the Black Cross Navigation and Trading Company, as well as the Negro Factories Corporation, grocery stores, a restaurant, and a publishing house in order to fund his ambitious quest to redeem Africa for African American resettlement. Thus, while his militancy alarmed many at first, he gained wider support by tying the idea of Africa centrally to black American unity as well as to industrial and commercial self-reliance and pride. But a skillfully presented platform was not the only reason for UNIA's expansion. The growth of Garvey's organization was proportionate to postwar disillusionment and the disturbing increase of racial violence throughout the South, as in the infamous red summer of 1919, and northern metropolises. Poor money management ended his rise in 1922 as he was convicted of mail fraud.

Nevertheless, Garvey was considered by many to be a prophet and, at the very least, the most vociferous advocate of an Afrocentric political philosophy that continued to shape the ancestral imaginary of African Americans from the Harlem movement to the present day. After all, though his methods were often bombastic his message seemed to encompass those voiced from various political and social quarters of African America: that all people of African ancestry, no matter how disconnected across the globe, have a common origin, which could and perhaps should unite them to pursue a collective self-governance that would compete with colonial western powers as equals.

NOTES

1. Audrey Fisch, *American Slaves in Victorian England: Abolitionist Politics in Popular Literature and Culture* (Cambridge: Cambridge University Press, 2000), p. 10.
2. George Hutchinson, *The Harlem Renaissance in Black and White* (Cambridge, MA: Harvard University Press, 1995), p. 106.
3. Brent Hayes Edwards, *The Practice of Diaspora: Literature, Translation, and the Rise of Black Internationalism* (Cambridge, MA: Harvard University Press, 2003), p. 141.
4. Nathan Irving Huggins, ed., *Voices from the Harlem Renaissance* (Oxford: Oxford University Press, 1976), p. 6.
5. Willis Richardson, "The Hope of a Negro Drama," *Crisis* 19 (1919), 338.
6. James Weldon Johnson, *The Book of American Negro Poetry* (1922; New York: Harcourt, 1931), p. 41.
7. Alain Locke, ed., *The New Negro* (1925; New York: Simon and Schuster, 1992), p. 7.
8. "Report of a Madison Square Garden Meeting," in *The Marcus Garvey and Universal Negro Improvement Association Papers*, ed. Robert A. Hill, 8 vols. (Berkeley: University of California Press, 1983), vol. 2, p. 499.
9. Jan Rogozinski, *A Brief History of the Caribbean from the Arawak and Carib to the Present* (New York: Facts on File, 1992), p. 265. See also Hans Schmidt, *United States Occupation of Haïti 1915–1934* (New Brunswick, NJ: Rutgers University Press, 1995).
10. Arnold Rampersad, *The Life of Langston Hughes*, vol. 1: 1902–1941: *I, Too, Sing America* (New York: Oxford University Press, 1986), p. 202.
11. Quoted in ibid. p. 205.
12. Quoted in ibid. p. 207.
13. Edwards, *The Practice of Diaspora*, p. 20; *Opportunity: A Journal of Negro Life* 4 (1026), 334.

14. Winston James, *Holding Aloft the Banner of Ethiopia: Caribbean Radicalism in Early Twentieth Century America* (New York: Verso, 1998), p. 76.

15. W. A. Domingo, "Gift of the Tropics," in *The New Negro*, p. 341.

16. Irma Watkins-Owens, *Blood Relations: Caribbean Immigrants and the Harlem Community, 1900–1930* (Bloomington: Indiana University Press, 1996), p. 94.

17. Joyce Moore Turner, *Caribbean Crusaders and the Harlem Renaissance* (Urbana: University of Illinois Press, 2005) p. 71.

18. Mark Naison, *Communists in Harlem during the Depression* (New York: Grove, 1983), p. xv.

19. William J. Maxwell, *New Negro, Old Left: African-American Writing and Communism between the Wars* (New York: Columbia University Press, 1999), p. 16.

20. Harold Cruse, *The Crisis of the Negro Intellectual* (New York: Morrow, 1967), p. 63.

21. Maxwell, *New Negro*, p. 88.

22. Quoted in ibid. p. 33.

23. Ibid. p. 145.

24. Rampersad, *Hughes*, p. 266.

25. Cheryl Wall, *Women of the Harlem Renaissance* (Bloomington: Indiana University Press, 1995) p. 49.

26. Ibid. p. 34.

PART II

Major authors and texts

4

DAVID KRASNER

Negro drama and the Harlem Renaissance

Dramatists of the Harlem Renaissance (c. 1916–35) sought to eradicate the legacy of minstrelsy. American minstrelsy began in the late 1820s and consisted in white actors applying burnt cork to their faces in degrading portrayals of African Americans. This created a cultural lexicon of stereotypes. Eliminating the century-long shroud of minstrel theater became one of the goals of Harlem Renaissance dramatists. Willis Richardson, author of the first African American non-musical drama on Broadway, said in 1919 that "When I say Negro plays, I do not mean merely plays with Negro characters," but dramas portraying "the soul of a people."[1] Indeed, it was part of the "New Negro" agenda to lay bear the "people's soul." Plays conveyed the principles of the "New Negro" by portraying characters having moral values, familial bonds, education, dignity, integrity, and work ethic. "Negro life," Alain Locke noted in his "Introduction" to the era's influential *The New Negro* (1925), "is not only establishing new contacts and founding centers, it is finding a new soul."[2]

Creating the New Negro "soul" onstage, however, proved no simple undertaking. Several factors had to be considered, among them: how should blacks be portrayed – with idealization or bluntness; and what was drama's function – to protest racism or to convey the ordinary folk? James Weldon Johnson added in 1928 that the African American author "faces a special problem which the plain American author knows nothing about – the problem of the double audience; it is a divided audience, an audience made up of two elements with differing and often opposite and antagonistic points of view."[3] There was also the issue of white playwrights dramatizing African American life. Ridgley Torrence's *Three Plays for a Negro Theatre* (1917), Eugene O'Neill's *The Dreamy Kid* (1919), *Emperor Jones* (1920), and *All God's Chillun Got Wings* (1924), Ernest Culbertson's *Goat Alley* (1922), Paul Green's *In Abraham's Bosom* (1926) and *No 'Count Boy* (1929), DuBose Heywood's *Porgy* (1926 novel adopted into a play in 1927), Edward Sheldon's *Lulu Belle* (1926), Em Jo Basshe's *Earth* (1927), and Marc

Connelly's *Green Pastures* (1930) were well-known white-authored plays with black-related themes. Critics considered it imperative for African American writers to create their own dramatic canon. Beginning in 1925, two major African American periodicals, *The Crisis* and *Opportunity*, held annual playwriting contests to encourage this end. However, defining "Negro Drama" proved to be an enormous challenge. Drama critic Theophilus Lewis remarked in 1927 that there "must be a clear understanding of what the term Negro drama means."[4] The need to discover the meaning of "Negro Drama" caused activist Anna Julia Cooper to invite Alain Locke to attend a gathering of intellectuals in Washington, DC in order to "tell us just what constitutes a race drama and how may we know it when we find it?"[5]

W. E. B. Du Bois devised "four fundamental principles" of "Negro Drama" in 1926, which at the time carried considerable influence. He asserted that plays of a "real Negro theatre" must be: "1. *About us*. That is, they must have plots which reveal Negro life as it is. 2. *By us*. That is, they must be written by Negro authors who understand from birth and continual association just what it means to be a Negro today. 3. *For us*. That is, the theatre must cater primarily to Negro audiences and be supported and sustained by their entertainment and approval. 4. *Near us*. The theatre must be in a Negro neighborhood near the mass of ordinary Negro people."[6] These remarks occurred during the high point of the debate over "Negro Drama." Alain Locke, James Weldon Johnson, Montgomery Gregory, and Zora Neale Hurston maintained that the realistic depiction of ordinary "folk" would be effective. The "real future of the Negro drama," Locke wrote, "lies with the development of the folk play. Negro drama must grow in its own soil and cultivate its own intrinsic elements; only in this way can it become truly organic, and cease being a rootless derivative."[7] Du Bois dissented, arguing that "All Art is propaganda."[8] He believed art should be ideological and instrumental in dismantling racism. Locke saw matters differently. He warned against the "propaganda play," maintaining that it was not the purpose of drama "to solve problems or reform society."[9] He challenged propaganda not on the grounds of its ineffectuality; he acknowledged that the "literature of assertion and protest did perform a valuable service," since it "encouraged and vindicated cultural equality." However, he believed protest drama fostered "melodramatic sentimentalism" over "pure self-expression," thereby repressing "folk forms and traditions."[10]

Locke and James Weldon Johnson looked to nineteenth-century German Romanticism as their model for black folk drama, as well as Ireland's early twentieth-century Little Theatre Movement for a theatrical paradigm. Locke advocated "racial reciprocity," a relativistic and cosmopolitan idea derived from German folk nationalist Johann Gottfried von Herder, who claimed that each race must make its own contribution.[11] Johnson urged drama and literature to convey a "racial spirit" similar to what the folk playwright John Millington Synge "did for the Irish." Johnson enjoined authors to express "the imagery, the idioms, the peculiar turns of thought, and the distinctive humor and pathos, too, of the Negro, but which will also be capable of voicing the deepest and highest emotions and aspirations, and allow of the widest range of subjects and the widest scope of treatment."[12] Johnson and Locke wanted to inculcate a Whitmanesque celebration of vernacular culture set within the framework of black American peasantry. Others believed the development of Negro Drama would evolve into a National Negro Theater. Montgomery Gregory, artistic director along with Locke of Howard University's theater program, wrote in *The New Negro* that the "ideal is a national Negro Theater where the Negro playwright, musician, actor, dancer, and artist in concert shall fashion a drama that will merit the respect and admiration of America. Such an institution must come from the Negro himself, as he alone can truly express the soul of his people." He added that "The only avenue of genuine achievement in American drama for the Negro lies in the development of the rich veins of folk-tradition of the past and in the portrayal of the authentic life of the Negro masses of to-day."[13] In the late 1920s and early 1930s Locke advocated formalism in drama and literature that anticipated the "New Criticism" which arose during the mid-twentieth century. African American authors, he said, should depict "simplicity, calm dignity and depth of folk art." Artists should additionally "fuse class consciousness with racial protest, and express proletarian sentiment in the genuine Negro folk idiom."[14] Depth, symmetry, and simplicity were among the hallmarks of New Criticism. In his Introduction to *Plays of Negro Life* (coedited with Gregory), he urged dramatists to provide "greater emotional depths," and in "The Saving Grace of Realism," he wrote that the "typical Negro author is no longer propagandist on the one hand or exhibitionist on the other," but rather promotes "sobriety, poise and dignity . . . the dominant keynotes of the developing Negro themes."[15]

Zora Neale Hurston maintained that Locke, Johnson, and others would violate the essence of Negro folk drama if they looked to Europe or white critical tradition for models. The "real Negro theatre," she wrote in her 1934 essay "Characteristics of Negro Expression," is "in the Jooks and the cabarets."[16] For Hurston the black aesthetic of the rural South could attain parity not by copying white models but by cultivating and remaining faithful to its own *Volksgeist* ("folk spirit"). Jook joints, honky-tonks, rural churches, and everyday southern life set the stage for pure folk drama. She wanted to hew closely to a slice-of-life ambience, insisting that only by returning to the roots of the black experience lodged in southern, rural communities can black folk art flourish. Hurston circumvented the symmetry, restraint, and proletarian folk drama of the 1930s that had been the bailiwick of Locke's theories by stressing the preference of African Americans for "mimicry," "asymmetry," and "will to adorn." Mimicry itself was the everyday art of black culture, with its elaborate rituals and storytelling folklore. It was also an ongoing process. "Negro folklore," she said, "is not a thing of the past. It is still in the making."[17] Hurston, contra Locke, advocated adornment, angularity, and a ludic incorporation of folk humor. Mimicry and embellishment – the antithesis of New Critical thinking – would reveal the "real Negro drama." For Hurston, the Harlem Renaissance focus on urbanity and modernity devalued the experience of southern folk ritual and in doing so marginalized what was essential, namely the art of rural storytelling.

The issue of folk versus propaganda was no mere academic debate. African American playwrights had limited opportunities; to succeed they needed the support of "race leaders." White producers and publishers looked to these leaders for advice and solicitation. Locke and Du Bois shepherded many novice playwrights to artistic maturity; Locke referred to himself as "the philosophical mid-wife to generations of young Negro poets."[18] As tutelary figures, Locke and Du Bois possessed enormous influence owing to the recognition they had received. Their prestige leveraged publication and the sponsorship of productions. Authors conformed or faced ostracization. Many theaters of the period, such as Du Bois' Krigwa Little Theatre of Harlem, Krigwa Players of Washington, DC, Maud Cuney Players of Boston, Dixwell Players of New Haven, The Dunbar Dramatic Club of New Jersey, Chicago's Ethiopia Art Theatre, and the Gilpin Players of Cleveland (renamed the Karamu Theatre), took sides on the issue of folk or propaganda as the preferred medium of African American theater. Among the most successful African American theater companies of the period was Anita Hill's Lafayette Theatre of Harlem (c. 1916–28).

Du Bois himself plunged into production with his pageant *The Star of Ethiopia*. It was drama on a grand scale. With a large cast and crew, it opened in October 1913 at the 12th Regiment Armory in New York. It was subsequently produced in Washington, DC in 1915, Philadelphia in 1916, and Los Angeles in 1925. The manner of its production was influenced by the rising interest in American pageantry, which extolled the virtues of ethnic pride. Du Bois, reacting against D. W. Griffith's film *Birth of a Nation* (1915, based on Thomas Dixon's 1905 play *The Clansman*), believed that African Americans had something to add to the American landscape. He saw pageantry as an opportunity for African Americans to reveal their cultural contributions. Pageantry, he reasoned, provided a propaganda platform with artistic foundation. In 1926 he founded the Krigwa Little Theatre Movement in Harlem devoted to racial uplift.

A common theme was lynching. Angelina Weld Grimké's *Rachel*, performed in 1916 by the Nathaniel Guy Players of Washington, DC, and published in 1920, was the first extant play to shed light on lynching's aftermath. Grimké (1880–1958) was the daughter of Archibald Grimké, lawyer, activist, and President of the American Negro Academy from 1903 to 1919. Originally titled *Blessed Are the Barren*, her three-act play concerns a sensitive and educated African American woman. Rachel is energetic yet melancholic. She plans to marry her brother's friend, John Strong, and raise a family. Her mother tells her that their family history had experienced violence. A decade earlier Rachel's father, publisher and civil rights advocate, had spoken out against a lynching. In retaliation, a white mob had lynched him and his oldest son. Violence continues to be a factor in her own life as Rachel discovers Jim Crow through the experiences of her adopted son Jimmy. Torn between the desire for motherhood and fears for Jimmy's safety, she calls off the marriage. Rachel rejects Strong's overtures on the grounds that raising a child in a hateful world is unsafe. *Rachel* is an expression of grief over lynching's brutality. It is almost operatic in its ebullient passion and overflowing sentiment. This turgid but heartfelt drama explores the consequences of intolerance for prospective mothers. Grimké writes: "If, then, the white women of this country could see, feel, understand just what effect their prejudices and the prejudices of their fathers, brothers, husbands, and sons were having on the soul of the colored mothers everywhere, and upon the mothers that are to be, a great power to affect public opinion would be set free and the battle would be half won."[19] In addition to this play she wrote *Mara*, which remains unpublished.

Grimké's protest play was the original focal point of the debate over propaganda and folk. In 1916 the NAACP organized a playwriting contest, with Du Bois and Locke among the judges. The winning drama, Grimké's *Rachel*, received a production. Gregory called the play "the first attempt to use the stage for race propaganda in order to enlighten the American people relative to the lamentable condition of ten million colored citizens in this free republic."[20] Locke opposed it. In his letter of resignation, which he sent to Grimké's father, he noted "an utter incomparability of point of view – something more than mere difference of opinion – indeed an abysmal lack of common meeting ground between myself and the majority of the members."[21] The battle lines had been drawn.

The aftermath of World War I left disillusionment. African Americans believed that their admirable military service would improve their lot with respect to citizenship and justice. Instead, racial antagonism hardened. Two one-act plays, Alice Dunbar-Nelson's *Mine Eyes Have Seen* (1918) and Mary P. Burrill's *Aftermath* (1919), concern soldiers and war. Dunbar-Nelson (1875–1935), widow of poet Paul Laurence Dunbar, was a poet, editor, and women's rights advocate. She published *Mine Eyes Have Seen* in the April issue of *The Crisis*. The political drama concerns one dilemma: whether to close ranks and serve in the military, or resist service for a country that denies equality. It takes place in a tenement and consists of Chris, whose draft number has been posted, his physically handicapped brother, his girl friend, a Jewish radical friend, an Irish neighbor widowed by the war, and a muleteer ready to reenlist and fight again. *Aftermath* by Mary Burrill (1884–1946), another play concerning the war, was published in the socialist journal *Liberator*. It is set in a cabin in South Carolina and the stage is replete with a family Bible and signs of a poor but dignified home. The circumstances center on Mam Sue, an elderly woman who must come to terms with her returning grandson. John has distinguished himself on the battlefield of World War I only to discover upon his homecoming his father's lynching. Like Burrill's play, Joseph Seamon Cotter's *On the Fields of France* (1920) takes up the war, showing two soldiers, black and white, dying together. Burrill also wrote *They That Sit in Darkness* (1919), published in *Birth Control Review*.

Two of the most prolific dramatists of the era were Willis Richardson and Georgia Douglas Johnson. Richardson (1889–1977) was raised in Wilmington, North Carolina. His family left in 1898, following race riots. They moved to Washington, DC, where Richardson attended the city's well-known M Street High School under the guidance of Mary Burrill. He was accepted to Howard University but lacked financial means. He worked instead as a government clerk in the Engraving and Printing Department, studying playwriting by correspondence course. His one-act, *Chip Woman's Fortune*, was produced by Chicago's Ethiopian Art Theatre and directed by Raymond O'Neil in 1922. When it came to New York in 1923 it was the first non-musical drama by an African American to receive a Broadway production.

During the 1920s and 1930s Richardson wrote nearly fifty plays. His principal objective was to present what he termed the "peasant class of the Negro group."[22] Under Locke's influence, Richardson wrote "folk" dramas, the most successful being *Chip Woman's Fortune*. It deals with a black family experiencing financial hardship. Silas has lost his job over a misunderstanding concerning a Victrola. The "chip woman," Aunt Nancy, has been caretaker for Silas' ailing wife, Liza, in exchange for free room-and-board. Silas, facing unemployment, asks the "chip woman" to leave; he can no longer support her. The family is rescued when the chip woman's son returns from prison. Aunt Nancy was saving money to get him back on his feet. Since Silas and Liza have been generous to his mother, the son agrees to hand the money over to Silas to repurchase the Victrola and restore his job. Richardson's next play, *Mortgaged*, was produced by the Howard Players in 1924, under the direction of Gregory and Locke. Like his play *House of Sham* (1929), it criticizes the selfishness of a black middle class having lost touch with its roots. His *Compromise: A Folk Play* (1925) was published in Locke's *The New Negro*. Like much of Richardson's work such as *Broken Banjo* (1925, *Opportunity* first prize winner), *Compromise* is about the "peasant class." A black woman's son is "accidentally" killed by a white man; another son seeks revenge. The play depicts the complexity of life among the downtrodden. In 1951 Rowena Jeliffe, producer of Cleveland's Karamu Theatre, wrote a letter to Richardson regarding *Compromise*, which can be taken as a description of his work in general: "I had then and still have the deepest respect for the dignity and majesty with which you portrayed the likes of simple, humble people."[23]

Georgia Douglas Johnson (1877–1966) was part of the "genteel movement" in poetry and letters. She, like Richardson, was born in the South (Atlanta) and moved to Washington, DC, with her husband Henry Lincoln Johnson when he received a government appointment. His financial security allowed his wife the opportunity to write, though he objected on the grounds that a woman's role is child-rearing not literature. When he died in 1925, Johnson became the most influential female playwright of the Harlem Renaissance. She turned her home – referred to as the S Street Salon for "Saturday Nighters" – into one of the most renowned intellectual meeting grounds for artists and scholars. Among her regulars were Locke, Du Bois, Gregory, Grimké, Richardson, Hurston, Burrill, and Marita Bonner. Her most significant contributions were her "lynching plays," five protest one-acts: *A Sunday Morning in the South*, *Blue-Eyed Black Boy*, *Safe*, *And Yet They Paused*, and *A Bill To Be Passed*.

There are two versions of Johnson's *A Sunday Morning in the South*. They were submitted to the National Play Bureau of the Federal Theatre's Work Project Administration somewhere between 1935 and 1939. The play is set in a kitchen of Sue Jones' home. Sue is grandmother to Tom and Bossie Griggs, ages nineteen and seven. The play takes place, as the title suggests, during an ordinary Sunday morning breakfast before church. The background of church bells can be heard, and in the second version "Amazing Grace" is clearly audible. The setting is meant to convey the sense of a family that is upright, moral, and religious. Tom is hard-working and ambitious. Sue's friend Liza drops by on her way to church. They gossip about local events. A black man apparently attacked a white woman the night before.

Sue and Liza agree that the assailant should be punished, but mob rule is not the way to go about it. The characters are law-biding, humble people with Christian values. For Sue and Liza, black criminals like all criminals need to be held accountable. But legal recourse, not lynching, must dispense the law. However, justice is non-existent. The police arrive accusing Tom of the crime. Tom's seemingly airtight alibi – he was home by 8 p.m. and everyone in the house saw him – is ignored. The victim identifies Tom as the assailant, though with considerable hesitation, saying he merely "looks something like" him. The fact that Tom fits the profile proves sufficient evidence for the police. Sue beseeches them with a reality all too familiar: "Mr. Officer, that white chile aint never seed my grandson before – All Niggers looks alike to her; she so upset she dont know what she's saying."[24] Events lead up to Tom's being lynched. *Sunday Morning in the South*, like Johnson's other one-acts, is an admonitory work, depicting the terror of lynching. Albeit contrived, it is a taut drama imbued with foreboding and suffering.

Johnson, more than any Harlem Renaissance dramatist, was under the influence of Alain Locke. Jeffrey Stewart documents their connection, noting that "If Johnson helped Locke cope with the death of his mother, Locke was the critic who provided the sympathetic counsel, pre-publication revisions, and inspired forwards that helped establish Georgia Douglas Johnson as one of the bright lights on the Renaissance horizon."[25] Locke's emphasis on "folk drama" did not go unnoticed by Johnson in her *Plumes* (1927, *Opportunity* first prize winner). It deals with a poor mother who must decide whether to pay for her terminally ill daughter's medical attention or use the money for her funeral. Like most of Johnson's plays, the kitchen-sink milieu provides the realistic backdrop. Johnson explores the superstitions of the poor, forged in the very "folk root" tradition Locke advocated.

Like Johnson, the playwrights of the Harlem Renaissance oscillated between folk and protest drama. Garland Anderson (1886–1939) wrote the second African American non-musical drama on Broadway. *Appearances* (1925) is a protest play concerning a bellboy falsely accused of rape. This courtroom melodrama contains long passages where characters plead for justice. Anderson, himself a San Francisco bellboy, used his considerable business savvy to raise capital for the production. The *New York Times* called it a "finely conceived, crudely wrought protest against lynch law" yielding "moments of power and a great many moments of ponderousness and stiffness."[26]

Zora Neale Hurston (1890–1960) wrote *Color Struck* (1925, published in *Fire!!* in 1926), *Spears* (1926), and *The First One* (1926), as well as *Mule Bone* (1931) with Langston Hughes, although this was left incomplete owing to their falling out.[27] *Color Struck* is located in Jacksonville, Florida. Emma is dark skinned. Her lover, John, pursues light-skinned Effie, Emma's rival in the cakewalking dance contest. In four scenes Hurston examines the issue of color consciousness in the black community. *Mule Bone* is a musical sketch concerning two hunters quarreling over a turkey they both claim to have shot. Hurston wrote several unpublished plays: *Meet the Mamma* (1925, a musical), *De Turkey and De Law* (1930), *Cold Keener* (1930, a revue consisting of nine comedic skits), *Woofing* (1931), *Lawing and Jawing* (1931), *Fiery Chariot* (1931), *Poker* (1931), *Forty Yards* (1931), *Spunk* (1935, the play), and *Polk County: A Comedy of Negro Life on a Sawmill Camp* (1944, written with Dorothy Waring). Some of these short plays were incorporated into two Broadway productions: *Fast and Furious* (1931) and *The Great Day* (1932 on Broadway and reproduced under different titles such as *From Sun to Sun*, *Singing Steel*, and *All de Live Long Day* throughout the 1930s). In these works Hurston stressed folkloric humor and everyday southern life.[28]

Eulalie Spence (1894–1981) wrote fourteen plays. Among those extant were *The Fool's Errand*, *Hot Stuff*, *Her*, and *Undertow* in 1927. Her plays, along with *The Church Fight* (1926) by Ruth Ada Gaines-Sheldon (1872–?) and Hurston's ribald one-acts, were among Harlem Renaissance comedies. Both Spence and Gaines-Sheldon avoided conflict, looking instead to everyday life in the church for material. Spence, who was Du Bois' friend, often took issue with him in regard to the latter's insistence on protest drama. Marita Bonner (1899–1971) was an exceptionally gifted short story writer and playwright. She graduated from Radcliff in English and Comparative Literature. Different in style if not in spirit from other Harlem Renaissance playwrights, her dramatic works were written in a staid, imagistic, and incantatory language that defies naturalistic interpretation. *The Purple Flower* (1927), *Exit: An Illusion* (1927), and *The Pot Maker: A Play To Be Read* (1929) portray characters vividly human yet surreal in their situations and ambience (*Purple Flower* and *Exit* received first prize in the *Crisis* play-writing contest). *The Purple Flower* is an expressionist drama in the style of German playwrights Georg Kaiser and Ernst Toller. Likely her knowledge of German provided access to Expressionist themes prevalent during the 1910s and 1920s. Her plays are explorations of racial conflict utilizing imaginative staging.

Frank Wilson (1886–1956) was an actor and vaudevillian. His play, *Meek Mose: A Comedy Drama of Negro Life* (1928), was produced on Broadway by drama critic and theatre manager Lester Walton. The story builds on the biblical notion that the "meek shall inherit the earth." Mose suffers patiently through a series of woes to triumph at the end when oil is found on his land. Walton and Wilson had hoped the play would initiate a National Negro

Theater. They enlisted the help of New York's Mayor Jimmy Walker to provide a speech before the show calling for financial support.

Novelist Wallace Thurman (1902–34) and William Jourdan Rapp, a white editor of *True Story Magazine*, co-wrote *Harlem: A Melodrama of Negro Life in Harlem* (1929). The play was originally titled *Black Mecca*, and then *City of Refuge*, carrying the subtitle *An Episode of Life in New York's Black Belt*. It was based on Thurman's short story *Cordelia the Crude, a Harlem Sketch*, about a sixteen-year-old prostitute. The play enjoyed ninety-three performances on Broadway, making it one of the most successful African American dramas up to that time. The three-act melodrama proved noteworthy for its realistic vernacular, depiction of Harlem life, and diversity of characters. Its large cast of twenty-six created a panorama of hard-working citizens and gangsters, religious mothers and numbers runners, Christians and hustlers. Cordelia "Delia" Williams is the toothsome daughter of the virtuous Williams family. She is drawn to the fast lane. The Williams family migrated north hoping for better wages. Instead, they encounter unemployment, crowded tenements, and speakeasies. Inevitably this eventuates in certain generational conflicts. Cordelia has aspirations for stardom but mostly she associates with numbers runners and ostentatious hoods. This upsets her religious parents. In Act I the Williams home is overtaken by a "rent party," festivities held to raise rent money. Delia follows gangster Roy Crowe to his apartment in Act II. This assignation is interrupted by Kid Vamp, former boxer and powerful numbers-game banker. Vamp accuses Crowe of selling him out to the white mob. When Crowe confesses, Vamp kills him and then tries to pin the murder on Basil Venerable who has a crush on Delia. Act III returns to the Williams home where the mother prays for her daughter's salvation and the father rues the day she was born. What makes the play exceptional is its vivid dialogue. Thurman and Rapp capture the argot popularized during the Jazz Age. Brooks Atkinson's *New York Times* review called the play "perhaps the most informalist melodrama in months with its high jinks, sizzling dancing, kicks on the shins and family jars, and its facility for tossing the facts of life around liberally. Not for some time have the natural processes become so firmly entangled in the warp and woof of the dramatic art. It is a rag-bag drama and high-pressure blow-out all in one."[29] Black critics were also impressed. Langston Hughes described the play as "a compelling study ... of the impact of Harlem on a Negro family fresh from the South." Theophilus Lewis went even further, saying that *Harlem* is "a spirited melodrama" introducing "an innovation in the treatment of the Negro character on the American stage." Its characters, he added, "are not abnormal people presented in an appealing light but everyday people exaggerated and pointed up for the purposes of melodrama."[30]

Francis Hall Johnson (1888–1970), known primarily as a choral director, wrote *Run Little Chillun* (1933), subtitled a "folk play." It was a Broadway success running for 126 performances. Moreover, it was reproduced by the Federal Theatre of Los Angeles from 1935 to 1937. The subject is religion in the Deep South. Jim Jones, a minister's son, is torn between his doubts and Baptist devotion. Two other significant dramatists of the early 1930s were May Miller (1899–1995) and Shirley Graham (1896–1977, wife of W. E. B. Du Bois). Miller wrote a variety of plays including historical pageants, children's theatre, and folk dramas examining interracial themes and lynching. Her best-known works, *Graven Images* (1929), *Stragglers in the Dust* (1930), *Riding the Goat* (1930), *Nails and Thorns* (1933), *Harriet Tubman* (1935), and *Sojourner Truth* (1935), were preoccupied with historical and moral issues. With Willis Richardson she edited two anthologies, *Plays and Pageants of Negro Life* (1930) and *Negro History in Thirteen Plays* (1935). Graham's most significant contribution was *Tom-Tom* (1932), a three-act play that was made into the first all-black opera to receive a professional production.

Shepard Randolph Edmonds (1900–83) was known throughout the South as the "father of black educational theatre" and "Dean of the Black Academic Theatre."[31] He chaired three Drama Departments during the 1930s and 1940s. His effort to cultivate a southern grass-roots theatre was premised on Booker T. Washington's educational principles of work ethic, propriety, Christian virtue, and racial uplift. Edmonds' dramas in particular foregrounded southern, agrarian culture, with its ingrained fraternalism, community resilience, kinship ties, church fellowship, and rootedness to the land. His work was largely in response to the dismissal by many, if not most, writers of southern black life. His intent was to express pride in southern regionalism and vernacular. He wrote forty-eight plays, nineteen of which were published in three collections: *Shades and Shadows* (1930), *Six Plays for a Negro Theatre* (1934), and *The Land of Cotton and Other Plays* (1942).

Myrtle Smith Livingston (1902–73) took up the issue of race mixing in her play *For Unborn Children* (1926). This theme had been explored earlier by O'Neill's *All God's Chillun Got Wings* (1924), Georgia Douglas Johnson's *Blue-Eyed Black Boy* and *Blue Blood* (c. late-1920s). But it was Langston Hughes (1902–67), known primarily as a poet and essayist, whose most successful play, *Mulatto* (1935), elevated this theme to a new artistic dimension. *Mulatto* ran for 373 performances on Broadway and two more seasons on the road. The play suffered from questionable rewriting of the last act by its producer Martin Jones. However, the popularity of its message made it an important landmark in African American drama (the play was adapted into an opera, *The Barrier*, by Jan Meyerowitz in 1951). Hughes was not only a playwright, but a producer and director. He helped create the Karamu Playhouse in Cleveland, and assisted in the establishment of African American theaters in Los Angeles and New York. Hughes wrote protest plays such as *Scottsboro Limited* (1931), which examined the trial of nine black men falsely accused of rape in Alabama. He fought against discrimination and unemployment in his plays *Angelo Herndon Jones* (1936), *The Organizer* (1938), and *Don't You Want to Be Free* (1938). He also wrote satires, *Scarlet Sister Barry* (1938) and *Limitations of Life* (1938).

Mulatto takes place on a Georgia plantation during the 1930s, though its tone and content make it appear distinctly antebellum. Colonel Norwood is a recalcitrant white patriarch of three children by his black mistress, Cora. Norwood's stubbornness and racism conflict with his paternal feelings; he condescends toward his three children – William, the oldest, Sallie, the youngest, and Robert, an eighteen year old, precocious and rebellious – yet he supports them financially. Robert has the temerity to challenge his father's authority by entering through the front door. Robert and Norwood clash with the animus eventuating in Norwood being killed. A white mob seeks to exact revenge on Robert. The melodramatic emphasis on heightened emotion, pitch-battle climaxes, and passion was common in the dramas of the 1930s. What sets the play apart is the theme of interracial romance that spills into a father–son imbroglio.

The period's effort to deal with sensitive issues in a dignified way occasionally conveyed weighty moralizing and contrivance. The plays, however, displayed creative sophistication and revealed aspects of black life heretofore unseen on the American stage. Theophilus Lewis described it best when he said, "The Negro stage should be a vital force in the spiritual life of the race; it should constantly delight Negro men and women . . . and . . . exalt . . . and it should crystallize that delight and exaltation in a form worthy of being preserved as part of our racial contribution to the general culture of mankind."[32] Such dramatists laid the foundation for theater about, by, for, and near African Americans.

NOTES

1. Willis Richardson, "The Hope of Negro Drama," *Crisis* 19.1 (November 1919), 338.
2. Alain Locke, "Foreword," in Locke, ed., *The New Negro* (New York: Macmillan, 1992), p. xxvii.
3. James Weldon Johnson, "The Dilemma of the Negro Author," *American Mercury* 15.60 (December 1928), 477.
4. Theophilus Lewis, "Main Problems of the Negro Theatre," *Messenger* 9.7 (July 1927), 229.

5. Anna Julia Cooper, postcard to Alain Locke (12 May, c. 1920s), Alain Locke Papers, Moorland-Spingarn Research Center, Howard University, Box 164–21, folder 53.

6. W. E. B. Du Bois, "Krigwa Players Little Negro Theatre," *Crisis* 32.3 (July 1926), 134.

7. Alain Locke, "The Drama of Negro Life," *Theatre Arts Monthly* 10.10 (October 1926), 703.

8. W. E. B. Du Bois, "Criteria of Negro Art," *Crisis* 36.2 (October 1926), 290.

9. Alain Locke, "Review of 'Goat Alley,'" *Opportunity* 1.2 (February 1923), 30.

10. Alain Locke, "The Negro's Contribution to American Art and Literature," *Annals of the American Academy of Politics and Social Science* 140.229 (November 1928), 240, 241.

11. Alain Locke, "The Contribution of Race to Culture," *The Student World* 23 (1930), 349–53; reprinted in L. Harris, ed., *The Philosophy of Alain Locke: Harlem Renaissance and Beyond* (Philadelphia: Temple University Press, 1989), pp. 201–6.

12. James Weldon Johnson, "Preface," in *Book of American Negro Poetry* (New York: Harcourt, Brace, & Co., 1922), pp. xl–xli.

13. Montgomery Gregory, "The Drama of Negro Life," in *The New Negro*, pp. 159, 160.

14. Alain Locke, "Propaganda or Poetry?," *Race* 1.2 (Summer 1936), 73.

15. Alain Locke, "Introduction," in *Plays of Negro Life*, ed. Alain Locke and Montgomery Gregory (New York: Harper and Brothers, 1927), n.p.; Locke, "The Saving Grace of Realism," *Opportunity* 12.1 (January 1934), 8.

16. Zora Neale Hurston, "Characteristics of Negro Expression," in Nancy Cunard, ed., *Negro* (1934; New York: Continuum, 1996), p. 31.

17. Ibid., p. 27.

18. Alain Locke, "Autobiographical Sketch," in Horace M. Kallen and Sidney Hook, eds., *American Philosophy: Today and Tomorrow* (New York: Lee Forman, 1935), p. 312.

19. Angelina Weld Grimké, "'Rachel' The Play of the Month: The Reason and Synopsis by the Author," *Competitor* 1.1 (1920), 52.

20. Montgomery Gregory, "A Chronology of Negro Theatre," in *Plays of Negro Life*, p. 414.

21. Alain Locke, "Letter to Archibald Grimké," Locke Papers, Moorland-Spingarn; quoted in Samuel Hay, *African American Theatre: An Historical and Critical Analysis* (New York: Cambridge University Press, 1994), p. 81.

22. Willis Richardson, "Characters," *Opportunity* 3.30 (June 1925), 183.

23. Rowena Jeliffe, "Letter to Richardson," December 18, 1951, Richardson File, Billy Rose Theatre Collection, New York Public Library at Lincoln Center, Astor, Lenox, and Tilden Foundations.

24. From the second version of *A Sunday Morning in the South*, National Play Bureau, Federal Theatre, George Mason Special Collection and Archive, Project, 1–8. The first version says "Mr. Officer, she aint seed him befo – All Niggers looks alike to her – that white girl aint never laid eyes on my grandson befo."

25. Jeffrey Stewart, "Alain Locke and Georgia Douglas Johnson, Washington Patrons of Afro-American Modernism," *George Washington University Washington Studies* 12 (1986), 37.

26. *New York Times*, October 15, 1925, p. 27.

27. For a survey of *Mule Bone* drafts, see Rachel A. Rosenberg, "Looking for Zora's *Mule Bone*: The Battle for Artistic Authority in the Hurston–Hughes Collaboration," *Modernism/Modernity* 6.2 (April 1999), 79–105. For an alternative opinion of the dispute, see Henry Louis Gates, Jr., "A Tragedy of Negro Life," in George Houston Bass and Gates, eds., *Mule Bone: A Comedy of Negro Life* (New York: Perennial, 1991). It also contains letters known as the "Mule Bone Controversy," pp. 157–283.

28. The plays can be accessed at http://memory.loc.gov/ammem/znhhtml/znhhome.html.

29. Brooks Atkinson, "Harlem: An Episode of Life in New York: Black Belt," *New York Times*, February 21, 1929, Sec. 1, p. 30.

30. Langston Hughes, "Harlem Literati of the Twenties," *Saturday Review of Literature* 22 (June 22, 1940), 13; Theophilus Lewis, "If This Be Puritanism," *Opportunity* 7.4 (April 1929), 132.

31. James Hatch and Errol Hill, "Educational Theatre," in *A History of African American Theatre* (Cambridge: Cambridge University Press, 2003), p. 263; profile in Henry Williams, ed., *The American Theatre: The Sum of Its Parts* (New York: Samuel French, 1971), p. 378.

32. Theophilus Lewis, "The Theater," *Messenger* 8.7 (July 1926), 214.

5

MARK WHALAN

Jean Toomer and the avant-garde

In 1923, amongst the many reviews of Jean Toomer's *Cane*, came two of very contrasting opinion. Disdaining "certain innovators who conceive language to be little more than a series of ejaculatory spasms," the *Minneapolis Journal* suggested "if the Negro (and the south) is to become really articulate its new writers must seek better models than those Mr Toomer follows."[1] In contrast, the African American critic Montgomery Gregory, writing in the first issue of *Opportunity*, soon to become the pre-eminent forum for the incipient New Negro Renaissance, waxed more lyrical:

> Fate has played another of its freakish pranks in decreeing that southern life should be given its most notable artistic expression by the pen of a native son of Negro descent ... Verse, fiction and drama are fused into a spiritual unity, an "aesthetic equivalent" of the Southland ... "Cane" is not OF the South, it is not OF the Negro; it IS the South, it IS the Negro – as Jean Toomer has experienced them.[2]

Despite their differences in opinion, these reviews nonetheless shared the evaluative criteria that characterized the reaction to *Cane* – and determined its importance – both in 1923 and in most of the subsequent (and voluminous) criticism devoted to it. Both were concerned with the effectiveness of the formal innovations and formal eclecticism of the work; with how well Jean Toomer had found either a voice or an "aesthetic equivalent" for the South; and to what degree Toomer was a "representative man," a figurehead and a model for subsequent African American writing. The reviews also suggest a critical terrain that would figure largely in the decade; the interest in "the folk," the politics of the observer – namely who had the authority to observe, and how one's situation affected what could be seen; and the political value of formal experimentalism. *Cane* was one of the first texts to pose these issues for the writers, periodicals, and audiences of the New Negro Renaissance, and it was widely admired by the new generation of African American authors emerging in the 1920s. Unique and challenging, the "spasms" of what proved to be Toomer's only major work were far from the aesthetic dead-end predicted by the *Minneapolis Journal*.

Part of this uniqueness sprang from Jean Toomer's own social position. As he wrote in 1928, "I have never lived within the 'color line,' and my life has never been cut off from the general course and conduct of American white life."[3] This liminality, and his refusal to accept the ever-hardening application of the "one-drop rule" in social conduct, meant that from at least his early twenties he "passed from the one [racial group] to the other quite naturally, with no loss of my own identity and integrity" (56). Although Toomer exaggerated this social mobility later in his career, his ability to mix with disparate and diverse artistic and intellectual communities – communities separated as much by aesthetic principle as by race – undoubtedly formed the basis for *Cane*'s stunning formal complexity and range. It also underpinned his complex meditation on racial liminality in *Cane*, a facet which, as George Hutchinson notes, "remained virtually invisible to critics for over half a century."[4]

A key part of that diverse social mixture was Toomer's childhood in an environment steeped in the most contemporary debates and ideas in African American culture and politics. Born in 1894 and deserted by his father before he was a year old, Toomer spent most of his youth in the home of his maternal grandfather, P. B. S. Pinchback. Pinchback was a part of the "Negro Four Hundred," the elite African American middle class of Washington, which Toomer referred to as a "natural and transient aristocracy."[5] Pinchback had been acting Governor of Louisiana during reconstruction, and this background gave Toomer access to the African American intelligentsia of the city that congregated around Howard University and the Dunbar High School. During the early 1920s, and after several misadventures at various northern universities and colleges, Toomer based himself back in Washington. Now committed to writing (he had briefly considered becoming a musician), he sent drafts of poetry and thoughts on issues of racial politics to his friends Alain Locke and Georgia Douglas Johnson, and was a guest at their houses. He attended reading groups on the history of slavery attended by the poet Clarissa Scott, the author and Howard Librarian E. C. Williams, and the playwright and teacher Mary Burrill. He used these connections to get an (ultimately disappointing) introduction to W. E. B. Du Bois; it was also these contacts that led him to briefly consider editing a magazine devoted to African American culture. He also used these connections to land a temporary job as the substitute school principal for the all-black Sparta Agricultural and Industrial Institute in Georgia in 1921, a job which proved crucial in the genesis of *Cane* and which he romanticized in all his recollections of it. As he later remarked on his first sustained experience of the rural South:

> Here was red earth, here pine trees, and smoke or haze in the valley. Here was cane or cotton fields, here cabins. Here was the south, before cities. Here were Negroes, people of the earth, and their singing. Never before had I heard spirituals and work songs. Here I heard them in their native setting, and they were like a part of me. At times I identified with the whole scene so intensely that I lost my own identity.[6]

As *Cane* demonstrates, Toomer was fascinated by black preindustrial culture in the South, the work songs that set the tempo for field labour and the spirituals that testified to the emancipatory yearnings – both physical and metaphysical – of an enslaved people. Along with many other authors and anthropologists in the 1920s, he was attracted to how these forms relied on improvisation and interpretation, in contrast to the increasingly standardized and schematized consumer economy driving both the postwar economic boom and the great migration. *Cane*, in this respect, represented what he called a "swan-song," as "the folk-spirit was walking in to die on the modern desert" (*Wayward* 123). He was also attracted to the way these folk forms established community, both in the call-and-response dynamic of the work song and the field holler, and the ancestral community of slavery they established for all people of African descent in the USA. Accordingly, the field cry of "eoho" echoes across *Cane*, from "Cotton Song" to "Calling Jesus" and "Harvest Song"; under the guise of gathering in the cotton harvest the work song pattern of "Cotton Song" calls all African Americans to participate in the collective labour of establishing freedom. His interest contained elements of celebration, and elements of salvage. In "Song of the Son," for example, Toomer establishes himself as a cultural saviour; "just before an epoch's sun declines / Thy son, in time I have returned to thee, / Thy son, I have in time returned to thee" (*Cane* 14). In becoming the planter of a "singing tree / Caroling softly souls of slavery," he claims to preserve in poetry this oral heritage of the black South, and it was this sentiment that made "Song of the Son" a favourite amongst anthologists of Negro writing in the 1920s.

However, Toomer's collection was far from being an anti-modern, nostalgic lament for the concreting over of a rural, oral culture: accordingly, it is not the straightforward elegy for an organic and foundational "folk culture" that various African American cultural nationalists in the 1920s sometimes pretended it was. This is partly because, as Charles Scruggs and Lee Vandemarr have suggested, the "terrors of American history" are never far from the vivid landscapes and lyrical folksongs of Toomer's Georgia. The relation between the rural African Americans Toomer portrayed and the red

Georgian soil was not one of nurture and organic connection, but one of enforced servitude and ambivalence; he later drew the distinction "between the wish to return to nature, and the desire to touch the soil. Nature ... is a virginal tract of land. The soil is tilled land, saturate with the life of those who have worked it," and the subtext of *Cane* is the brutal and enslaved nature of that "saturation."[7] These terrors of history are often tacit, or signalled by ellipsis, such as the silence that surrounds the whereabouts of Karintha's baby in the first story of the collection. At other times they are shockingly explicit, such as the way that the ritualized burning of a black man in the act of lynching is inextricable from the discursive construction of white female beauty in the South in "Portrait in Georgia," whereby the woman's "slim body" is "white as the ash / of black flesh after flame" (*Cane* 29).

Crucially, the most developed character in *Cane*, Ralph Kabnis, is paralyzed by his inability to relate to southern history in the form of Father John, the ex-slave who lives in the cellar of Fred Halsey's workshop. Indeed, Kabnis's inability to face this "father of hell" results in his "misshapen, split-gut, tortured, twisted words" (104, 110). The threat of violence and the memory of violence – often an institutionalized violence – is a constant pressure in Toomer's South; as Kabnis thinks, "things are so immediate in Georgia" (86). Moreover, this violence does not run merely along racial lines, as many of the most evocative portraits of part one of *Cane* are of abused women. As Vera Kutzinski observes of the women in *Cane*, "that they are mysterious, elusive and sexually disturbing is a function not of their 'nature' but the male narrators' need carefully to filter out emotionally and ideologically troubling histories of sexual and economic abuse, along with obvious differences in social class, which would (and do) interfere with these figures' ability to represent cultural and spiritual purity and wholeness."[8] As many critics have noted, this issue of the "spectatorial artist" and how the northern, male, middle-class observers of part one frame, interpret and desire these women makes thematically explicit the question of what type of "cultural work" occurred in the 1920s when working-class, rural black women enter literary representation.[9] As such, the position (and the selectivity) of the observer – a topic of interest which united contemporary anthropology and modernist aesthetics – becomes a troubling problem for Toomer, and a vital issue for considering how what Toomer's friend Waldo Frank called the "buried cultures" of America's racial minorities could be brought into the current of contemporary literature.

If Toomer drew heavily on black folk culture in *Cane* – both on its formal resources and on its figurations of suffering, oppression, and resistance – he also engaged in a more substantial way than any other figure of the New Negro Renaissance with the ideas of the white avant-garde. Imagism and futurism, Robert Frost's suggestive evocations of place in his understated language (along with his supple use of traditional verse forms), and Sherwood Anderson's lyric, open-ended short fiction and his ear for the rhythms of speech were all important influences on Toomer's style. So too were the psychological exteriorizations of the drama of Eugene O'Neill, and the lively imagery of Lola Ridge's poetry. Most significant, however, was the prose and cultural criticism of Waldo Frank. As Toomer admitted, "He is so powerful and close, he has so many elements that I need, that I would be afraid of downright imitation if I were not so sure of myself."[10] Toomer and Frank shared a fascination with the spiritual and political charge that inhered in the meeting of strangers from across social divides; in the importance of symbol to demonstrate how the metaphysical is anchored in the mundane; and in the importance of moulding prose to fit the contours of subjective experience – for as Frank said, "our standard of reality is an accumulating, gyrating and disappearing flux of subjective contributions."[11] Moreover, both shared a Whitmanesque sense of the prophetic and socially inclusive powers of the artist; as Frank exclaimed with typical grandeur and egotism, "the life of America is a stupendous symbol of the human chaos which such an artist beholds in all life ere the transfiguring magic of his unitary vision has been worked upon it."[12]

Aspects of Frank's cultural criticism also appealed to Toomer. In *Our America* (1919), Frank had followed Van Wyck Brooks's lead in seeing the dominance of the "Pioneer" and the "Puritan" mentality in American life as deeply detrimental to American collectivity in privileging material gain above cultural and spiritual connection. Moreover, Frank saw this legacy as inherently racialized, the result of an Anglo-Saxon cultural hegemony. Consequently Frank, along with several contemporary anthropologists such as Edward Sapir, felt lessons could be learned from what they perceived to be more culturally and spiritually rich and complex ways of life in North America, particularly from the Native American tribes in the Southwest and their interactions with Spanish culture, which had been "buried" by Anglo-Saxon cultural dominance.[13] Frank hoped these "buried cultures" could help effect a revolution akin to those that had occurred in Europe, wherein a "deep potential energy – religious, aesthetic – which is simply the love of life and which, applied by suffering and education to the level of practical demands, [became] indefeasibly the kinetic energy of revolt."[14]

Toomer was attracted to this brand of lyrical revolution, which built on his commitment to socialist ideas evident from his 1919 publications in the socialist paper *The Call*, and also on his attendance at the "worker's university," New York's Rand School, in 1918.[15] It also offered him a political application for what he had experienced in Georgia. As Toomer told Frank in his first letter to him in 1922, "In your *Our America* I missed your not including the Negro," and he let his work speak for itself in suggesting how rural African American culture might be exactly the type of "buried culture" that had so fascinated Frank in 1919. Accordingly, Frank was soon planning a revised edition of *Our America* to include a section on Negro culture, with Toomer graciously suggesting "What little I know is freely open to you" (*Letters* 31, 49). As 1922 progressed, Frank became Toomer's most important and intimate literary comrade; they addressed each other as "brother" in their prolific correspondence, and read and edited each other's work. Toomer introduced Frank to the African American culture of the rural South in their trip to South Carolina in the summer; Frank returned the favor by providing formal suggestions of how individual text-pieces could interrelate in his 1922 short story cycle *City Block*. He also introduced Toomer to the publishers Boni and Liveright, and provided several other contacts in the white avant-garde.

Perhaps the most significant of these was Gorham B. Munson, editor of the little magazine *Secession*. As Malcolm Cowley later recollected, the postwar "younger generation" – including writers who coalesced around *Secession* such as e.e. cummings, Kenneth Burke, Hart Crane, and Matthew Josephson – held "a new interest in form ... one can forecast safely that our younger literature will be at least as composed as a good landscape."[16] In keeping with this new interest, Munson spoke of *Secession*'s attraction to the "cerebral" qualities of art, in particular "abstractness, the concomitant of form" – a preoccupation also evinced by his work on theorizing the process of reader-response – in contrast to the more "emotional, instinctive" properties of Frank.[17] Toomer was instructed by these distinctions, and was also interested in Munson's refusal to condemn industrialization and its production of mass culture, a rejection Frank had embarked upon fairly completely in *Our America*. In his largely laudatory critical study of Frank, Munson sided with the Dadaists connected with *Secession* in averring that Frank's groundwork for a lyrical revolution in American culture had overlooked a crucial resource, suggesting that mass culture and mechanical technologies such as the skyscraper, the movies, and electric light may well represent the "peculiar genius of the American people thrusting into a new age."[18] In an open letter to Munson, Toomer would sound almost like a Futurist in echoing that sentiment, describing Washington as "pregnant, warm, dynamic, tensioned, massed, jazzed, lovable ... I had been in every powerhouse in the city before I dragged myself into the Corcoran Gallery."[19]

Consequently, Toomer began to become more interested in the fusion of cultures then forming the milieu of black urban life, a milieu that was growing rapidly and erratically owing to the Great Migration. In early

1922 he described black migrants to American cities as "a pseudo-urbanized and vulgarized, a semi-Americanized product," but by early 1923 he saw them as "jazzed, strident, modern. Seventh Street [a major black thorough-fare in Washington] is the song of crude new life. Of a new people. Negro? Only in the <u>boldness</u> of its expression. In its healthy freedom. American" (*Letters* 36, 116). This attitude was evident in the (sometimes violent) vibrancy and gaudiness of the middle section of *Cane*, set in Washington and Chicago. The "bootleggers in silken shirts" driving Cadillacs in "Seventh Street," the ethereal, jazzy Crimson Gardens nightclub in "Bona and Paul," the open play of fantasy, desire and a degree of performative identity in black theaters in "Theater" and "Box Seat," all indicated Toomer's belief that black urban life was a crude, inventive, vivid and revitalizing force for the future of American culture. As with his portrayal of the South, it is not an unbridled celebration; the black middle class's adherence to what he referred to as the "Anglo-Saxon ideal," an ideal which stressed both white supremacy and the primacy of materialism, comes in for severe criticism, as does the ability of urban geography and planning to stratify and segregate according to class and race in highly effective ways. These concerns are also evident in Toomer's minor work of the period, particularly his story "Withered Skin of Berries" and the drama "Natalie Mann." Despite these reservations, how-ever, Toomer's interest and faith in this "New People" – what he would later call the "Negro Emergent" – would last long beyond his *Cane* years.

What would not, however, was his willingness to identify himself as a member of that group. Throughout 1922 and early 1923 he discussed his "Negro blood" with several correspondents, and wrote an essay identifying his "Negro descent."[20] But by the fall of 1923 he was responding hotly to his publisher Horace Liveright's accusation that he was "dodging" the facts of his racial identity, an accusation prompted by Toomer's reluctance to be labeled a Negro in *Cane*'s publicity material. "My racial composition and my position in the world are realities which I alone may determine," he informed Liveright, a statement that flew in the face of the ever more stringent legal codes then policing the color line (*Letters* 171). In later autobiographies Toomer would blame those he felt had sought to pin him to a Negro identity; the primary culprit here was Waldo Frank, who he charged with leaving a telling ambi-guity over his racial identity in the preface to *Cane* (*Wayward* 126). By the early 1930s, Toomer was refusing to allow parts of *Cane* to be published in anthologies of Negro writing. A year later, in a statement accompanying his marriage to the white author Margery Latimer, he would affirm that "There is a new race in America. I am a member of this new race. It is neither white nor black nor in-between. It is the American race ..."[21] This affirmation under-pinned his finest late poem, "Blue Meridian" (1936), which prophesies the transcendence of racial categorizations and the arrival of "the man of blue or purple / Beyond the little tags and small marks" (*Wayward* 232). Yet the nationally syndicated newspaper coverage of his marriage – "Negro who wed white writer sees new race" was one headline – was a grimly ironic reminder of how far his position was from the laws and social conventions of the time.[22] This aspect of Toomer's life led to him being hailed as a pioneer in challenging racial essentialism by some, and as a person who had selfishly abandoned the fledgling New Negro Renaissance by others; and it formed one of the two important shifts his career took in late 1923 and 1924.[23]

The other was his embrace of the teachings of Georges I. Gurdjieff, an Armenian mystic whose theory for the "harmonious development of man" proposed that the instincts, intellect, and emotions must work in balance to allow a person to become whole and to undergo further – and higher – development. Gurdjieff's theories became highly popular in western avant-garde circles for individuals seeking spiritual – and effectively apolitical – solutions to the many social and cultural anxieties and conflicts that afflicted the 1920s. By the end of 1923 Toomer had become disaffected with the spiritual thinness of literary New York, weary of the vacuous debates and posturing he felt to be rife. Soon, however, a pamphlet outlining the work at Gurdjieff's institute at Fontainebleau, France, and a demonstration of "sacred dances" by a Gurdjieff group in New York supervised by Gurdjieff and A. R. Orage, seemed to provide answers. As he remembered, "Here was a work that indicated what must be done in order to achieve a balanced development. Here was a work whose scope was greater and more complete than anything I had dreamed of. Here, in fine, was truth" (*Wayward* 131).

By July of 1924 Toomer had sailed for France and Fontainebleau, and begun a life involved in the Gurdjieff work which lasted in a fully committed form until 1935, and which marked the entirety of the rest of his intellectual career. It also marked a change in his approach to writing, which became more didactic and denotational. As P. D. Ouspensky, one of Gurdjieff's disciples, explained, "In real art there is nothing accidental. It is mathematics ... The artist knows and understands what he wants to convey and his work cannot produce one impression on one man and another impression on another."[24] Although it is open to debate just how fully Toomer subscribed to this theory of "objective" art, after 1924 his work moved away from the fertile indeterminacy of his highly figurative style, and from the direct socio-economic concerns of the *Cane* period. Although Toomer continued to have poetry published in avant-garde magazines, and wrote several significant essays, publishers consistently rejected the novels he wrote after 1924. The only other book-length project that came to print was his privately issued collection of aphorisms, *Essentials*, which appeared in 1931.

However disappointing African American authors found Toomer's apostasy from the New Negro Movement, the contribution of *Cane* to the New Negro Renaissance from what Toomer called his time engaged in "Negro study" was a powerful one, effecting a manifold influence on the writing of the subsequent decade (*Letters* 31). W. E. B. Du Bois cautiously welcomed Toomer as "a writer who first desired to emancipate the colored world from the conventions of sex," and Toomer's frank treatment of sex and sexuality, particularly how they were intimately interrelated to the formation of racial and class identity, set the tone for much of the work that considered this topic in the Harlem Renaissance (*Cane* 171). In his seminal defence of the unique qualities of black American culture, Langston Hughes praised *Cane* for its "truly racial" contribution to American literature, by which he doubtless meant its sophisticated adaptation of black musical forms into literary usage – demonstrating how a modernist embrace of these forms could overcome the "racial mountain" of slavishness to Anglo-Saxon, bourgeois aesthetic taste.[25] Moreover, Toomer's use of the hidden, the secret, the indeterminate, and the overdetermined symbol in his work presented a model of political engagement and social critique which transcended the limitations of "protest fiction," for as James Baldwin would later famously write, *Cane* demonstrated that "only within [a] web of ambiguity, paradox, this hunger, danger, darkness, can we find at once ourselves and the power that will free us from ourselves."[26] *Cane*'s status as the product of a conjunction of avant-garde ideas and folk culture, as a cornerstone of any canon of American modernism and New Negro writing, and as an index to one of the most unusual biographies in contemporary American writing all participate in its ambiguity, paradox, danger, and darkness, its continuing ability to unsettle, astonish, and provoke.

NOTES

Permission is gratefully acknowledged to reproduce manuscript material from the Jean Toomer Papers, James Weldon Johnson Collection, Beinecke Rare Book and Manuscript Library, Yale University.

1. *Minneapolis Journal*, October 14, 1923. Review and publicity material in Jean Toomer Papers, Box 26 Folder 612. Jean Toomer Papers are hereafter abbreviated to JTP.
2. From *Opportunity* 1 (December 1923), 374–5. Reprinted in Jean Toomer, *Cane*, ed. Darwin T. Turner (New York: Norton, 1988), pp. 165–6.
3. "The Crock of Problems," in *Jean Toomer: Selected Essays and Literary Criticism*, ed. Robert B. Jones (Knoxville: University of Tennessee Press, 1996), pp. 55–9, at 56.
4. "Identity in Motion: Placing *Cane*," in Geneviève Fabre and Michel Feith, eds., *Jean Toomer and the Harlem Renaissance* (New Brunswick, NJ: Rutgers University Press, 2001), pp. 38–56, at 53.

5. Jean Toomer, *The Wayward and the Seeking: A Collection of Writings by Jean Toomer*, ed. Darwin T. Turner (Washington, DC: Howard University Press, 1982), p. 85.

6. "On Being an American," JTP Box 20 Folder 513, p. 38.

7. JTP Box 60 Folder 1411.

8. "Unseasonal Flowers: Nature and History in Placido and Jean Toomer," *Yale Journal of Criticism* 3 (1990), 153–79, at 169.

9. See Susan L. Blake, "The Spectatorial Artist and the Structure of *Cane*," *CLA Journal* 17 (June 1974), 516–34; reprinted in *Cane*, pp. 217–23; Laura Doyle, *Bordering on the Body: The Racial Matrix of Modern Fiction and Culture* (Oxford: Oxford University Press, 1994); and Nathan Grant, *Masculinist Impulses: Toomer, Hurston, Black Writing, and Modernity* (Columbia: University of Missouri Press, 2004).

10. *The Letters of Jean Toomer, 1919–1924*, ed. Mark Whalan (Knoxville: University of Tennessee Press, 2006), pp. 90–1.

11. Waldo Frank, "Note on the Novel," in *Salvos: An Informal Book about Books and Plays* (New York: Boni and Liveright, 1924), pp. 223–31, at 227.

12. Waldo Frank, "The Artist in Our Jungle," in *In the American Jungle, 1925–36* (New York: Farrar and Rinehart, 1937), pp. 149–53, at 152.

13. See Edward Sapir, "Culture, Genuine and Spurious," 1924; reprinted in *Selected Writings of Edward Sapir in Language, Culture and Personality*, ed. David G. Mandelbaum (Berkeley: University of California Press, 1949), pp. 308–31; and Susan Hegeman, *Patterns for America: Modernism and the Concept of Culture* (Princeton, NJ: Princeton University Press, 1999).

14. Waldo Frank, *Our America* (New York: Boni and Liveright, 1919), p. 231.

15. See Charles Scruggs and Lee VanDemarr, *Jean Toomer and the Terrors of American History* (Philadelphia: Pennsylvania University Press, 1998), p. 48.

16. Malcolm Cowley, *Exile's Return* (New York: Viking Books, 1956), pp. 99–100.

17. Gorham Munson, *The Awakening Twenties: A Memoir-History of a Literary Period* (Baton Rouge: Louisiana University Press, 1985), p. 168.

18. Gorham Munson, *Waldo Frank: A Study* (Boni and Liveright: New York, 1923), p. 25.

19. "Open Letter to Gorham Munson," *S4N* 25 (March 1923), n.p.; reprinted in *Jean Toomer: Selected Essays and Literary Criticism*, pp. 19–20, at 19. See also Mark Whalan, "Jean Toomer, Technology, and Race," *Journal of American Studies* 36 (2002), 459–72.

20. Jean Toomer, "The South in Literature," 1923; reprinted in *Jean Toomer: Selected Essays and Literary Criticism*, pp. 11–16, at 12.

21. "A New Race in America," 1931; reprinted in *A Jean Toomer Reader: Selected Unpublished Writings*, ed. Frederik L. Rusch (New York: Oxford University Press, 1993), p. 105.

22. See Cynthia Kerman and Richard Eldridge, *The Lives of Jean Toomer: A Hunger for Wholeness* (Baton Rouge: Louisiana State University Press, 1987), p. 202.

23. One admirer of Toomer's stance on this issue is Frederik L. Rusch; see his "The Blue Man: Jean Toomer's Solution to His Problems of Identity," *Obsidian* 6.3 (1980), 38–54. A critical reaction to Toomer's refusal of a black identity

is Robert B. Jones, *Jean Toomer and the Prison House of Thought: A Phenomenology of the Spirit* (Amherst: University of Massachusetts Press, 1993).

24. P. D. Ouspensky, *In Search of the Miraculous* (London: Routledge and Kegan Paul, 1950), pp. 26–7.

25. Langston Hughes, "The Negro Artist and the Racial Mountain," 1926; reprinted in *The Norton Anthology of African American Literature*, ed. Henry Louis Gates Jr. and Nellie Y. McKay (New York: Norton, 1997), pp. 1267–71, at 1270.

26. James Baldwin, "Everybody's Protest Novel," 1949; reprinted in *Notes of a Native Son* (London: Penguin, 1995), pp. 19–28, at 21.

6

CHERYL A. WALL

"To tell the truth about us": the fictions and non-fictions of Jessie Fauset and Walter White

Jessie Fauset once told an interviewer that she, Walter White, and Nella Larsen became novelists after reading T. S. Stribling's *Birthright*, a novel that depicted the return of a newly minted black Harvard graduate to his southern hometown. His efforts at racial uplift flounder; his end is predictably tragic. Versions of this story had been told before, notably in Charles Chesnutt's novel *The Marrow of Tradition* and W. E. B. Du Bois' short story "Of the Coming of John" in *The Souls of Black Folk*, for example. But Stribling, a white author writing on the cusp of the Harlem Renaissance, found an unusually responsive audience. His black readers noted that response as well as the fallacies in Stribling's fiction, which suggested that the protagonist's tragedy is his black ancestry, while his ambitions derive from his "white blood." Fauset and White knew better. Deigning to speak for her peers, Fauset reasoned: "here is an audience waiting to hear the truth about us. Let us, who are better qualified to represent that truth than any white writer, try to do so."[1] White responded similarly, when he observed that Stribling had written his story from the outside. When White's friend H. L. Mencken challenged him to write a better book, he began work on *The Fire in the Flint*. Like *Birthright*, it depicts a northern-trained black physician who brings his skills to uplift a rural southern community. Many of the novel's details are drawn from White's experiences as the assistant field secretary of the National Association for the Advancement of Colored People (NAACP). For Fauset and White, the commitment to a single verifiable truth both inspires and cripples their fiction. Their non-fiction, by contrast, remains powerful.

That they would share an artistic vision is not surprising, given how much else they had in common. In an era when most African Americans scrambled to make ends meet, they enjoyed a measure of privilege. Fauset in Philadelphia and White in Atlanta belonged to the sliver of Negro society that might be termed elite. Such terminology denoted status rather than wealth. Fauset was a gifted student, while White made barely passing grades, but their college degrees further set them apart from the masses. Most strikingly, they joined the staff of the NAACP within a year of each other. White became assistant field secretary in 1918, after James Weldon Johnson recruited him, and Du Bois, who had known White's family in Atlanta, vouched for him heartily. Before she became literary editor in 1919, Fauset had contributed to *The Crisis*, almost from the time of its founding by Du Bois in 1910. She had also been active behind the scenes in the organization; in 1916 she had been considered for an executive post. Certainly Du Bois knew who she was. While a Cornell University undergraduate, she wrote to thank him for *The Souls of Black Folk*, that she recognized immediately as the pathbreaking book it was. Eager now to join the staff of the preeminent civil rights organization, Fauset and White were deeply committed to its work.

They believed, moreover, that the struggle for equal rights could be waged in the artistic arena as well as through the legal and political system. They recognized that the time was ripe. Despite White's best efforts to publish his novel *The Fire in the Flint* first, Fauset's *There Is Confusion* appeared a few months earlier. Locke greeted it as "the novel the Negro intelligentsia have been clamoring for."[2] After praising White's ingenious plot and well-drawn characters, Carl Van Vechten remarked that the novel's restraint and subtlety "almost lifted it into the realm of art."[3] Contemporary reviews agreed that these novels were more important for what they said than for how they said it. Fauset and White were not deterred. She published three additional novels; he published one more as well as two important non-fiction books.

Subsequently neither Fauset nor White has won great acclaim for their fiction, though Fauset's has belatedly received sympathetic readings from some feminist critics.[4] But scholars have come to appreciate the contributions both made as mentors. As literary editor, Fauset could and did publish most of the writers of the Harlem Renaissance in *The Crisis*; essays and poems by Marita Bonner, Arna Bontemps, Langston Hughes, and Anne Spencer appeared regularly. White's role was unofficial, but he was an indefatigable networker, who arranged meetings between white publishers and black writers; his interventions advanced the careers of Countee Cullen, Rudolph Fisher, Nella Larsen, Claude McKay, and Dorothy West. Of course, White's popularity in the 1920s owed much more to his extraordinary acts of personal courage as he investigated lynchings throughout the South than to his literary work. Fauset evidently admired that courage; a subplot in *Confusion* features a black woman who investigates lynchings. Yet the historical record documents little interaction between them. One reason is that during Fauset's years at *The Crisis*, White was on the road, traveling incognito under the cover of his light skin, documenting mob violence. It is also likely that differences in age, temperament, and personal style mitigated against the formation of a bond. So too did their contrasting views on women's rights. Yet, as reevaluations of their careers make clear, they in their different ways made signal contributions to African American and American culture.

Born in 1882 in Fredericksville, New Jersey (now Lawnside), Fauset grew up in Philadelphia. After her mother's death, her father, a minister, encouraged her to excel. She did. In 1905 she graduated from Cornell University, having been elected to Phi Beta Kappa. She later earned the MA in Romance Languages from the University of Pennsylvania and studied at the Sorbonne. Despite these sterling credentials, Fauset could only find employment in the segregated schools of Baltimore and Washington, DC. Indeed so limited were the options for professional black women that at M Street High School her colleagues included two of the first three black American women to earn the PhD.

In Washington, she belonged to a circle of literary women including Georgia Douglas Johnson, Alice Dunbar-Nelson, Angelina Weld Grimké, and May Miller. When she became literary editor of *The Crisis*, she helped put their work into print. She also commissioned painters Gwendolyn Bennett, Effie Lee Newsome, and Laura Wheeler Waring to design covers for issues of *The Crisis*. After moving to New York in 1919, she began to shepherd the careers of Countee Cullen, Langston Hughes, and Jean Toomer. Her initiative led *The Crisis* to become the premier venue for African American writers in the early 1920s. After she left in 1926, many writers found *Opportunity*, the official journal of the Urban League, to be more receptive to their work.

In Harlem Fauset and her sister Helen Lanning became popular hosts. Langston Hughes remarked that at their parties when guests spoke about Florence, they meant Italy not Alabama. But Fauset had a lighter side. She was an usher for the popular Broadway show *Shuffle Along*, and an accomplished dancer herself. When she married Herbert Harris in 1929, the black press highlighted her membership in Delta Sigma Theta sorority as much as her novels. Being taken seriously as an artist was a special challenge for a black woman.

Yet Fauset wrote in multiple genres. Before becoming a novelist she was a poet, short story writer, book reviewer, and translator. She was a particularly gifted essayist, who knew how to construct an argument and turn a phrase. Many of her essays appeal to sentiment without turning sentimental as her fiction often does. Generally, she enlivened her essays with the kind of telling detail that too rarely turns up in her novels. The essays reveal, moreover, her willingness to grapple with new cultural and political concepts. Through these one can chart the process by which a woman conditioned by background and training to accept a very conservative social ethic assimilated a good many progressive ideas. She reported on nationalism and Egypt as well as the convention of the National Association of Colored Women, an activist group of black women reformers. She penned prose portraits of prominent artists such as comedian Bert Williams and painter Henry Ossawa Tanner. In keeping with the Pan-African politics of *The Crisis* she also profiled outstanding men of African descent across the world. "The Emancipator of Brazil" (co-authored with Cezar Pinto) told the story of Jose Do Patrocinio, the son of a Catholic priest and a black woman, a journalist, and a staunch abolitionist. Born in Guadeloupe, Joseph Boulogne Saint-George, "Chevalier of France," made his name in France as a composer, violinist, and swordsman. In "Looking Backward," an essay on Reconstruction, "the single finest instance of the effort of a nation to set immediately right an ancient wrong," Robert Brown Elliott, a congressman from South Carolina, is the avatar of nobility. Like all these men, Elliott presented in Fauset's phrase, a "model . . . of the possibilities of our race."[5]

Fauset continued to explore those possibilities as a woman. In 1921 she attended the Second Pan-African Congress and shared her impressions with *Crisis* readers; she responded with enthusiasm to an experience rich in history and drama and one in which very few women took part. The Congress had met in three European capitals – London, Brussels, and Paris – after which a delegation was sent to the League of Nations in Geneva. In her account, Fauset attempts to convey the flavor of these cities while reminding her readers that the wealth and the children of Africa had made much of the Old World charm possible. She described the conditions in various parts of Africa and drew broad parallels between the problems of colonialism in Africa and segregation in the United States.

Also in 1921 she joined Du Bois in publishing *The Brownies' Book*, a magazine for children, regrettably short-lived, that conveyed the cosmopolitan vision of both its editors. It published short stories and poetry, African folk tales, games, puzzles, and monthly historical features. Among the figures profiled were Alexander Dumas, Harriet Tubman, Alexander Pushkin, Benjamin Banneker, and Phillis Wheatley. A column by Du Bois, "As the Crow Flies," covered current events on a level incredibly sophisticated for a children's magazine. "The Judge" was Fauset's column, that offered political commentary, advice, and recommendations for further reading. As managing editor, Fauset solicited manuscripts from a list of contributors that reads like a who's who of the Harlem Renaissance. Weldon Johnson published poetry; Willis Richardson, whose folk drama *Compromise* appeared in

The New Negro, contributed two plays; folklorist/biographer Arthur Huff Fauset (her half-brother) profiled Blanche K. Bruce, a political leader during Reconstruction. Frequent contributor Hughes was represented not only by his poems, but by an early play, "The Gold Piece," and his offering to the playtime feature, "Mexican Games." Larsen's "Scandinavian Games" was her first publication.

On these publishing ventures, Fauset worked side by side with Du Bois, whom she admired for his erudition and political commitment. Although he left the academy when he founded *The Crisis*, Du Bois remained an activist scholar, who continued to write books and maintain an extensive speaking schedule. These commitments kept him on the road. Working in his shadow, Fauset received little credit for her contributions to the publications whose mastheads led with his name. However, Fauset was often the editor in fact. Her respect for her boss notwithstanding, she was confident in her own editorial judgments.

Fauset solicited contributions to *The Crisis* from virtually every writer of the Harlem Renaissance. She recognized the experimental talents of Hughes and Toomer. When "The Negro Speaks of Rivers," later one of Hughes' signature poems, arrived in the mail, she took it to Du Bois and wondered how it was possible that such a prodigious talent had escaped their notice. When the nineteen-year-old poet moved to New York in 1921 to attend Columbia University, Fauset sought him out and became a loyal mentor. Fauset paid $5.00 to publish Toomer's "Song of the Son," that became the central poem of his path-breaking volume, *Cane* (1923), but cautioned him to strive for greater clarity. Though neither Hughes' innovations with blues and jazz poetry nor Toomer's experiments with imagism and free verse were her preference, she encouraged talent wherever she recognized it. She helped Douglas Johnson prepare her first volume, *The Heart of a Woman* (1922), for publication. In less formal, but telling ways, she promoted the work of Dunbar-Nelson, Weld Grimké, and especially Anne Spencer, who rarely left her home in Lynchburg, Virginia, where she regularly hosted black luminaries as they traveled through the segregated South. In her poetry Spencer often invents a world in which racism and sexism do not exist, or in which some unexpected source of beauty transforms the ugliness of social reality. Fauset was eager to put her poems in print.

Joanna Marshall, the protagonist of *There Is Confusion*, insists "that if there's anything that will break down prejudice it will be equality or perhaps even superiority on the part of colored people in the arts."[6] Fauset shared this belief with White and other leaders of the New Negro Movement. For Joanna Marshall however, the modest success she achieves on the vaudeville stage is a disappointment. As a young girl, she has aspired to the greatness exemplified by Harriet Tubman and Sojourner Truth in the stories her father told. But racism makes it impossible for her to achieve her grand ambitions for the stage. After years of striving for theatrical success, she contents herself with marriage to a physician. Her creator kept the faith. Fauset published four novels, along with short stories, poems, reportage, reviews, translations, and essays. Tellingly, several of Fauset's black female characters are artists: Angela Murray in *Plum Bun* (1928) is a painter; Laurentine Strange in *The Chinaberry Tree* (1931) a seamstress, and Marise, a character in *Comedy American Style* (1933), a performer whose transatlantic career seems inspired by Josephine Baker's. Despite the challenges of racism and sexism, these characters strive to realize their twin dreams of becoming artists and advancing the struggle for racial equality.

Angela Murray is forced to withdraw from art school in Philadelphia, when her white classmates discover she is black. She passes for white when she moves to New York to continue her studies. She justifies the decision easily: "'Why should I shut myself off from all the things I want most, – clever people, people who do things, Art' – her voice spelt it with a capital – 'travel and a lot of things which are in the world for everybody but which only white people, as far as I can see, get their hands on.'"[7] Repeatedly, Angela, who believed that artists were more tolerant than other people, is disillusioned. Rachel Powell, the one visibly black student in her class, is gifted and highly disciplined, yet alienated by and from her peers. In a plot sequence derived from an actual incident involving sculptor Augusta Savage, Rachel wins a competition for a fellowship abroad; when the donors learn that she is black, they revoke the award and explain that they are interested "not in Ethnology but in Art" (359).

Angela lives in Greenwich Village, then New York City's artists' quarter, and visits her darker-skinned sister, Virginia, in Harlem. The novel contrasts the purposeful New Negroes in Harlem with the self-absorbed white artists downtown. Nevertheless Angela does not consider Harlem a viable home for serious artists, because the black community is too poor to support their work.

Passing into the white world of bohemian Manhattan forces Angela to understand the impact of sexism on women's lives. She observes the constricted ambitions of the young white women with whom she studies. She observes as well the compromises that define their personal lives. In one of the novel's most compelling passages, "She remembered an expression 'free, white and twenty one,' – this was what it meant then, this sense of owning the world, this realization that other things being equal, all things were possible ... She knew that men had a better time of it than women, colored men than colored women, white men than white women" (88). Although

Angela's analysis is apt, she exaggerates the degree of her own freedom and independence. She is soon seduced and abandoned by Roger Fielding, a rich blond aristocrat, whose racist attitudes toward blacks and sexist attitudes toward women coincide perfectly. Fauset modernizes the oldest plot in the tradition of the novel in English not only by adding the aspect of race, but by giving her protagonist artistic ambitions. However, the novel ends conventionally with the heroine's marriage.

The Chinaberry Tree explicitly reworks literary conventions. It draws on the Oedipal myth to represent the sexual traumas of slavery and their legacy on families who do not know their kin. The foreword is somewhat misleading, in its promise that the novel depicts the "breathing spells, in-between spaces where colored men and women work and love and go their ways with no thought of the 'problem.'"[8] Zora Neale Hurston had a similar goal in her novels that are less engaged with interracial conflict than with life within the African American community. Yet black communities in these fictions live under history's shadow. The plot of *The Chinaberry Tree* begins with the love affair between the wealthy white Colonel Holloway and the black servant woman, Sal, who choose to love each other despite the sanction against it. As in her earlier novels, Fauset explores the hierarchies of race and gender that limit the freedom of black women. No doubt Fauset's insistence that her characters manage to work and love despite their oppression tells the truth about them, but the novel does not *show* us this truth convincingly.

The elaborate structure of Fauset's final novel, *Comedy: American Style*, announces its ambition. Reflecting Fauset's longstanding attraction to theatrical tropes, it is divided into six sections: the Plot, the Characters, Teresa's Act, Oliver's Act, Phebe's Act, and the Curtain. Also consistent is the view that racism is a burden that blacks simply must overcome before they can get on with life. What is new and promising is the novel's antiheroine, Olivia Cary. A self-hating woman, a conniver, a shameless traitor to the race, and most shockingly, an unloving mother, Olivia is a new character in African American literature. Deliberately revising elements in the narratives of race men such as Du Bois (*Souls of Black Folk*) and Weldon Johnson (*The Autobiography of an Ex-Colored Man*), Fauset creates the anti-race woman. Living in a small Massachusetts town, like the protagonists of Du Bois and Johnson, Olivia experiences the shock of racial recognition when she is called "nigger" by a playmate. She determines never to experience such humiliation again. She aims to escape white bigots by separating herself from black people.

When Olivia recognizes that she will be unable to escape completely herself – she decides that marriage to a light-skinned African American physician is preferable to marrying a white man of lower status – she resolves that her children will be free of any racial stigma. Her hopes are thwarted when her third child, a son and namesake, betrays the mark of blackness. Her son Oliver "meant shame. He meant more than that; he meant the expression of her failure to be white."[9] Unflinchingly, she acts out her hatred of her son (and of herself). Alternately banishing him from the family home or asking him to remain to impersonate a Filipino butler for her white friends, she drives him to suicide.

Through Olivia, the novel depicts racism's endless capacity to wound and to make victimizers of its victims. But it is a portrayal drawn very much from the outside; Fauset declines to develop the character from within. When Alain Locke, among others, criticized the novel's characters for being one-dimensional types, Fauset defended herself by explaining that she had based them on a real family. Perhaps that fact dissuaded her from exploring Olivia's innermost feelings. Whatever the reason, Fauset is so reluctant to imagine an interior life for her protagonist that she does not assign Olivia her own "act."

Despite publishing four novels in ten years, Fauset could not sustain a career as a writer. She returned to the high school classroom. Then she and her husband left Harlem for the New Jersey suburbs. By the time of her death in 1961, Jessie Fauset's contributions to the Harlem Renaissance had been largely forgotten.

White remained one of the best-known African Americans in the country until his death in 1955. Ironically, as the Civil Rights Movement for which he had done so much to lay the foundation succeeded, White disappeared from public memory. Although scholars of the Harlem Renaissance have cited his role as a mentor – David Lewis names him as one of the six individuals who produced the cultural awakening – he only became the subject of a full-length biography (by Kenneth Janken) in 2003. The biography corrects some of the personal myths that White created in his autobiography, *A Man Called White*, published in 1948, when he rode the crest of fame.

The facts are impressive enough. His mailman father and schoolteacher mother raised him in a comfortable home on the edge of Atlanta's black community. Although he did not narrowly escape death during the Atlanta riot of 1906, as he later claimed, White was deeply affected by the event. As he later reflected, "I knew then who I was. I was a Negro, a human being with an invisible pigmentation that marked me a person to be hunted, hanged, abused, discriminated against, kept in poverty and ignorance, in order that those whose skin was white would have readily at hand a proof of their superiority."[10] After graduating from Atlanta University, he began a career in insurance and real estate. Then, after helping to found the local branch of the NAACP (the board was all-male), he moved to New York City in 1924 to begin his career at organization headquarters.

Within three weeks of being hired, he went on his first investigative mission, an activity that no one had anticipated would be part of his job. But the terror of lynching pervaded the South. White, whom observers often mistook for a Caucasian, benefited from the cover of his light skin. Passing from one community to another until his identity was discovered, he interviewed white perpetrators and black victims. These forays into dangerous territory proved White's courage as well as his capacity for innovative thinking and leadership. On his initial expedition to rural Tennessee, he used the cover of a traveling salesman who sold hair-straightener. In his pocket he carried press credentials from the *New York Post*, the paper's publisher Oswald Villard Garrison, an heir of William Lloyd Garrison and a board member of the NAACP. White reported his findings in an article, "The Burning of Jim McIlheron: An NAACP Investigation," in *The Crisis* in May 1918. The details were riveting, and soon White was on the road again.

In "The Work of a Mob,"[11] he documented the burning of Mary Turner, a black woman, nine months pregnant, who determined to find out who had lynched her husband and bring them to justice. White was able to speak to witnesses and identify participants, including seventeen members of the mob. To gain these interviews, he clearly put his life on the line. Two other signal investigations centered on Helena and Elaine, Arkansas, where attacks on blacks were spurred by black sharecroppers' efforts to organize the Progressive Farmers' and Householders' Union which would negotiate higher prices for their crops and obtain itemized statements of debits and credits from landowners. At least twenty-five blacks were murdered. The authorities then arrested hundreds more blacks on charges of *their* plotting to murder whites. Twelve black men were condemned to death, while an additional eighty were sentenced to prison. Armed with press credentials from the *Chicago Daily News*, White secured an interview with the governor of Arkansas as well as with whites in Helena. When his identity was discovered, he had to outrun a lynch mob himself. Eventually the Supreme Court overturned the conviction of blacks in the Arkansas riot cases on the grounds that their right to due process, guaranteed under the Fourteenth Amendment, had been violated. Critics attacked White's penchant for drama and what they saw as self-promotion. Arguably, White sought publicity not so much for himself as for the larger cause. Although the NAACP failed to win passage of an anti-lynching law, they did win public relations victories when prominent white Americans, including former President Woodrow Wilson, publicly condemned lynching.

White's investigations became recruiting tools for the NAACP that rewarded White with hefty raises and special perks. Like Fauset, he accompanied Du Bois to the Pan-African Congress in 1921. But the experience seems not to have elicited a similarly engaged response. White's spirit was not cosmopolitan. But it was passionate. After *Birthright* was published, several of his friends, notably H. L. Mencken, the journalist, satirist, and champion of American vernacular English, encouraged White to put his experiences in a novel.

The only attribute that keeps Kenneth Harper, the protagonist of *The Fire in the Flint*, from being the prototypical New Negro is his naiveté. Southern-born and bred, but educated in the North (the first Negro intern at Bellevue), he is a veteran who has lived in post-war Paris. When he returns to Central City, Georgia to practice medicine, he plans to follow his father's advice about race relations: "the best way to get along with white people is to stay away from them."[12] He acknowledges the insults of Jim Crow, but, despite all evidence to the contrary, believes that only bad Negroes are lynched. He lacks patients, because blacks are reluctant to patronize a Negro doctor. Yet to perform surgeries, he has to rely on the goodwill of his black predecessor, Dr. Williams, a buffoon, and the local white physician, an incompetent. While his brother Bob is embittered by the prejudice he encounters after taking over his father's contracting business, Harper wonders that black sharecroppers do not hire a lawyer to represent them against cheating landlords.

White recognized that many white readers shared Harper's naiveté. The events of the novel serve to educate them. Blacks live in terror of the economic violence inflicted by their landlords and the physical violence threatened by the Ku Klux Klan. White men harass and abuse black women at will. Blacks who protest are lynched. White drew the vivid details of the plot from his investigative reporting. For example, Harper becomes involved with the Negro Farmers' Cooperative and Protective League, that is based on the Progressive Farmers' and Householders' Union in Arkansas that had been at the center of the Supreme Court case. White is on shakier ground when he invents details for the novel. Critics lambasted the novel's stilted love scenes with good reason.

However, the difficulty White encountered in finding a publisher for his novel was not based on the quality of his fictive imagination. White originally submitted his manuscript to Charles Doran, who eventually rejected it in part because his friend and author, the humorist Irvin S. Cobb, who specialized in "darky" stories, found it offensive. The publisher felt that White had not been fair to the "other side," that is to the decent white people in the South. White had in fact gone to considerable length to depict tolerant white men like Judge Stevenson, who may be the novel's most noble character. But the judge, like the men and women he represents, is totally ineffectual. *The Fire in the Flint* ends with two lynchings. In the first Bob is murdered and burned after he takes revenge against the white men who rape his sister. In the second, Dr. Harper is lynched for being the "troublemaker" he has inadvertently become.

When Doran turned down the novel, Alfred A. Knopf quickly signed it up. Knopf was on his way to becoming a legend in US publishing. The quality of his books was outstanding, both for their writing and for their manufacture. H. L. Mencken was Knopf's good friend. He and Carl Van Doren urged Knopf to publish White, as White would later urge Knopf to publish Larsen. Networker that he was, White also engaged the support of novelist Sinclair Lewis, who offered White writerly advice and then a blurb for the book. After these interventions, *The Fire in the Flint* was successful enough that Knopf urged White to try another novel.

Flight (1926) is more romance than documentary. Like *Plum Bun*, it explores passing, but the exploration is less psychological than Fauset's. The courageous protagonist, Mimi Daquin, named after the heroine of *La Bohème*, is a New Orleans Creole. The novel idealizes the fluid biracial Catholic culture that contrasts vividly with the more racially rigid Protestant culture of Atlanta, where Mimi finds herself during the 1906 race riot. She returns to New Orleans. Later, when she finds herself pregnant, she decides not to marry the weak father of her child and embarks on a journey that takes her to Philadelphia and to Harlem, where she lives with an aunt and socializes with the New Negro elite until an acquaintance from Atlanta recognizes her. She calculates that passing for white will not only enable her escape but create new opportunities. It does, as Mimi succeeds in her career as a seamstress and "French" dress designer for a New York fashion house. Mimi marries a wealthy white man, Jimmie Forrestor, who turns out to be a bigot. Despite her desire to acknowledge her past, Mimi recognizes that she cannot. However, when she views a black history pageant in Harlem, she decides to leave her husband and the false life they have led. After she retrieves her son, who is being raised as white, she reclaims her identity as a Negro: "'Free! Free! Free!' she whispered exultantly as with firm tread she went down the steps. '*Petit* Jean – my own people – and happiness!' was the song in her heart as she happily strode through the dawn."[13]

Critics were not impressed. Harlem Renaissance iconoclast Wallace Thurman wrote a damning review in *The Messenger*. Another young writer, poet Frank Horne, was almost as dismissive in *Opportunity*. White complained to editor Charles Johnson, who solicited a second review by White's friend Larsen. She found much to praise.

With his wife Gladys, White became a fixture on the Harlem social scene. At their Sugar Hill apartment, they regularly entertained the famous and talented, including the concert singers Paul Robeson, Roland Hayes, and Jules Bledsoe; the artist Miguel Covarrubias; the Weldon Johnsons, the Sinclair Lewises, and Carl Van Vechten and his wife Fania Marinoff. According to White's daughter Jane, George Gershwin debuted *Rhapsody in Blue* (1924) on the family's piano. White corresponded with many leading cultural figures and enjoyed hobnobbing with the elite. As his fame grew, he expanded his circle to include European visitors to New York including Konrad Bercovici, Nancy Cunard, Sergei Eisenstein, and Rebecca West. Not only did he like to drop names, he rarely missed a chance for self-promotion. In 1927 he was awarded a Guggenheim Foundation Fellowship. He did not complete the novel he had planned to write in France, but he finished *Rope and Faggot: A Biography of Judge Lynch* (1929).[14]

Apart from Ida Wells-Barnett, whose pioneering efforts White does not acknowledge, no one was better qualified than he to document the crime of lynching in the United States. In the decade between 1918 and 1927, White reports 454 lynchings; 416 of the victims were black. He gives locations and statistics, but asserts that "figures alone could not possibly tell the entire story."[15] Culling information from newspaper accounts and court records as well as his own investigations, White fills in horrific details of the brutal and sadistic violence that attended these crimes, the impact of the public spectacle they became, and the indifference of the legal system. He delves into the underlying causes of lynching that he locates in social history, religious traditions, group psychology, economics, and scientific racism. White's tone blends righteous anger and biting irony, as when he writes "in September 1925 a mob of Georgians, not content with murdering sane Negroes, actually broke in a state asylum at Milledgeville and lynched a violently insane Negro"(33). He notes with regard to his reliance on local newspaper stories that they doubtless minimized the horror they reported. He is scathing in his depiction of the rural South as a site of unbridled ignorance, in the throes of poverty and religious fanaticism.

In response to the illness and retirement of Weldon Johnson, White deepened his commitment to the NAACP. By 1930, he was the man in charge. He continued to engage in activism through the arts – by endorsing the Broadway production of *Green Pastures*, a depiction (some felt a caricature) of black folk religion based on the novel by DuBose Heyward and by monitoring the representation of blacks in Hollywood film. Although the NAACP Image Awards were established long after White left the scene, he was their progenitor. White was doubtless more popular with the public than with his colleagues. They faulted him for his imperious manner and his elitism. He and Du Bois clashed frequently, over both ideology and management style. In 1934, having forced Du Bois out of the organization, White could claim the soubriquet, "Mr. NAACP," which he owned for the rest of his life.

NOTES

1. Marion Starkey, "Jessie Fauset," *Southern Workman* 61 (May 1932), 218.
2. W. E. B. Du Bois and Alain Locke, "The Younger Literary Movement," *Crisis* 27 (1924), 162.
3. Quoted in Edward Waldron, *Walter White and the Harlem Renaissance* (Port Washington, NY: Kennikat Press, 1978), p. 64.
4. Many studies of the Harlem Renaissance pay short shrift to Fauset and White. For biographical information and critical analysis on both, see Ann Douglas, *Terrible Honesty: Mongrel Manhattan in the 1920s* (New York: Farrar, Straus, Giroux, 1995); George Hutchinson, *The Harlem Renaissance in Black and White* (Cambridge, MA: Harvard University Press, 1995); David Levering Lewis, *When Harlem Was in Vogue* (New York: Knopf, 1989). For more on Fauset, see Ann duCille, *The Coupling Convention: Sex, Text, and Tradition in Black Women's Fiction* (New York: Oxford University Press, 1993); Susan Goodman, *Civil Wars: American Novelists and Manners, 1880–1940* (Baltimore: Johns Hopkins University Press, 2003); Jacqueline McClendon, *The Politics of Color in the Fiction of Jessie Fauset and Nella Larsen* (Charlottesville: University Press of Virginia, 1995); Deborah McDowell, *"The Changing Same": Black Women's Literature, Criticism, and Theory* (1995); Nina Miller, *Making Love Modern: The Intimate Public Worlds of New York's Literary Women* (New York: Oxford University Press, 1998); Carolyn W. Sylvander, *Jessie Redmon Fauset: Black American Writer* (Troy, NY: Whitson, 1981); Cheryl A. Wall, *Women of the Harlem Renaissance* (Bloomington: Indiana University Press, 1995). For more on White, see Kenneth Robert Janken, *White: The Biography of Walter White, Mr. NAACP* (New York: New Press, 2003); Gilbert Jonas, *Freedom's Sword: The NAACP and the Struggle against Racism in America, 1909–1969* (New York: Routledge, 2005); Waldron, *Walter White and the Harlem Renaissance*; Robert L. Zangrando, *The NAACP Crusade against Lynching* (Philadelphia: Temple University Press, 1980).
5. "The Emancipator of Brazil," *Crisis* 21 (1921), 208–9; "Saint-George, Chevalier of France," *Crisis* 22 (1921), 9–12; "Looking Backward," *Crisis* 23 (1922), 125–6.
6. Jessie Fauset, *There Is Confusion* (1924; Boston: Northeastern University Press, 1989), p. 97.
7. Jessie Fauset, *Plum Bun* (1928; Boston: Beacon Press, 1990), p. 78. Subsequent references to this edition will be cited parenthetically.
8. *The Chinaberry Tree* (1931; Boston: Northeastern University Press, 1995), p. xxxi.
9. *Comedy: American Style* (1933; College Park, MD: McGrath Publishing Co., 1969), p. 205.
10. *A Man Called White: The Autobiography of Walter White* (New York: Viking Press, 1948), p. 11.

11. Walter F. White, "The Work of a Mob," *Crisis* 16 (1918), 221–3.
12. Walter White, *The Fire in the Flint* (New York: Alfred A. Knopf, 1924), p. 17.
13. *Flight* (New York: Alfred A. Knopf, 1926), p. 300.
14. Scholars recently discovered his unpublished novel titled "Blackjack."
15. *Rope and Faggot: A Biography of Judge Lynch* (1929; Notre Dame, IN: University of Notre Dame Press, 2001), p. 22.

7

MARK A. SANDERS

African American folk roots and Harlem Renaissance poetry

Our contemporary celebration of African American culture, especially our concern for "authentic" blackness and the vernacular, owes much to the New Negro era. From Hip Hop, to movies depicting black inner city life, to spoken-word poetry, to "Chitlin' Circuit" theater, and beyond, black folk expression (either rural or urban) has come to serve as the sign of black cultural identity. Yet the centrality of the vernacular was not always evident in the longer history of African American letters. To be sure, the vernacular has always held a place in African American literary expression, but through the eighteenth and nineteenth centuries standard English and Anglo-American literary models were the norm (indeed the ideal for many) in addressing both African American and white audiences. It was the Harlem Renaissance that radically relocated the folk, indeed reinvented an African American literary vocabulary based on folk forms, idioms, and patterns of speech; and in doing so, the Harlem Renaissance bequeathed a legacy that would shape African American literature throughout the twentieth century and up to the present day.

The legacy of Harlem Renaissance artistry begins in the larger context of the New Negro Movement, the late nineteenth-, early twentieth-century political and cultural movement to reclaim the civil rights guaranteed through Reconstruction legislation. The New Negro generation created political organizations, published magazines and newspapers, attended colleges and universities in unprecedented numbers, and pursued professional careers all in the name of African American equality, inclusion, and full citizenship. Equally as important, the era institutionalized black history and historical research. New Negroes founded institutions for the creation and preservation of black history; they wrote histories that celebrated black heroes and heroines, documented crucial African, Afro-Caribbean, and African American contributions to world culture, and ultimately put the lie to black essentialism. Furthermore, as we will see, African American folk culture would play a major role in reconstructing a cultural past that would help lay claim to full citizenship.

But what, for New Negro intellectuals and artists, was African American folk culture? Folk culture consisted of material objects, cultural practices, and linguistic idioms and forms created by poor and working-class African Americans in both rural and urban settings throughout the eighteenth, nineteenth, and twentieth centuries. Material objects included quilts, jewelry, toys, musical instruments, etc.; while cultural practices and linguistic forms included work songs, seculars, field hollers, shouts, spirituals, blues, tall tales, aphorisms, dance songs, children's rhymes, toasts, sermons, gospel music, the blues, jazz, playing the dozens, lies, sounding and signifying, etc. Arguably the most ubiquitous folk source, music, could include varying mixtures of the following elements: descending pentatonic scale, homophonics (as apposed to heterophonics), blue notes, syncopation (in standard time, accents on 2 and 4 rather than on 1 and 3), antiphonal or call-and-response dynamics, and vernacular instrumentation. In addition to marching band or dance hall instruments, vernacular instrumentation could include readily available tools and other materials such as wash boards, wash tubs, gourds, spoons, cooking kettles, hollow logs, sticks, animal skins drawn over kettles or hollow logs, etc. Folk instrumentation also included orchestral instruments such as violins and bass violins as well as the African-derived banjo.

For New Negroes, folk culture held great promise both politically and artistically; indeed many New Negroes saw folk culture as an essential element of a usable past, a history of heroic resolve in the face of one of the cruelest forms of slavery in history. Through spirituals, enslaved African Americans sang about enslaved Hebrews and so celebrated a god of liberation, a god that championed the slave and the oppressed; and through secular songs, aphorisms, and tall tales they could check the despotic power of slave owners and explore the ways by which the physically weak could outwit and overpower the physically strong.[1] In a larger sense, blacks were able to create a culture that both reflected and celebrated the richness of the humanity of black lives, a complexity that slavery (and its attending forms of black representation) actively denied.

Thus, this culture, rich with expressive possibilities, served as a source for all of the arts of the era. Music, theatre arts, graphic arts, film, and literature culled folk sources in order to depict African American life with accuracy, with complexity, and above all sensitivity for its inherent humanity. Against the backdrop of racist caricature in all forms of mainstream American popular culture, this final point becomes more significant. For New Negroes sought to redress the cultural expressions that legitimized lynchings, disfranchisement, peonage, and Jim Crow. More specifically, the plantation tradition and minstrelsy, dating from the antebellum period to World War II, portrayed African Americans either as loyal retainers filled with love and devotion for their masters, or as child-like buffoons in need of constant supervision. The mammy and Uncle Tom placed loyalty to the master and his family above their own families, in some cases above life itself. On the minstrel stage, dancing, comic capers and the broken English of the happy-go-lucky darky (variations on the sambo figure) played out a fantasy of debased and inconsequential black being. In literature and on stage, both traditions played on folk forms, language, and types in service to black caricature. Surviving well into the twentieth century, the zip coon, sambo, mammy, Uncle Tom, pickaninnie, etc. were also the vocabulary of advertising, vaudeville, and mainstream film. They were the dolls children played with; they sold the meals Americans ate. In short, all forms of American popular culture aped folk forms and created folk types in the general assertion of black absence, depravity, and sub-humanity. Relative to the politics of segregation and disfranchisement, American popular culture constructed blacks as ultimately deserving of political exclusion; it depicted them as the antithesis to the legitimate participants in a democratic society.

In response, New Negro artists reconstructed folk culture as a rich artistic source, and offered it as an essential element of American democratic identity. Indeed, in the preface to *The Book of American Negro Poetry* (1922) James Weldon Johnson makes the broader and specific claim for folk culture, going so far as to argue that its lore is the *only* truly American folklore.[2] For Johnson, the African American possessed a "transfusive quality," the ability "to suck up the national spirit from the soil and create something artistic and original" (Johnson, "Preface to the First Edition" 20). Although New Negroes continued to argue over the relative value of specific folk forms, most agreed that part of the African American claim to citizenship was its cultural and artistic gifts to the nation. For Johnson, African American folklore (represented in the Uncle Remus stories) and spirituals served as the two folk-derived gifts to the nation. Du Bois anticipated Johnson when in *The Souls of Black Folk* (1903) he too offered the "sorrow songs" as black cultural achievement and essential contribution. In addition, playwrights, novelists, and poets including Langston Hughes, Zora Neale Hurston, James Weldon Johnson, Jean Toomer, Sterling A. Brown, Claude McKay, Eric Walrond, Rudolph Fisher, and many more looked to folk culture as a means of representing dimensions of black life never before explored in literature.

As prose writers and poets alike began to look to folk sources, New Negro poets faced a particular challenge: a crisis in poetic language for addressing African American life.[3] Their immediate predecessors of the mid to late nineteenth century – James Edwin Campbell, Daniel Webster Davis, Paul

Laurence Dunbar, Frances E. W. Harper, etc. – had left them little in the way of usable models for poetic representation. On the one hand, Campbell, Davis, and Dunbar had worked within the nineteenth-century dialect tradition that by 1922 had been condemned by Johnson for its inability to render anything more than humor and pathos (Johnson "Preface to the First Edition" 41). Dunbar himself admitted to the artistic dead end of dialect, confessing to Johnson that he worked in the tradition to "gain a hearing" but could not remake it to account for the broader expressive abilities of the black vernacular.[4]

On the other hand, Harper worked in a tradition of Victorian sentimentality that tended to reduce the palpable realities of black peonage to lifeless abstractions of injustice.[5] Both traditions were inadequate for the teeming realities of black life confronting New Negro poets; thus these artists literally had to invent a new poetic language, new forms, and symbolic vocabulary largely based on a more thorough exploration of folk culture.

Thus, a number of New Negro era poets took up the challenge to reconstruct dialect, to reclaim the black vernacular, in order, again, to engage in the ongoing cultural war over black representation. For example, Claude McKay's first collection, *Songs of Jamaica* (1912), was in Jamaican folk dialect, and Roy Garfield Dandridge wrote two collections very much in the old Dunbar-styled dialect tradition; but it was Jean Toomer, James Weldon Johnson, Sterling A. Brown, and Langston Hughes who defined the folk-based poetic legacy that the Harlem Renaissance would pass on to ensuing generations of black poets. Although, of the four, James Weldon Johnson was the first to publish a folk-based poem ("The Creation" in *The Freedman* 2, 1920), it was Toomer who established the broader possibilities of literature based on folk sources, thus providing a foundation. Through his prose, Johnson provided a critical framework for using folk sources, then contributed the enduring example of *God's Trombones*, capturing both the oral and the aural performance of folk sermons and church services. Moving in a different direction, Sterling Brown fused secular folk forms and western prosody to explore folk subjectivity. And finally, Langston Hughes reclaimed dialect, invented jazz poetry, and celebrated the blues, all in service to a broader, deeper, and more complex rendering of African American life.

Jean Toomer

In 1923 Jean Toomer published *Cane*, a collection of sketches, short stories, poetry, and drama largely focused on African American rural folk culture. Pulling from his experiences teaching at the Agricultural Industrial Institute in Sparta, Georgia, experiences that put him in intimate contact with the folk, Toomer wrote a paean to the culture, lamenting that "The folk-spirit was walking in to die on the modern desert. That spirit was so beautiful. Its death was so tragic ... And this is the feeling I put into 'Cane.'"[6] Toomer viewed modernization, mechanization, and black migration out of the rural South as signs of the demise of black folk culture; thus he tried to capture in *Cane* both the beauty of the culture and the tragedy of its passing.

As the first of the New Negro poets and writers to publish a volume based on folk culture, Toomer's portraits in *Cane* helped to make subsequent New Negro writing on the folk possible. Arna Bontemps commented that younger writers "went quietly mad"[7] over *Cane*, and Sterling Brown wrote to Toomer confessing, "I look upon *Cane* as one of the most influential forces in the artistic awakening of the Negro and as one of the most beautiful and moving books of contemporary American literature" (Byrd, *Jean Toomer's Years* 183).

Part of the artistic success of the volume stems from a vision of the transformative power of folk-based literature, a potential in transformation based on a specific theory of spiritual wholeness. Toomer held that individuals could grow to harmonize intellect, emotions, and body, into a spiritual whole capable of resisting the corrosive effects of modernization. For Toomer, *Cane* reflected the modern dilemma for African Americans and folk culture, asserting dislocation, dissipation, and loss, while signaling the possibility of synthesis and transcendence. Indeed, the very structure of *Cane* – moving from the rural South to the urban North and Midwest and back – and the crescents marking the beginning of each section, formally and visually sustain this ongoing tension between wholeness and perpetual fragmentation.

The first section introduces the milieu of the rural black South, focusing on the plight of black women, particularly in terms of sexual exploitation, racism, and the lack of self-awareness.[8] In each of the sketches, the central figures – Karintha, Becky, Carma, Fern, and Esther – experience psychic trauma owing to the male-dominated culture that surrounds them, and thus fail to acquire a level of self-awareness necessary to resist the culture. The impressionistic style Toomer uses depicts emotional reality rather than physical, stresses sense and feeling over action. Indeed the affinity between environment and psychic states suggests sketches as prose poems rendering the psychic and emotional landscape.

Furthermore, the actual poems function to heighten this impressionistic effect by further elucidating mood, theme, and image of the surrounding sketches. According to Bernard Bell, they function as transition pieces, highlighting the thematic connections between sketches.[9] For example, "Reapers" and "November Cotton Flower" function as "companion poems" for "Karintha," by reasserting "the haunting appeal and religious core" of the sketch, and "Face" and "Cotton Song" amplify the "religious symbolism" found in "Becky."[10] But more specifically the poems – through compression of language – effect a higher level of metaphoric density or concentration that serves to render the lyric or aesthetic possibilities of folk culture in a manner and form commensurate with the inherent artistry of the culture itself. Thus, the poems not only sustain the central tension of the collection, but offer folk-derived lyricism as a possible resolution. Bell suggests that "Spirituals, folk songs, jazz, and poetry are vehicles for the attainment of this end" (Bell, "A Key to the Poems in *Cane*" 326), the harmony of mind, body, and emotion. Thus poetry, representing the spirituality of folk culture, is not simply a vehicle, but an emblem of Toomer's desired harmony.

It is important to keep in mind that Toomer published a number of these poems before publishing *Cane*, presenting his folk-referenced poetry in isolation, allowing them on their own to represent these aspects of folk culture heretofore ignored in literature. For example, "Face," "Portrait in Georgia," and "Conversion" were first published as a series – "Georgia Portraits" – in *Modern Review* 1 (January 1923). As a group, they employ imagist technique to render the deep psychic wounding of black women, perhaps emblematic of the larger trauma visited upon blacks in Georgia. The physical aspects – "Eyes–fagots, / Lips–old scars, or the first red blister"[11] – convey the emotional reality specific to lynching but also the larger psychic landscape: "grapes of sorrow / purple in the evening sun / nearly ripe for worms."[12] The specific victim of lynching also represents the group, ruthlessly attacked simply for who they are. Similarly, "November Cotton Flower," "Song of the Son," and "Georgia Dusk" were published prior to *Cane*, depicting the profound tragedy of racial oppression visited upon blacks, while illustrating the lyric possibilities (and thus hope) found in the artistic representation of folk culture and its plight.

Ultimately for Toomer, his poetry struck an ambivalent pose toward African American folk culture. Clearly he celebrated its inherent artistry, and thus its spiritual/psychic possibilities, particularly in the ongoing project of human development toward harmony. Nevertheless, for Toomer, folk culture was doomed; indeed *Cane* marks its final fading. Perhaps even more paradoxically, the deep psychic wounding Toomer found at the core of folk culture – indeed much of the source of its haunting beauty – ultimately threatens the final resolution in the wholeness he hopes that it will promote. Karintha, Becky, et al. can only hint at recuperation while the overriding élan they affect is one of tragedy. Furthermore, just as the two half crescents at the beginning of "Kabnis" gesture toward closure, they remain separated. Similarly, the drama itself suggests the possibility of Kabnis' rejuvenation through his contact with Father John (the sign of folk heritage); it also suggests that he remains frozen, cut off from history and thus unable to achieve wholeness (Sanders, "American Modernism and the New Negro Renaissance" 152).

James Weldon Johnson

As an educator, lawyer and political activist for the NAACP, James Weldon Johnson typified the combination of art and politics for New Negro writers. Johnson first articulated quite clearly that black writers should write about racial issues, about black lives, and necessarily then the vicissitudes of racial oppression (Johnson, "Preface to the First Edition" 7). For Johnson, an investment in the artistic depictions of the lived experiences of blacks led directly to a concern for the largest group of African Americans, poor and working-class blacks, still mostly in the deep South in the 1920s. Thus as the folk experience became a greater artistic concern, the forms of folk expression, too, held out greater possibility for Johnson. Indeed, in his autobiography, *Along This Way* (1938), Johnson articulates a vision of "serious" or "high" African American art based on folk culture, referring to "a realization of the importance of the American Negro's cultural background and his creative folk-art, and ... [of] the superstructure of conscious art that might be reared upon them" (Johnson, *Along This Way* 52). Previously, in his preface for *The Book of American Negro Poetry*, Johnson had articulated four major contributions to American culture that blacks had made, two of them being elements of folk culture. Some sixteen years later, he looked back at his artistic career and asserted folk culture as the basis of his best poetry and as the source of the most innovative and important New Negro writing.

Given the larger New Negro concern over the past and African American cultural history (most often represented by folk culture), Johnson identified an important yet neglected element of folk culture: folk sermons. In his preface to *God's Trombones*, he states that in the larger collection of folk forms sermons have gone overlooked, yet represent a vital dimension of African American culture.[13] For Johnson black preachers were the first to unify enslaved Africans as a New World people; they were the first to create a free space – the black church – where leadership and mobilization could develop; and it was the black preacher, through his sermons, who "for generations was the mainspring of hope and inspiration for the Negro in America" (Johnson, "Preface to the First Edition" 2–3). Furthermore, as a result of a trip to Kansas City where he had the opportunity to hear what he termed an "old-time Negro preacher" (11), Johnson began to combine the larger significance of folk sermons with his vision of New Negro art founded on folk culture. Hearing the natural poetry of the sermons, witnessing the drama of the performance (and its effects on the congregation), Johnson wanted to capture this unique form of black speech and cultural expression in verse. Indeed, the very title of the collection signals the philosophical/ prosodic approach to versified sermons, focusing on the human voice as a musical instrument, the trombone "possessing above all others the power to express the wide and varied range of emotions" (7). Just as the preacher chanted, intoned, shouted, moaned, and sang, Johnson's verse – like trombones – would capture the expansive possibilities in meaning these sermons represent.

After the inspiration of the sermon in Kansas City, Johnson set out to versify "classic" sermons such as "The Valley of Dry Bones" (based on chapter 37 of Ezekiel) or the "Train Sermon" that were passed from preacher to preacher and preached to numerous congregations across the South. So, too, the collection would highlight well-worn Judeo-Christian themes – fall and redemption, judgment, sin, and death – marking so many of these sermons. Similar to *Cane*, the collection would capture an aspect of folk culture Johnson felt was fading in the wake of modernity.

Like Toomer, too, Johnson would use standard English, rather than dialect, but for very different reasons. As we saw earlier, Johnson rejected the dialect tradition because it limited black expression to comic burlesque or maudlin sentimentality; but Johnson adds to this argument that the language of black sermons could not be represented through the dialect tradition because black preachers "spoke another language, a language far removed from traditional Negro dialect." For Johnson, this language was "a fusion of Negro idioms with Bible English," a language "saturated with the sublime phraseology of the Hebrew prophets and steeped in the idioms of King James English" (9).

Johnson represented this language with an inventive approach to form, heavily influenced by Old Testament poetics received through the King James translation. It is important to keep in mind too that Johnson, like all of his New Negro poet compatriots, was a Whitman devotee, seeing in his free verse an approach to multiple American voices, languages, and modes of singing, a formal model for his own poetry. Johnson combined a Whitmanesque and Old Testament approach to prosody, creating a form that could dramatize the performative dimensions of folk sermons. Mutlu Blasing provides an informing assessment of Old Testament verse form, one that helps to explain Johnson's own approach: "Biblical verse structures lines on the basis of phonetic, syntactic, *or* semantic parallelism, which includes contrasts and modifications as well as repetition and elaborations. The lines are units of thought, and all or any of these linguistic features may be used, together or interchangeably, to mark verse units."[14] Johnson ultimately effects this combination through a similar adaptation from the Bible. Instead of standard prosody, he uses "units of thought," often through similar parallelisms, repetitions, and improvization. For example, the third stanza of "Listen, Lord – A Prayer" features many of these characteristics:

> And now, O Lord, this man of God,
> Who breaks the bread of life this morning –
> Shadow him in the hollow of Thy hand,
> And keep him out of the gunshot of the devil.
> Take him, Lord – this morning –
> Wash him with hyssop inside and out,
> Hang him up and drain him dry of sin.
> Pin his ear to the wisdom-post,
> And make his words sledge hammers of truth –
> Beating on the iron heart of sin.[15]

Note the use of recognizable biblical diction – "breaks the bread of life" for example – along with a folk approach to metaphor: "And keep him out of the gunshot of the devil" (Johnson, *God's Trombones* 14). Furthermore, the dashes indicate "an audible expulsion of the breath" (Johnson, "Preface to the First Edition" 11), in reference to the performance, where the preacher may chant or even sing parts of the sermon, punctuating sections with dramatic breathing. These moments too create space for call-and-response, the interchange between preacher and congregation in which church members respond in affirmation and encouragement.

Finally, Johnson's approach to folk sermons, similar to what we will see in Hughes and Brown, created new poetic forms derived from folk forms, modes of expression, and sensibilities. Focusing on a neglected yet vital dimension of folk culture, Johnson's poetry sings with celebration of the African American tradition, one that for Johnson helped to sustain and preserve African American psychic life in the face of relentless assault.

Sterling A. Brown

Prior to his first and most successful collection of poems, *Southern Road* (1932), Sterling A. Brown had already published several celebrated poems in folk idioms and dialect and was recognized by Alain Locke and Louis Untermeyer as a pioneering voice in New Negro poetics. In order to write such poetry, Brown toured the rural South through the latter half of the 1920s, listening and taking note of local speech patterns and modes of cultural expression. He met Calvin "Big Boy Davis," a local blues singer who would become a mythic hero in one of Brown's most celebrated poems; he patronized dives and honky-tonks; he interviewed blacks from different walks of life, and so became intimately familiar with the cultural practices through which black communities invested their collective lives with meaning.

In turn, Brown wrote three books of poetry (along with essays, literary studies, and one anthology) that sought to reinvent poetic black vernacular and literary representation of African American culture. Thus Brown's portraits of southern black life are invested with a thorough sense of historicity. More than simply a static set of cultural artifacts, his use of dialect, his control of folk forms such as the blues, and his innovative use of the blues ballad depict folk culture as dynamic, ever evolving tools for affecting the present moment. Indeed, his personas are most often captured in the act of perpetual creation, using the cultural forms around them to reshape the past and the present, and thus in envisioning a future of greater possibility.

Southern Road, and its opening poem, "Odyssey of Big Boy," best illustrate Brown's approach to the folk. The collection as a whole takes as its overriding metaphor a dominant theme in nineteenth- and early twentieth-century African American folklore: the road, or more largely the promise of travel in pursuit of greater freedom and possibility. Echoing Walt Whitman's "Song of the Open Road" in its celebration of multiple indigenous voices, sounds, and expressive practices, *Southern Road* offers passage to the black southern landscape, a teeming cultural tapestry in the perpetual process of remaking itself in response to changing circumstances. Thus Brown's metaphor of the road first suggests access, the poet/observer's avenue to a largely unseen, unappreciated cultural milieu.

Yet in keeping with the folk implications of the road, the metaphor also signals black mobility, the act of changing location in order to improve one's material/political condition. At this historical moment of black migration from South to North, from rural to urban, the road (represented by trains, buses, automobiles, riding, walking, or running) suggested the ability to effect change, ultimately black agency, in its ability to shape the future.

In this sense, then, the metaphor expands to include the cultural and artistic ways in which African American folk "move" in order to occupy ever freer psychic spaces. More specifically, voice (singing, speaking, shouting, etc.), language, and form serve as interrelated elements. Brown's folk personas such as Sister Lou, Big Boy Davis, or Ma Rainey, use folk forms in order to explore their personal and communal histories and to assign them mythic or transcendent meaning.

"Odyssey of Big Boy" well illustrates the multiple implications of the road and African American folk culture in Brown's poetry. First, this blues ballad reinvents the folk ballad by taking the traditional form for chronicling the past deeds of cultural heroes and refashioning it in order to envision the future. Rather than addressing the past and established meaning, it is a ballad about the future and potential meaning.

As such, the ballad begins and ends with invocations of the future. Facing imminent death, the speaker intones:

> Lemme be wid Casey Jones,
>   Lemme be wid Stagolee,
> Lemme be wid such like men
>   When Death takes hol' on me,
>   When Death takes hol' on me.

Presenting John Henry as the sign of transcendence, he ends the poem with another look into the future.

> An' all dat Big Boy axes
>   When time comes fo' to go,
> Lemme be wid John Henry, steel drivin' man,
>   Lemme be wid old Jazzbo,
>   Lemme be wid ole Jazzbo ...[16]

Thus, as the meaning of the poem and Davis' life depend entirely on the present moment of vocalization, the voice itself serves as the road, the passage toward transcendent meaning; so too, this meaning relies upon folk cultural values. The history Davis relates is the classic black masculinist model of personhood based on "physical and psychological autonomy, mobility, and irrepressible vitality."[17] His chronicle of travel, physical work, and sexual conquest will hopefully prove a manhood just as outsized and romantic as that of John Henry or Stagolee; indeed, the poem ultimately asks for entry into the pantheon of folk cultural gods based on a similarly heroic life.

Where Davis' movement toward mythic meaning depends on the statement of deed, it also relies upon the form that statement takes. Here the five-line stanza with an elongated third line, and repeating final lines, adapts one of the folk ballad forms for "John Henry." Although the lines are one foot shorter, the essential form is the same, and thus Davis reconstructs himself rhetorically and poetically in the form of John Henry; he grafts his life and potential meaning onto a folk form that has enshrined John Henry's immortality. Not only does Davis (or Brown) demonstrate the potential of using folk forms in creating (or re-creating) meaning, the poem itself becomes a study of contingent black subjectivity: the perpetually present moment of a black psyche culling from its cultural landscape in order to re-create itself in expansive, more meaningful ways. Note, too, Brown's use of the vernacular. Here Davis' dialect more accurately reflects variations in intonation and psychological disposition, variations that deliver a fully complex, fully human black subject.

Brown's most famous poems from *Southern Road* – "Strong Men," "Southern Road," "When de Saints go Ma'ching Home," "Sister Lou," etc. – all explore black subjectivity in its use of folk culture to affect material and psychic conditions. Culling from the blues, spirituals, work songs, etc., they heroically reshape the present and the future. Thus, the road suggests the folk cultural continuum leading to mythic and liberating possibilities (Sanders, "Sterling A. Brown's Master Metaphor" 927).

Langston Hughes

Putting it succinctly, Gerald Early writes that Langston Hughes "made the whole business of modern Afro-American literature possible."[18] The sheer volume of his writings, his iconoclastic attitude toward black middle-class representation (and New Negro elites), and most importantly his concern for the lives and culture of poor and working-class blacks has made him the veritable icon of the Harlem Renaissance. His was "the project of constructing an entire literary tradition upon the actual spoken language of the black working and rural classes – the same vernacular language that the growing black middle class considered embarrassing and demeaning, the linguistic legacy of slavery."[19]

Moreover, Hughes' approach to folk culture, most often in an urban context, validated under-class blacks as legitimate poetic subject matter, and more generally celebrated a fuller range of black representation, one that would include the uglier or seamier sides of black life. Ultimately, for Hughes, the range (and thus honesty) itself worked to "affirm quietly the dignity and historicity of blacks."[20] Again, in keeping with larger New Negro ideals, Hughes' poetry asserted blacks as fully complex, fully human, and thus equals in the American democratic experiment.

Prior to 1926, the publication date of his first collection, *The Weary Blues*, Hughes had published several of his poems in the leading New Negro and mainstream magazines including *The Crisis*, *Opportunity*, and *Survey Graphic*; but when Knopf brought out *The Weary Blues*, the volume marked an important literary moment, followed the next year by the publication of *Fine Clothes to the Jew*. The two volumes marked a defining shift in New Negro poetics and the larger artistic stance relative to the vernacular and folk culture. Both volumes introduced jazz poetry to the Harlem Renaissance and mainstream literary scene, and both unapologetically explored the broadest range of African American life.

Extending Toomer's example, Hughes took up not only folk culture as subject matter, but the same forms of expression that defined and sustained it. More specifically, Hughes' attention to African American music – jazz and blues in particular – as folk expression and as poetic forms stands as perhaps his most important poetic innovation. Indeed, Arnold Rampersad regards Hughes' jazz poetry as "the only genuinely original achievement in form by any black American poet" (Rampersad, "Hughes' *Fine Clothes to the Jew*" 67). For example, "Negro Dancers" presents a black speaker celebrating his relationship (here expressed through dance and the love of jazz) in the idiom of jazz, conveying what Countee Cullen described as the "frenzy and electric heat of a Methodist or Baptist revival meeting":[21]

> Me an' ma baby's
> Got two mo' ways,
> Two mo' ways to do de buck!
>   Da, da,
>   Da, da, da!
> Two mo' ways to do de buck![22]

Complementing the enthusiasm of the speaker's statement, the pace of the lines, the repetition, and the use of "da" to connote syncopated rhythm, all work to replicate the kinetic intensity of dance hall jazz. Both form and statement fuse as they express joy and abandonment (ultimately, freedom and its attending connotations), and thus the power and potential of this urban folk form. (Hughes went on to write even more famous jazz poems after the Harlem Renaissance in *Montage of a Dream Deferred* (1951) and *Ask Your Mama* (1961), but for the New Negro era, his jazz poetry found in *The Weary Blues* invented the poetic vocabulary.)

Equally as important, Hughes helped to create blues poetry, with *Fine Clothes to the Jew* being the first volume to explore more widely its artistic possibilities. As Steven Tracy points out, Hughes bases his poetry primarily on the "classic" blues form made famous by singers and musicians such as Ma Rainey, Bessie Smith, and W. C. Handy.[23] This style employed the AAB verse form: first line as statement, second line as repetition of statement with slight variation, and third line as response or resolution relative to the problem posed by the statement. Hughes often changed the form slightly, breaking each line into two, making six lines rather than three-line stanzas. But the presentation of theme, repetition, and sense of resolution remain the same. The last stanza of "Lament over Love" serves as an apt example:

I'm goin' up in a tower
Tall as a tree is tall
Say up in a tower
Tall as a tree is tall.
Gonna think about ma man an'
Let ma fool-self fall.[24]

The lack of punctuation at the end of lines 1, 3, and 5, and the hard stops at the ends of lines 2, 4, and 6 replicate the units of meaning found in the classic blues form. So, too, the lyric compression echoes the folk idiom's gift of emotional intensity through verbal economy and formal simplicity. Thus, Hughes does not simply reproduce the form or feel of the folk idiom; he invents a poetics capable of an analogous ritual and ethos, thus a poetics promising similar possibilities for psychic recuperation and sustenance that the idiom has offered historically. Thus, in "Lament over Love," where the speaker contemplates suicide as a result of her despair, the act of transforming emotional wounds into art suggests that, rather than suicide, dogged survival will be the outcome of this episode. It is the song/poem itself that the speaker uses to impose order (indeed to extract meaning) from the emotional chaos caused by the break up of her love relationship.

Anticipating both James Weldon Johnson and Brown, Hughes identified the black church and African American worship as a vital dimension of folk culture and a rich source for poetry. In a number of poems, Hughes effects the emotional intensity of and psychic transformation he often found in African American religious services. Furthermore, a poem such as "Prayer Meeting" or "Sinner" reflects a vital way in which African Americans asserted themselves as spiritual beings deserving of God's love and grace. As "Prayer Meeting" begins by repeating, "Glory! Halleluiah! / De dawn's a-comin'!," the poem conveys the speaker's hope and relief realized through a night of prayer and fervent religiosity. Over and against the racism and economic violence bent on her psychic destruction, the speaker is able to find affirmation and assurance through religious ritual.

Finally, Hughes' use of vernacular in his blues and church-based poems is equally significant. In addition to claiming the agency and artistry of black music, his poems in the vernacular reclaim black English from the dialect tradition, presenting black voices fully capable of expressing the range and depth of their humanity.

Perhaps one of Hughes' earliest successes in dialect, "Mother to Son," best illustrates his renovation of the dialect tradition. Indeed, Rampersad identifies the poem as "nothing less than a personal reclamation of black dialect . . . [where] . . . black speech is invoked in the context of the race's courage, endurance, and sense of duty" (Rampersad, "Hughes' *Fine Clothes to the Jew*" 55). Recalling her trials and perseverance, the speaker tells her son:

> I'se been a-climbin' on,
> And reachin' landin's
> And turnin' corners,
> And sometimes goin' in the dark
> Where there ain't been no light.
> So boy, don't you turn back.
>
> (Hughes, *The Weary Blues* 107)

In the language of a poor long-suffering black woman, Hughes delivers a persona far removed from the limitations of humor and pathos; the poem in fact presents a fully realized black subject replete with complex dimensions including tenacity, endurance, sorrow, love, pride, and a compelling sense of hope for her son.

Finally, Hughes' full investment in African American culture, thus in vernacular and folk roots, helped to set the stage for the most innovative and compelling poetry of the New Negro era. Indeed, Hughes helped to forge the poetic language that not only would distinguish Harlem Renaissance poetics, but would look forward to ensuing generations. A whole host of poets – Gwendolyn Brooks, Robert Hayden, Margaret Walker, Bob Kaufman, Amiri Baraka, Michael S. Harper, Yusef Komunyakaa, and many more – have inherited the Harlem Renaissance approach to black orality, vernacular, and cultural forms. Indeed, in terms of approach to black culture, one could argue that the Harlem Renaissance never ended.

NOTES

1. Lawrence W. Levine, *Black Culture and Black Consciousness: Afro-American Folk Thought from Slavery to Freedom* (New York: Oxford University Press, 1977), pp. 81–133.
2. James Weldon Johnson, "Preface to the First Edition," in *The Book of American Negro Poetry*, revised edition (New York: Harcourt Brace and Company, 1931), p. 10.
3. Louis D. Rubin, Jr., "The Search for Language, 1746–1923," in *Black Poetry in America: Two Essays in Historical Interpretation* (Baton Rouge: Louisiana State University Press, 1974), pp. 1–35.
4. James Weldon Johnson, *Along This Way: The Autobiography of James Weldon Johnson* (New York: Viking Press, 1933), p. 160.
5. Mark A. Sanders, *Afro-Modernist Aesthetics and the Poetry of Sterling A. Brown* (Athens: The University of Georgia Press, 1999), p. 8.
6. Quoted from Rudolph P. Byrd, *Jean Toomer's Years with Gurdjieff: Portrait of an Artist, 1923–1936* (Athens: The University of Georgia Press, 1990), p. 12.
7. Arna Bontemps, "The Negro Renaissance: Jean Toomer and the Harlem Renaissance of the 1920s," in Herbert Hill, ed., *Anger, and Beyond: The Negro Writer in the United States* (New York: Harper and Row, 1966), p. 24.

8. Mark A. Sanders, "American Modernism and the New Negro Movement," in Walter Kalaidjian, ed., *The Cambridge Companion to American Modernism* (Cambridge: Cambridge University Press, 2005), p. 151.

9. Bernard Bell, "A Key to the Poems of *Cane*," in Therman B. O'Daniel, ed., *Jean Toomer: A Critical Evaluation* (Washington, DC: Howard University Press, 1988), p. 323.

10. Bernard W. Bell, "The Poems of *Cane*," in *Cane: Norton Critical Edition*, ed. Darwin T. Turner (New York: W. W. Norton & Co., 1988), p. 224.

11. Jean Toomer, "Portrait in Georgia," in *Cane: Norton Critical Edition*, ed. Darwin T. Turner (New York: W. W. Norton & Co., 1988), p. 29.

12. Jean Toomer, "Face," in *Cane: Norton Critical Edition*, ed. Darwin T. Turner (New York: W. W. Norton & Co., 1988), p. 10.

13. James Weldon Johnson, "Preface," in *God's Trombones: Seven Negro Sermons in Verse* (New York: Penguin Books, 1990), p. 1.

14. Mutlu Konuk Blasing, *American Poetry: The Rhetoric of Its Forms* (New Haven: Yale University Press, 1987), p. 136.

15. James Weldon Johnson, "Listen, Lord – A Prayer," in *God's Trombones: Seven Negro Sermons in Verse* (New York: Penguin Books, 1990), p. 14.

16. Sterling A. Brown, "The Odyssey of Big Boy," in *The Collected Poems of Sterling A. Brown*, ed. Michael S. Harper (New York: Harper and Row, 1980), pp. 20–1.

17. Mark A. Sanders, "Sterling A. Brown's Master Metaphor: *Southern Road* and the Sign of Black Modernity," *Callaloo* 21.4 (1998), 922.

18. Gerald Early, "Langston Hughes Keynote Lecture," in *Tuxedo Junction: Essays on American Culture* (New York: Ecco Press, 1989), p. 253.

19. Henry Louis Gates, Jr., "Preface," in Henry Louis Gates, Jr. and K. A. Appiah, ed., *Langston Hughes: Critical Perspectives Past and Present* (New York: Amistad Press, Inc., 1993), p. xi.

20. Arnold Rampersad, "Hughes' *Fine Clothes to the Jew*," in Henry Louis Gates, Jr. and K. A. Appiah, eds., *Langston Hughes: Critical Perspectives Past and Present* (New York: Amistad Press, Inc., 1993), p. 54.

21. Countee Cullen, "Review," in Henry Louis Gates, Jr. and K. A. Appiah, eds., *Langston Hughes: Critical Perspectives Past and Present* (New York: Amistad Press, Inc., 1993), p. 3.

22. Langston Hughes, "Negro Dancer," in *The Weary Blues* (New York: Knopf, 1926), p. 26.

23. Steven C. Tracy, "To the Tune of Those Weary Blues," in Henry Louis Gates, Jr. and K. A. Appiah, eds., *Langston Hughes: Critical Perspectives Past and Present* (New York: Amistad Press, Inc., 1993), pp. 69–93.

24. Langston Hughes, "Lament Over Love," in *Fine Clothes to the Jew* (New York: Knopf, 1927), p. 81.

8

JAMES SMETHURST

Lyric stars: Countee Cullen and Langston Hughes

Many people have considered the work of Countee Cullen and Langston Hughes to represent two antagonistic strands of Harlem Renaissance thinking about the role of the black artist, the nature of African American literature, and indeed whether something called "Negro Literature" existed. It is unquestionably true that the two poets themselves to some extent felt such an antagonism, as seen most famously in Hughes' 1926 essay "The Negro Artist and the Racial Mountain," that began with a sort of racial syllogism attributed to an unnamed Negro poet in which the statement "I want to be a poet – not a Negro poet" becomes "I would like to be white." While Hughes does not name the poet, the opening premise of this syllogism closely resembles a statement Cullen made during a 1924 interview in which he declared, "if I am going to be a poet at all, I am going to be POET and not NEGRO POET."[1]

Hughes, too, is well known as the progenitor of a new black vernacular lyric poetry, particularly the genre of blues poetry, while the statement "White folks is white" in the first line of Cullen's "Uncle Jim" represents practically the entirety of his published verse directly utilizing some version of a distinctly African American idiom. Though Cullen agreed that one could talk about poetry by Negro authors, he vigorously disputed notions of a distinct "Negro poetry," put forward not only by Hughes but also by such "midwives" of the Harlem Renaissance as Alain Locke and James Weldon Johnson:

> Negro poetry, it seems to me, in the sense that we speak of Russian, French, or Chinese poetry, must emanate from some country other than this in some language other than our own. Moreover, the attempt to corral the outbursts of the ebony muse into some definite mold to which all poetry by Negroes will conform seems altogether futile and aside from the facts. This country's Negro writers may here and there turn some singular facet toward the literary sun, but in the main, since theirs is also the heritage of the English language, their work will not present any serious aberration from the poetic tendencies of their times.[2]

Yet both Hughes and Cullen were the literary descendants of the turn of the century writers, particularly Paul Laurence Dunbar, who grappled with the political, cultural, and ideological impact of the rise of Jim Crow and the final collapse of most of the institutions and ideals of Reconstruction. Like many in the New Negro Renaissance, Langston Hughes (born 1902) and Countee Cullen (born 1903) were part of the first generation of black artists and intellectuals to grow up after the final triumph of Jim Crow in the South signaled by the infamous Supreme Court decisions that legitimated "separate, but equal" (Plessy v. Ferguson in 1896) and the various devices and strategies designed to restrict the access of African Americans to the ballot (Williams v. Mississippi in 1898) despite the continued presence of the Fourteenth and Fifteenth Amendments in the Constitution.

They also matured during the second wave of Jim Crow that saw the establishment of often extraordinarily rigid patterns of residential segregation in the cities of the North and South. This process began in earnest during the first decade of the twentieth century, greatly gaining in scope with the beginning of the "Great Migration" of African Americans from the country to the city, North and South, and from the South to the North. Cullen's foster father, Frederick Asbury Cullen, began the Salem Methodist Episcopal Church in a Harlem storefront with a handful of members in 1902 as part of an effort by the downtown St. Mark's Methodist Episcopal Church to reach the growing black community of Harlem still scattered in small pockets across the neighborhood.[3] By the time Cullen was adopted in 1918, Harlem's African American residents numbered in the several tens of thousands, replacing white Harlemites who fled what they frequently described as a black "invasion" (Osofsky, *Harlem* 109). When Hughes and his mother joined his stepfather in Cleveland in 1916, they lived in a basement apartment in the emerging ghetto on the East Side. This period saw not only the black population of Cleveland swell exponentially (308 percent between 1910 and 1920), but also a dramatic increase in segregation in the city. For example, despite the rapid growth of the African American community, the number of census tracts reporting no Negro inhabitants more than doubled from seventeen to thirty-eight. During this same period, the number of Cleveland's 112 elementary schools that were all-white went from seventeen to thirty. Where, in 1910, no census tract reported a Negro population greater than 25 percent, by 1920, ten were recorded as a quarter or more Negro with two over 50 percent.[4] As Hughes later noted, the World War I period also saw a concomitant local increase in Jim Crow practices in public accommodations despite Cleveland's history as a liberal city that frequently elected socialists to office.[5] Beyond the personal histories of Cullen and Hughes, Woodrow Wilson's increasing segregation of Federal jobs, the increasing number and intensity of violent racist incidents in the North and the South, and the growth of the Ku Klux Klan into a mass organization of millions that essentially ran governments of many southern and northern cities and states, attested to the growth of Jim Crow as a national phenomenon.

In short, by the time Hughes was in Central High School in Cleveland and Cullen in DeWitt Clinton High School in New York, Jim Crow was in many respects intensifying and reaching North in ways that went beyond the longstanding patterns of discrimination in employment, housing, education, and so on. Both, especially Hughes, credited the teachers and students at their predominately white high schools with doing much to introduce them to a larger artistic and intellectual life beyond the increasingly rigid boundaries of the ghetto. Yet even in Hughes' 1940 account of his days at Central High, there is a sense that it was a short moment of a school in transition. Within ten years of Hughes' graduation, he notes, only 3 percent of Central High's student body was white (*Big Sea* 29–30).

Given their coming of age during this second wave of Jim Crow, it is not surprising that both Hughes and Cullen looked back to Paul Laurence Dunbar as a crucial literary ancestor. Hughes in particular felt an early attachment to Dunbar's poetry, claiming that, other than Longfellow's *Hiawatha*, it was the only verse he liked as a young child (*Big Sea* 26). He also recalled that in his first serious efforts as a poet in high school, his two literary models were Carl Sandburg and Dunbar (*Big Sea* 28–9). As a mature poet, Hughes continued to acknowledge the impact of Dunbar on his work (and on the readers of his work, especially black readers), as in the collection *The Black Mother and Other Dramatic Recitations* (1931), a self-published chapbook aimed at the primarily African American audiences of his early reading tours in the South that declared the pieces to be in the tradition of Dunbar's vernacular work.

Far less is reliably known about Cullen's early life, which was apparently spent largely in Louisville, Kentucky. Still, it is clear that Cullen, too, saw Dunbar as a model. In part, the attachment of Cullen (and Hughes) to Dunbar stemmed from what Cullen called "his uniquity as the first Negro to attain to and maintain a distinguished place among American poets, a place fairly merited by the most acceptable standards of criticism" (Cullen, "Foreword" x–xi).

Dunbar's influence on Cullen and Hughes also derived from his "uniquity" as the best-known and perhaps the most powerful literary articulator of an African American dualism in the early Jim Crow era. African American dualism in its various expressions revolved around the notion that there were huge (and in many respects increasing) political, legal, social, cultural, and psychological contradictions between "Negro" and "American," so that the term "Negro American" might seem like an oxymoron. Like others in his age cohort, such as W. E. B. Du Bois and James Weldon Johnson, Dunbar was a product of a paradoxical time. He grew up during Reconstruction, came into young adulthood with the growth of Jim Crow, and achieved artistic success as the Supreme Court put its imprimatur on "separate, but equal." This bifurcated legal and political status was mirrored by a similarly double and ambivalent position in the simultaneous emergence of a relatively distinct African American transregional popular culture and of the linked and "mainstream" popular culture fueled significantly by the "coon song" and the related ragtime craze (in which Dunbar participated as a librettist).

The problem of dualism, whether in the Du Boisian semi-psychological sense of two more or less unintegrated consciousnesses existing simultaneously in one body or in a more strictly legalistic sense of post-Reconstruction Jim Crow segregation, is the problem of being a citizen and yet not a citizen (and, by extension, of being legally human and not quite human) in an increasingly urbanized, industrialized, and imperial United States. How does one respond? By proving oneself to be worthy or by withdrawing? Or through a sort of integration through self-determination in which African Americans force white people to recognize them as full citizens through political, educational, economic, and cultural self-development? And if one tries to represent the distinctly African (American) portion of this divided identity, what might that be? How does one represent and/or re-create black culture without being contaminated by the stereotypes of minstrelsy and plantation literature, by popular and so-called "high" culture appropriation or misappropriation? How does one deal with the doubleness of popular culture as seen in the cakewalk, ragtime, and the ambivalence of African American minstrelsy and "coon songs"?

Dunbar's engagement of these questions in "We Wear the Mask" is the most influential literary expression of African American dualism after *The Souls of Black Folk*. With the possible exception of "Sympathy" (and its famous dualistic line "I know why the caged bird sings!"), "We Wear the Mask" is almost certainly Dunbar's best-known and most anthologized poem today. Formally, it is a fairly straightforward rondeau – an old French form that enjoyed a vogue in English poetry at the end of the nineteenth century. The most arresting and most remembered aspect of the poem is, of course, Dunbar's metaphor of the mask. It may seem obvious, but, appropriately enough, this metaphor (and its relation to the logic of the poem) is more complicated than it might first appear. After all, the speaker of the poem identifies with a "we" who are compelled to mask "our" true identities and true emotions from "the world." Yet there is a sort of game of doubling in this revelation of concealment. The speaker weirdly stands outside him- or herself, describing the existence and something of the nature of "the mask" that he or she as part of the "we" wears. On the other hand, the speaker contradictorily proclaims that "the world" never really sees "us," only the disguise "we" put on. This confession would seem to involve a lowering of the mask – unless the revelation about the mask is a mask.

In other words, there is an endless regress in which the possibility of a double-consciousness is asserted, but without the comfort of any stable features or boundaries. This contradiction between concealment and revelation resembles that of Du Bois' notion of "the veil" and a "double-consciousness" that prevents or inhibits genuine African American self-reflection and self-consciousness, while provoking endless introspection about the nature of the self and identity. The metaphor of masking makes obvious the act of concealment and its coerced motivation, underpinning militant and historically pointed social criticism, suggesting a new way of reading African American minstrelsy and other forms of African American popular culture as well as Dunbar's own work. The metaphor of the mask invites (or challenges) the reader to change the way she or he reads apparently conventional dialect poems.

Also, can Dunbar the "high" poet exist without Dunbar the "dialect" or "popular" poet? If the so-called "low" or popular work did not exist, wouldn't the "high" poetry be less powerful, less well-defined? And, of course, without the "high" poetry and the split proposed between "real" and "mask," between "art" and box office rooted in a representation and/or re-creation of the African American voice, wouldn't the dialect poetry seem far shallower and much more easily conflated with the plantation tradition and the minstrel tradition in some uncomplicated way? In other words, "high" and "low," "standard" literary and "dialect," are inextricably linked and opposed. This strategy allowed Dunbar both to affirm himself as a poet and to re-create the black speaking subject on the page in a way that acknowledged the problems popular culture posed for the representation of the African American folk subject, while at least partially circumventing those problems. This opposition remained a potent paradigm for the New Negro era with its concern for representing "authentically" the racial (or national) self without being imprisoned by the implicitly or explicitly racist expectations of white readers, actual or potential, or of variously accommodationist black readers.

One trend within Harlem Renaissance poetry is a continuation of the radical democratic impulse that can be traced back to Phillis Wheatley. As Countee Cullen pointed out when questioned about his affinity for Keats:

> She turns to one of my poems, and indicts me for my love of Keats, for concerning myself with names like Endymion and Lancelot and Jupiter. It is on the tip of my tongue to ask why Keats himself should have concerned himself with themes like Endymion and Hyperion.[6]

Cullen's claim about his relationship to Greek myth was that it was exactly the same as Keats', and his relationship to Keats was exactly the same as that of white Americans: attachments formed through reading and education, not through biogenetic transmission. So what, he infers even if he is too polite to ask, gives a "white" American poet any more claim on Keats than Cullen, other than some pseudo-biological notions of race and pseudo-historical ideas of Europe and Africa? Cullen's implicit question resembles Du Bois' queries to white Americans in the final chapter of *The Souls of Black Folk*: "Your country? How came it yours?"[7] In short, he asserts full cultural citizenship, contesting pseudo-biological racist notions of artistic propriety and property. In the face of the intensification and extension of Jim Crow during Cullen's youth, this assertion of a larger cultural citizenship rests on a democratic spirit that transcends nation. At the same time that Cullen stakes a claim to citizenship in the republic of letters, he does not negate his particular position as a gay black man in the Jim Crow United States in which to be an active homosexual is to commit a crime for which one could be, and often was, jailed.

Dunbar's split between high and low allows Cullen to assert his cultural citizenship while addressing his particular subjectivity as he saw it. In his poetry Cullen assumed the split between high and low proposed by Dunbar (and other expressions of turn of the century African American dualism) and then rose above it by eliminating the low – at least so far as diction and syntax goes. Again and again, one finds in Cullen's poetry the idea of a divided self, and a divided society, where such explicit categories of identity as black and white, Negro and poet, pagan and Christian, and nature and civilization coexist and yet contradict or conflict with each other.

The depiction of warring selves threatening to tear asunder the black speaker clearly recalls Du Bois' *The Souls of Black Folk*. However, the notion that this conflict is a permanent condition of the speaker without even the possibility of resolution that Du Bois holds out resembles even more closely the split posed in Dunbar's poems. Because these warring selves seem in permanent conflict with each other without any likelihood (or even desirability) of lasting victory by one side or another, they are strangely linked through the mind, soul, and body of the poet so that they become at times indistinct or doubles of each other, yet always retaining at least a trace of conflict or division. This blurring and doubling is echoed by the androgynous and racially ambiguous figures of Charles Cullen (no relation to the poet) that illustrate Countee Cullen's collections *The Black Christ and Other Poems* (1929) and *Copper Sun* (1927) and the long poem *The Ballad of a Brown Girl* (1927).

As many have observed, much of Cullen's love poetry is not clearly marked by racial signs. However, it is worth pointing out that most of Cullen's first-person love lyrics not only lack racial markers but are unmarked as to gender as well. In short, these poems, often filled with loss, confusion, regret, and/or resentment, allow space for almost any sort of romantic pairing possible. When seen within the frame of Charles Cullen's illustrations, which both foreground and collapse together categories of race and gender, these poems are far from "universal" in some abstract sense, but instead quite personal and quite specific with regard to the condition of a gay black man in the early twentieth century.

For example, Cullen's best-known poem, "Heritage," is still seen in terms of various oppositions of paganism versus Christianity, nature versus civilization, Africa versus Europe, passion versus reason, and so on, resembling the various sorts of primitivism popular among Cullen's black and white contemporaries. There was of course a long-standing dichotomy between the secular and the sacred – as in the opposition of the blues and various sorts of sacred music – in African American culture which would give this poem a particular resonance for a black audience. And, obviously, the various dichotomies of the spirit and the flesh, nature and civilization, etc. have a long history in the so-called western world in general and the United States in particular.

Nonetheless, read in these ways, it is still hard not to think that the poet is more than a little overwrought and that there is an emotional discrepancy between the apparent subject of the poem and the poem's anguished rhetoric of a latent criminal against God and society who can just barely, for the moment, repress his evil desires. As with Cullen's "Yet Do I Marvel," which poses "poet" against "black," the reader is forced to ask whether there is such a dichotomy between blackness, as it were, and Christianity, between the laws of God and those of African American nature, between a generalized passion associated with Africa and reason. Similarly, the reader of "Yet Do I Marvel" might wonder why it is so marvelous in the sense of an awful strangeness that God should "make a poet black, and bid him sing." Yet it is also clear that some genuine and powerful emotions are at work in these poems' strange oscillations between repulsion and attraction, love and self-loathing – as they are in "Tableau," "Uncle Jim," and even "The Colored Blues Singer."

One clue the reader who is familiar with the literary scene of Harlem in the 1920s receives as to how to interpret these poems is the dedication of "Heritage" to Harold Jackman. Whatever Cullen's precise relationship to Jackman, it was well known during Cullen's lifetime that sexual attraction was an important part of their friendship. One might add here that the possibility that Cullen's foster father, a Methodist minister who was the subject of much speculation about his sexuality, was gay might also provide a new view of what "heritage" might mean, particularly with respect to the dichotomy of Christianity and homosexuality.[8]

If read within a black homosexual context, "Heritage" becomes paradigmatic of many of Cullen's poems. "Heritage" begins in a mythic landscape in which there is no contradiction between the speaker's sexuality and the demands of society and of God. Then there is a fall into a historical present in which the speaker's sexuality is in conflict with the society which the speaker inhabits and the God in whom the speaker believes. Again, this conflict, the subject's sense of alienation from a sexual "mainstream," is displaced onto a discourse of a sexualized racial difference. Finally, there is a realization that there will be no resolution to this contradiction in this world and that this sexuality can be suppressed or covert, but it cannot be either erased or overtly practiced – at least as far as the poem's speaker is concerned.

Of course, this could be read within a heterosexual context. But such a reading removes the immediacy and the power of the poem. Cullen was gay. He also was a Christian. While today there may be relatively orthodox Christian denominations which no longer consider homosexuality a terrible sin, this was not the case in Cullen's lifetime. Cullen, like another Christian gay poet, W. H. Auden, was obviously extremely conflicted about the demands of his religious beliefs and those of his sexuality. Similarly Cullen was an extremely social man in many respects. Though it is perhaps unfair to claim, as a number of critics do, that Cullen was too enamored of "bourgeois" culture in any simple manner – his endorsement of the Communist Party Presidential and Vice-Presidential candidates in 1932 would seem to undercut this notion – it is clear that "society," particularly of the black community where he lived, wrote, and taught (and where his foster father was a prominent minister), was important to him. Again, it is worth making the obvious point that homosexuality was outlawed and homosexuals were frequently prosecuted for their "crimes" in the 1920s and 1930s. There is obviously a huge difference between whispered comments, however deeply believed by the whisperers, and an open declaration of homosexuality. Certainly, Cullen's career in the New York public schools, where he began teaching in 1932, would have been impossible if he had made such a declaration. In short, "Heritage" is a poem of extreme personal anguish over a very specific aspect of the poet's nature that is in a real conflict with the poet's conscience and society and cannot be approached directly, but instead utilizes the language and tropes of dualism for expression.

Even more than Cullen, Hughes, like Dunbar, embodied a dualistic split within his early poetry, formally as well as thematically. However, both sides of this split could be seen as a sort of nationalism that is at odds with the internationalism of Cullen and Dunbar – though one might see in this nationalism a sort of challenge to the United States resembling that of Dunbar. Of course, one has to qualify the notion of Hughes' nationalism a bit. After all, even among the polyglot, peripatetic, and cosmopolitan artists and intellectuals of the Harlem Renaissance, Hughes stood out. His travels as an artist, activist, and merchant sailor, his friendship with artists and intellectuals around the world (especially those of Africa and its Diaspora), and his translations of such writers as Nicolás Guillén, Federico Garcia Lorca, Jacques Roumain, and Vladimir Mayakovsky (many for the first time in the United States) were exceptional. Nonetheless, the sort of nationalist split indicated by his early adoption of Sandburg and Dunbar as his literary models persisted in his work throughout the Harlem Renaissance – and, in some important respects, beyond.

Hughes' Sandburgian poems consist of free-verse catalogs, such as "The Negro Speaks of Rivers" and "Negro," and short imagistic portraits of urban life and scenes from Hughes' travels in the Americas, Europe, and Africa, such as "Mexican Market Woman" and "Young Singer." While Hughes uses an irregular end-rhyme in these poems more often than Sandburg, his diction shares with Sandburg's a plain, almost colloquial, but not conversational character. This diction is not marked particularly as African American, but is still like that of Sandburg (and Walt Whitman) a generic "American" language posed against a "high" literary diction like that of Cullen's that is more or less British in its derivation and alleged sensibility. While not as clearly "Red" as much of his writing in the 1930s, Hughes' 1920s verse drawing on the work of Sandburg prefigures the more self-consciously "proletarian" diction and themes of Hughes' "revolutionary" poetry during the Depression. The common "American" language of Hughes' Sandburgian poems in the 1920s evolves into Hughes' working-class "American" diction of the early 1930s. Interestingly, these Sandburgian poems, especially the longer free-verse catalogs, are often vehicles for Hughes' deepest musings on the nature of African American identity and its historical, cultural, and spiritual connection to Africa.

Hughes' early African American vernacular poetry is clearly indebted to the dialect poetry of Dunbar. As in Dunbar's dialect poems, Hughes' vernacular pieces make plain their identity as speech, generally either a folk monologue or song. It is true that Hughes' vernacular poems generally stake a claim to a certain sort of authenticity that is undercut in Dunbar's work where outside claims for the peculiar verisimilitude of the dialect poetry, whether by William Dean Howells or the Dodd, Mead Publishing Company, were posed against tropes of masking, deformity, and imprisonment. However, Dunbar's stance is closer to that of Hughes than might be seen at first glance.

One way in which Hughes attempted to reclaim vernacular poetry from the limitations of minstrelsy, "coon songs," and the plantation school of dialect literature during the Harlem Renaissance was to anchor it in identifiably black "folk" and popular forms, especially the blues, gospel music, jazz, and various sorts of sacred and secular rhetoric. Sometimes, as in his famous "The Weary Blues," a work from the 1926 collection of the same name that is often taken to be the beginning of the sub-genre of "blues poetry," the black folk voice of a blues singer is framed by the slightly colloquial, but more or less "standard" English of a somewhat alienated African American intellectual. One way in which the song of the blues singer is protected from confusion with popular culture misappropriations is through the eye- and ear-witness of the speaker of the poem, guaranteeing the authenticity of the performance:

> Droning a drowsy syncopated tune,
> Rocking back and forth to a mellow croon,
>   I heard a Negro play
> Down on Lenox Avenue the other night.   (*Collected* 51)

Interestingly, the speaker of the poem is both an insider and an outsider, one who has a special affinity for the singer and his music and yet is somewhat distant from the singer at the beginning of the poem. One might say that the tension set up by this sort of alienation from the folk that an implicit authorial consciousness seeks to overcome marks the entire collection. However, the speaker enters into the music and is by the end of the poem so bound up with the bluesman that the speaker is inside the singer's bed-room (and head) after the show is over:

> The singer stopped playing and went to bed
> While the Weary Blues echoed through his head.
>   (*Collected* 51)

The authenticity of the scene of the re-creation of the folk voice is guaranteed both by the speaker's original distance allowing a sort of objective account and by the speaker's final identification with the singer demonstrating a deeper understanding of the folk spirit contained in (really produced by) the music, as well as a potential if not altogether happy healing of the split consciousness of the speaker.

   This authenticity is also guaranteed by the form, the rhythmic stresses, the rhyme scheme, and the tropes of the blues itself, a musical genre associated with African Americans that was, by the 1920s and the enormous growth of the recording industry, widely recognizable throughout the United States (and beyond). While the actual rhyme schemes, lineation, and patterns of rhythmic stresses of the early blues varied, Hughes interpolated an adap-tation of the common AAB blues verse into the second strophe. In this variation of the blues stanza, the first line is repeated in the second line (sometimes, as in "The Weary Blues," with a slight difference or "worrying"), followed by a different, but rhyming, concluding line. Generally, there would be a slight pause or caesura in the middle of these lines. Hughes broke the lines in two at the caesura so that his typical blues poetry stanza was six lines instead of three. This adapted version of the AAB stanza became the standard for blues verse in American poetry throughout the twentieth century. Hughes, and later such poets as Sterling Brown and Waring Cuney, saw in this form a key building block for a distinctly African American lyric poetry that utilized the blues much as "high" poetry in Western Europe had adapted such song forms as the sonnet, the ballad, the rondeau, and the villanelle. In this, Hughes echoed, anticipated, and influenced the sense of much modernist poetry in the United States, that, as Ezra Pound argued in his 1934 *ABC of Reading*, "music begins to atrophy when it departs too far from the dance; that poetry begins to atrophy when it gets too far from music."[9]

Nonetheless, as in the work of Dunbar, there remains a split between authentic uses of African American folk and popular culture and minstrelized misappropriations and misreadings of black culture. In Hughes' vision, this distinction rests on a dialectical relationship between tradition and innovation. One might say that in Hughes' view innovation is one of the marks of the authentic African American popular culture. In "Negro Dancers," for example, a black dancer announces that "Me an' ma baby's/ Got two mo' ways,/ Two mo' ways to do de Charleston!" (*Collected* 44). It is this innovation that, both the dancer and the speaker of the poem suggest, distinguishes the true African American expressive spirit from white imitation and misappropriation. The notion of the crucial and inextricable relationship between cutting-edge black creativity and a cultural continuum reaching from the urban ghetto through the rural South to, in a more distant and attenuated manner, Africa, remained a centerpiece of Hughes' poetry for the rest of his career.

Interestingly, Hughes' second collection of poetry, *Fine Clothes to the Jew* (1927), largely finesses the question of the troubled relationship between the black artist and the folk through a composite portrait of the black working class and the floating world of rounders, grifters, prostitutes, and gamblers, of the urban African American communities. Even more than in *The Weary Blues*, Hughes negotiates the problems presented by popular-culture and high-culture representations of the black poor by embedding their stories and their voices in a wide variety of "authentic" black forms, especially the blues, but also gospel songs, ballads, street calls, church testifying, overheard conversations, and so on.

Still, the notion of a divide both within the black intellectual–artist and between the black intellectual artist and the folk remained a theme in Hughes' poetry into the 1930s. As Hughes moved more and more into the cultural and political world of the communist left with the deepening of the Great Depression, however, the divided speaker is stirred into a communion with the folk, now something more like the working class, not so much through the power of African American culture, but through a forced contact with reality, or what the communists used to like to call life itself. For example, in the final poem of the 1931 collection *Dear Lovely Death*, "Aesthete in Harlem," the long and peripatetic search of a black artist for "Life" is finally and unexpectedly realized when the "aesthete" finds "Life" "stepping on my feet" on a Harlem street (*Collected* 128). It might be added, however, that Hughes' poetry in the early 1930s remained in many respects divided into three strands: a more directly Dunbarian poetry of racial uplift primarily aimed at the black audiences he encountered on the reading tours to African American schools, churches, reading circles, and so on, that he began during this period; a less racially inflected, class-based revolutionary poetry aimed at a radical audience who read *New Masses*, *The Harlem Liberator*, *The Anvil*, and other journals of the left and the proletarian literature movement; and a more literary sort of verse aimed at readers of modern literature. Of course, these categories overlapped to a certain extent. Hughes would often slip one of his revolutionary poems into his readings before black audiences on his tours. His poetry in left journals often addressed racial and colonial oppression, placing those issues (as did the Communist Party and the Comintern) as central concerns of the national and international class struggle. Sometimes, perhaps most notably in his poetic "jazz play" *Scottsboro Limited* where he attempted to openly combine elements of African American expressive culture with the "mass chant" form of the communist workers theater movement, Hughes gave his revolutionary work a more distinctly "Negro" inflection. Still, it was not really until the Popular Front era in the second half of the 1930s that Hughes successfully integrated the different strands of his poetry.

The sense of a split, of two warring selves within a single body, is even more pronounced in Hughes' early fiction, showing a persistent concern with (and insecurity about) the fluidity of racial, sexual, and class identity. His earliest adult stories published in the late 1920s, based on his experience as a merchant sailor and much influenced by D. H. Lawrence's modernist fiction of class, gender, and sexual conflict and confusion in Britain, are full of the contradictions of an African American narrator, whose predicament is not that Africa is, to quote the 1930 poem "Afro-American Fragment," "so long, so far away," but that it is right at hand. Or rather the narrator suffers the existential dilemma of arriving in West Africa with a multinational crew of "Greeks, West Indian Negroes, Irish, Portuguese, and, Americans" and finding it "so long, so far away" and frighteningly, if often movingly present at the same time. The indigenous peoples of Africa consider him an outsider, and frequently identify him with his "white" and "brown" shipmates. Of course, the confusion that the narrator experiences is not completely unique, as his fellow sailors from the United States, black and white, attempt to reconfigure "American" racial, gender, and sexual practices for an African context as white sailors "defend the honor" of African prostitutes assaulted by fellow seamen even as the narration is suffused with an understated outrage about intersecting racism, sexual exploitation, colonial oppression, and class conflict that leaves him feeling as both insider and outsider simultaneously. One finds something of this conflict in Hughes' first novel, the coming of age story *Not Without Laughter* (1930). There the protagonist Sandy moves between the women of his radically divided family, consisting of his grandmother (the sort of folk Negro Mother figure that Hughes most famously invoked in the poem "From Mother to Son"), his mother (a loving, but somewhat dim and self-absorbed domestic worker married to a usually absent and somewhat layabout blues singer, Sandy's father Jimboy), his aunt Tempy (a stiff, middle-class "race woman" who despises the culture of the black folk), and his Aunt Harriet (a disreputable classic blues singer who nonetheless provides the money for Sandy to continue his education).

As different as the works of Hughes and Cullen appear in many respects, then, both address the questions of political and cultural citizenship and filiations posed by turn of the century writers, particularly Dunbar, adopting and adapting in their different ways the dualistic models of those writers as the United States became increasingly segregated. Cullen's work as a poet substantially decreased after the early 1930s, but his perceived stance as literary internationalist, if not always his actual poetry, remained powerful, both in the production of black poetry and in the understanding of the Harlem Renaissance, as critics saw Cullen emblemizing one pole of the movement. These models also left a large mark on the literary output of Hughes throughout the rest of his long career as he became arguably the most widely accomplished American writer, working in poetry, short and long fiction, children's literature, drama, musical theater, autobiography, journalism, translation, and combinations of genres difficult to classify, considerably influencing the work of black writers into the twenty-first century.

NOTES

1. Margaret Sperry, "Countee P. Cullen, Negro Boy Poet, Tells His Story," *Brooklyn Daily Eagle*, February 10, 1924.
2. Countee Cullen, Foreword to *Caroling Dusk: An Anthology of Verse by Negro Poets*, ed. Countee Cullen (New York: Harper and Brothers, 1927), p. xi.

3. Gilbert Osofsky, *Harlem: The Making of a Ghetto* (New York: Harper and Row, 1966), pp. 84–5.
4. Kenneth L. Kusmer, *A Ghetto Takes Shape: Black Cleveland, 1870–1930* (Urbana: University of Illinois Press, 1976), pp. 158–64.
5. Langston Hughes, *The Big Sea* (1940; New York: Thunder's Mouth Press, 1986), p. 51.
6. Countee Cullen, *My Soul's High Song: The Collected Writings of Countee Cullen* (New York: Anchor Books, 1991), p. 568.
7. W. E. B. Du Bois, *The Souls of Black Folk*, ed. David W. Blight and Robert Gooding-Williams (1903; New York: Bedford Books, 1997), p. 190.
8. George Chauncy, *Gay New York: Gender, Urban Culture, and the Makings of the Gay Male World, 1890–1940* (New York: Basic Books, 1991), pp. 264–5.
9. Ezra Pound, *The ABC of Reading* (1934; New York: New Directions, 1960), p. 14.

9

MARGO NATALIE CRAWFORD

"Perhaps Buddha is a woman": women's poetry in the Harlem Renaissance

An essay "On Being Young – a Woman – and Colored" (1925), written by Marita Bonner, offers a profound glimpse into the ethos of women's writing of the Harlem Renaissance. At the end of this essay Bonner muses, "Perhaps Buddha is a woman," as she decides that the image of Buddha may best describe what it meant in 1925 to be "young – a woman – and colored."[1] The image of the brown Buddha presents the young "colored" woman as contained but somehow moving in spite of the appearance of stasis. Bonner writes, "Like Buddha – who, brown like I am – sat entirely at ease, entirely sure of himself; motionless and knowing, a thousand years before the white man knew there was so very much difference between feet and hands. Motionless on the outside. But inside?" (112). This image captures the complexity of Harlem Renaissance women's poetry. "On Being Young – a Woman – and Colored" was published the same year, 1925, as the pivotal, male-oriented anthology *The New Negro*. As opposed to Locke's archetype of the "New Negro," Marita Bonner makes Buddha her prime archetype for the young "colored" women emerging in 1925. The very image of the "colored" female Buddha evokes a peaceful hybrid fusion of the old and the new as opposed to Locke's vehement differentiation between the "Old Negro" and the "New Negro." The female Buddha is imagined as the best way to counter the stereotypes that deny black women's aesthetic sensibilities and femininity. Bonner wonders why a black woman must be viewed as a "feminine Caliban craving to pass for Ariel" (111). This notion of the black woman passing for Ariel, presumably an image of refined white womanhood, illuminates the nexus of gender, class, and race constraints negotiated by women poets of the Harlem Renaissance. Forty years before the focus on intersections of race and gender by black women battling the blindspots of many white women in second-wave feminism, these black women poets confronted the need to analyze the real differences as well as the real similarities between black women and white women. These poets often reclaimed the femininity that antiblack racism denied black women. The women's

126

poetry of the Harlem Renaissance, in comparison to the women's poetry in the 1960s and 70s Black Arts Movement, may seem tame on the "outside" and yet the question remains, "But inside?"

In the poem "For Saundra" (1968), the Black Arts poet Nikki Giovanni insists that "these are not poetic / times," after imagining a black woman being asked why she does not write about the sky and trees.[2] When Harlem Renaissance women poets make nature one of their main subjects, they sometimes insist on the sheer freedom of being able to write a poem about the beauty of nature as opposed to being burdened by heavy racial or gendered themes. Their nature poems that do address race tend to revolve around the expression of racial pride. Their nature poems about gender, however, include more than celebrations of womanhood; there are pivotal poems that critique the imagined naturalness of gender. Georgia Douglas Johnson's poem "Black Woman" (1922), for example, defies the natural desire to procreate, the literal idea of mother nature. When the speaker in "Black Woman" insists, "I must not give you birth," Johnson suggests that the mother cannot celebrate the birth of a black child in an antiblack world.[3] In "Black Woman" Johnson denaturalizes women's desire to become mothers. When she describes herself as the "mother of Negro poets," it is clear that her role as a poet was overdetermined by the very gender norms that she sought to subvert. This poem was given the title "Motherhood" when originally published in *The Crisis*, and renamed "Black Woman" when published in *Bronze: A Book of Verse* (1922). The move away from the title that evokes universal womanhood is a key sign of the gender and race terrain navigated by black women poets of this era. This poem gains a different emphasis when read through the lens of the title "Black Woman." The dual titles reveal the "double jeopardy" of black women, a foreshadowing of the principal theory of gender and race in 1970s black feminism.[4] In addition to predating this intervention in second-wave feminism, Johnson also compli-cates the idea that the goal would be the constant articulation of the inter-sections of race and gender. "Motherhood" and "Black Woman," the two different presentations of this poem, suggest that the duality of gender and race sometimes led to experimentation with the privileging of race or gender.

In poems explicitly addressing white women, there is a great emphasis on the need to understand intersections of race and gender. In the poem "A Brown Aesthete Speaks" (1928), written by Mae V. Cowdery, the white women addressed by the speaker as "you" assumes that the "brown aesthete" imitates white women and desires whiteness. The speaker of this poem reminds the white woman that the servitude of black women has effaced their femininity. The speaker urges the white woman to reconsider the charge of imitation (the notion that the refined black woman is imitating white women). This poem captures the aesthetic warfare that black women engaged in as they fought against the insidious equation of whiteness and highbrow culture. Cowdery begins the poem with a statement that defies both transformation and stasis: "No: I am neither seeking to change nor keep myself; / Simply acting upon new revelations."[5] She rejects the idea of an essence that does not change as well as the discourse of transformation undergirding Locke's theory of the New Negro. In the opening essay of *The New Negro*, Locke writes, "In the very process of being transplanted, the Negro is becoming transformed."[6] As opposed to Locke's differentiation between the New Negro and the Old Negro, Cowdery moves from the paradigm of new versus old identities to a focus on new ways of seeing ("new revelations"). The black woman who straightens her hair, Cowdery insists, is experimenting with aesthetics, not desiring whiteness. The speaker in the poem reminds the white woman addressee that when white women experiment with their hair, they are not accused of being imitators. The speaker inquires,

> Did I carp when you created beautiful curls,
> Becoming curls, to deck your Marcian bob?
> Or of the Bob itself?
> [...] Did I charge that you were aping me?
> (Why should I
> Or why should anyone?)
> I only thought that you were questing Beauty.   (89)

In this poetic dialogue with white women, Mae Cowdery captures the more nuanced aspects of the relation between white and black women. Many black women poets of this era represented white women as both their comrades and their nemesis. Cowdery refers to white women as "friend" after she defends the "brown aesthete" against the critical gaze of white women. A more genuine friendship is imagined as Cowdery presents aesthetic experimentation as the bond that connects white and black women.

In his preface to one of Georgia Douglas Johnson's volumes of poetry, *An Autumn Love Cycle* (1928), Alain Locke situates these black women poets outside the aesthetic experimentation of modernism. When Locke sets these poets outside modernist experimentation, he fails to think about the larger experimentation in fashion and style that transcends racial boundaries. Cowdery presents white and black women as experimenting with style and fashion in a manner that complicates the black/white divide. The white women assume "black" hairstyles and the black women alter their hair to achieve "white" curls. Beauty, in this poem, is defined as transformation. Locke does recognize that these poets defy a facile feminism that approaches the didactic. In his preface to *An Autumn Love Cycle*, he recognizes that these poets both participate in and subvert the 1920s and 30s discourse of feminism, that which he refers to as "doctrinal feminism" (Johnson, *Selected Works* 195). As one of the "race men," Locke claims, in this preface, the right to define the black woman's agenda. Even as he occupies this space of appropriation, he also identifies one of the distinguishing features of Harlem Renaissance women's poetry, the non-self-conscious feminism that explored gender without developing an explicit protest. Locke writes, "And here she succeeds where others more doctrinally feminist have failed; for they in over-sophistication, in terror of platitudes and the commonplace, have stressed the bizarre, the exceptional, in one way or another have overintellectualized their message and overleapt the common elemental experience they would nevertheless express" (195). The lack of this overintellectualization is striking in "A Brown Aesthete Speaks." Mae Cowdery refuses to overintellectualize the pure performance and fantasy of the "brown aesthete" who is accused of desiring whiteness because of her aesthetic preferences. With a matter-of-fact tone, Cowdery explains the unavoidable allure of the aesthetic impulse and the reasons why aesthetics cannot be reduced to the ideological. The "brown aesthete," Cowdery insists, is only accused of imitation when investments in beauty are analyzed as investments in racial hierarchy. Cowdery complicates the assumption that the aesthetic is necessarily ideological.

Alice Dunbar-Nelson's "The Proletariat Speaks" (1929) is another compelling example of the interrogation of aesthetics and ideology in women's poetry of this era. Dunbar-Nelson, like Cowdery, honors the simplicity and naturalness of the desire for beauty. In this poem she refuses to think too critically about the very fantasy of beauty. Instead she emphasizes the tragedy of the proletariat's lack of access to this beauty and the inability of poverty to stifle the proletariat's desire for beauty. Three of the stanzas in this poem begin with the words "I love beautiful things," followed by stanzas that begin with the following qualifiers: "And so I work / In a dusty office," "And so I eat / In the food-laden air of a greasy kitchen," "And so I sleep / In a hot hall-room whose half-opened window, / Unscreened, refuses to budge another inch" (Honey, *Shadowed Dreams* 75–6). In the 1920s, five decades after enslaved Africans were emancipated from their literal reduction to commodities, the assertion by a black woman poet that "I love beautiful things" was a bold defiance of the whitewashing of beauty and femininity. As Dunbar-Nelson underscores the slippage between the proletariat's aesthetic taste and the material conditions of her life, the protest element of the poem emerges subtly through the wry tone.

The sarcasm in the lyric poetry of Alice Dunbar-Nelson begs to be compared to the poem "Sympathy" (1899), written by her first husband Paul

Laurence Dunbar, which includes the famous lines "I know why the caged bird sings." "I Sit and Sew" (1927), written by Alice Dunbar-Nelson, is the sarcastic version of "Sympathy." The gist of "I Sit and Sew" is that the caged bird does not sing; the speaker is caged and her self-expression is a "little useless seam," not a song (Honey, *Shadowed Dreams* 74). In "To a Poet and a Lady" (1907), Paul Laurence Dunbar trivializes the gender shackles that Harlem Renaissance women poets sometimes lifted and sometimes simply tilted in order to create their art. In this poem, as Dunbar addresses Lida Keck Wiggins, he wonders if women sing simply for the "love of singing."[7] As opposed to the vexed "singing from the cage" in his most famous poem "Sympathy," that seems to represent his own position as a black male poet, the "love of singing" presented in "To a Poet and a Lady" is a black male poet's romanticized notion of a woman's natural inclination to be a "wife-poet." The notion of a "wife-poet" emerges when Dunbar writes,

> You think you are working for wealth and for fame,
> But ah, you are not, and you know it;
> For wife is the sweetest and loveliest name,
> And every good wife is a poet!   (336)

To the extent that Alice Dunbar-Nelson's marriage to Paul Laurence Dunbar continues to overdetermine critics' interest in her work, she is the archetype of the "wife-poet." The sarcasm, however, in her poems such as "I Sit and Sew" reveals that she did not accept the notion that every "good wife is a poet" (336). Paul Laurence Dunbar in "To Alice Dunbar" (1903) proclaims that Alice is the "bride for eternity" (Braxton, *Collected Poetry* 330). Gloria Hull's groundbreaking biographical work on Alice Dunbar-Nelson has proven that her multiple marriages and lesbian affairs defy the traditional understanding of the "good wife" and the "bride for eternity." The nature of the protest in her poetry is the tone and tenor of a stereotypical sarcastic wife. In "I Sit and Sew" she presents the type of sarcastic wife who is not necessarily critiquing patriarchy as she critiques the complacency of women. The speaker in "I Sit and Sew" yearns to participate in the war:

> This little useless seam, the idle patch;
> Why dream I here beneath my homely thatch,
> When there they lie in sodden mud and rain,
> Pitifully calling me, the quick ones and the slain?   (74)

In contrast to this representation of the desire to be a part of the war, many of the nature poems written by Harlem Renaissance women epitomize the struggle not to be overdetermined by ideological warfare, to escape the "shadow" over black women. In "The Task of Negro Womanhood," an essay in the seminal anthology *The New Negro* (1925) Elise McDougald explains this "shadow over" black women in the following manner.

> She is conscious that what is left of chivalry is not directed toward her. She realizes that the ideals of beauty, built up in the fine arts, have excluded her almost entirely. Instead, the grotesque Aunt Jemimas of the streetcar advertisements proclaim only an ability to serve, without grace or loveliness. Nor does the drama catch her finest spirit. She is most often used to provoke the mirthless laugh of ridicule; or to portray feminine viciousness or vulgarity not peculiar to Negroes. This is the shadow over her. (370)

McDougald delineates the social script of "negro womanhood" in 1925. Black women viewed as vulgar Aunt Jemimas were placed outside the constructs of white womanhood in a manner comparable to the public restroom signs in the Jim Crow South that only included the options "Women," "Men," and "Colored." As McDougald emphasizes the denial of black women's "grace or loveliness," she argues that black women in this era were often placed outside the very category of "women." This denial is powerfully addressed in the women's poetry of this era. In "Lady, Lady," one of the few poems written by a woman in *The New Negro*, Anne Spencer tenderly addresses the "dark as night" women whose tenderness has been effaced by their toil. The "dark as night" woman's hands are described as "crumpled roots" that, through her toil, are "bleached poor white":

> Lady, Lady, I saw your hands,
> Twisted, awry, like crumpled roots,
> Bleached poor white in a sudsy tub. (148)

Images of nature, in this poem, are used to denaturalize race; the word "roots" describes the transformation of "dark as night" bodies into that which is "bleached poor white." In *The New Negro*, this poem appears on the same page as "The Black Finger," written by Angelina Grimké. In contrast to the "crumpled roots" in "Lady, Lady" and the use of images of nature to denaturalize race, images of nature in "The Black Finger" are used to reinforce the "natural" beauty of blackness. Grimké pays homage to a

> straight black cypress,
> Sensitive,
> Exquisite,
> A black finger
> Pointing upwards. (148)

Grimké grants the signifier "black" as much force as it has during the Black Arts Movement. Her image of the black finger foreshadows the 1960s icon of the black power fist.

This poem "The Black Finger" also blurs the boundaries between the genre of nature poetry and protest poetry. The central use of nature in protest poetry reveals that the women poets were often blurring the distinction between nature as the feminized subject and protest as the domain of men. As the women poets make images of nature a key part of protest poetry, they articulate frustration, and sometimes, even rage, in the unlikely medium of the lyric and odes to nature. A focus on nature also leads Harlem Renaissance women poets to an expression of ambivalence toward modernist primitivism as they confront the imagined connection between blackness and the primitive. A conversation about the modernist cult of the primitive is embedded in the women's poetry of this era. Many of these women poets responded explicitly to the white gaze that often celebrated blackness through an elevation of their imagined primitive nature (their raw desire, their untainted purity, their hyper-sexuality). A poem entitled "Epitome" (1930), written by Ruth Dixon, is one of the most compelling representations of Harlem Renaissance women poets' ambivalent relation to modernist primitivism. After creating a caricature of white people's obsession with the "negro primitive," Dixon ends the poem by confessing,

> And yet – to you, my fairer ones,
> I am indebted – and somewhat appeased.
> I hold not light the tribute you have given,
> When in the peons of my race,
> When in its outcasts and its prostitutes,
> You find not filth
> But souls divine and beautiful.
>
> (Honey, *Shadowed Dreams* 83–4)

This confession is a prime example of the complication of identity politics that fueled Harlem Renaissance women's poetry. The move, at the end of this poem, to the expression of an appreciation of the white primitivist gaze signals an identity politics that claims the right to identify as both the protestor (the speaker who critiques the stereotypes in primitivist depictions of blackness) and the sympathizer (the speaker who realizes that primitivism was, in many ways, a move away from unadulterated antiblack racism). The white discovery of the beauty of the "Negro" is first presented as self-serving adoration:

> You fawn, you worship, you adore;
> You see a human god and goddess
> Hitherto unknown.
> They show a new and interesting life –
> Souls of lust embroidered to your liking –
> Not shaming gazing eyes

But feeding them,
Not piercing human hearts
But salving sores of pride.   (83)

The reference to the sham of transcendence of race, the white creation of a
black "god or goddess," is followed by the speaker's assumption of the stance
of a black god. In the final confessional stanza that begins "And yet," the
speaker states, "to you, my fairer ones." The word "my" signals that as Dixon
critiques white primitivism she discovers a subject position in which she is
both the indignant body on which these primitivist stereotypes have been
written and the social critic who has a point of view that can empathize with
both the "peons of my race" and "my fairer ones."

When women poets of this era seized the position of the social critic, they
developed analyses of the interplay of race, gender, and the "New Negro"
discourse that add many layers to Locke's framing narrative in *The New
Negro*. When Ruth Dixon, for example, likens the "new and interesting life" of
the "New Negro" to "Souls of lust embroidered to your liking," she addresses a
gender-specific white gaze. The white women both chastised and defended in this
poem use the very stereotypes placed upon themselves as their means of objecti-
fying the "Negro." In Alice Dunbar-Nelson's poem "I Sit and Sew" the critique of
the needlework tied to women becomes a type of universal feminism as opposed
to a focus on the specificity of black or white women. The reference to "souls of
lust embroidered to your liking," in "Epitome," focuses on white women's
participation in the constructions of the black primitive. The poem underscores
that, in the primitivist script, black women signified raw and uninhibited desire.
One common thread in the black women's poetry of this era is the uncovering of
a quite different image of black women, an image of black women as "contained." In "To Usward" (1924), Gwendolyn Bennett captures this ethos when
she writes, "[L]et us be contained / By entities of Self" (Honey, *Shadowed
Dreams* 104). As these poets fought against the images of the wild black
woman, their poetry was often "contained" even as they developed alternative
ventilation systems that would allow their poems to "breathe" without what
Toni Morrison refers to as the "eruption of funk."[8] Whereas black women blues
singers of this era expressed raunchy desire and sexuality with an openness that
would match the primitivist script, the women poets of this era insisted on their
right to be subversive in a subdued manner. A poem entitled "The Mask"
(1927), written by Clarissa Scott Delany, explores black women's empathetic
response to the contained nature of other black women. Delany writes:

So detached and cool she is,
No motion e'er betrays
The secret life within her soul,

The anguish of her days.
. . .
But once a woman with a child
Passed by her on the street,
And once she heard from casual lips
A man's name, bitter-sweet.

Such baffled yearning in her eyes,
Such pain upon her face!
I turned aside until the mask
Was slipped once more in place.   (144)

The representation of the need to overcome repression coexists in this body of poetry with the representation of the shared understanding of the reasons why black women in the 1920s and 30s were claiming the demureness and containment associated with respectability and racial uplift.

In 1929 Alice Dunbar-Nelson inveighs against the "'sewer literature' which has offended the nostrils of those to whom literature is a beautiful dignified mistress and not a strident, disheveled gutter-snipe" (88).[9] Dunbar-Nelson views literature itself as the "dignified mistress," not the "strident, disheveled" mistress, but in a larger sense the black women poets of this period fought to represent black womanhood as a "dignified mistress" as well as a "strident" mistress. When Georgia Douglas Johnson, in a *Pittsburgh Courier* review, is described as "absolutely feminine," it is clear that the poets' fight against the defeminization of black women coexisted with their being pigeonholed in the constructs of "white" femininity.[10] The impossible struggle was the seizure of the femininity that had been coded "white" even as they wrestled to rebuke the repression embedded in this "dainty" femininity. A comparison of the poems "Interlude" (1936), written by Mae V. Cowdery, and "Magalu" (1927), written by Helene Johnson, encapsulates the larger move to make room for images of the black "beautiful dignified mistress" as well as images of the non-repressed black woman. Cowdery begins "Interlude" with an expression of black women's desire for a certain gentility even if that sense of order is rather fleeting within the larger hectic pace of their lives. At the very beginning of the poem, the speaker announces with frank simplicity,

I like this quiet place
Of lawns and trees well kept
And bright geometric gardens.
                    (Honey, *Shadowed Dreams* 193)

In comparison, in "Magalu," Helene Johnson inveighs against the type of pristine order that would replace "riotous" passion and sheer openness. At the end of "Magalu," the speaker queries,

> Would you sell the colors of your sunset and the fragrance
> Of your flowers, and the passionate wonder of your forest
> For a creed that will not let you dance?
>
> (Honey, *Shadowed Dreams* 101)

As opposed to the black "dignified mistress" who needs neat lawns, at least, as an "interlude," the speaker, in "Magalu," hopes that Magalu will never trade the "passionate wonder of your forest" for the sanitized comfort of "geometric gardens." Just as Nella Larsen, in *Quicksand*, includes a key scene in which Helga Crane pauses, in the midst of dancing, to remind herself that she is not a "jungle creature," Helene Johnson, in "Magalu," uncovers the psychological effects of the oversexualization of black women in modernist primitivism. In "Magalu" the speaker is enjoying the beauty of nature when she stumbles upon a young black woman who is being counseled by a male religious authority figure, presumably a priest. The "creed that will not let you dance" is represented in this poem as religious doctrine, but, in a larger sense, it is the crisis of black womanhood that can only be fully understood through a rediscovery of the discussions of race and gender in such poems as Anne Spencer's "Letter to My Sister" (1927).

The crisis, in "Letter to My Sister," is represented as the navigation of a "dangerous" situation in which the only option for "sisters" may be the creation of personal hiding places. After beginning the poem with the words "It is dangerous for a woman to defy the gods," Spencer ends the poem with the image of a hiding place. She writes,

> This you may do:
> Lock your heart, then, quietly,
> And lest they peer within,
> Light no lamp when dark comes down
> Raise no shade for sun;
> Breathless must your breath come through
> If you'd die and dare deny
> The gods their god-like fun.
>
> (Honey, *Shadowed Dreams* 51)

The rediscovery of Harlem Renaissance women's poetry is a means of excavating some of these hiding places. Poems such as "Letter to My Sister" are direct expressions of the need to hide the interior in a protective exterior. The poem "Bottled" (1923), written by Helene Johnson, includes the question "But inside?," the same question Marita Bonner poses while describing the black female Buddha in her essay "On Being Young – a Woman – and Colored" (1925). In "Bottled," Johnson defies the imagined difference between the dancing black body and the dignified black person. As the speaker in the poem watches a white gaze watch a young black man dance, she notices the face of the dancer and then realizes that the dance is experienced by the dancer as "dignified / and slow. No, not slow either. / Dignified and *proud!*" (Honey, *Shadowed Dreams* 97). The dancer is "bottled," on display as much as African sand is on display within the 135th Street library exhibit, but the speaker is able to see his self-image, his sense of dignity, once she imagines him in a jungle. The "jungle" is reclaimed as the natural location of the "poor shine's" dance. When the speaker mentally transports him from 135th Street to the African jungle, she revels in her ability to see past the "tricks" that make his dance a spectacle. The last lines of the poem are

> Trick shoes, trick coat, trick cane, trick everything – all glass –
> But inside –
> Gee, that poor shine!
>
> (98)

The speaker's discovery of an authenticity in the midst of this trickery demonstrates the overcoming of the binary between the "dignified mistress" and the "strident gutter-snipe," Dunbar-Nelson's descriptions of the dichotomous archetypes that shape the crisis of black femininity. In "Bottled" Helene Johnson envisions a dance that is entirely "dignified" and entirely evocative of the "jungle."

The poets celebrate the primitive even as they critique the imagined natural connection between blackness and the primitive. Some of the celebrations of the primitive lead to images of a delicate beauty that exists within the "jungle." This delicate beauty is in sharp contrast to the defeminization of black women that Marita Bonner describes as the "feminine Caliban" ("On Being Young" 111). In the poem "To a Dark Girl" (1923), written by Gwendolyn Bennett, this delicacy is conveyed in the following lines: "Something of old forgotten queens / Lurks in the lithe abandon of your walk" (108). The litheness of the "dark girl" is rendered remarkable owing to the fact that "something of the shackled slave / Sobs in the rhythm of [her] talk" (Honey, *Shadowed Dreams* 108). This image of the "dark girl" who moves with an elusive grace in spite of the shackles reveals Bennett's desire to counteract the plentiful images of the heaviness of "mammy." Bennett avoids a sugarcoating of the heaviness of black women's oppression through her focus on the shackles as well as the litheness. The prevalent popular culture images of black women, in the 1920s, were either mammy caricatures or oversexualized "jezebels." Countering these images, Bennett inserts the image of the black woman who attains a state of delicacy and feminized grace precisely through the way that she moves through her oppression. This assumption of grace, in the midst of the heaviness, is the serious message hidden in the light-heartedness and humor of the short poem "Wild Roses" (1927), written by Mary Effie Lee Newsome:

> What! Roses growing in a meadow
> Where all the cattle browse?
> I'd think they'd fear the very shadow
> Of daddy's big rough cows.
>
> (Honey, *Shadowed Dreams* 210)

The potentially trite idea of the black woman as a rose gains much more depth when understood as these women poets' attempt to carve out a space for the serious consideration of the dignity of black womanhood.

The tender touch, the granting of the "roses," is a part of the signifying difference, the specificity, of Harlem Renaissance black women's poetry. This tenderness does not cancel out the "strident" counterpart that, as Alice Dunbar-Nelson testifies, has been set apart from the "dignified mistress." These women poets negotiated the crisis of black womanhood by experimenting with different ways of writing "race poems," "gender poems," and "nature poems." This constant negotiation is most apparent when Georgia Douglas Johnson's poem entitled "Motherhood" is renamed "Black Woman," possibly in an effort to make room for a focus on both race and gender. The experimentation with the boundaries between "nature poems" and "race poems" is most apparent when the poets use images of nature to question the imagined naturalness of racialized ideas of progress. In "Sonnet to a Negro in Harlem" (1923), for example, written by Helene Johnson, nature is tied to the "Negro" who is the object of the praise, and then the naturalness of urban sophistication is called into question when the speaker asserts, "You are too splendid for this city street" (Honey, *Shadowed Dreams* 99). Some "nature poems" are also the prototypical "race poems" as the poems locate a space in which to describe both the beauty of nature and the ugliness of racial oppression. This difficult space is fully achieved in Anita Scott Coleman's poem "Portraiture" (1931):

> Flames strip their branches,
> Flames sear their limbs,
> Flames scorch their trunks.
> Yet stand these trees
> For their roots are thrust deep
> In the heart of the earth.
> Black men are the tall trees that remain
> Standing in a forest after a fire.
>
> (Honey, *Shadowed Dreams* 199)

The "tall trees" are both the site of the trauma and the sign of the resilience of the black men. Six decades after the emancipation of slaves, this poem raises compelling questions about African Americans' relation to nature after the historical legacy of lynching and being forced to "work the land." The "nature poems" of the Harlem Renaissance women poets are often attempts to find beauty within a historical landscape of trauma. Many decades after the Harlem Renaissance, as Alice Walker thinks about the trauma attached, as a result of slavery, to "fields," she creates the character Shug Avery who asserts, "I think it pisses God off if you walk by the color purple in a field somewhere and don't notice it."[11] This attempt to locate an aesthetic experience in the midst of the historical landscape of pain is at the heart of these poets' struggle to disassociate delicateness from constructs of white womanhood.

This delicateness is brought to the surface in the poem "Trees at Night" (1925) in which Helene Johnson offers a feminized counterpart to the phallic image of black men as "tall trees" in "Portraiture." The "slim sentinels" in this poem are "fragile pinnacles / Of fairy castles" (Honey, *Shadowed Dreams* 220). The fragility, however, is rendered beautiful precisely because it expresses an urgency and a refusal to be passive ("The trembling beauty / Of an urgent pine"). Reconsiderations of beauty abound in the conversation between these women poets. In a poem simply titled "Beauty" (1930) Octavia Beatrice Wynbush thinks about the beauty that "lurks"; this use of this word highlights the unexpected nature of the subtle aesthetic warfare that shapes Harlem Renaissance women's poetry. The speaker in the poem "Beauty" confesses that

> beauty lurks for me in black, knotted hands,
> Hands consecrated to toil that those who come
> Behind them may have tender, shapely hands;
> And beautiful are shoulders with bearing heavy burdens stooped
> That younger shoulders may grow straight and proud.
>
> (Honey, *Shadowed Dreams* 120)

The image of the "tender, shapely hands" created by the "beauty" of the "toil" of the "black, knotted hands" foregrounds these poets' attempt to locate tenderness and beauty in the rough-hewn womanhood historically forced upon black women.

In a 1929 review of Georgia Douglas Johnson's poetry, published in *The Crisis*, Anne Spencer captures the challenge posed by this insistence on representing tenderness and elegance while combating the peculiar simultaneous defeminization of some black women and oversexualization of others. Spencer, in this review of *An Autumn Love Cycle* (1928), insists that "Lovers are the only persons left to us of any elegance at all" and praises Johnson for "writ[ing] of love without hypothecating atavistic jungle tones: the rumble of tom-tom, voodoo ebo, fetish of sagebrush and high spliced palm tree."[12] Spencer decides that the poetic representation of the crisis of black womanhood demands a tone of passion and fury that somehow escapes the snares of the stereotypes of the black primitive. Although Spencer focuses on Georgia Douglas Johnson's delicate maneuver around the allure of primitivism, the larger ethos of Harlem Renaissance women's poetry was overdetermined by this maneuvering. Spencer's description of Johnson's achievement resonates as a way of understanding the dialogue between these women poets, the call and response and the signifying difference that might constitute a tradition. The work of poets such as Georgia Douglas Johnson, Helene Johnson, Anne Spencer, Gwendolyn Bennett, Alice Dunbar-Nelson, and Angelina Weld Grimké fully exemplifies the complexity of the form and content of Harlem Renaissance women's poetry. The call and response between their poems is most resonant when the more strident poems are compared to the more subdued ones. As they traverse the terrain between exuberance and containment, rage and racial uplift, they articulate a collective enlightenment about the crisis of black womanhood. As Marita Bonner muses, "Perhaps Buddha is a woman."

NOTES

1. Venetria K. Patton and Maureen Honey, *Double-Take: A Revisionist Harlem Renaissance Anthology* (New Brunswick NJ, and London: Rutgers University Press, 2001), p. 112.
2. Nikki Giovanni, *Black Feeling, Black Talk, Black Judgment* (New York: Morrow Quill Paperbacks, 1979), pp. 88–9.
3. Georgia Douglas Johnson, *The Selected Works of Georgia Douglas Johnson* (New York: G. K. Hall, 1997), p. 119.
4. The groundbreaking 1970 anthology *The Black Woman*, edited by Toni Cade Bambara (New York: New American Library, 1970), makes "double jeopardy" the central description of what it means to be black and female.
5. Maureen Honey, ed., *Shadowed Dreams: Women's Poetry of the Harlem Renaissance* (New Brunswick, NJ and London: Rutgers University Press, 1989), p. 88.
6. Alain Locke, ed., *The New Negro* (1925; New York: Touchstone, 1997), p. 6.
7. Joanne M. Braxton, ed., *The Collected Poetry of Paul Laurence Dunbar* (Charlottesville and London: University Press of Virginia, 1993), p. 336. This poem was written to Lida Keck Wiggins and first published in *The Life and Works of Paul Laurence Dunbar*, ed. Lida Keck Wiggins (Naperville, IL and Memphis, TN: J. L. Nichols Co., 1907), pp. 116–17.
8. In *The Bluest Eye* (1970), Toni Morrison describes the "thin brown girl" who fights against the potential "erupt[ions]" of "Funk." Toni Morrison, *The Bluest Eye* (1970; New York: Plume/Penguin, 1994), p. 83.

9. This statement appears in one of her "As in a Looking Glass" columns in the Washington *Eagle*. This column is dated June 4, 1929 and is located in the Alice Dunbar-Nelson collection in the University of Delaware library.

10. Geraldyn Dismond in this column writes, "From the place she occupies in the Negro renaissance, I had expected to see a brusque, cold-blooded individual whose efficiency and belief in sex equality would be fairly jumping at one. I imagined she was engrossed in herself and work, sophisticated and self-sufficient ... All of which was wrong. She is very sensitive, retiring, and absolutely feminine" (Geraldyn Dismond, "Through the Lorgnette," *Pittsburgh Courier*, October 29, 1927).

11. Alice Walker, *The Color Purple* (New York: Simon and Schuster, 1982), p. 203.

12. The review appeared in *The Crisis*, 36 (March 1929), 87. The quoted passage appears in Gloria T. Hull, *Color, Sex, and Poetry: Three Women Writers of the Harlem Renaissance* (Bloomington and Indianapolis: Indiana University Press, 1987), p. 178.

10

A. B. CHRISTA SCHWARZ

Transgressive sexuality and the literature of the Harlem Renaissance

Elaborately costumed crossdressers at Harlem drag balls, public wedding ceremonies for black lesbian couples, speakeasies entertaining racially and sexually mixed crowds with illicit drinks and sexually explicit performances – transgressive sexuality clearly represented a visible facet of life during the Harlem Renaissance. This glossy and racy image of Harlem fits the sexualized cliché of the "roaring twenties" as a decade of abandon and sexual revolution. Dramatic changes in the urban sexual and racial landscapes indeed occurred in the early twentieth century: thousands of African Americans migrated to the northern urban centers, the "New Woman" emerged, and same-sex desire was reconceptualized. Until then explained by the phenomenon of gender inversion – effeminate men desire other men and "mannish" women desire other women – and represented by easily identifiable "inverts," types such as "fairies"/"pansies" or "mannish-acting" women, same-sex desire was now increasingly linked to a discrete and less visible category: homosexuality. Older theories of same-sex interest as inextricably linked to gender inversion, however, persisted. While the police and urban anti-vice societies attempted to suppress "immoral" sexual activities, New York's freshly emerged metropolis Harlem was largely exempt from policing efforts and consequently developed into a popular vice district. Striving for racial uplift, the black bourgeoisie tried to counteract this development by exerting pressure on the black community, but they lacked the power to successfully police Harlem.[1]

In this environment of competing social forces and racial and sexual transformations, the Harlem Renaissance developed. Representing no less than a new, cultural strategy that was to pave the path for African Americans' achievement of equal rights, the Renaissance movement and its protagonists were fraught with expectations. Black intellectual leaders like W. E. B. Du Bois and Alain Locke demanded seriousness and writers' acceptance of their task of representation. The so-called "Talented Tenth" was to concentrate on the creation of new and positive images of African

141

Americans. One might consequently assume that transgressive sexuality played barely any role in the Renaissance movement and its literature. However, as Henry Louis Gates, Jr. summarizes, the Harlem Renaissance "was surely as gay as it was black."[2] Many Renaissance participants were indeed same-sex interested. Most of them were covertly gay (for example Alain Locke and Countee Cullen) or bisexual (for example Claude McKay and Wallace Thurman). Only the bohemian Richard Bruce Nugent dared to openly display his same-sex desire. Speculations abound in the case of Renaissance icon Langston Hughes, who apparently had hetero- and homosexual relationships but shielded his private life from public gaze. Hidden from the eyes of the black bourgeoisie that remained vigilant while willing to overlook Renaissance participants' sexual indiscretions providing a respectable façade was maintained, a secret gay network, headed by Locke, existed. Harlem Renaissance participants such as Cullen, McKay, and Nugent were to varying degrees involved in the network, which was based on same-sex interest outside a context of gender inversion. Black lesbian networks also seem to have existed, but there was no similarly advantageous structure specifically for same-sex interested Renaissance women like Angelina Weld Grimké and Alice Dunbar-Nelson. Moreover, faced with gender discrimination and often burdened with family obligations, female Renaissance authors in general experienced more repressive living and writing conditions than their male counterparts.[3]

Homo- and bisexuality – the main issues addressed in this chapter – but also other transgressive sexualities such as interracial coupling, cross-class bonds, and incest are represented in a surprisingly large amount of Harlem Renaissance works. The presentation of transgressive sexuality, ranging from encodings to explicit depictions, differed decisively depending fundamentally on writers' sexual status and on the basic question whether they identified with the Harlem Renaissance and accepted the responsibility of representation. The openly gay Nugent thus tended to portray same-sex desire explicitly. McKay and Thurman rejected any prescription of respectability, while the closeted "poet laureate" Cullen adhered to a "best-foot-forward" policy – a path also chosen by the majority of Harlem Renaissance women.

Women-loving women

Provocative portrayals of female sexuality played a minor role in the work of female Renaissance authors. This can partly be ascribed to their social background. Most female Harlem Renaissance contributors were northern bred and belonged to the black bourgeoisie that believed in racial uplift. Furthermore, many of the best-known female Renaissance writers such as

Dunbar-Nelson or Jessie Fauset belonged to a somewhat older generation. Another central reason for black women writers' reticence regarding depictions of sexuality can be seen in the persistent myth of black women's lasciviousness promulgated during and after slavery. Most female Renaissance writers feared an implicit confirmation of stereotypes. Zora Neale Hurston, a southerner with no connections to the black bourgeoisie, represented a rare exception. She felt free to present outspoken black heroines such as Janie Crawford, the protagonist of *Their Eyes Were Watching God* (1937), who seeks sexual fulfillment with men across class and age boundaries. Compared to the era's blueswomen, the 1920s' outrageous black female stars, Hurston however seems tame. In "Prove It On Me Blues" (1928), Ma Rainey for instance claimed to go out with friends who "must have been women 'cause I don't like no men"[4] – a line virtually impossible for female Renaissance writers.

The black bourgeoisie strove to control black women's sexual image – particularly as thousands of single black female migrants poured into the northern cities. Black women were ideally positioned as "mothers of the race," responsible for the future of black America. Lesbians were consequently regarded as a disaster: they undermined the aim of racial uplift, posed a threat to African Americans' future by rejecting a reproductive role, and were additionally suspected of corrupting black youth. Given this sensitivity regarding black female sexuality, it does not surprise that particularly transgressive sexuality played a minor role in the works of female Renaissance writers.

As Gloria T. Hull shows, only personal papers and unpublished works of Grimké, who remained single, and Dunbar-Nelson, who married three times, indicate that these women were same-sex interested. Clearly, one needs to distinguish between works intended for publication and others created for the private realm when discussing the role of transgressive sexuality in Harlem Renaissance women writing. While Dunbar-Nelson and Grimké largely silenced lesbian issues in works intended for publication – Grimké even resexed pronouns – both created poetry that expressed same-sex passion. Apart from "You! Inez!," only fragments of Dunbar-Nelson's romantic secret poetry are extant, but several of Grimké's unpublished poems survive. These love lyrics, addressed to women, usually speak of unfulfilled longing and frustrated desire.[5]

Nella Larsen's novel *Passing* (1929) can be read as incorporating a lesbian narrative. Larsen – not known to have been same-sex interested – here achieved what can be described as a successful layering of race and (homo-) sexuality. The novel is on the surface simply about racial passing: the passing protagonist Clare reestablishes contact with the black community after a chance reunion with her childhood friend Irene. Yet a closer reading indicates an interwoven lesbian subplot. Readers are presented with a dramatic tale in which Clare increasingly gets involved in Irene's life and which ends with Clare's mysterious death. Racial passing was a conventional subject in 1920s literature and might indeed, as Deborah E. McDowell notes, constitute a "protective cover"[6] shielding the far more transgressive story of Clare and Irene's same-sex attraction. In contrast to the women's marriages, which seem unemotional, passion is involved whenever the two women meet. In Clare's letters to Irene, in which she speaks of "wild desire," sexual overtones are clearly audible (145). Even physical intimacy is evident: visiting Irene in her bedroom, Clare "drop[s] a kiss on [Irene's] dark curls" – a display of affection which causes Irene to experience "a sudden inexplicable onrush of affectionate feeling" (194). Ending the story with Clare's death, Larsen, as suggested by McDowell, not only followed a "safe" passing plot, but also safely disposed of the story's centre of transgressive desire. Significantly, however, Larsen's racial tale constitutes more than a ploy for a prioritized lesbian story as Larsen produced a multiple layering of themes and played with the idea of "passing" which is, after all, about fluid, unstable identities.[7]

The *Fire!!* venture

When the Niggerati, a group of rebellious young Harlem Renaissance writers and artists, decided to voice their dissatisfaction with what they regarded as the elitist and assimilationist direction the movement was taking, they opted for a modern outlet – the little magazine *Fire!!*, published in 1926 with the intention to cause outrage among black critics. Transgression of moral and aesthetic boundaries linked most contributions. Thurman and Nugent opted for the extreme of transgressive sexuality: "Cordelia the Crude," Thurman's story about a sixteen-year-old girl who lives in an urban environment characterized by immoral excesses and becomes a prostitute – outrageous given black critics' sensitivity regarding black women's sexual image; and Nugent's "Smoke, Lilies and Jade," the first overtly homoerotic story published by an African American.

"Smoke, Lilies and Jade" was provocative in terms of content and form. Nugent linked fragments of his protagonist's thoughts in a modern elliptical stream-of-consciousness style so far undared by black writers. The result is a story with clear decadent markings and a protagonist – Alex – who rejects any kind of work ethic and spends his time smoking and indulging in sex and sexual visions. Focusing on Alex's erotic encounter with the attractive Latin Adrian ("Beauty"), Nugent openly depicted same-sex passion and sexual contact between men. Same-sex desire, while crucial in Nugent's story, however represents just one transgressive issue among others such as decadent idleness and bisexual polygamy. Alex is thus infatuated not only with Beauty but also with Melva, concluding in the end that "one *can* love two at the same time" (*Gay Rebel* 87).

In the same way that "Smoke, Lilies and Jade" stood out in *Fire!!*, Nugent's many other portrayals of transgressive sexuality – in paintings and literary works – exceeded those of other Renaissance writers. Given his sexual explicitness, the majority of Nugent's works remained unpublished during the Renaissance era. But even his few published pieces are often sexually transgressive, as evident in the short story "Sahdji" (1925), which tells the exotic tale of Numbo, who seems to be in love with the chieftain's son Mrabo. Nugent's unpublished works surpass this level of transgression. In his Bible stories, he conflated religion and homosexuality by presenting same-sex attraction as the uniting force between Jesus and his disciples. In the novel "Geisha Man," Nugent widened his transgression of sexual norms by telling a tale featuring same-sex passion, sado-masochist desire, and incestuous longing. Significantly, Nugent in his works not only transgressed sexual boundaries but also dissolved binaries of race and gender to an extent unsurpassed by other Renaissance writers even in *Fire!!*

The *Fire!!* venture certainly represents the climax of a portrayal of transgressive sexuality in published Harlem Renaissance literature. The magazine eventually failed: it proved a financial disaster, a substantial amount of copies was lost in a fire, and the Niggerati never received the attention they had vied for. But *Fire!!* clearly indicates the extent to which sexual dissidence constituted part of the younger Renaissance writers' transgressive strategies.

Homosexual stereotypes

While stereotypes of homosexuals play barely any role in Nugent's oeuvre, McKay, Hughes, and Thurman largely relied on specific types when explicitly depicting same-sex interested characters. Nugent himself served as a model for a sexually transgressive type – Paul Arbian, an African American version of the bisexual Greenwich Village artistic type – in Thurman's novel *Infants of the Spring* (1932). Given the centrality of gender inversion in public discourses on homosexuality, it does not surprise that the "invert" is the main type of homosexual presented in the works of Hughes, Thurman, and McKay. All three writers refused to create solely respectable images of African Americans and were intent on portraying their versions of "real" black life.

In contrast to female Renaissance writers, McKay opted for explicit representations of lesbians in his work. McKay's references to lesbianism are usually linked to the stereotype of the butch, unattractive lesbian. In his novel *Home to Harlem* (1928), McKay included both a dismissal and a somewhat half-hearted defense of women-loving women: The sexually "wholesome" black protagonist Jake believes that lesbians are "bulldykers" – a slang expression for lesbians – and "all ugly womens," while the less "manly" black intellectual Ray challenges this opinion: "Not *all*. And [bulldyker is] a damned ugly name" (*Home to Harlem* 155). Interestingly, McKay racialized his portrayal of lesbians. Reflecting his version of primitivism that distinguishes between whiteness which is linked to perversion, impotence, and weakness, and blackness which is related to vitality, potency, and "healthy" sexuality, McKay's works exclusively feature white lesbians. In McKay's most negative portrayal of lesbianism, the short story "Highball" (1932), the black pianist Nation's unsympathetic white wife Myra organizes parties behind his back with her white female companion Dinah. Somewhat reminiscent of Larsen's work, the women's meetings are sexually charged encounters, whereas Myra and Nation seem physically distant. Yet while Larsen's narrator Irene indulges in Clare's sexual attractiveness, McKay took up the stereotype of the lesbian as the unattractive "other" of femininity by describing Myra as "a rather coarse-fleshed woman, with freckled hands . . . and lumpy hair of the color of varnish" (*Gingertown* 106) and her friend Dinah as vampire-like.

Without specific racial connotations, Hughes and Thurman sometimes rather casually incorporated homosexual stereotypes in their works. Thurman thus introduced the effeminate Bobby at the very end of his novel *The Blacker the Berry* (1929) as a somewhat disgusting and weak character, and Hughes' play *Little Ham* (1935) features a ridiculous "EFFEMINATE YOUTH" (63) and a "MASCULINE LADY" (63) who speaks in a "bass voice" (71). These are sexually transgressive figures contemporary readers could easily recognize. Both authors went even further in their depiction of negative stereotypes of gay men and lesbians by presenting "the homosexual" as child molester, thereby reiterating a combination of same-sex interest and "perversion" repeatedly featured in contemporary news stories. Intending to ridicule the black bourgeoisie's uplift efforts, Thurman in *The Blacker the Berry* placed his stereotypical lesbian character – an older woman seeking to convert and corrupt young women – in the center of a supposedly safe haven for newly arrived single female migrants. When looking for accommodation in Harlem, the novel's protagonist Emma Lou encounters a "spinster type" (*The Blacker the Berry* 108) who runs a boarding house for women. Clearly displaying sexual interest, the older woman "placed her hand on Emma Lou's knee, then finally put her arm around her waist" (108). Emma Lou rejects the woman's passes, but the house's other young female inhabitants appear to have already been corrupted. In his novel *Not Without Laughter* (1930), Hughes presented a fairy as a despicable child molester. While otherwise refraining from value judgments regarding morally transgressive characters such as bootleggers, gamblers, or pimps in his work, he portrayed the "small yellow man with a womanish kind of voice" (*Not Without Laughter* 282) who aggressively approaches the young black male protagonist Sandy as the epitome of disgust and a typical brand of sexual "deviant" who targets boys.

The figure of the pansy plays a different role in McKay's work. McKay presented pansies together with female prostitutes as dominant and widely accepted elements of Harlem's sexually transgressive landscape who both target "manly" men. McKay's pansies are "painted boys" (*Home to Harlem* 210) who, while not cross-dressing, display distinct signifiers of femininity. Casual sexual involvement with pansies is presented as socially acceptable in *Home to Harlem*. Pansies do not seem to challenge the structure of sexual relations, as in a coupling of "manly" men and pansies male meets quasi-female, resulting in a variety of the male/female dichotomy which seems all-important. This is also the case with the sexually transgressive type of the "wolf," a hyper-manly variety of homosexual. In *Home to Harlem*, Billy Biasse represents a wolf who displays a strong and aggressive masculinity and "eats his own kind" (139) – his sexual relations are exclusively with men. Billy prefers pansies and thus apparently also does not disturb Harlem's sexual structures. He is considered somewhat "queer" by other men, but his high masculine status earns him respect. Moreover, he displays self-confidence, claiming to be "the happiest, well-feddest wolf in Harlem" (138).

"Romance in Marseilles" (1930) stands out in McKay's literary presentation of transgressive sexuality. Its central homosexual types are the well-built "wolf" Big Blonde and his partner, a somewhat freakish white pansy. In Marseilles they are exposed to homophobic aggression – an unjust treatment which leaves its marks on Big Blonde, who eventually breaks down in tears. Harlem, it seems, is more tolerant of homosexuality than white Marseilles. While McKay presented white and black pansies and wolves, he apparently distinguished among them along racial lines, befitting his overall primitivist positioning of white perversion versus black naturalness. In *Banjo*, McKay seemed far more willing to delve into negative stereotypes in his depiction of pansies, whom he criminalized and whose movements he described as "smirking" and "minc[ing]" (87). While in Harlem black effeminate gay men are part of a "natural" black sexuality, in Marseilles white pansies' sexuality seems just as "unnatural" as that of other white men. Focusing on the type of the invert, McKay could be said to have reaffirmed the effeminate stereotype of gay men just as Hughes and Thurman did, yet while certainly strengthening negative stereotypes of lesbians, he painted a more neutral picture of pansies and wolves and to some extent naturalized them.

Loving comrades

Less likely to be spotted by readers than the obvious and, given the clear distinction between the types portrayed and the authors themselves, "safe" portrayals of stereotypical homosexuals, the "love of comrades," same-sex desire among men unconnected to gender inversion plays a role in Hughes' and McKay's works. The concept of "loving comrades" can be traced to Walt Whitman, famous not only for his free-verse style but also for his celebration of male same-sex bonding.[8] Whitman's works quickly attracted the attention of same-sex interested men. Significantly, they also influenced the intellectual and sexual coming-of-age of Harlem Renaissance participants. McKay, for instance, was introduced to Whitman by his white mentor Walter Jekyll, who initiated the young Jamaican into the cultural concept and potentially also the physical side of male same-sex relationships.[9] Whitman was also highly valued by Hughes who, when starting on a sea journey as a mess boy, threw all of his books over board in an act of intellectual liberation, saving only his copy of *Leaves of Grass*.[10]

Whitman's ideal of a "manly love of comrades"[11] seems reflected in Hughes' tales and poems about sailors and the waterfront – a suitable context in light of sailors' hyper-masculine image. Hughes contrasts manly seafaring with its effeminate "other" in his autobiography *The Big Sea* (1940) and in the short story "The Little Virgin" (1927), in which an "unmanly" crew member is excluded from what Hughes' narrator describes as a "strange comradeship, a strict fraternity" ("The Little Virgin" 327) among the sailors. In this way, Hughes constructed the all-male camaraderie at sea as a "manly" framework for same-sex experiences. Viewed in this context, Hughes' maritime-themed works, for instance the poem "Long Trip" (1926), in which sailors "dip and dive, / Rise and roll" (*Collected Poems* 97) – movements potentially describing sexual motions – offer possibilities for gay readings.

In his early Jamaican poetry volumes *Songs of Jamaica* (1912) and *Constab Ballads* (1912) and in the short story "When I Pounded the Pavement" (1932), which center on the Jamaican constabulary, McKay constructed a similar framework for male camaraderie. While not offering the glamorous freedom of life at sea, the police compound represents an exclusively male space, a "depot of men" (*Gingertown* 208). Allowing for a constant provision of young men, the constabulary could be read as a sheltered cruising ground. Within this setting, two types of camaraderie can be identified. On the one hand, there is a general bond linking recruits, who do "everything in common, drilling, eating, bathing, dressing, sleeping" (208). Although supervised, this intense homosocial bonding has homoerotic potential. On the other hand, intimate bonds between two men feature prominently. Presented in a sentimental fashion, this is the case in McKay's Jamaican poetry – particularly in a series of three emotional poems about a narrator's intimate relationship with the recruit "Bennie" which is destroyed when Bennie is transferred. In "When I Pounded the Pavement," McKay presented an intimate same-sex bond in the constabulary compound, where acquaintances "extended to ripe comradeship" (*Gingertown* 208), without sentimentality. Yet this relationship also fails, indicating the constabulary's twisted character: it constitutes a legitimate same-sex space allowing for intimate contacts, but the very nature of police work seems life- and love-destroying.

In *Home to Harlem* and *Banjo*, McKay's male protagonists form an exclusively black homosocial haven. McKay positioned black male camaraderie as a necessary counterweight against the "corrupting" forces of a white-defined civilization and heterosexual relationships or, more generally, women, who are presented as exploiters of men's sexual desire. Next to a more general level of black male camaraderie, closer bonds are discernible. The "manly" Jake shares a "big friendship" (*Home to Harlem* 168) with Ray, the intellectual, who, while initially standing apart owing to his "white" education, quickly joins in the spirit of black camaraderie. Interestingly, Ray is the only character explicitly identified with same-sex desire: he admires Jake in his sleep and furthermore has visions of "[s]weat dripping bodies of black men naked under the equatorial sun" (*Banjo* 67). *Home to Harlem* is framed by the heterosexual narrative of Jake's pursuit of the black Felice, but the story of the two loving comrades Jake and Ray seems equally important. Forced to part, Jake declares "I likes you" and "looked into Ray's eyes with frank savage affection" (*Home to Harlem* 209). Their unexpected meeting in Marseilles depicted in *Banjo* is presented in even more intimate terms: they "embraced and kissed" (292). At the end of *Banjo*, when the more general camaraderie between the beach boys disintegrates as the group disperses, Whitman's vision of loving comrades who wander free seems to come true: Ray and the novel's rough and manly protagonist Banjo embark on a vagabondage from which women are on Banjo's insistence excluded.

Gay poetics

While male Renaissance writers referred to the dominant sexually transgressive figure of the prostitute in their poetry, their verse is generally devoid of explicit references to homosexuality. Cullen and McKay subscribed to classic poetic aesthetics which per se excluded sexual explicitness. Same-sex desire is often concealed in the poetic work of Hughes, McKay, Cullen, and also Nugent, whose only extant explicitly gay poem seems to be "Who Asks

This Thing?," in which the speaker dares to "wear [his] love for all to see" and declares: "He walks alone who walks in love with me" (*Gay Rebel* 90).

As Gregory Woods points out, depictions of attractive men are a good starting point for an exploration of the Renaissance's gay poetics.[12] McKay's "handsome bronze-hued lad" (*Selected Poems* 76), featured in "Alfonso, Dressing to Wait at Table, Sings" (1922), is an eye-catcher, but Hughes' maritime-themed poems and particularly his poem "Boy" (1928), which describes a young man as "solid with strength / And lovely as a young tree / All his virile length,"[13] certainly stand out in this context. In other poems, same-sex love is expressed in what can be described as the culturally accepted form of mourning. In his elegiac "Poem [2]" (1925), Hughes opened up a gay space by letting his speaker mourn a lost friend. He specified the speaker's friend as male and framed the poem with the statement "I loved my friend" (*Selected Poems* 52) – a "safe" option as the form of the elegy to some extent legitimizes the expression of love for another man. In his epic poem "The Black Christ" (1929), Cullen combined mourning with a religious and brotherly theme, thereby widening the space available for the expression of same-sex love and desire. Cullen's narrator admires his brother Jim's looks and, after Jim is falsely accused of rape and eventually murdered, mourns his death, touches him, and voices his affection. In "Judas Iscariot" (1925) – a reinterpretation of the story of Judas not as a traitor but as Christ's dedicated servant – Cullen again chose a religious theme, presenting Christ as linked to Judas by same-sex attraction and love.

Cullen also employed dedications to create gay poetic spaces. In his famous poem "Heritage" (1925), dedicated to his intimate friend Harold Jackman, he asked "What's your nakedness to me?" (*Color* 37) – a question that can be read as directly addressing Jackman. Similarly, Cullen dedicated poems to his intimate friends and/or lovers Llewellyn Ransom ("The Shroud of Color"), Donald Duff ("Tableau"), and Edward Perry ("More Than a Fool's Song"). Sometimes, however, it seems necessary to uncover literary codes or strategies to explore the gay dimension of Harlem Renaissance poetry. Cullen seems to have included references to a terminology of "friendship," a specific gay discourse employed in Locke's gay network, which was based on a fusion of terms emanating from a Greek discourse of homosexuality with Whitmanesque expressions – all indicating an interpretation of male same-sex love as "manly" and "healthy." References to this coded language seem evident for instance in "Sonnet," where the "noblest way" (*My Soul's High Song* 247) of love is mentioned, and in "Love's Way" (1927), where it is stated that "Love's is the nobler way" (*My Soul's High Song* 161) – potential evocations of the coded term for homosexuality – "noble friendship." Hughes, in contrast, played on double meanings, as evident in "Joy" (1926). While the "Joy" the speaker refers to can be read as a woman's name – a man searches for his lover "Joy" and eventually "found her" with the "butcher boy" – it can also be read as "happiness": the presumably male speaker finds joy "In the arms of the butcher boy" (*Collected Poems* 63), an extraordinarily explicit yet simultaneously camouflaged gay reference.[14]

The creation of gay poetic space through multiple meanings could indeed be viewed as a central strategy of same-sex interested Harlem Renaissance poets. Particularly the image of the dream and the themes of oppression and resistance seem to serve authors well in this context.[15] In Hughes' maritime-themed "Water-Front Streets" (1926), sailors themselves could represent the dreamy freight on the "dream ships" (*Collected Poems* 96) the speaker observes. Or maybe the ships' destinations – they are heading to where "life is gay" – turn the vessels into "dream ships." The image of a usually unspecified, unfulfilled dream that is dangerous yet simultaneously requires protection repeatedly appears in Harlem Renaissance poetry, for instance in Hughes' "Star Seeker" (1926), McKay's "Courage" (1922), and Cullen's "For a Poet" (1925). Given the context of the Harlem Renaissance, racial readings of these dreams as visions of African Americans' liberation and equality seem feasible. But gay readings, in which a life without homophobic repression is envisioned, also seem valid, indicating the possibility of a transference between the topics of race and (homo-)sexuality. The multitude of Renaissance poems dealing with the theme of a usually unspecified oppression and resistance against repression, such as McKay's famous call to arms "If We Must Die" (1919) or Hughes' "Shadows" (1923), in which people confined to darkness escape from the shadows, equally invite such multiple readings. Even when the topic of race seems foregrounded, as in Nugent's "Shadow" (1925), gay readings seem feasible – particularly in light of Nugent's statement that while "Shadow" was "considered a race poem" he thought of it as a "soul-searching poem of another kind of loneliness."[16] Like Nella Larsen, the male poets of the Harlem Renaissance displayed mastery in the layering of meanings and themes, creating works which often only at second sight reveal a gay dimension.

Homosexual miscegenation

As Kevin Mumford argues, "Sex across the color line is never just sex."[17] In light of African Americans' mass migration to the northern urban centers, anti-miscegenation sentiment swelled up as a blurring of racial identities was feared. The sexual color line was thus policed, and interracial sex was defined as a form of transgressive sexuality endangering, as with homosexuality, the reproduction of the "race" – by white and black Americans. Larsen took up this issue in *Passing* (1929) and in *Quicksand* (1928), where she presented black female protagonists who display moral outrage when confronted with consensual interracial relationships. Befitting his dissident image, McKay provocatively included the controversial topic in his fictional work – for instance in "Nigger Lover" (1932), a short story about a white female Parisian prostitute who only targets black men. In McKay's poem "One Year After" (1922), the color line represents an almost unsurmountable barrier for two lovers. One might also read Cullen's frequent poetic treatment of outlawed and doomed love in an interracial context. In "The Love Tree" (1927), for instance, he portrayed a couple forced to deny and bury what is presented as an illicit love. Again, a transference between race and sexuality seems possible, or, widening the scope, one could also imagine a combination of an interracial and a homosexual union: a case of "homosexual miscegenation" – a twofold crossing of boundaries.[18]

The relationship between the white Swede Stephen and the black intellectual Raymond which constitutes a central story line in Thurman's novel *Infants of the Spring* can also be read as a case of homosexual miscegenation. The factor race, however, seems to be of no significance for their relationship, which is depicted as an intense companionship between like-minded intellects. While Thurman revealed the men's "frankly acknowledged affection for one another" (*Infants of the Spring* 34), he emphasized that "[t]heir greatest joy came when they could be alone together and talk" (35). By avoiding any sign of physical intimacy, Thurman lifted their relationship to a platonic level which, also given the fact that Thurman himself for a while shared his room and bed with his white Scandinavian lover Harald Jan Stefansson, seems somewhat unconvincing. Just like Thurman displayed homosexual and heterosexual interest in his life, Raymond and Stephen are identified with heterosexual desire next to their same-sex attraction. What remains is a sense of indeterminacy indicative of Thurman's "resistance to easy characterization."[19]

The openly gay Nugent also presented cases of interracial same-sex desire in his works – for instance in the aforementioned "Bastard Song" and in the Bible story "The Now Discordant Song of Bells," in which the white catamite Carus desires Caspar, the black member of the Magi, reveling in his exotic "otherness." More surprisingly, Cullen openly portrayed interracial same-sex coupling in his poems "Uncle Jim" (1927) and "Tableau" (1925). Again, Cullen layered themes, foregrounding the topics of race and youth. By starting off "Uncle Jim" with a debate between the black speaker and his uncle about "[w]hite folks" (*My Soul's High Song* 143), Cullen created a racial framework which seems to divert attention from his later depiction of the speaker's happy same-sex relationship. It is not explicitly stated that the speaker's "friend" is white, yet this can be inferred from the poem's context. Significantly, the young men's happiness seems threatened as the speaker cannot help remembering Uncle Jim's warning that "[w]hite folks is white" – interracial contacts seem doomed. In "Tableau," an early poem by Cullen characterized by a youthful spirit, accompanied by a highly suggestive illustration by white artist Charles Cullen (not related), and dedicated to Cullen's white intimate friend and potential lover Donald Duff, this gloomy assessment is rejected. The poem's homoerotic component is evident already in the first two lines: "Locked arm in arm they cross the way, / The black boy and the white" (*Color* 12). The two young men, whose youth might serve to signal sexual innocence to homophobic readers, clearly "cross" boundaries – on a racial and a sexual level. Their transgressive connection has caught the attention of hostile black and white observers who disapprovingly watch the illicit couple. Despite Cullen's application of an imagery that appears threatening and indicative of potential physical violence, the poem ends on a surprisingly positive note as "lightning...blaze[s] the path of thunder," blazing, as might be said, a trail for others who dare to transgress racial and sexual boundaries.[20] The implication in "Tableau" is that gay men can overcome the barrier of race and thus advance race relations – a very positive outlook on same-sex relations which seems exceptional in Cullen's work.

Clearly, transgressive sexuality plays a significant role in the literature of the Harlem Renaissance. The movement's voices of sexual dissidence, sometimes plainly, at other times barely audible, do not form a harmonious chorus, but a wealth of material awaits readers willing to pay attention to this transgressive dimension of the Harlem Renaissance.

NOTES

I am indebted to Wigan Salazar for his never-failing support of my Harlem Renaissance studies. Many of the details treated in this chapter are taken from A. B. Christa Schwarz, *Gay Voices of the Harlem Renaissance* (Bloomington: Indiana University Press, 2003).

1. See George Chauncey, Jr., *Gay New York: Gender, Urban Culture and the Making of the Gay Male World, 1890–1940* (New York: Basic, 1994), pp. 124–5, 244–67.
2. Henry Louis Gates, Jr., "The Black Man's Burden," in Michael Warner, ed., *Fear of a Queer Planet* (Minneapolis: University of Minnesota Press, 1993), p. 233.
3. See Gloria T. Hull, *Color, Sex & Poetry: Three Women Writers of the Harlem Renaissance* (Bloomington: Indiana University Press, 1987), pp. 12, 95–7.
4. Ma Rainey, "Prove It on Me Blues." *Down in the Basement*, Milestone MLP-2017.
5. See Hull, *Color*, pp. 21, 22, 26, 95–7, 140–1, 145.

6. Deborah E. McDowell, "'It's Not Safe. Not Safe at All': Sexuality in Nella Larsen's *Passing*," in Henry Abelove, Michèle Aina Barale, and David M. Halperin, eds., *The Lesbian and Gay Studies Reader* (New York: Routledge, 1993), p. 624.
7. Ibid.
8. For an overview of the gay dimension of Whitman's works see Robert K. Martin, "Whitman, Walt," in *The Gay and Lesbian Heritage: A Reader's Companion to the Writers and Their Works, from Antiquity to the Present* (New York: Holt, 1995), pp. 736–42.
9. See Wayne F. Cooper, *Claude McKay: Rebel Sojourner in the Harlem Renaissance. A Biography* (New York: Schocken, 1990), pp. 30–1.
10. See Arnold Rampersad, *The Life of Langston Hughes*, vol. 1 (New York: Oxford University Press, 1988), p. 72.
11. Walt Whitman, "For You O Democracy," [1867], in *Walt Whitman: The Complete Poems*, ed. Francis Murphy (London: Penguin, 1975), p. 150.
12. Gregory Woods, "Gay Re-readings of the Harlem Renaissance Poets," in Emmanuel S. Nelson, ed., *Critical Essays: Gay and Lesbian Writers of Color* (New York: Harrington Park-Haworth, 1993), pp. 128–32.
13. Langston Hughes, "Boy," *Carolina Magazine* May 1928, 38.
14. See Woods, "Gay Re-readings," p. 136.
15. Ibid. pp. 129–35.
16. Audiotape recording of interview with Richard Bruce Nugent conducted by Thomas H. Wirth, 1983, tape #2.
17. Kevin J. Mumford, *Interzones: Black/White Sex Districts in Chicago and New York in the Early Twentieth Century* (New York: Columbia University Press, 1997), p. xi.
18. See Woods, "Gay Re-readings," p. 135.
19. Granville Ganter, "Decadence, Sexuality, and the Bohemian Vision of Wallace Thurman," *MELUS* 28 (2003), 85.
20. See also Alden Reimonenq, "Countee Cullen's Uranian 'Soul Windows,'" in Emmanuel S. Nelson, ed., *Critical Essays: Gay and Lesbian Writers of Color* (New York: Harrington Park–Haworth, 1993), pp. 150–1.

CHARLES SCRUGGS

Sexual desire, modernity, and modernism in the fiction of Nella Larsen and Rudolph Fisher

Critics of the Harlem Renaissance often pair Nella Larsen with Jessie Fauset, but Nella Larsen and Rudolph Fisher make a better literary pair than do Fauset and Larsen. Like Claude McKay and Wallace Thurman, both Larsen and Fisher believed that sexual desire is a primary force in human nature but one shaped by the ubiquitous presence of modernity. One manifestation of modernity, of course, is popular culture – cabarets, film, and pulp fiction. And as modernists, Larsen and Fisher saw that popular culture was a source of modernism, especially American modernism. For instance, as murder mysteries, Larsen's *Passing* (1929) and Fisher's *The Conjure Man Dies* (1932) are indebted to a modernist conception that a lowbrow literary genre like a detective novel might reveal, in Raymond Chandler's famous phrase, a "hidden truth."[1] In *Quicksand* (1928), Larsen makes use of another aspect of popular culture (both cinematic and literary), the sensational story of the "tragic mulatta," but her allusion to Hemingway's *The Sun Also Rises* (1926) reinterprets that story as an examination of love in a post World War I universe. Finally, in Fisher's *The Conjure Man Dies*, the clue to the murderer's identity lies not in rational analysis (which presupposes Newtonian order) but in a comic blues song about sexual desire heard daily on Harlem's streets. Echoing Plato's *Symposium*, all three novels treat sexual desire as the engine in the human machine that can either destroy the self or create the possibility for transcendence, either personal or communal.

Hazel Carby claims that *Quicksand* "contains the first explicitly sexual black heroine in black women's fiction."[2] Making her mulatta protagonist, Helga Crane, "explicitly sexual" was a risky thing for Larsen to do in the 1920s. White writers and film makers (such as D. W. Griffith) depicted the mulatta as Jezebel, a free-floating libido that threatened white domesticity and white male virtue. Lydia Brown (Mary Alden) in Griffith's *The Birth of a Nation* (1915), Lissa in Vara Majette's *White Blood* (1924), and Madame Duvall in Frances Mocatta's *The Forbidden Woman* (1928) are examples from popular culture of mulattas whose sexuality is so excessive that it borders on insanity. Black writers and film makers revolted against this pulp fiction image of black femininity. Their mulattas are educated, sophisticated, vulnerable, victimized, and sexless. Rena Walden in *The House Behind the Cedars* (1900), Sappho Clark in Pauline Hopkins' *Contending Forces* (1900), and Sylvia Landry (Evelyn Preer) in Oscar Micheaux's film *Within Our Gates* (1919), his answer to *The Birth of a Nation*, are sometimes "tragic" but always chaste.

One exception to this rule is *The Scar of Shame* (1927), a film with an all black cast and produced by a black production company. This cinematic melodrama features a mulatta, Louise Howard (Lucia Lynn Moses) who, like Helga Crane, has a dubious family background, runs hard against the barrier of caste within the race, and ends her life by sinking into a sexual and moral abyss. And like Helga, she undergoes a series of metamorphoses, depicted first as a vulnerable woman, then as a *femme fatale*, and finally as a victim of "environment." What is unique about *Quicksand* is the way Larsen complicates her mulatta, Helga Crane, by giving her psychological and social depth and by making her condition modern: she is alone in a world she never made. Specifically, Helga is educated, sophisticated, and an object of desire, but she also is a creature of desire. Because she is sexually driven in ways that she doesn't understand and refuses, at times, to acknowledge, her tragic end lies in a combination of forces – personal, social, and environmental – in which the issue of victimization is a two-way street.

Early in the novel, Helga poses the question, "But just what did she want?" She imagines it to be "happiness," but her "conception of it had no tangibility."[3] Because of her troubled racial past, Helga wants a world outside of history, but what she finds is that there is no escape from history, either from American history or from the bewildering landscape of modernity. Her mode of protection much of the time is what Meredith Goldsmith calls her "commodity aesthetic." In Naxos, Helga constructs a genteel life out of "material objects"[4] – clothing, furniture, books. In Copenhagen, she allows herself to be made over and put on sexual display by her aunt and uncle; she is outfitted with low-cut dresses, loopy earrings, and sexy shoes. It is a persona that expresses her sexuality as a form of power, but it also blinds her to her own desires, a point made clear in the novel when Helga refuses to see the truth in Axel Olsen's painting of her. Although the portrait reflects Olsen's own sexual fantasy of Helga, it also depicts what Helga cannot see in herself, that she is a creature of desire. That "disgusting sensual creature" in the painting "with her features" (McDowell, ed. 89) becomes the return of the repressed by the novel's end.

Throughout, Helga is looking for a "home" (McDowell, ed. 30), but just when she thinks she has found it, discontent drives her to search for a new place. That discontent hides a primal fear, the fear of being "engulfed." Late in the novel, Larsen refers to Helga's anger at "the quagmire in which she had engulfed herself" (McDowell, ed. 133). It is a word or situation that Larsen had used in two previous short stories. In "Freedom," an unnamed protagonist is desperate to leave his wife, "to get out of the slough into which his amorous folly had precipitated him."[5] One day he abandons her, only to find out a year later that she has died. His freedom becomes a nightmare; her death throws him into a "mental chaos that was engulfing him" and leads to his suicide (Larson, ed. 17). In "The Wrong Man," wealthy socialite Julia Romley goes to a dance on Long Island with her husband and unexpectedly confronts an abyss. The man who had once kept her as his mistress is there. She meets him in the summerhouse in the dark, begging her former lover not to reveal the truth, only to realize she is talking to a stranger. The stranger swears not to reveal her secret, but the impact of the story lies in the fact that the secret, being expressed, is like the world lying in wait to swallow her whole.

Forty-one years after *Quicksand* was published, psychiatrist R. D. Laing in *The Divided Self* (1969) would use the same language to describe "ontological insecurity" as a symptom of the modern human condition. The fear of "engulfment" occurs when the individual lacks a stable self and feels "dread" when threatened by the "absorption" of another person or by the world itself. Laing says that "the dread of engulfment" is the fear of "being caught and dragged down into the quicksand."[6] Larsen's brilliance is to connect Helga's downward spiral to both interior and exterior space. She perceptively links Helga's psychological fear of "engulfment" with a social landscape that is continually shifting in and out of focus. Each place Helga lands repeats that "magic sense of having come home" (McDowell, ed. 43), but what she doesn't understand is that each new place presupposes a new social context of unforeseeable conditions.

The accelerating pattern of Helga's descent into the abyss is at first slow and then sudden. In the beginning, Harlem for Helga is paradise, but gradually she feels that she is suffocating in a claustrophobic space. Fleeing to Denmark, she breathes the free air of the Old World, only to find that the disappearance of one set of limitations is replaced by the appearance of another. After refusing an advantageous marriage in Denmark, she returns to Harlem with a strong sense of *déjà vu*. At a cocktail party Robert Anderson kisses her passionately, but what for him is a momentary lapse of self-control becomes for Helga a release of suppressed, torrential desire. Reeling from Anderson's rejection, she seduces and then marries a Baptist preacher from the South, the Reverend Mr. Pleasant Green. Returning with him to his church in Alabama, Helga believes that religion and the "simple happiness" of a pastoral world outside of history will give her happiness (McDowell, ed. 114). Yet her happiness is short-lived, as the quicksand that swallows her is both her unleashed sexual desire and the masculinely defined space in which it is expressed. The American pastoral has become a trap in which Helga recapitulates the historical nightmare of slavery. All her beauty is now put to the service of being a breeder.

Larsen sustains an element of mystery about Helga to the very end, but she does hint at what Helga needs to survive in a world of mutability and contingency. It is not simply the shield of "callousness" that Robert Anderson advocates (McDowell, ed. 20), nor the "commodity aesthetic" she adopts. Rather, she needs a self that can adapt to the world's shifting circumstances and that would enable her, like Hemingway's bullfighter, to hold the "purity of line through the maximum of exposure."[7] In a Harlem cabaret, Helga observes Robert Anderson dancing with Audrey Denney, a minor but significant character. Audrey dances with "pulsing motion" to "wild music from the heart of the jungle," but her dance is a combination of both "grace and abandon" (McDowell, ed. 62). "Grace and abandon" is an oxymoron that suggests a tension between Eros and artifice, between energy and order. Overcome by desire, all Helga hears is the "wild music" and all she sees are "two figures, closely clinging." What she doesn't see is what she desperately needs: the graceful movement of the dance. Audrey transforms the "wild music," and its erotic potential to expose her to the "maximum," into fluid motion. For a brief transitory moment, the dancer is the dance.

Helga, however, refuses to see the various levels of reality in the cabaret. For one thing, the jazz in the Harlem cabaret is not simply "wild" but music, and it reflects an improvisation that plays with a linear conception of time and a static notion of space.[8] In Louis Armstrong's words, jazz is music "that's never played the same way once" (qtd. in Werner 132). As such, it mirrors the shifting kaleidoscope of the cabaret, its "moving mosaic" (McDowell, ed. 60). Failing to see the artistic improvisation in either the dance or the music, Helga rushes from the cabaret in despair. That same blindness occurs in Copenhagen when she views a vaudeville show made up of her fellow African Americans whose "cavorting" on stage fills her with disgust and dread (McDowell, ed. 83). Yet she cannot look away. She returns repeatedly to the "Circus" to gaze upon the "gesticulating black figures" who throw "their bodies about with a loose ease!" To her, the performers are both on display, as she is in Copenhagen, and naked, revealing something that should be concealed. The spectacle recalls a racialized past that embarrasses her and exposes a sexuality that she refuses to claim. What she doesn't see is that the spectacle is a performance. The figures express themselves "with a loose ease" within the limitations of the vaudeville skit, just as Audrey danced with "grace and abandon" within the freedom of the music. They are both improvising, creating a provisional order out of limitation or chaos.

At the end of the novel, as Helga becomes biologically trapped by child-birth, she desperately clings to high culture, especially literature, as a kind of moral anchor. The last story she has read to her by her nurse before her fifth pregnancy is Anatole France's "The Procurator of Judea." The story is a fitting commentary upon Helga's tragic blindness to her own life, especially to her own sexual life. The "procurator" is Pontius Pilate, now an old man, who is worried that history will not do him justice. The irony of the story is that his memory is myopic. His concerns are with Roman history. He has no idea that he will be remembered by a post-Roman western civilization as the killer of Christ, whom, he tells his friend, he "cannot call ... to mind" (McDowell, ed. 132).[9] So, too, Helga fails to see that her identity and her history are not static, for the mosaic is always "moving," changing shape like an amoeba. To survive in the world one has to adapt to it like an actor in a play whose part keeps changing, one day a dancer like Audrey Denney, another day a clown like the vaudeville actors.

Larsen's second novel *Passing* is a mystery story that opens up more mysteries than it solves. The novel begins with the premise that "passing" is a form of theatricality and ends with the theme that "passing" conceals the essential mystery of human identity and human desire. Clare Kendry is beautiful, "white," and married to a white banker named John Bellew who does not know her ancestry. Irene Redfield, her "friend" whom she hasn't seen in twelve years, has remained within the race. The novel deals with their reconnection, Clare's desire to "pass" back into Irene's world, and Irene's betrayal of Clare. Through the use of cinematic flashbacks and flashbacks within flashbacks, Larsen constructs a detective story that lacks definitive closure, but this openness makes possible the revelation of other truths.

One truth that remains controversial is Irene's sexuality. Does her para-noia over Brian and Clare hide a latent sexual desire for Clare (McDowell, ed. xviii)?[10] Although critics argue over this point, one thing about Irene's sexuality is obvious. It has been replaced by her desire for safety and "secur-ity" which she refers to as "the most important and desired thing in life" (McDowell, ed. 235). A seemingly inconsequential scene with Brian under-scores this theme. Irene says that their son has learned some "dreadful jokes" about sex on the school playground, and Brian's angry response resonates beyond the specific situation: "The sooner and the more he learns about sex, the better for him. And most certainly if he learns it's a grand joke, the greatest in the world. It'll keep him from lots of disappointments later on" (McDowell, ed. 189). Brian's bitterness suggests that he knows he is only a pawn in Irene's master plan for domestic tranquility and social status within the black elite. Because he was once sexually attracted to a woman who is now a philistine, he is now forced to remain a doctor because it gives her a socially respectable and affluent position within the race. Also, the joke is on him because she is no longer interested in sex, as hinted in the fact that they have separate bedrooms (McDowell, ed. 224).

Irene worries about her son hearing "dirty jokes" because she sees sexual desire as uncontrollable, something that threatens her intelligent design for her family. Thus she can imagine an affair between Brian and Clare because Clare has said that she is "not safe," meaning she will not live by "any proper morals or sense of duty," and Brian suffers from "restlessness," wishing to flee to Brazil to escape not merely racist America but the domestic trap in which Irene has placed him (McDowell, ed. 210, 178). Paradoxically, Irene is both attracted to and appalled by Clare's desire to live on the edge. On the one hand, Clare represents "some wild ecstasy that she has never known" (McDowell, ed. 235). On the other hand, she associates Clare with the "menace of impermanence" (McDowell, ed. 229), the very thing she fears in her pursuit of safety, security, and permanence. The key moment in the novel is Irene's rejection of Clare's Dionysian energy for Apollonian order, and yet the novel's irony is that Irene's sexual desire will out in any event. As Freud famously noted, it takes the form of an aggressive instinct akin to murder.[11]

Irene complains of Clare's selfishness, her "having way" (McDowell, ed. 153), but it is Irene who has the "having way." Her husband Brian, she claims, is always "wanting things he can't have," but she is determined to "have" the things that she wants. She refuses to consider his desire to go to South America: "She belonged in this land of rising towers. She was an American. She grew from this soil, and she would not be uprooted" (McDowell, ed. 235). Although Irene claims to be loyal to the "race," what she's loyal to is American capitalism, "the rising towers." The image also has sexual implications, for Irene has assumed a masculine identity by becoming the head of her household. She insists upon directing "for their own best good the lives of her sons and her husband." She identifies with the phalli of the towers, an identification Brian refers to when he calls sex "the biggest joke of all."

Irene's surnames – her maiden name and her married name – are indications of her "American" character: "Westover" and "Redfield." The "west" being "over," Irene redefines the agrarian dream ("soil") as urban energy. She is ready to turn the fields red with blood to protect her turf. Larsen links the vertical "towers" with the horizontal house, the domestic "soil" that Irene will do anything to preserve. The house is an image of bourgeois aggressiveness and acquisitiveness, not an innocent image of family values. The link between "soil" and "towers" is a brilliant one, for it echoes the ending of *The Great Gatsby* in which the "green breast of the new world" is transformed overnight into Dutch commerce (New Amsterdam) and then Wall Street.[12]

So does Irene push Clare from the window to her death at the end of the novel? Certainly Irene is capable of murder, at least a thought-crime, once she thinks that Brian and Clare are having an affair: "If Clare should die! Then – Oh it was vile! To think, yes, to wish that! ... But the thought stayed with her" (McDowell, ed. 228). The thought is not the act, but then Clare does die and Irene passes out before we find out if the thought became the act. But one thing is certain: Irene does murder Clare indirectly by not informing Brian or Clare that Bellew had met her and Felise the previous afternoon. Felise is too dark to pass for white, and since she is in the company of Irene, Irene knows he can put two and two together. By remaining silent, Irene commits the sin of omission; it is the absent act that fulfills the thought. Larsen was no Marxist, but she saw with Marx that the discreet charm of the bourgeoisie hid the killer instinct.

Sexual desire in *Passing* then cannot be reduced to a simple theme. It is triangulated by the three major characters, all of whom desire on different planes. If Irene desires Clare, that desire turns to murder. Brian's desire for South America is a reflection of a desire for a world elsewhere, and Clare's desire for Brian, if it in fact exists, is a reflection of her desire to live in multiple worlds and to live multiple lives.

Sexual desire is also tied to social class. Throughout the novel, Irene assumes a moral superiority over Clare because Irene is grounded in the black bourgeoisie whereas Clare's father was an alcoholic janitor. Moreover, Irene has not married outside the race for "gain," whereas Clare is a selfish opportunist and a parvenu. Clare has married up but her world at the top is unstable. If the secret of her racial identity is revealed, it is a sudden descent to the bottom, and yet Irene's world is grounded on an illusion, especially as it concerns what Larsen calls her "security of place" (McDowell, ed. 190). Consider the scene early in the novel in which Clare invites Irene and a mutual friend Gertrude over to tea. At the outset, Irene seems to be the most sympathetic of the three. Both Gertrude and Clare have married white men for money, whereas Irene has married a black doctor. Our perspective changes when Gertrude, whose husband knows she's black, tells the story of someone they once knew who converted to Judaism. Clare and Gertrude assume that their mutual friend became a black Jew for a social advantage. Irene responds with righteous indignation: "It evidently doesn't occur to either you or Gertrude that he might possibly be sincere in changing his religion. Surely everyone doesn't do everything for gain" (McDowell, ed. 169). Clare doesn't miss the insult, nor the self-compliment made at her own and Gertrude's expense. What Clare urges Irene to consider is whether any person's motives are as simple and pure as the word "sincere" would indicate. Does not everyone on some level "pass"? A key theme in the novel is that Irene's "passing" is something fixed and inflexible; she claims to be a race woman but in fact embraces those "rising towers" as though they were her lovers. In contrast, Clare acts out her utopian impulse to live in a world where racial categories vanish, and she dies for her desire.

For Larsen, the utopian impulse remained an individual matter: the life you saved could only be your own. For Fisher, especially in his short stories, creating the Beloved Community in Harlem was never guaranteed but remained possible. The short story "Miss Cynthie" makes its point by signifying upon the first Hollywood movie to use sound, *The Jazz Singer* (1927). In the film Jewish Jakie Rabinowitz (Al Jolson) is on his way to becoming a Broadway star as Jack Robin. Anticipating his future fame, Jack boasts to his audience in a coffee house that "you ain't heard nothing yet," a line that overnight became the film's tag line. Later, as Jack is about to become famous as a "jazz singer," he wears black face and sings a sentimental song about his "Mammy," knowing that his Jewish mother is in the audience. When his mother hears him sing his song *about* her, she tells her brother that "he belongs to the whole world now."

Fisher puts the line "you ain't seen nothing yet" in David Tappen's mouth as he is showing his grandmother, Miss Cynthie, the architectural wonders of modern Harlem.[13] She has just arrived from Georgia and is impressed with the large buildings, especially the large churches. David, however, is taking her to the Lafayette theater to see him perform in a song and dance routine, not quite what the deeply religious Miss Cynthie expected. Her first impression of the theater is that it is a temple of sin. She is shocked by the stage's scantily dressed women and its bawdy humor. Yet when David sings a song to her, one she taught him in childhood, she changes her mind. The point of Fisher's allusion to *The Jazz Singer* is that David doesn't need black face to sing to the woman who nurtured him. His rendition of the song also implies that an urban reshaping of the past need not be a break with the past; rather, there is a continuity between folk traditions and modern interpretations of them. In *The Jazz Singer*, black face allows Jack Robin to finesse his relationship to American culture via mass culture. As Michael Rogin has noted, when he wears black face, Jakie/Jack can claim both a Jewish mother and a black "Mammy," but in fact he has neither. For black face is also Jack's way of saying that he's not Jewish but a white man. If you can put on burnt cork, you can also take it off.[14]

Like "Miss Cynthie," *The Conjure Man Dies* tries to find a utopian space within the historical reality of the Diaspora and the complex and often devastating presence of modernity. The novel opens with the lines from a blues song made famous by Jack Teagarden in 1931: "You Rascal You." Its lyrics, which will recur throughout the novel, are comic though its theme is deadly. The "rascal" in the song is the singer's wife's lover, and the singer wants him dead: "*I'll be glad when you're dead, you rascal you.*" The significant line in the song for the novel is not the singer's vengeful intent but one that poses a question: "*What is it that you've got/Makes my wife think you so hot*?" That question points to the mystery of Eros, the theme that haunts the novel.

The novel centers upon the "murder" of a conjure man, Frimbo, who turns out to be the king *in absentia* of the African kingdom of Buwongo. The "murder" is the novel's red herring, for the murderer has killed Frimbo's servant by mistake, thereby making Frimbo one of the four detectives trying to solve the crime. The other three detectives are Dr. John Archer, police detective Perry Dart, and Bubber Brown who is a working-class detective specializing in "monkey-business."[15] At the outset, Fisher uses the format of the classical detective tale, the murder taking place in the enclosed space of a house in Harlem, but as the novel develops, the "mean streets" of Dashiell Hammett's ground-breaking, hard-boiled detective novel *The Maltese Falcon* (1930) complicate the nature and end of detection.

Sexual desire is at the heart of the hard-boiled detective novel. Its overwhelming and persistent presence challenges the straightforward formula of crime being a "a game or puzzle" to be solved.[16] *The Maltese Falcon* begins as a puzzle (who killed Miles Archer?) but soon focuses on the sexual warfare between Sam Spade and Brigid O'Shaughnessy. Indeed, that warfare leads Spade to solve the crime of Archer's murder. Fisher's Dr. Archer is modeled on Sherlock Holmes and both he and Perry Dart operate as classical detectives, attempting to solve the crime of Frimbo's "murder" through ratiocination, empirical evidence, and the scientific method. So absorbed are they in their analysis of clues that they overlook the obvious. They both assume, on meager evidence, that sexual desire is not a factor in the crime, that Frimbo was a "woman hater" (*Conjure Man* 25, 93). For a different reason, Frimbo, too, considers sex to be no more important than "blowing one's nose," essential to "comfort" but trivial compared to his love of science (268). However, "blowing one's nose" is an act that will, eventually, get him killed. It is only the ex-street-cleaner/garbage collector Bubber who knows, as does Hammett's Sam Spade, what motivates human nature in general and city life in particular: "Don't matter how bad business gets, lovin' still goes on; and long as lovin' is goin' on, cheatin' is goin' on too" (49).

As is true of blues music, "business" and "monkey business" are intimately connected in the novel, the word "business" occurring multiple times in many contexts. Samuel Crouch the undertaker is all businessman, so cold hearted that he's pleased that his wife Martha had collected the rent before Frimbo died (88). Yet we discover that is not all Martha collected. While Crouch, the house's owner, was taking care of business, Frimbo was taking care of Crouch's business. That his wife is only one of Crouch's "possessions" (93) explains why Martha seeks consolation in Frimbo's bed, but she, as the novel's *femme fatale*, also points to the novel's real crime. That crime is articulated by the novel's most complex character: Frimbo.

On an obvious level, Frimbo's metamorphosis in the New World, including his mysterious death and rebirth, illustrates the American theme of the reinvention of the self. On a deeper, symbolic level, his memory of the Malindo, the feast of procreation that he witnessed as an adolescent in Africa, is connected to the fate of Africans in the New World. The organic wholeness he describes in the past is set against the Diaspora of the present; it is a memory of a lost order that echoes T. S. Eliot's Fisher King in *The Waste Land* (1922) who has "shored these fragments against my ruins."[17] Frimbo's nostalgic remembrance of the Malindo should also be juxtaposed with Casper Gutman's historical account of the Crusades in *The Maltese Falcon*, a pilgrimage of greed and "loot" whose ultimate manifestation was the slave trade.[18]

Frimbo tells Archer that the Malindo is a ritual reenacted every year. It is a rite of initiation for the young and a reminder to the adults of the source of the living tissue of the community. It occurs within a circle, the symbol of eternity (having no beginning and no end) and of the cosmos. The individuals in the community are mortal, but the community itself is renewed through sexual desire. The fire burning on the periphery of the ring is the fire that burns away mutability. The snake that emerges from the box is Damballah, the life force, not the symbol of evil as in Christianity.[19] The ring itself, which expands and contracts, is not simply the vagina but that which makes the invisible visible: a child mysteriously appears in the arms of the warrior and is transferred to the waiting arms of a maiden. She leaps from the fire with the child and offers it to the members of the community, who become its parents. Thus the sexual act is not a private affair, nor is it secular (for pleasure alone). In the nation of Buwongo, it is an expression of the community, reflecting the health of the polis and the sacred well springs of life.

In the New World, Frimbo lives a divided life, tied to the Old World through memory and yet transformed by the city. He confesses to Archer that he renounced his kingship of Buwongo because he loved the "adventure" of city life and that he wanted to embrace the intellectual tradition of western civilization (*Conjure Man* 215). Educated at Harvard, he comes to believe that modern science, especially the philosophy of determinism, has allowed him to escape the empirical world of cause and effect. His delusion is also compounded by something he has brought with him from the Old World: the rite of the gonad (269). Injecting himself with an extract from human testicles, he thinks that he has acquired a knowledge of the past, thereby permitting him to control the present and predict the future.

What he doesn't see is that the gonad is a part separated from the whole – testicle from penis, penis from body, body from community. Like the fragments found as clues to the murder, the rite of the gonad is a microcosm of the Diaspora. As a symbol of modernity, it also replaces the mythical with the physical. Moreover, it is exclusively a male rite. The Malindo expresses an equal partnership in the sexual act; both male and female powers are necessary for the community's cohesiveness. In contrast, Frimbo compartmentalizes his sexual life and remains oblivious to the effect that his sexual behavior has on others. It makes Crouch abandon his normal prudence, consuming him with a maddening rage. As the object of Frimbo's careless hedonism and Crouch's jealous possessiveness, Martha is the cause over which blood is shed. She is the goddess Erzulie (*Tell My Horse* 143–4), the Malindo's revenge on those who would trivialize the life force.

In *The Conjure Man Dies* the segmented space of the house symbolizes the lost organic order of the Malindo. The top two floors – second and third – are rented by the "pyschic" Frimbo, whereas Crouch uses the first floor for his undertaker establishment. The cellar contains the furnace, not only an important element in the plot but a parody of the fire of the Malindo, as are Frimbo's "artificial logs" in his fireplace (*Conjure Man* 213). The space of the house mirrors Harlem society in two ways, the divided self and the divided society. On one level, Frimbo and Crouch symbolize the gap between mind and body. On another level, the gap between them mirrors the gap between the Harlem Renaissance intellectuals and the business community. The fact that Crouch puts the Christian "chapel" in the basement adds another dimension to Harlem's fragmentation.

The house also reflects the enigma of Frimbo's character. In the room where he keeps human testicles in jars, he also places a television apparatus that attaches to the horizontal light in his consultation room. With his television monitor, he spies upon his clients. When he tells Archer about the Malindo, he not only becomes Walter Benjamin's "storyteller," he is having a face to face relationship, but hiding in another room as he watches his clients, he is engaging in surveillance. As Walter Benjamin notes, "looking at someone carries the implicit expectation that our look will be returned by the object of our gaze," but "the camera records our likeness without returning our gaze."[20] Here precisely is Frimbo's dilemma. Although he wants to believe that he represents a holistic medicine, combining both ancient and modern ways of healing, he may be only a confidence man, hiding behind smoke and mirrors. His preoccupation with the rite of the gonad and his own blackness isolates him not only from his patients but from reality itself. In Africa, black is the color of the universe, but in America his color becomes the source of his paranoia. "Why Frimbo was black" is the question that becomes his obsession (230). However, when he translates that question into the difference between Archer's skin color and his own, he exposes the "hidden truth" at the heart of the novel: "You are almost white. I am almost black. Find out why, and you will have solved a mystery" (230). As a detective, Frimbo can define the mystery (the mystery of "race"), but he cannot, as indeed no one can, locate its origin or point to its solution.

Bubber is the detective who ultimately finds the missing part that leads to the revelation of who murdered whom, but his discovery is not a celebration of street wisdom over intellectual wisdom. A doctor himself, Fisher identifies with Dr. Archer's passion for empirical evidence and his desire to "fit conclusions to the facts, not facts to conclusions" (78). Masters of the scientific method, Dr. Archer and Detective Dart assemble a mass of clues – fingerprints, bone (femur used as a club), bridge (teeth), handkerchief – to find the killer. They are all parts separated from their contexts, and through the process of ratiocination the two detectives hope to reconstruct the origin of the crime. Behind the classical detective tale is the Enlightenment tradition: Isaac Newton, natural law, and the clock-maker God. But the modern world is no longer a clock but a "moving mosaic" whose surface is always in flux. The modern city appears in "masquerade," a word that occurs in the novel as often as "business." Crouch, we remember, commits the crime disguised as Easley Jones, a railroad porter, who worries if "my wife . . . was true *to* me or f'ru *with* me" (129). What his masquerade exposes is that Eros is the great leveler, that social class (and, by implication, race) is a kind mystification, a sleight of hand. Crouch indulges in a form of "passing," and if he can pass for a Pullman porter, what keeps a Pullman porter from passing as him? Or for that matter, what keeps an illiterate guy like Bubber from passing as a detective? Archer and Dart can only solve the crime if they have someone like Bubber sifting through the garbage and poking into furnaces.

Bubber and his friend Jinx Jenkins are modeled on vaudeville caricatures or the newly popular radio show *Amos 'n' Andy*,[21] but we should not be misled by their verbal insults. Playing the "dozens" both hides and expresses a deep affection for the other, and it also serves another purpose. Frimbo retreats to science to escape his "blackness." Bubber and Jinx make jokes about it. Their verbal dexterity may be a sign that the lost order of the Old World is not completely lost. When Bubber enters the Hip-Toe club on Lenox Avenue looking for Doty Hicks, he encounters a female singer who says to the rotund Bubber, "You're short and broad, but sweet, oh Gawd!" Without missing a beat, Bubber, "who was as much a child of the city as she," responds: "You're long and tall and you've got it all" (103)! Here rhyming slang creates a bond that bridges the gap between self and other, male and female. Eros is made the basis of a momentary community; language in the city becomes a new kind of urban folklore.

The blues song that begins and ends the novel suggests something of Fisher's optimism about Harlem's future. Not only does the comic song reveal Frimbo's murderer, but its theme, language, and tone unite the community. It says in essence that love will kill you if you let it, but the humor of the song suggests something about the resiliency of human nature. The humor functions as a replacement for the lost world of the Malindo in which Eros too was seen in a larger context than individual desire.

Throughout his stories and novels, Fisher examines Harlem from multiple perspectives, sometimes taking a hard view, sometimes a soft view. At times he can be as realistic in his depiction of black urban life as Richard Wright; at other times, he can wrap his portrait of the city in pink ribbons. His first novel, *The Walls of Jericho* (1928), is a portrait, even possibly the germ of a screenplay, of an idealized Harlem. Indeed, Fisher ends *The Walls of Jericho* with a deliberate allusion to the ending of F. W. Murnau's *Sunrise* (1927), one of the best-loved films of the 1920s. Shine's van "Bess" climbs over a "crest beyond which spread sunrise like a promise." The van carrying Linda and Shine is seen against a "background of light" before it drops "abruptly out of vision, into another land" (293). In *Sunrise*, it is the Woman from the City (Margaret Livingston), the film's *femme fatale*, who disappears over the hill in a cart, leaving the rural landscape to the lovers as the sun rises on their happiness. The farmer and his wife have weathered the storm of the city and of nature and now form a perfect picture of family values in this pastoral world. For Fisher, however, utopian space lies in the city, not the country, and it is to that utopian space that his lovers, Linda and Shine, return.

Nella Larsen lacked Fisher's optimism and his faith in the black masses. She could never write a novel like *The Walls of Jericho* or a story like "Miss Cynthie." However, it is doubtful Fisher could have created a character like Helga Crane or Irene Redfield. His sense of the gothic was almost always undercut or qualified by comedy and/or melodramatic resolution. He had planned to write a series of detective novels, using both Dr. Archer and Perry Dart, but only got as far as writing a short story, "John Archer's Nose." Indeed, the short story is a literary form at which he excelled.[22] Although Larsen was an indifferent short story writer, her two novels haunt the imagination. No one who has read *Quicksand* and *Passing* can ever forget Helga, Irene, and Clare. They remain three of the most complex and interesting characters in the fiction of the Harlem Renaissance and all of American literature. Larsen's talent was to use domestic melodrama to express gothic themes, and in this sense she foreshadows Toni Morrison's *Beloved* (1987). Once considered minor writers, both Larsen and Fisher have emerged as two great literary figures of the Harlem Renaissance.

NOTES

1. Raymond Chandler, "The Simple Art of Murder," *Atlantic Monthly* 174 (December 1944), 59.
2. Hazel Carby, "It Jus Be's Dat Way Sometime: The Sexual Politics of Women's Blues," *Radical America* 20 (June–July 1986), 11.
3. Deborah McDowell, ed., *Quicksand and Passing* (New Brunswick, NJ: Rutgers University Press, 1986), p. 11.
4. Meredith Goldsmith, "Shopping to Pass, Passing to Shop: Consumer Self-Fashioning in the Fiction of Nella Larsen," in Lisa Botshon and Meredith Goldsmith, eds., *Middlebrow Moderns: Popular American Women Writers of the 1920s* (Boston: Northeastern University Press, 2003), pp. 266, 270.
5. Charles R. Larson, ed., *An Intimation of Things Distant: The Collected Fiction of Nella Larsen* (New York: Doubleday, 1992), p. 14.
6. R. D. Laing, *The Divided Self* (New York: Pantheon Books, 1969), pp. 45–7.
7. Ernest Hemingway, *The Sun Also Rises* (1926, New York: Scribner, 2003), p. 172.
8. Craig Werner, *A Change is Gonna Come: Music, Race & the Soul of America* (New York: Penguin, 1999), p. 134.
9. Anatole France, *Mother of Pearl*, trans. Frederic Chapman (New York: John Lane Co., 1927), p. 26.
10. Also, see Judith Butler, "Passing, Queering: Nella Larsen's Psychoanalytic Challenge," in *Bodies That Matter: On the Discursive Limits of "Sex"* (New York: Routledge, 1993), p. 180. Brian Carr, "Paranoid Interpretation, Desire's Nonobject, and Nella Larsen's *Passing*," *PMLA* 119 (March 2004), 287–91.
11. Sigmund Freud, *Civilization and Its Discontents*, trans. James Strachey (1929; New York: W. W. Norton, 1961), p. 68.
12. F. Scott Fitzgerald, *The Great Gatsby* (1925; New York: Simon and Schuster, 1995), p. 189.
13. John McCluskey, ed., *The City of Refuge: The Collected Stories of Rudolph Fisher* (Columbia: University of Missouri Press, 1987), p. 72.
14. Michael Rogin, *Blackface, White Noise: Jewish Immigrants in the Hollywood Melting Pot* (Berkeley: University of California Press, 1996), p. 112.
15. Rudolph Fisher, *The Conjure Man Dies* (1932; Ann Arbor: University of Michigan Press, 1992), p. 49.
16. John G. Cawelti, *Adventure, Mystery, and Romance: Formula Stories as Art and Popular Culture* (Chicago: University of Chicago Press, 1977), p. 99.
17. T. S. Eliot, *The Waste Land and Other Poems*, ed. Frank Kermode (New York: Penguin, 1998), p. 69, line 30.
18. Dashiell Hammett, *The Novels of Dashiell Hammett* (New York: Knopf, 1965), p. 376.

19. Zora Neale Hurston, *Tell My Horse* (1938; Berkeley, CA: Turtle Island, 1983), pp. 137–42; Janheinz Jahn, *Muntu: An Outline of the New African Culture*, trans. Marjorie Grene (New York: Grove Press, 1961), p. 43.

20. Walter Benjamin, "On Some Motifs in Baudelaire," in *Illuminations*, trans. Harry Zohn (New York: Schocken Books, 1969), p. 188.

21. First aired on radio in 1926, the show was originally called *Sam 'n' Henry*. By 1927, it was enormously popular with whites and blacks alike. As *Amos 'n' Andy*, the show made its debut on March 19, 1928. Its white creators, Charles Correll and Freeman Gosden, were also the voices of the two black characters who first migrated from Alabama to Chicago (as Sam and Henry) and then from Chicago to Harlem (as Amos and Andy). http://www.otr.com/amosandy.html.

22. Larsen wrote three short stories, but they are weak efforts compared to her novels. They can be found in *An Intimation of Things Distant: The Collected Fiction of Nella Larsen*. She was accused of plagiarism for her story "Sanctuary." See Thadious Davis, *Nella Larsen: Novelist of the Harlem Renaissance* (Baton Rouge: Louisiana State University Press, 1994), pp. 348–53.

12

WILLIAM J. MAXWELL

Banjo meets the Dark Princess: Claude McKay, W. E. B. Du Bois, and the transnational novel of the Harlem Renaissance

The most notorious bad review of the Harlem Renaissance peaks with an upset stomach and an itch for soap. In an installment of his regular "Browsing Reader" column in *The Crisis*, W. E. B. Du Bois accused Claude McKay's *Home to Harlem* (1928) of being nasty, brutish, too long, and largely unhygienic. "[F]or the most part," Du Bois confessed, McKay's best-selling novel "nauseates me, and after the dirtiest parts of its filth I feel distinctly like taking a bath."[1] Several features of *Home to Harlem* inspired this unusually embodied instance of reader response criticism. The novel fed the lechery of debased white bohemians, charged Du Bois, a smart set eager to project its own fantasies of "utter licentiousness" onto "black Harlem," and powerful enough within the New York publishing industry to do so in wide public view. McKay satisfied this small but influential constituency for transracial pornography with rare skill, Du Bois allowed, summoning "every art and emphasis to paint drunkenness, fighting, lascivious sexual promiscuity and utter absence of restraint in as bold and as bright colors as he can." Yet gilding the lily of decadence did not make for lean, harmoniously integrated fiction. *Home to Harlem* was "padded," deprived of a logical plot or "any artistic unity." It cried out for a well-wrought, well-scrubbed sequel free from a "dirty subject" and supplied with a "strong, well-knit as well as beautiful theme." Before any such sequel was forthcoming, Du Bois' review inspired a blistering private letter from McKay. Questioning the elder statesman's basic credentials as a critic and author of mimetic fiction, McKay mockingly pitied Du Bois' removal from "real life" forced by his role as a racial advocate.[2] "I should not be surprised when you mistake the art of life for nonsense and try to pass propaganda as life in art!," McKay pronounced. "Yours for more utter absence of restraint," he snapped in his signature line, convinced that down his road of excess lay classic realism rather than short-lived titillation or Negrophilic special pleading.

Du Bois' review and McKay's rejoinder have long been favorites of Harlem Renaissance scholarship. And for good reason: over and above their quotable vehemence, they illuminate a major fault-line in the history of the New Negro in New York. To adopt the evolutionary vocabulary of historian David Levering Lewis, the Du Bois–McKay clash dramatizes the split between the "Talented Tenth Renaissance" and the succeeding "Negro Renaissance" built by its freethinking charges.[3] The former, "Talented Tenth" stage of the rebirth, represented by Du Bois, set the scene of official Harlem from 1924 to mid-1926, and was sponsored by the Civil Rights magnates of the National Urban League (NUL) and the National Association for the Advancement of Colored People (NAACP) (xvii). In the face of public skepticism and pushy erotic daydreaming, this stage depended on a mainly non-lascivious collaboration between the well-heeled white liberals Zora Neale Hurston dubbed "Negrotarians" and the educated African American elite Du Bois himself labeled the "Talented Tenth" (xvii). The latter stage of the rebirth, the "Negro Renaissance," represented by McKay notwithstanding his foreign address and relatively advanced age, led the formal arm of black Manhattan culture from late-1926 until the Harlem Riot of 1935. This was a renaissance moment "increasingly dominated by the African-American artists themselves" – the "Niggerati," in the vulgate of Hurston's uptown Latin – whom the Negrotarian–Talented Tenth alliance had originally cultivated as proof of black capacity for full US citizenship (xvii–xviii). In the Du Bois–McKay quarrel over *Home to Harlem*, scholars have thus found vivid illustration of a movement in conflict and transition, shifting uneasily from one leadership class and one developmental rung to another, from a forthrightly reformist to a more self-consciously aesthetic staff and strategy.

No less significant for the ongoing historical reconstruction of the Harlem Renaissance, however, is Du Bois' overlooked review of the fictional sequel to *Home to Harlem* he had recommended that McKay produce. *Banjo*, the thick expatriate *Story without a Plot* McKay published in 1929 despite his general disdain for Du Bois' advice, struck the "Browsing Reader" as "a better book" than *Home*, and a more thoughtful one.[4] *Home to Harlem*'s gravest flaws had not been repaired in *Banjo*, Du Bois admitted. McKay's subtitle conceded that his work was "in no sense" a coherent novel, and he had furnished morally upright readers with cause to refill the tub: "Here are a lot of people whose chief business in life seems to be sexual intercourse, getting drunk, and fighting." All the same, McKay's "race philosophy" practically outweighed these uncorrected errors. Raised in the West Indies as "a direct descendant from Africa," he had come to know both Harlem and Europe, "and he philosophizes about the whole thing." McKay, in short, had matured into a mindful "international Negro." While not a taut piece of fiction, his *Banjo* shone as a "sort of international philosophy of the Negro race," a series of prizable meditations on black life considered as a transnational, transatlantic, and Diaspora-wide affair.

Du Bois did not say so explicitly, but McKay's follow-up to *Home to Harlem* had the virtue of entering Du Bois' orbit while escaping the earlier novel's Manhattan-centric gravity. *Banjo* retraced the worldly steps of Du Bois' own long fiction of 1928, *Dark Princess: A Romance*, a work calculated to seize the momentum of the renaissance back from McKay and other "Niggerati." In his *Story without a Plot*, McKay's "utter absence of restraint" targeted national boundaries as well as received bourgeois ideas of sexual and literary comportment. As a result, his race philosophy and fictional geography aligned themselves more closely than ever before with Du Bois' loftiest aspirations for New Negro outreach. Regardless of the brawl over *Home to Harlem*, Du Bois seems to have appreciated that *Banjo* joined *Dark Princess* in leading the fiction of the Harlem Renaissance on the headiest of foreign voyages. Du Bois' welcoming review of McKay's second novel thus deserves a higher profile as twenty-first-century critics reenvision the Harlem Renaissance as a global happening in addition to a sequence of New York stages. If this renaissance was in fact an international circuit reaching beyond what Alain Locke called the "parapets of prejudice and ... cramped horizons" of American racism,[5] then the flash of sympathy between the rebirth's Massachusetts-born grand old man and its Jamaican-born *enfant terrible* becomes a weighty episode of diasporan connection. Here, black internationalisms recognize their family resemblance across national limits as well as Harlem battle lines, in the process enlarging the imaginative scope of both the New Negro Movement and the longer lineage of black radicalism.

Banjo and *Dark Princess* are hardly the only fictions of the Harlem Renaissance to record the nomadic enthusiasms of the New Negro. As critic Brent Hayes Edwards explains, black intellectuals eagerly scrutinized the League of Nations and kindred western international institutions as they emerged in the wake of World War I, building by the 1920s "a multilingual and 'cosmopolitan' black print culture" of their own in the interstices of counter-international organizations such as Du Bois' Pan-African Congress and Marcus Garvey's Universal Negro Improvement Association (UNIA).[6] The imaginative products of this black print culture addressed the far reaches and corner pockets of the African Diaspora in Europe and the Americas – not least between the covers of those high-profile texts of African American literary modernism "considered to be paradigmatic articulations of Harlem" (293). Nella Larsen's *Quicksand* (1928), for example, the novel praised for good behavior in the very same issue of *The Crisis* that lambasted

Home to Harlem, transports its changeable protagonist from New York to Copenhagen and back again. The anxious drama of Larsen's second novel, *Passing* (1929), fitfully turns on the specter of a Harlem doctor's relocation to Brazil. *Tropic Death* (1926), the remarkable story collection by the Guyanese-Barbadian-Panamanian expatriate Eric Walrond, explores what Edwards terms "the intricacies of imperialism and labor migration in the Caribbean basin" (293). Even *Home to Harlem* focalizes a generous helping of its narration through Ray, an authorial double in the form of a well-educated Haitian immigrant to Afro-America. Little wonder, given this onslaught of expeditionary representation, that the most provocative modern European theory of the intellectual was moved to assess the global implications of Harlem cosmopolitanism. Composed as far from 125th Street as an Italian jail cell, the *Prison Notebooks* (written 1929–35) of Marxist philosopher Antonio Gramsci took time to ask whether the diasporic consciousness of the "surprising number of negro [*sic*] intellectuals who absorb American culture and technology" would result in a liberating black Zionism, or in the employment of African Americans as "agents" of US imperialism in "the conquest of the African market."[7]

The resolutely anti-imperialist transnationalism of *Banjo* and *Dark Princess* is nonetheless distinctive, breaking from all the renaissance fictions above in its unorthodox but assiduous black radicalism. Critic George Hutchinson is not wrong to mark the idiosyncratic differences of genre and ideology declared in the respective subtitles of Du Bois' and McKay's texts. On the one hand, Du Bois' *Romance*, a book unembarrassed to dedicate itself to the "Queen of Faerie," crosses a prose form "identified with feudal social structures" with the fantasy of a noble Marxian "High Command."[8] On the other hand, McKay's *Story without a Plot* ties an insatiably digressive picaresque tale to the everyday resistance of the lowborn, the unattached, and the proudly vulgar. Yet *Banjo*'s self-referential mention of "barbarous international romance"[9] concurs with Du Bois' review in splitting the difference between the two texts, and their greatest significance to the Harlem Renaissance lies in their underlying affinity. Both books aimed to resupply the New Negro Movement with militant prospects during its most aestheticized "Negro Renaissance" stage. Both accordingly insisted that the trope of the self-defending, left-leaning New Negro fashioned around the Red Summer of 1919 did not forever fade when the "Talented Tenth Renaissance" endorsed the soft-shell policy of "civil rights by copyright," or incremental black progress pursued through cultural means.[10] Both books expressed their militant revivalism through a common stock of transnational tropes and narrative hinges, even as each fabricated a distinct version of the "generic searching and mixture" that fictions of black radicalism frequently imagine as the proper register of the hard-to-imagine, politically redeemed future.[11] While the intellectual networks binding the modern black Diaspora were ironically tightened by "a series of self-defeating and abortive collaborations, a failure to translate even a basic grammar of blackness,"[12] the books together testify that the most radical interwar variant of this grammar was also structured by shared terms – terms seductive enough, in fact, to lure the dissonant likes of Du Bois and McKay into a singular form of joint authorship.

State-sponsored and adversarial transnationalisms

Paul Gilroy, the influential mapmaker of the "Black Atlantic," notes that the expressive culture of the modern black West is given to transposing the negative meanings of enforced movement. The transatlantic distribution of African peoples throughout Europe, the Americas, and the Caribbean creates the possibility of a truly cosmopolitan, multiethnic, and multinational Pan-Africanism, but only because of the equal breadth of the trade in West African slaves that flourished from 1450 until the end of the nineteenth century. "A concern with the Atlantic as a cultural and political system" was imposed on black thinkers by the multiple routes of the Middle Passage, scattering African lives and cultures around the ocean's shores.[13] Transforming imposition into possibility, and obligatory migration into voluntary pilgrimage, is thus perhaps the primary task of the black artist as internationalist. "What was initially felt to be a curse – the curse of homelessness or the curse of enforced exile," Gilroy explains, must be "affirmed [and] reconstructed as the basis of a privileged standpoint from which certain useful and critical perceptions about the modern world become more likely" (111).

In McKay's case, the period culminating in *Banjo* was one in which reconstructing the perceptual advantages of mandatory exile was no mere philosophical problem. National and imperial discipline enforced what McKay glossed as the international flight of his "vagabond soul," and Locke less flatteringly described as his "chronic and perverse truancy" from the home town of the Harlem Renaissance.[14] The long trek through Europe and North Africa that McKay launched soon after *Harlem Shadows* (1922), the book that launched Harlem Renaissance poetry, was something of a compulsory black Atlanticism: McKay could not have made it home to Harlem had he tried. Following his stay in the Soviet Union in 1922–23, the FBI issued orders to stop and search McKay to officials in every major American port. Though McKay did not tempt fate and attempt to reenter the USA until 1934, Bureau agents in Baltimore promptly advertised their diligent search for the renaissance man in a memo addressed to a young J. Edgar

Hoover, boasting of a "Local Police Department" on the "lookout" for one "Claude McKay (Colored)."[15] As he polished the manuscript of *Banjo* in Morocco in 1928, McKay discovered that his involvement with local anti-colonialists had stirred a similar wariness on the part of French police, who questioned him aggressively in hearing range of the British consul and contemplated various deportation strategies. Soon afterward, British authorities denied him entrance into Gibraltar, driving him back to Morocco to await page proofs from Harper and Brothers in Tangiers. From a frank letter written by a contact within the British government, McKay subsequently determined that the Foreign Office retained "a full record of [his] political and other activities" and would bar his admission to his native Jamaica along with all other "British Colonial and Protectorate Territories."[16] The McKay of the *Banjo* years, his travels regularly policed, was thus provided with every opportunity to perceive that black radical internationalists cultivated vagabond souls at the cost of criminalizing many chosen movements, and coercing some others. The curse of homelessness and enforced exile was not confined to the enslaved past, the bygone world of removal from Africa, but would need to be redeemed anew in an era of advanced, defensive imperialism. Both obligatory migration and voluntary pilgrimage could take place within the same twentieth-century instant, McKay learned, for black transnationalism braved redoubled western harassment even as it drew on the promise of western globalist reforms such as the League of Nations.

If *Banjo* is any indication, both obligatory migration and voluntary pilgrimage could also find room within the same twentieth-century black text. The pivotal story line of McKay's *Story without a Plot* concerns a small society of black docker-drifters who amble their way through the French port city of Marseilles. Though roaming is their daily business, these non-surfing "Beach Boys" return again and again to *La Fosse*, or the ditch, a densely packed red-light district in the Vieux Port quarter whose historical original would be destroyed by the Nazis for harboring French resistance fighters during World War II.[17] McKay fills out his cast of Mediterranean Beach Boys with an eye to the widest diasporan range. There is Bugsy, a dark-complected black nationalist from the Caribbean; the gently drunken Dengel, from Senegal; Goosey, a "high yellow," or light-skinned, middle-class African American; Malty, a West Indian more interested in music than radical politics; and Taloufa, a Nigerian unable to choose between Garveyism and the guitar. At the head of McKay's transnational band is an audacious escaped African American southerner, Lincoln Agrippa Daily, whose banjo-playing lends him the nickname that provides the book's title; and Ray, a Haitian intellectual refugee from *Home to Harlem*, here lodged even closer to McKay's narrative perspective. In *Banjo*'s first chapter, the

Beach Boys' will-to-travel is couched within a rank and file of needful rambling, a motley interracial assembly instructed by their motherlands that they cannot go home again:

> They were all on the beach, and there were many others beside them – white men, brown men, black men. Finns, Poles, Italians, Slavs, Maltese, Indians, Negroids, African Negroes, West Indian Negroes – deportées from America for violation of the United States immigration laws – afraid and ashamed to go back to their own lands, all dumped down in the great Provençal port, bumming a day's work, a meal, a drink, existing from hand to mouth, anyhow any way, between box car, tramp ship, bistro, and bordel.   (6)

In *Banjo*'s final chapter, the Beach Boys' will-to-travel is resharpened by a tightly aimed, racially pointed instrument: the mass issuance to black sailors of seamen's papers labeled "Nationality Doubtful" (312). The "chief topic of serious talk among colored seamen in all the ports," these papers removing a cardinal badge of modern identity are swiftly perceived as a concrete lesson on race and European citizenship: "Colored subjects were not wanted in Britain" (311). Yet the move to deprive the Beach Boys of the national belonging that paradoxically eases their international wandering also sparks an abstract radical history lecture. In Ray's authoritative judgment, western immigration and police officers, the belligerent unconscious of their imperial nations, "were strong-armed against the happy irresponsibility of the Negro in the face of civilization" (313). These enforcers of the same powers that "had despoiled [blacks] of their primitive soil" in Africa, that "had uprooted, enchained, transported, and transformed them to labor under its laws," had gone on to decide they could not tolerate joyful traveling within their own national "walls" (313–14). The countries of the West had created black vagabondage through the slave trade, but now sought to repulse or redirect it when invested with black free will – in *Banjo* as in McKay's life before it.

McKay's novel is thus framed by chapters in which tramping, particularly in shades of black, is revealed as a target for "the clubbers of helpless vagabonds" on the front lines of western discipline (314). In the nearly 300 pages sewn between these chapters, however, McKay presents countless sketches and discussions of black internationalism redeemed. Surprisingly, given McKay's early hajj to the Soviet Union, *Banjo* shows little attachment to the revisionist twentieth-century Marxism that fused Pan-African vistas with the program of the Communist International. McKay's own pioneering early-1920s role in the invention of progressive "Comintern" reports and theses on the "Negro Question" is transparently discounted,[18] with Ray preferring "the fine intellectual prerogative of doubt" to youthful dreams of "the association of his race with the social movements of the masses of civilization milling through the civilized machine" (324). Ray elsewhere admits his instinctive hatred for the white portion of the "proletarian spawn of civilization," and ingeniously transubstantiates this hatred into the springboard of his untethered revolutionary leftism: "I became a revolutionist because I have not only suffered with them, but have been victimized by them – just like my race" (270). Garveyism fares no better than organized communism as a suitable platform for emancipated black cosmopolitanism, even despite its greater representation among the Beach Boys, who compose a sampler pack of Black Atlantic ideologies as well as Black Atlantic nationalities. The UNIA's Jamaican head, declares Banjo, was little more than a fool unable to ward off the strong arm of civilization's police: "'Marcus Garvey was one nigger who had a chance to make his and hulp other folks make, and he took it and landed himself in prison'" (76). *Banjo*'s favored emplotting of liberation instead takes its cues from the incohesive, unsystematic movements of its title character. The Garvey-averse Banjo is the symbol, keeper, and bard of a free-form "dream of vagabondage" (11), a serial impulse toward "'going on the fly'" (317) in search of the best that has been heard and tasted freely. Banjo's mobile dream is fueled by a balanced disdain for regular wage labor and aristocratic leisure, for middle-class individualism and sober radical collectives. At his book's conclusion, just pages after the news that the Beach Boys may be frozen by devious seamen's papers, the formal indiscipline of McKay's *Story without a Plot* reveals its disciplined service to black globetrotters. "'Come on pardner,'" Banjo prods Ray in the text's last sentences, "'Wese got enough between us to beat it a long ways from here'" (326) – enough story, too, to outrun both fixity and predicted movement through ceaseless extension. In a *Story without a Plot* that is also a story without an end, McKay finally outruns a civilization resolved to stop the black vagabondage it has started.

For its part, Du Bois' personal reckoning with the not-so-secret policing of black travel arrived well after *Dark Princess*, and took the form of an arrested, rather than imperative, internationalism. For the first eight years of the 1950s, the "father of Pan-Africanism" was stripped of his passport and blocked from visiting any part of the Diaspora outside US territory, his American patriotism rendered doubtful by a late-life embrace of the Soviet Union. All the same, Du Bois' *Dark Princess*, his own favorite of his imaginative works, shares *Banjo*'s creative attention to each leg of the black transnational journey – the forced and the voluntary – and represents both, in common with McKay's fiction, as pressing modern concerns. "The Exile," the first of four parts of Du Bois' global *Romance*, begins with the "cold white fury" of an unjustly expelled African American intellectual.[19]

Matthew Towns stands on the deck of the *Orizaba*, a liner bound from New York to Antwerp, in no mood of Black Atlantic celebration. Once a Talented Tenth archetype at the University of Manhattan, his pursuit of a medical degree has been derailed by his inability to enroll in a required course in obstetrics. "'Do you think white women patients are going to have a nigger doctor delivering their babies?'," the Dean sputters, pushed into ugly frankness by Matthew's refusal of pity (4). Du Bois' hero takes the bitter truth not lying down, but on the run, recognizing that he is "a man outcast in his own native land!" (7). To his mother, an emblem of the buried royalty of the folk South who aptly makes her home in Prince James County, Virginia, Matthew curtly announces his solution to the nation's Negro problem: "'I'm through. I cannot and will not stand America longer. I'm off'" (5). Where he is off to is unimportant, a thing of "sheer accident" (5). That he is quitting the country is enough – under his own power but without a choice, and thus a proper exile according to Du Bois' withering recalculation of the Talented Tenth's native odds.

As Brent Hayes Edwards observes, the four numbered parts of *Dark Princess* are prefaced by carefully chosen dates, with the flight of Du Bois' "Exile" set in August 1923.[20] In Du Bois' own busy career, this date marked a journey to the Third Pan-African Congress in Lisbon, Portugal, and the "momentous first trip to Africa, to Liberia and Sierra Leone" that he took immediately after (235). In his 1940 autobiography *Dusk of Dawn* – there would be another – Du Bois claimed that his proudest day arrived on January 1, 1924, when "the United States made a gesture of courtesy, a little thing . . . but one so unusual it was epochal. President Coolidge . . . named me, an American Negro traveler, Envoy Extraordinary and Minister Plenipotentiary to Liberia . . . the special representative of the President of the United States to the President of Liberia, on the occasion of his inauguration."[21] Edwards wonders "how much of an echo we might hear between Du Bois' pompous title and the ridiculous epithet he confers on the Queen of Fairie in the dedication to *Dark Princess*" (235): namely, "Commander of the Bath; Grand Medallion of Merit; Litterarum Humanarum Doctor; Fidei Extensor; etc., etc." A note of self-parody as well as affectation may inhere in the text's inaugural date, providing a needed – though obscurely self-referential – cue to levity at the entrance into 300 demanding pages.

Considerably more overt, by contrast, is the direction to readers furnished by the coincidence of Matthew's departure to Europe and the moment of both the Third Pan-African Congress and the Fourth Congress of the Comintern, the latter the 1922–23 meeting at which McKay issued his influential "Report on the Negro Question." Du Bois' desire to convert Matthew's directionless exile into an ideal of purposeful cosmopolitanism is signaled by the open reference to this golden season of black internationalism. And it is clinched by the sumptuous (inter)state dinner which concludes the book's first part. Attended by deft white servants at a Berlin table "sheer with lace and linen, sparkling with silver and crystal," Matthew is introduced to the full beauty of the Indian Princess Kautilya he has met only that afternoon, and to the promise of an underground revolutionary International to rival the Comintern's, piloted by a floating directorate of all the Darker Races of the World (18). The ghost of McKay's communist past hovers above the well-appointed room, as the princess speaks of an "astonishing," inspirational Moscow "report on the Negroes of America" (22). The dinner-jacketed luxury, comically unsuited for a meeting of anticolonial insurgents, announces Du Bois' peculiar intent to synthesize communist and Talented Tenth politics, not to mention the hostile prose genres of the romance and the radical tract. Just as important, all the Du Boisian finery adds sensual ornament and erotic tension to a crucial narrative hinge also found in *Banjo*: the transition from a "state-sponsored" black transnationalism, forced by the racial exclusions of Euro-American national and imperial power, to a self-directed, adversarial black transnationalism, dedicated to unmaking precisely the former. In *Dark Princess*, this privileged turn and term within the imaginative grammar of black radicalism becomes a voluptuous object of elevated desire. Ironically assimilating the carnality of McKay's *Home to Harlem*, Du Bois' fiction uses every art and emphasis to relibidinalize black internationalism in as bold and as bright colors as he can.

Decolonized and other marriages

In one of Anglophone modernism's oddest brief encounters, Wyndham Lewis, the very model of the British modernist as fascist, devoted a section of his study *Paleface: The Philosophy of the "Melting Pot"* (1929) to none other than *Dark Princess*. Lewis casts Du Bois' book as a specimen of the "exceedingly partisan and bellicose attitude" adopted by black opponents of that "shallow cocksureness shown by many Palefaces."[22] He concedes his pride in discovering that Princess Kautilya is asked for her impression of Vorticism, the blasting and bombardiering avant-garde movement he superintended from London in 1914–15. Yet Lewis derides Kautilya's opinion to the effect that all the fractious "isms" of twentieth-century European art have schooled themselves in African aesthetics: "'The Congo,' said the Princess, 'is flooding the Acropolis'" (20). On the same disapproving note, he ends his survey of Du Bois' romance with the complaint that therein "Coloured Peoples are urged to develop a consciousness of *superiority*," a mere "change in [the] *colour*" of racial hierarchy, "rather than its total abolition" (41).

Lewis's unexpectedly acute reading of *Dark Princess*'s color complex finds its likeliest support in the ornate regal marriage that concludes the text's fourth and final part, "The Maharajah of Bwodpur." Here, the Dark Princess who holds this title stands at the altar "dressed in eastern style, royal in coloring, with no concession to Europe" (307). Her intended, a thoroughly resurrected Matthew, finds himself elevated into "the God-man, the Everlasting Power, the eternal and undying Soul" while rushing to the ceremony in a private airplane (305). Their love child, his existence revealed by Kautilya only at the wedding ceremony, is heralded from the surrounding "forest, with faint and silver applause of trumpets":

> "King of the Snows of Gaurisankar!"
> "Protector of Ganga the Holy!"
> "Incarnate Son of the Buddha!"
> "Grand Mughal of Utter India!"
> "Messenger and Messiah to all the Darker Worlds!" (311)

There is plenty of self-conscious superiority to go around in this climactic sequence, which makes the princess's Berlin dinner party look like a fast-food picnic. But not all of it is aimed at inverting the color hierarchies of western racism in a compensatory case for dark-skinned beauty and nobility. At bottom, the eccentric, synthetic pomp of Du Bois' marriage scene – futurist–Orientalist in aesthetics, royalist–communist in politics, and Hindic–Christian in religion – celebrates the union between "the red-black South and the yellow-brown East" he had earlier summoned in his contribution to Locke's *New Negro* anthology.[23] Through a political allegory tightly entwined with a romantic fantasy, *Dark Princess* finally projects a redeemed black transnationalism confident enough to nurture Afro-Asian alliance, a thing of spiritual syncretism and mutual anti-imperial self-interest. In the child of Kautilya and Matthew, the brown Messiah who incarnates the alliance's liberated future, a starry-eyed Du Bois foretells the coming of the 1955 Bandung Conference which gathered newborn African and Asian nations, the heyday of anticolonial struggle in the twentieth century.[24]

Both Bandung and marriage allegories would seem to be the farthest thing from McKay's mind and its arrant distaste for prophecy. *Banjo*'s dream of black vagabondage refuses most styles of accredited heterosexuality, whether normative, compulsory, or merely long-lasting. As critic Tom Lutz suggests, Ray's arrival in Marseilles prompts Banjo "to spend time with him instead of [his] women and make various protestations about the relative importance of male over female companionship."[25] The Haitian intellectual in turn embraces Banjo's brand of black vernacular music and black vernacular comradeship, discovering that he and other Beach Boys "possessed more potential power for racial salvation than the Negro literati, whose poverty of mind and purpose showed never any signs of enrichment, even though inflated above the common level and given an appearance of superiority" (322). Ray, his conclusions rhyming with McKay's, learns to choose the black vanguard of the lower depths over that of the Talented Tenth, and for reasons of racial renaissance as much as individual amusement. Tutored by the boys of the Ditch, he cobbles together a New Negro ethic adequate to an era of irregular decolonization, grasping "how to exist as a black boy in a white world and rid his conscience of the used-up hussy of white morality" (322). That this antiquated white morality is figured as a "used-up hussy" emphasizes the fact that McKay's alternative is as homosocial as it is racial; as Lutz notes, it is no accident that his text ends with Ray and Banjo lighting out for the territory free from women and the narrative resolution of marriage, restaging on French soil the typically "anti-social" American novelistic conclusion outed by Leslie Fiedler's *Love and Death in the American Novel* (1960) (59).

Yet it is nonetheless telling that Ray nearly misses the trip, insisting that "[i]t would have been a fine thing if we could have taken Latnah" (326), a passionate working girl with whom Banjo has lived, and Ray has slept. With her carefully nebulous "Near Eastern" identity – "I don't know whether she is Arabian or Persian or Indian. She knows all languages" (10) – Latnah serves as *Banjo*'s own Dark Princess, and McKay's text, no friend of settled heterosexuality, is nonetheless hesitant to abandon the potential for black–brown anti-imperial union she represents. Even in the ambiguous, untraditional affair between Ray and Banjo, moreover, McKay makes hay from the trope of the decolonized marriage earlier employed by Du Bois, cementing radical ties between Afro-America and the black Caribbean through the Boys' erotically charged affection. "'My twinkling stars, but this Marcelles is a most wonderful place foh meeting-up'": so says Banjo during his initial encounter with Ray, smitten with the Haitian's command of French and similar tokens of intraracial diversity (64). In such politically resonant love matches between the differently colonized, as in the common narrative hinge between state-sponsored and adversarial transnationalisms, McKay and Du Bois each inhabits a cherished strand of the other's sweeping radical fiction. Each stands alone on his title page, and stands in opposition to the other in almost every field beyond the book. But their colloquy throughout *Banjo* and *Dark Princess* attests that shared terms as well as necessary misrecognitions composed the lingua franca of Harlem Renaissance internationalism at its most inventively militant.

NOTES

1. W. E. B. Du Bois, "Review of Nella Larsen's *Quicksand*, Claude McKay's *Home to Harlem*, and Melville Herskovits' *The American Negro*," *Crisis* 35 (June 1928), 202.
2. Claude McKay to W. E. B. Du Bois, June 18, 1928, quoted in Wayne F. Cooper, *Claude McKay: Rebel Sojourner in the Harlem Renaissance. A Biography* (Baton Rouge: Louisiana State University Press, 1987), p. 244.
3. David Levering Lewis, "Introduction," in Lewis, ed., *The Portable Harlem Renaissance Reader* (New York: Viking, 1994), pp. xvii–xviii. Subsequent quotations will be noted parenthetically in the body of the chapter.
4. W. E. B. Du Bois, "Review of Claude McKay's *Banjo* and Nella Larsen's *Passing*," *Crisis* 36 (July 1929), 234.
5. Alain Locke, "The New Negro," in Locke, ed., *The New Negro* (1925; New York: Atheneum, 1992), p. 14.
6. Brent Hayes Edwards, "Three Ways to Translate the Harlem Renaissance," in Geneviève Fabre and Michel Feith, eds., *Temples for Tomorrow: Looking Back at the Harlem Renaissance* (Bloomington: Indiana University Press, 2001), p. 293. Subsequent quotations will be noted parenthetically in the body of the chapter.
7. Antonio Gramsci, *Selections from the Prison Notebooks*, ed. and trans. Quintin Hoare and Geoffrey Nowell Smith (New York: International Publishers, 1971), p. 21.
8. George Hutchinson, "The Novel of the Negro Renaissance," in Maryemma Graham, ed., *The Cambridge Companion to the African American Novel* (New York: Cambridge University Press, 2004), p. 65.
9. Claude McKay, *Banjo: A Story without a Plot* (1929; New York: Harcourt Brace Jovanovich, 1957), p. 69. Subsequent quotations will be noted parenthetically in the body of the chapter.
10. David Levering Lewis, "Parallels and Divergences: Assimilationist Strategies of Afro-American and Jewish Elites from 1910 to the Early 1930s," in Jack Salzman, ed., *Bridges and Boundaries: African Americans and American Jews* (New York: Braziller, 1992), p. 29.
11. Brent Hayes Edwards, *The Practice of Diaspora: Literature, Translation, and the Rise of Black Internationalism* (Cambridge, MA: Harvard University Press, 2003), p. 233.
12. Edwards, "Three Ways to Translate the Harlem Renaissance," p. 291.
13. Paul Gilroy, *The Black Atlantic: Modernity and Double Consciousness* (Cambridge, MA: Harvard University Press, 1993), p. 15. Subsequent quotations will be noted parenthetically in the body of the chapter.
14. Claude McKay to Harold Jackman, March 10, 1928, quoted in McKay's *Complete Poems*, ed. William J. Maxwell (Urbana: University of Illinois Press, 2004), p. xi; Alain Locke, "Spiritual Truancy," review of Claude McKay's *A Long Way from Home*, *New Challenge* 2 (Fall 1937), 81–5, at 82.
15. Federal Bureau of Investigation, March 23, 1923, Claude McKay file, no. 61–3497.
16. Daisy Postgate [Her Majesty's Office of Works] to Claude McKay, December 18, 1930, quoted in McKay's *Complete Poems*, p. xvii.

17. Edwards, *The Practice of Diaspora*, p. 189.
18. For an account of McKay's influence on the "Theses on the Negro Question" issued by the Fourth Congress of the Comintern, see William J. Maxwell, *New Negro, Old Left: African-American Writing and Communism between the Wars* (New York: Columbia University Press, 1999), pp. 63–93.
19. W. E. B. Du Bois, *Dark Princess: A Romance* (1928; Jackson: University Press of Mississippi, 1995), p. 3. Subsequent quotations will be noted parenthetically in the body of the chapter.
20. Edwards, *The Practice of Diaspora*, p. 235. Subsequent quotations will be noted parenthetically in the body of the chapter.
21. Quoted in Edwards, *The Practice of Diaspora*, p. 235.
22. Wyndham Lewis, *Paleface: The Philosophy of the "Melting Pot"* (London: Chatto and Windus, 1929), p. 29. Subsequent quotations will be noted parenthetically in the body of the chapter.
23. W. E. B. Du Bois, "The Negro Mind Reaches Out," in Locke, ed., *The New Negro*, p. 408.
24. For a reflection on the importance of the Bandung Conference, particularly in the thought of Du Bois, see Bill V. Mullen, *Afro-Orientalism* (Minneapolis: University of Minneapolis Press, 2004), p. 59.
25. Tom Lutz, "Claude McKay: Music, Sexuality, and Literary Cosmopolitanship," in Saadi A. Simawe, ed., *Black Orpheus: Music in African American Fiction from the Harlem Renaissance to Toni Morrison* (New York: Garland, 2000), p. 58. Subsequent quotations will be noted parenthetically in the body of the chapter.

13

CARL PEDERSEN

The Caribbean voices of Claude McKay and Eric Walrond

The Caribbean

Claude McKay and Eric Walrond have long been regarded as important figures of the Harlem Renaissance. They were not African Americans, however. McKay, born in Jamaica, and Walrond, born in present-day Guyana and raised in Barbados and Panama, were part of a large contingent of migrants from the Caribbean who came to the USA in the late nineteenth and early twentieth centuries. Their Caribbean origins had a profound influence on their attitude toward American race relations as well as on their literary development.

The impact of Caribbean immigrants on the Harlem Renaissance was widely noted at the time. As early as 1919, the editor Fenton Johnson wrote that "We of America owe much to the West Indian ... In every field of American life we find the West Indian pushing ahead and doing all in his power to uphold the dignity of the Negro race."[1] Yet there has been a tendency to subsume writers like McKay and Walrond into the American canon without taking full account of their Caribbean origins. There is a need to reclaim them for Caribbean literary history and to see them as precursors of major contemporary writers such as Derek Walcott, Caryl Phillips, Jamaica Kincaid, and Edwidge Danticat, who were born in the Caribbean but have lived in the USA for much of their writing lives.

In his last novel, *Banana Bottom* (1933), Claude McKay described the beginning of the twentieth century in Jamaica as a period of "inquietude" (45). That was somewhat of an understatement. Jamaica and other British colonies in the Caribbean were undergoing profound social, economic, and political upheavals that would contribute to the massive migration that took place from the 1890s to the 1920s.

McKay and Walrond spent their formative years on two islands that were deeply affected by the transition from a slave to a free economy after slavery was abolished in all British possessions in 1838. Sugar was the driving economic force in Jamaica and Barbados, two of the most successful islands of the black gulag archipelago in the Caribbean. From the mid-nineteenth century, the boom in the world sugar economy made Jamaica, Barbados, and other British possessions in the Caribbean single-crop societies using slave labor to process the precious commodity. The post-Emancipation era coincided with an increase in world sugar production that caused a drop in sugar prices that affected planters and former slaves in the Caribbean alike.

The process across the Caribbean was uneven. Planters in much of the Hispanic Caribbean and in Guyana and Trinidad made adjustments to the vagaries of the world sugar market, while many of the British colonies such as Barbados and Jamaica suffered. Economic hardship was compounded by a series of natural disasters such as earthquakes and hurricanes that periodically plagued the Caribbean.

Jamaican society after the 1860s was divided by geography and class. The Morant Bay riots of 1865 prompted fears among the Jamaican colonial authorities that Jamaica might devolve into a second Haiti with black rule. The governor's response to the unrest was consequently completely out of proportion to the threat. Accordingly, the British government imposed direct rule from London, called Crown Colony government, on the island in 1866. By the end of the nineteenth century, only a few islands remained outside this new political structure. Crown Colony government reinforced the widespread view that Afro-Caribbeans were unable to govern themselves. The divisions in Jamaican society were also reflected in geographical patterns. The well-to-do white and colored middle classes populated the coastal areas while the increasingly impoverished black peasantry retreated into the interior sections of the island or migrated to urban areas to find work. Between 1881 and 1911, the population of the capital, Kingston, increased by 55 percent.[2]

Not all blacks endured hardship in equal measure, however. Claude McKay was born in 1889 in the village of Nairne Castle, Clarendon parish, the son of a relatively prosperous farmer.[3] Despite the family's economic security, the course of McKay's early life in Jamaica epitomizes to some degree the social and cultural changes that were taking place on the island. His father passed on African tales to his children and through his occupation made McKay aware of the fickleness of the world market and its impact on agricultural development in Jamaica. His brother, U'Theo, a schoolteacher, introduced McKay to British literature and philosophy. As a youth, McKay came under the sway of an upper-class Englishman, Walter Jekyll. Jekyll had come to Jamaica in 1895 and was an avid collector of Jamaican folksongs and stories, some of which he published in *Jamaican Song and Story* (1907). Jekyll introduced the young McKay to German philosophy and poetry and urged him to write poetry in Jamaican dialect.

In the political sphere, McKay became familiar with free thought, widespread in Britain at the time, and Fabian socialism, whose most prominent disciple on the island was no less a figure than the Governor, Sydney Oliver.

These four seemingly disparate influences merged in McKay's early verse. Just before leaving for the United States in 1912, McKay published two volumes of poetry, *Songs of Jamaica* and *Constab Ballads*. His poetry remained bound to classical forms such as the sonnet. Yet the content of McKay's verse expressed the social conflicts and economic oppression that characterized Jamaica in the first decades of the twentieth century. Poems like "Hard Times" recorded the daily drudgery of the peasant class, while others like "Quashie to Buccra" touched on the sensitive topic of race relations.[4]

McKay's early dialect verse was part of the development of a national literature free from the constraints of the British literary tradition. Another early Jamaican poet, Thomas MacDermot, edited a series called the All-Jamaica Library, whose goal it was "to present to a Jamaican public ... a literary embodiment of Jamaican subjects. Poetry, Fiction, History and Essays, will be included, all dealing with Jamaica and Jamaicans and written by Jamaicans."[5] Throughout the Caribbean, similar stirrings of literary independence were in evidence in the first decades of the twentieth century. In Trinidad in the 1920s, C. L. R. James' realist fiction of the poor barrack-yards shocked polite Trinidadian society in much the same way as McKay's work did in Harlem.

Eric Walrond was born in 1898 in Georgetown, the capital of British Guiana (which changed its name to Guyana after independence in 1966).[6] His father was Guyanese, his mother Barbadian. Walrond was uprooted at a very young age. His father left for Panama in 1906 and his mother brought him and his siblings back to her birthplace. His mother was a member of the fundamentalist Christian Protestant sect the Plymouth Brethren. Walrond spent only five years on Barbados before his mother decided to uproot the family once again and join her husband in Panama. At that point, construction of the Panama Canal was well underway. The Canal project was perhaps the most visible marker of the US presence in the Caribbean in the wake of the Spanish American War. Many migrants from the islands flocked to the Isthmus to work on the project. McKay commented on this migratory flow in his 1912 poem "Peasants' Way o' Thinkin'":

> We hea' a callin' from Colon
> We hea' a callin' from Limon
> Let's quit de t'ankless toil an' fret
> Fe where a better pay we'll get.[7]

In Panama, Walrond eked out a living as a journalist, a profession he held onto after his arrival in New York in 1918.

Migrations

McKay and Walrond were part of a wave of Caribbean immigrants that escaped the natural disasters and economic decline of the islands and came to the United States in search of educational opportunity and/or gainful employment. From 1899 to 1932, 107,892 black immigrants came to the USA. By 1930, the year James Weldon Johnson published *Black Manhattan*, almost a quarter of Harlem residents came from the Caribbean.[8] It is significant that McKay did not travel directly to New York, but went instead to the rural South. He enrolled at Booker T. Washington's Tuskegee Institute with the intention of becoming an agronomist and returning to Jamaica to help improve economic conditions there. Discouraged by the rigid discipline of Tuskegee, McKay abandoned his plans and went to New York City. Here he quickly fell in with two groups at either end of Manhattan: radical Greenwich Village intellectuals and Caribbean and African American writers and intellectuals in Harlem.

Like many other Caribbean immigrants coming from societies in which blacks formed the majority, McKay was shocked by the viciousness of US racism. His reaction to the East St. Louis race riot of 1917 prompted one of his most famous poems, "If We Must Die." This poem bears the hallmark of most of McKay's verse after he abandoned Jamaican dialect: conventional form and radical content. The defiance expressed in "If We Must Die" anticipated some of the central concerns of the Harlem Renaissance: a sense of pride and a refusal to accommodate passively to white prerogatives.

In between McKay's and Walrond's arrival in the United States came another Caribbean immigrant who was to have a profound effect on the development of black nationalism in the 1920s and beyond. Marcus Garvey came to New York from Jamaica in 1916, bringing his black nationalist Universal Negro Improvement Association with him. Like McKay and Walrond would do later, Garvey traveled to England in 1912. The center of the Empire was an entirely different world from the provincial Jamaica he had left. On the boat bound for England, he read Booker T. Washington's autobiography *Up from Slavery*. In London, Garvey met the editor of *The African Times and Orient Review*, Mohamed Ali Duse, a Sudanese-Egyptian, who opened his mind to Pan-Africanism and introduced him to African history. These dual influences from an African American leader who, despite his accommodationist proclivities, encouraged black economic advancement, and an African who promoted black internationalism remained with Garvey throughout his life.

Garvey's black nationalism struck a chord among Africans in Africa and in the Diaspora. By 1924, the UNIA could boast of an estimated 6 million members spread throughout the Americas and Africa. In this sense, the UNIA was a truly transnational organization, promoting ties between the various branches around the world. Garvey welcomed delegates from the Caribbean and Africa to his headquarters in New York. McKay and Walrond could not but take into account the power and influence of their fellow Caribbean immigrant, though they approached him in different ways. Walrond became a journalist for the UNIA publication *The Negro World*, serving as first an assistant and then an associate editor from 1921 to 1923. However, from looking at the articles Walrond wrote for *The Negro World*, it is clear that he saw himself in the role of journalist and literary critic rather than as a propagandist for Garveyism. Indeed, as early as 1922 Walrond was complaining in the pages of Henry Ford's *Dearborn Independent* that African American writers were turning away from an examination of black folklife in favor of propagandistic tracts. When Walrond finally did offer an assessment of the Garvey movement, the tone was anything but flattering. In two articles, "The New Negro Faces America," published in *Current History* in February 1923, and "Imperator Africanus. Marcus Garvey: Menace or Promise?" published in *The Independent* in 1925, he focuses on the development of black leadership in the United States. For Walrond, the problem facing the New Negro was the lack of a broad-based organization with leaders attuned to African American race and a recognition of the place of African Americans in the modern world. According to Walrond, Washington was out of step with the times, W. E. B. Du Bois was too elitist, and Garvey was, simply, a "megalomaniac." Recognizing Garvey's achievement in forging an organization of uprooted southern blacks and immigrant Afro-Caribbeans, Walrond nevertheless repudiated the psychological panacea of the Back-to-Africa movement and roundly criticized Garvey's various business dealings. In short, Garvey emerged from these articles as having the potential for being a true leader, but one who squandered it on "fairy dreams" of African repatriation and grandiose schemes of black enterprise in the United States.

McKay, like Walrond, held a grudging admiration for Garvey, but kept his distance from the UNIA. In "Garvey as a Negro Moses," published in *The Liberator*, McKay assessed the appeal of Garvey's ideology. He concluded that Garvey's "spirit is revolutionary, but his intellect does not understand the significance of modern revolutionary developments."[9] In light of Garvey's Caribbean background, where blacks suffered from economic oppression and a prejudice based more on class than race, McKay found it difficult to comprehend Garvey's rejection of the struggle of black workers. McKay's article reflects the frustration of Cyril Briggs's African Blood Brotherhood in attempting to infiltrate the Garvey movement and win its membership over to the international communist movement.

Despite Garveyism's global reach, McKay felt that its ideology was too narrow and the UNIA needed to work in consort with other international revolutionary movements. To that end, McKay arranged for meetings held in the offices of *The Liberator* that brought black and white, American and Caribbean radicals together. Among those Caribbeans attending were Briggs from Nevis; Richard Moore from Barbados, who together with W. A. Domingo from Jamaica edited *The Emancipator*; and Otto Huiswoud of Dutch Guinea, who in 1923 would be the American Communist Party's official delegate to the Fourth Congress of the Comintern, and the Danish West Indian Hubert Harrison, who had joined the Socialist Party when he came to the United States in 1911. McKay wrote in his autobiography *A Long Way from Home* (1937) that the first meeting was devoted to "making the Garvey Back-to-Africa Movement . . . more class conscious" (109), something that Walrond would no doubt have applauded. Although nothing concrete came of these meetings, they demonstrate the ties between Caribbean intellectuals from Harlem and the Greenwich Village white radical set.

McKay's negative assessment of Garvey was nevertheless tinged with admiration for his achievements, and in 1940, in a biographical essay on Garvey in *Harlem: Negro Metropolis*, he concluded that Garvey provided blacks all over the world with "a finer feeling of race consciousness . . . If Marcus Garvey did not originate the phrase, New Negro, he at least made it popular" (177).

McKay's conception of the goals of the international revolutionary movement set him apart from the Bolshevik cause that he cautiously supported, however. Writing of the Irish revolution in *The Liberator*, McKay made it clear that "I love to think of communism liberating millions of city folk to go back to the land."[10] In his speech at the Fourth Congress of the Comintern, McKay expressed doubts about recruiting southern blacks to the communist cause, but praised the work of the Third International in fighting for the emancipation of all the workers of the world regardless of race. McKay summed up his views on the significance of the Bolshevik Revolution for blacks in the article "Soviet Russia and the Negro," published in *The Crisis*. The inability of western society to deal with the "Negro Question" was contrasted by McKay with the Soviet Union, which, owing to historical and demographic reasons, exhibited a natural solidarity with the aspirations of blacks and other subject peoples similar to that he saw in the Irish revolution. However, as his affinity with the dissident Soviet poet Sergei Essenin demonstrated, McKay, no doubt with his native Jamaica in mind, was at odds with the notion of a proletarian revolution and looked to those who worked the soil as a potential revolutionary force.

McKay published poems in the literary journal *Seven Arts* and the radical magazine *The Liberator*. As co-editor of *The Liberator*, he clashed with Michael Gold over the issue of proletarian art. Vehemently disagreeing with Gold's desire to, in McKay's words, make *The Liberator* "a popular proletarian magazine, printing doggerels from lumberjacks and stevedores and true revelations from chambermaids" (138) McKay left the magazine in 1922. He joined the Workers' Party, a quasi-communist organization. During a prolonged stay in London, McKay grew close to Sylvia Pankhurst's *Workers' Dreadnought* and published poems as well as articles dealing with the experience of black soldiers in Great Britain after World War I. Paradoxically enough, the poems McKay published in *The Workers' Dreadnought* for the most part failed to rise above the level of the doggerel he objected to in *The Liberator*. In 1922, he attended the Fourth Congress of the Comintern in Moscow along with another Caribbean, Otto Huiswoud. McKay gave a speech to the Congress, in which he praised the work of the Third International in its fight for the emancipation of all the workers of the world regardless of race. McKay's involvement in these various movements reflects the transnationalist bent of many of the Caribbean immigrants to the USA.

McKay's Caribbean voice found expression in some of the verse he published during the 1920s. Gone, however, were the experiments with dialect that suffused his Jamaican poetry. Gone, too, was the incisive cataloguing of peasant hardship and displacement. Employing classical poetical forms, McKay looked to the island of his birth with longing and nostalgia. The poem "The Tropics in New York" (1922) is a case in point. The first lines, with a litany of fruits such as bananas, avocados, tangerines, and mangoes, evoke the fecundity of the land. This sensory experience is undermined when it is made clear that these fruits lie behind a window in New York. The fruits of the Caribbean are detached commodities and have become a part of memory. The poet ends by weeping with pangs of longing for his homeland.

McKay did not forsake his "angry" verse, however. The sheaf of poems included in Alain Locke's anthology *The New Negro* (1925) contained verse expressing his outrage at the sad state of race relations in the United States (McKay was furious when Locke changed the title of one of the poems from "White House" to "White Houses" which McKay felt tempered his message).

Locke's anthology reflected the influence that Caribbean immigrants had on the Harlem Renaissance. Locke intended the volume to demonstrate the rise of blacks in the Diaspora as a cultural and transnationalist force in the postwar era. Walrond's story "The Palm Porch" was included alongside McKay's poetry. Arturo Schomburg from Puerto Rico and W. A. Domingo contributed essays that pointed to the past and future of the Caribbean presence in the United States. Domingo saw the growing links between Afro-Caribbean radicalism and African American support for liberation movements in the Caribbean and Africa as a positive sign for the future. Schomburg stressed the importance of studying the Caribbean and African American past in order to strengthen black identity for the present and future.

The presence of the Caribbean in New York, in political organizations as well as in literature and culture, inspired some African Americans to explore the culture of the islands. In the 1930s, Langston Hughes visited Cuba and Haiti and Zora Neale Hurston traveled to Jamaica and Haiti.

McKay's concerns over events in the Caribbean are evident in the three novels he published between 1928 and 1933: *Home to Harlem*, *Banjo*, and *Banana Bottom*. Taken together, these novels can be read as a trilogy that explores the lives of Africans in the Diaspora in the early twentieth century: from the interwar urban culture of Harlem, to migrants brought together in a French seaport in the Mediterranean in the late 1920s, to the rural culture of Jamaica at the beginning of the century.

McKay was clearly preoccupied with the American occupation of Haiti from 1915 to 1934 and sought to provide a counterimage to the traditional view of Haiti as the repository of chaos and savagery. It is no accident that Ray, a main protagonist in McKay's first two novels, is from Haiti, and not Jamaica. Ray had left Haiti after his father had been jailed for speaking out against the US occupation and his brother had been killed by US Marines. In *Home to Harlem*, Ray offers a diasporic interpretation of world history by going back to the ancient African civilizations of Dahomey, Benin, and Abyssinia, and praising the Haitian Revolution (1791–1804) which created the first black republic in the Western Hemisphere. Most of the reviews of the novel chose to focus on what many felt was McKay's gratuitous portrayal of the seamy side of Harlem life and so largely ignored the Caribbean element.

In a review in *The Crisis*, W. E. B. Du Bois claimed that McKay's second novel, *Banjo*, offered nothing less than an "international phiosophy of the Negro race."[11] In this novel, African diasporic cultural exchange takes place not in Harlem, but in Marseilles.

Situated between Europe and Africa, Marseilles was a center not only of world commerce but of cultural interchange. McKay stresses the modern, international character of Marseilles through his alter ego Ray, the Haitian intellectual.

McKay subtitled *Banjo* "a novel without a plot" and the lack of any rigid narrative is central to McKay's conception of the new black philosophy. The gang of the Ditch, made up of blacks from the United States, the Caribbean, and Africa, are often described as drifters, and their drifting suits a world in flux in the modern age. Clearly, McKay feels that the only way to survive the twists and turns of the modern age is to possess a fluid adaptive capability, while retaining a strong sense of identity. The simultaneous phenomena of structure and improvisation that characterize black musical expression create a solid bulwark of cultural defense against appropriation and exploitation. The ongoing conflict between civilization (respectability) and what McKay terms bawdiness (obscenity, sexual drive) is played out in the physical space of Marseilles, between the respectable east and the degenerate west, the low-lying and low-life section of the Ditch, populated by sailors and migrants from around the world.

It is in the Ditch that Banjo, from the American South, decides to form a group of musicians to play at the bars and cafés by the waterfront. The efforts to form this group provide the only narrative drive of the novel, and it is striking that McKay at several instances voices his opposition to joining specifically political movements. Goosey, the Garveyite, who is "squeamish" about the kind of music the group should play, is contrasted with the West African Taloufa, who "loved all music with a lilt" (102). It is the politics of cultural dissemination and not social organization that is paramount in McKay's conception of a Pan-African sensibility. The links between Africans, West Indians, and African Americans are forged by folk and music tradition, and not political ideology. This tradition, extending from Africa to the Diaspora, is characterized by rhythmic variations, not rigid ideological doctrines:

> They played the "beguin," which was just a Martinique variant of the "jelly-roll" or the Jamaican "burru" or the Senegalese "bombé."..."Beguin," "jelly-roll," "burru," "bombé," no matter what the name may be, Negroes are ever so beautiful and magical when they do that gorgeous sublimation of the primitive African sex feeling. In its thousand varied patterns, depending so much on individual rhythm, so little on formal movement, this dance is the key to the African rhythm of life. (105)

McKay's sensitivity to the cultural force of these interrelated music and dance forms is marred by his efforts to link them with what he calls "the primitive African sex feeling." In doing so, he commits the same error that his intellectual disciples, Francophone *nègritude* writers like Aimé Césaire and Léopold Senghor, were guilty of: a biological determinism that ultimately contradicts the openness McKay sees in African diasporic culture. Ray's close relationship with Banjo in the novel exemplifies the connection McKay sees between black musical and literary expression. Here again McKay emphasizes the transatlantic nature of black literary tradition: Ray, with his Haitian background, is keenly aware of his Caribbean heritage, is trying to write about his experiences in the United States and Europe, and has read a classic of African literature, René Maran's *Batouala*. In his diatribes against the gentility of the African American intelligentsia, and the Martinican student who applaudes the banning of Batouala on his native island, Ray allies himself with the gang of the Ditch, who draw on musical traditions which are also disparaged by the black cultural elite in the United States and the Caribbean.

With the short stories set in Jamaica that form part of the collection *Gingertown* (1932) and in his last novel *Banana Bottom* (1933), McKay returns to his native land. *Banana Bottom* is a critical meditation on the conflicts that drive Jamaican society around the turn of the century. He portrays the waning influence of missionaries such as the married couple the Craigs, who take the main protagonist, Bita Plant, under their wing. Years before Zora Neale Hurston's novel of black rural culture in Florida, *Their Eyes Were Watching God* (1937), McKay described the resilience of the black peasantry in the interior of Jamaica. Bita Plant has received a proper British education abroad and returns to the small village of Jubilee ready to continue the work of the Craigs. However, she grows increasingly intolerant of their narrow-mindedness and artificiality, and finds herself drawn toward the indigenous culture of the island. Unfortunately, McKay injects a thinly veiled Walter Jekyll in the figure of Squire Gensir, as a mentor for Bita. Gensir represents the kind face of British colonialism, adopting a patronizing attitude toward his protégée in order to make her realize her intimate connection with the Jamaican folk.

In spite of these flaws, McKay's last novel is a penetrating examination of a Jamaica caught between the colonial legacy of the past and the profound social and economic changes taking place at the dawn of the twentieth century, where some inhabitants of Jubilee are forced to leave Jamaica to work on the Panama Canal, and where the farmers fall victim to the fluctuations of a fickle world market, much the same as the motley group portrayed in *Banjo* succumb to the power of world commerce.

Two years before McKay published his first novel, Walrond published his only collection of short stories, *Tropic Death*. Whereas McKay did not return to a Caribbean setting before his last novel, the stories in *Tropic Death* are all set in Guyana, Barbados, and Panama. When *Tropic Death* was published in 1926, it stood out from other fiction of the period. McKay had published a smattering of poetry expressing a longing for his island home. A number of essays dealing with the Caribbean had graced the pages of African American newspapers, magazines, and anthologies. But here, at the height of what was to become known as the Harlem

Renaissance, was a fictional work written by a Caribbean immigrant, set entirely in the Caribbean basin, and with most of the dialogue in Caribbean dialect. Americans, if they did appear, were unwelcome intruders, tourists on cruise ships deriving pleasure from black boys diving for coins. However, the Caribbean Walrond depicted in the ten stories that make up *Tropic Death* is far from the tourist haven that still characterizes American perceptions of the region. Walrond's Caribbean is beset by displacement, deprivation, and desperation. Mysterious deaths, remote settings, and Caribbean religious rituals like obeah and voodoo lend a gothic quality to the stories. *Tropic Death* is both a modernist literary experiment and an incisive critique of the debilitating force of British imperialism and American neocolonialism.

Most of the stories in the volume have a timelessness about them and could easily describe the hardships of the black lower classes in parts of the present-day Caribbean. However, there are sporadic hints that place the stories in the first decade of the twentieth century – the soldier of fortune returning from South Africa to his plantation in Barbados after the end of the Boer War (1899–1902) in "The Vampire Bat," the coronation of King George V and Queen Mary in 1911 in "Tropic Death," and of course references to the construction of the Panama Canal (1904–14).

In a nod to Jean Toomer's slim volume of sketches, poems, and stories from the American South, *Cane* (1923), Walrond introduces the setting of the first story, "Drought," with the following words: "It wasn't Sepia, Georgia, but a backwoods village in Barbados" (190).

In this first story, drought sucks the life out of the tropics, leaving the dry, white marl that kills the child Beryl, who attempts to quell her hunger pains by eating it. The black peasants of Barbados eke out a meager existence by working the white earth in a quarry, but nevertheless maintain the customs of polite English society, taking tea in the afternoon. Whiteness literally drains the life out of the peasantry.

In "Vampire Bat," the colonized wreak vengeance on the colonizer when the plantation owner Bellon Prout is killed by a vampire bat that is described as "weirdly interchangeable" with a black child (252).

"The Wharf Rats" provides an interesting parallel to McKay's later novel *Banjo* about black migrant laborers in Marseilles. The laborers of Walrond's story are described as a "motley crew," "dusky peons of those coral isles in the Caribbean ruled by Britain, France, and Holland" (210). The life of one wharf rat is cut senselessly short when he is attacked by a shark while diving for coins thrown from a cruise ship.

Even though most of the stories of *Tropic Death* are drawn from Walrond's childhood and youth in Guyana, Barbados, and Panama, the title story is the most autobiographical. A young boy, Gerald Bright, is the son of a devout member of the Plymouth Brethren, who takes him on a harrowing trip to Panama to reunite with his father.

Walrond continued his involvement with Harlem journals after leaving the editorial staff of *Negro World* and worked as business manager of *Opportunity* from 1925 to 1927. In the middle of his tenure at the journal, Walrond helped put together a special issue on the Caribbean. The journal also stressed the international character of the New Negro Movement, as Locke had done two years before:

> The Anglo-African, that is the English-speaking Negro, both in America and in the British possessions, is becoming internationally minded with regard to his blood brethren. The World War, the Pan-African Congresses, fostered with prophetic vision by Dr Burghardt Du Bois, the phantasmagoria of the Garvey program, René Maran's *Batouala*, increase in European travel, had forced the international thought both upon the Negro intellectuals and the Negro masses.[12]

Unlike McKay, Walrond did make it back to the Caribbean. In 1928, he traveled to a number of islands. Walrond's next book project after *Tropic Death* was to be a non-fictional work, *The Big Ditch*, on the building of the Panama Canal. He went to France in 1929 to work on it.

As far as is known, nothing ever came of Walrond's project on the Panama Canal, though he did write several articles on Panama for Spanish and French publications during his stay in France from 1929 to 1933.

In 1933 he moved to London. The year after, Marcus Garvey transferred the headquarters of the UNIA from Jamaica to London. There, he started publication of a magazine, *The Black Man*. Walrond began writing for *The Black Man* in 1936. His articles on England examine the lives of black seamen living in segregated enclaves in Cardiff, Liverpool, Tyneside, and London and criticize British colonial policies. In this respect, Walrond seemed to be moving away from classical Garveyism, with its notions of black capitalism and racial politics, toward a more class-based, anti-capitalist worldview. His articles reveal that Walrond maintained his distance from Garveyism even while contributing to the official organ of the UNIA.

Both McKay and Walrond faded into obscurity toward the end of their lives. McKay died, sick and penniless, in Chicago in 1948. Walrond died in London in 1966. They never returned to the Caribbean.

Legacy

The Caribbean presence during the Harlem Renaissance was strong and long-lasting, and affected many aspects of life in Harlem in the

1920s – political movements as well as social and cultural life. The influence of writers like McKay and Walrond went far beyond the confines of Harlem, however. *Banjo* had a marked impact on black Francophone intellectuals in Paris in the 1930s. *Banana Bottom* has been widely regarded as one of the first examples of the modern Caribbean literary tradition. If anything, this Caribbean influence is stronger today than in the 1920s, especially in Florida and New York. Dominicans are now the largest single ethnic group in New York City. New York is also home to a sizeable number of immigrants from McKay and Walrond's home islands of Jamaica and Barbados. A number of writers born in the Caribbean either have settled in the United States or have lived there for longer periods – Derek Walcott from St. Lucia, Jamaica Kincaid from Antigua, Paule Marshall from Barbados, Edwidge Danticat from Haiti, Caryl Phillips from St. Kitts, and Fred D'Aguiar from Guyana. Much of their work covers ground first traversed by McKay and Walrond. Jamaica Kincaid's first novel *Annie John* (1986) is clearly indebted to *Banana Bottom*. Caryl Phillips' itinerant wanderings, recorded in *Atlantic Sound* (2000), harken back to the travels of McKay and Walrond. Owing to modern means of transportation and communication, most recent immigrants, unlike McKay and Walrond, maintain close ties with the islands of their birth. Unlike McKay and Walrond, whose work was relatively marginalized during their lifetimes and has received belated recognition as an integral part of the Harlem Renaissance through work done by black studies scholars from the 1970s onwards, the work of current Caribbean writers who live or have lived in the United States is widely appreciated. Perhaps the most prominent example is Nobel Prize winner Derek Walcott from St. Lucia, who has lived in Boston for much of his life.

Claude McKay and to a lesser extent Eric Walrond are firmly ensconced in the pantheon of Harlem Renaissance literary luminaries. This position has tended to downplay their Caribbean origins and their singular contribution to the development of a distinct Caribbean voice in contemporary literature. Increasingly, however, they are achieving recognition as Caribbean writers. For example, a short story from McKay's *Gingertown*, "The Strange Burial of Sue," was anthologized in a volume of stories from the Caribbean called *Rhythm and Revolt: Tales of the Antilles* (1995). *The Routledge Reader in Caribbean Literature* (1996) includes some of McKay's early dialect poetry. A new anthology *"Look for Me All Around You": Anglophone Caribbean Immigrants in the Harlem Renaissance* (2005) includes work by McKay and Walrond.

It is worth noting that McKay spent only about twenty-two of his fifty-nine years in the United States, and lived outside of Harlem for most of the 1920s. Walrond was in the United States for ten years and left in 1928, never to return. To be sure, both McKay and Walrond were heavily involved in the literary debates and political activities associated with the Renaissance, but their writings and political affiliations reflect their Caribbean backgrounds. They deserve to be seen as part of a postcolonial Caribbean tradition.

NOTES

1. Winston James, *Holding Aloft the Banner of Ethiopia: Caribbean Radicalism in Early Twentieth-Century America* (London: Verso, 1998), p. 1.
2. Ibid. p. 22.
3. For biographical details on McKay, see Wayne Cooper, *Claude McKay: Rebel Sojourner in the Harlem Renaissance* (Baton Rouge: Louisiana State University Press, 1987); Tyrone Tillery, *Claude McKay: A Black Poet's Struggle for Identity* (Amherst: University of Massachusetts Press, 1992); and Winston James, *A Fierce Hatred of Injustice: Claude McKay's Jamaica and His Poetry of Rebellion* (London: Verso, 2000).
4. For excerpts and discussion of McKay's Jamaican poetry, see James, *Fierce*.
5. Quoted in Alison Donnell and Sarah Lawson Welsh, *The Routledge Reader in Caribbean Literature* (London: Routledge, 1996), p. 27.
6. For details of Walrond's life, see the introduction to Louis J. Parascandola, ed., *"Winds Can Wake Up the Dead": An Eric Walrond Reader* (Detroit: Wayne State University Press, 1998).
7. James, *Fierce*, p. 214.
8. James, *Holding Aloft*, p. 12.
9. Claude McKay, "Garvey as a Negro Moses," in Wayne Cooper, ed., *The Passion of Claude McKay* (New York: Schocken Books, 1973), p. 67.
10. Claude McKay, "How Black Sees Green and Red" in Cooper, ed., *Passion*, p. 61.
11. Du Bois quoted in Melvin Dixon, *Ride Out the Wilderness* (Champaign: University of Illinois Press, 1987), p. 49.
12. Quoted in Michael J. Dash, *Haiti and the United States* (New York: St. Martin's Press, 1988), p. 47.

14

J. MARTIN FAVOR

George Schuyler and Wallace Thurman: two satirists of the Harlem Renaissance

One of the effects of the Harlem Renaissance was to bring people of disparate backgrounds together in common cause. Such was the case with George Schuyler and Wallace Thurman, two of the era's major satirists. Schuyler was born in Providence, Rhode Island in 1895 and raised in Syracuse, New York. He started writing while serving in the United States Army and moved on to a long and controversial career that lasted until his death in 1977. Wallace Thurman was born (1902) and raised in Salt Lake City, Utah; he was educated at both the University of Utah and the University of Southern California before coming to New York City in 1925. Thurman's career was both exceptional and tragically short; he died of tuberculosis in 1934. Despite their different backgrounds, both writers ended up moving in important Harlem Renaissance literary and intellectual circles from 1925 onwards. By the same token, both Schuyler and Thurman ended up adopting significant and very complex roles as intellectual champions of some of the movement's prime ideals and as satirical excoriators on the age's foibles and excesses. Thurman and Schuyler took seriously the discussions of race and culture that circulated all around them, but they refused to see the major social and aesthetic concerns of the time as anything that could be easily understood, corrected, or improved. Their interventions into the political and artistic discourses of the 1920s and 30s were meant to counteract the romanticization of Harlem at that time and provide for their readers a healthy skepticism toward issues of race, color, nationalism, and conformism.

George Schuyler is most famous for his 1931 novel *Black No More*, a satirical book which is part science fiction, part roman à clef and part political thriller. His second novel, *Slaves Today: A Story of Liberia*, has been less studied and discussed. Schuyler also published several novellas and short stories – including *Black Empire* (published serially from 1933 to 1938) – in the *Pittsburgh Courier* under the pseudonym Samuel I. Brooks. The *Courier* was an important African American newspaper with a national circulation and an organization with which Schuyler had a long history as a reporter, columnist, and editor. Wallace Thurman is best known for his 1929 novel *The Blacker the Berry* and his 1932 book *Infants of the Spring*. Along with these novels, he authored the stage play *Harlem* and co-founded two important, if very short-lived, literary journals, *Harlem* and *Fire!!*. In virtually all their writings what ties Schuyler and Thurman together is a caustic wit directed at the customs, mores, and politics of their contemporaries.

One may argue that it is precisely this use of humor and these attacks on convention that have rendered Schuyler and Thurman as "marginal" or "minor" figures within the Harlem Renaissance. Because their characters may come off as ciphers, types, or caricatures to a reader expecting a certain type of social realism in a novel, several critics have underestimated the significance of these writers. Bernard Bell, for instance, concludes that "their goal was a form of humanism that sought to lift lower-class blacks out of their ethnic community to the spurious perfection of assimilation in the larger white community."[1] As we shall see on closer inspection of their works, however, the very idea of assimilation strikes both Schuyler and Thurman as something that is, on the one hand, always already achieved amongst all classes of African Americans and, on the other, an absurd notion that only serves to stifle the individual's creative and expressive potential. Dexter Gordon, tracing African American humor to an origin in southern folk culture, claims that "Blacks transplanted to the cities used humor to celebrate their folk culture [and] by the 1930s this celebration became a protest against racism."[2] Yet this "return" to roots as a prime motivator is difficult to argue in the cases of Thurman and Schuyler, given their migration to Harlem from decidedly non-southern and non-folk locales.[3] Even their contemporary, the poet Sterling Brown, characterized their work – within ten years of its publication – as showing "little depth of character" and having the "flippancy of many literati" and "the carelessness of the hedonist and the lighter touch of the satirist." In the end, for Brown, these works are "good-natured 'spoofs.'"[4] Yet I would not want to minimize the role that satire plays in African American literature or the very serious way that Schuyler and Thurman felt about comedy. Indeed, one of the things Thurman and Schuyler most deeply felt about the Harlem Renaissance was that it was in itself dangerously faddish, superficial, and intellectually suspect, especially among its self-proclaimed leaders. Their satires seek to expose the foundational weaknesses of New Negro cultural assumptions. In the end we might productively extrapolate from Terrell Scott Herring's observation on Thurman's *Infants of the Spring* that such satires work "as modern allegories, [their] characters do function as ciphers in order to illuminate the various clashing problematics of the New Negro Movement."[5] Such satire functions to alert its reader to the intellectual incongruities that we might gloss over or naturalize in everyday life.

George Schuyler and Wallace Thurman's urge to satirize did not arise in a cultural vacuum. Their work is meant not simply to be amusing or mean spirited but rather to address under- or unexamined cultural assumptions. Their mode of writing has historical precedent within African American literary history, and it found inspiration and support in one contemporary, white American in particular, the author and journalist H. L. Mencken, perhaps most noted for his acerbic coverage of the Scopes evolution trial in 1925. In 1926 Mencken was lauded as "the most powerful personal influence on this whole generation of educated people," and his influence certainly extended across the color line.[6] Students of African American literature may most vividly remember Mencken's influence from an anecdote Richard Wright recounts in his autobiography *Black Boy*; Wright tells of his fascination with Mencken but not being allowed to check out books from a segregated library. His solution to this dilemma is to borrow a white man's library card and forge a note that reads: "Will you please let this nigger boy . . . have some books by H. L. Mencken?"[7] Critic Eleanor van Notten argues that while attending USC, Thurman's "most important discovery was the work of H. L. Mencken" and that "not only was Thurman fascinated by Mencken's relentless assaults on the so-called American 'booboisie,' but he was attracted to the idea of the artist-iconoclast . . . at odds with the inherently stupid masses."[8] Examples of Mencken's influence on Thurman's writing can be found in *Infants of the Spring*, in which he writes: "Fifty Percent of [African Americans] never think about [racial identity]. They go about their business, happy in their menial jobs, enjoying themselves while and as they may. The rest . . . the educated minority and middle class have that memorable American urge to keep up with the Joneses."[9] Such a sentiment clearly echoes Mencken's own appraisal of American politics more generally, and any close study of Thurman and Schuyler reveals that this type of satiric take on American culture on either side of the color line occurs rather frequently.

George Schuyler was sometimes known as the "Black Mencken," and indeed his articles appeared "more frequently in [*American Mercury*, the significant journal of cultural and literary criticism] in the final six years of Mencken's editorship than [those of] any other writer, white or black."[10] Indeed, critic John Gruesser attributes much of Schuyler's influence during his lifetime to his "unprecedented access to mainstream publications, such as H. L. Mencken's *American Mercury*."[11] Mencken himself published a number of significant Harlem Renaissance writers in the *American Mercury*, and had correspondence with such figures as W. E. B. Du Bois, Countee Cullen, James Weldon Johnson, Walter White, and Claude McKay even as he rejected the young Ernest Hemingway for publication. He retained a special fondness for Schuyler, however, whom he later called "the most competent Negro journalist ever heard of" and "the best columnist, of any race, now in practice in the United States."[12] In return, Schuyler describes Mencken as "always favorably disposed toward Negro writers who had anything to say" and was honored to have been asked by Mencken to write an article on race in America that "was an irreverent, slashing appraisal which so delighted Mencken he made it the lead article."[13] Although Mencken was a powerful role model and patron, he was not the only influence on Thurman and Schuyler.

Both Wallace Thurman and George Schuyler served as associate editor of *The Messenger*, a publication founded by A. Philip Randolph and Chandler Owen, which sought to challenge the NAACP's *Crisis* (under Du Bois' editorship) for influence in the African American intellectual community. Having set itself up as a radical voice, *The Messenger* takes on particular significance because it "addressed issues of racial and cultural amalgamation more boldly than did any other publication, and it did so within the context of addressing the 'Americanness' of African American culture in provocative and often satirical fashion."[14] Within this context, then, Schuyler and Thurman not only took up the pressing and popular issues of the day, but found an outlet by which they could question political and cultural assumptions within an established institutional framework. Being a central part of *The Messenger* staff afforded Schuyler and Thurman the luxury of both creating and critiquing Harlem Renaissance ideologies and aesthetics since such journals were "absolutely integral to the dissemination and institutionalization of New Negro art."[15]

From that position of editorship, Schuyler and Thurman took particular delight in striking out at both emerging and established questions of aesthetics, particularly as they related to the representation of African Americans. Part of their scorn was directed toward a supposedly intellectual milieu that they felt was populated by apologists, propagandists, hacks, and outright cowards. Thurman writes in *Fire!!*, a journal for young African American artists which he co-founded: "Why Negroes imagine that any writer is going to write what Negroes think he ought to write about them is too ridiculous to merit consideration."[16] The very idea of a "proper" way to represent blackness looms as an intellectual failure too great even to deserve his analysis; the fact that African American and white liberal intellectuals were attempting to put forth such programs of representation caused Thurman to lash back with unforgettable satirical wit. Schuyler, too, fought bitterly against this kind of racialist thinking. He decried the very idea of a "Negro art" as something separate from art in general, saying that "such nonsense is probably the last stand of the old myth palmed off by

Negrophobists" and "that there are Negroes who will lend this myth a helping hand need occasion no surprise." Ultimately Schuyler called for a complete reassessment – indeed an absolute rejection – of "African American" art as a distinct category which "must be rejected with a loud guffaw by intelligent people."[17] A variety of artists and intellectuals, it seemed to these satirists, were abandoning their responsibilities to think for themselves and create a new social order. Rather, they were content to rehash clichés. Thurman and Schuyler thought intellectuals should go beyond making the race anew; it was their responsibility to challenge the validity of "race" altogether.

Both Thurman and Schuyler were driven by the modernist ethos of making things anew and rebelling against the obsolete structures of the past. These authors' major works, then, become a catalog of iconoclasm. In the era of the "New" Negro, Schuyler and Thurman offer continual correctives to where they see the movement stalling or going astray. Indeed, in their deepest critiques they want to ask us to reconsider the ideas of both newness and blackness and judge whether they are useful cultural concepts. At one moment in Thurman's *The Blacker the Berry*, the heroine Emma Lou muses to herself that "she should have read that Harlem number of the *Survey Graphic* issued two or three years ago. But Harlem hadn't interested her then."[18] The reference is to the issue of *Survey Graphic* magazine that was eventually turned into Alain Locke's volume *The New Negro*, and here the irony is several-fold: first, that a resident of Harlem would actually look to a magazine to explain it; that the New Negro is a kind of manufactured fad which published itself into a momentary prominence; and that what Emma Lou would encounter in those pages would be the very same people – artists and intellectuals – whom she meets in parodic form in the course of the novel, including Tony Crews (Langston Hughes), Cora Thurston (Zora Hurston), and Walter Truman (Wallace Thurman himself). The plot of *The Blacker the Berry* revolves around Emma Lou Morgan, a young woman from Idaho, who goes to college in southern California before migrating to New York City.[19] Emma has heard of Harlem as an almost magical place where a great diversity of African Americans can live and thrive. What she discovers, however, is that for a dark-skinned woman, there is nothing "new" there. All the inter- and intraracial color prejudices remain. She is still exploited economically and emotionally. She remains trapped in a world where race, color, class, and gender represent insurmountable barriers. In *Infants of the Spring*, the character Paul Arbian worships great artists, but remains stuck within the walls of "Nigerati Manor" when it comes to his own work. This house where the central characters live and work is far from a productive salon, generating ground-breaking works of art, music and literature. Rather, it is a kind of intellectual ghetto occasionally patronized by elites who have little genuine interest in advancing the careers of African American artists, except as they might be able to produce hackneyed "racial" art. Van Notten has noted that this novel "can no longer simply be interpreted as a parody of the Harlem Renaissance ... [but one] must also study the documentary value of *Infants of the Spring*, a text which deals with Harlem's first avant-garde and America's first black bohemia."[20] I would suggest that the novel is, in fact, both parody *and* documentary. Indeed, that is what makes it effective satire. The very avant-garde with which Thurman was associated was, in his own estimation, worthy of caustic ridicule.

Schuyler, too, militates in his fiction against a New Negro intellectual culture which he saw as not bent on innovation or racial "uplift," but rather as clichéd and self-serving, especially among the elites. One of the major figures of the novel *Black No More* is Dr. Junius Crookman, an African American physician who discovers and markets a medical process for literally transforming African Americans into blond-haired, blue-eyed Nordics. The premise of the book is that no sane African American would prefer to remain phenotypically black when s/he could be guaranteed to become white. That, as such, is already a satire of race-pride and race-consciousness which we often associate with the Harlem Renaissance. Schuyler pushes his satire even farther, however, by drawing sneering parallels between Crookman, a New Negro entrepreneur bent on making a buck off the American racial problem, and a number of thinly disguised race leaders of the day. Schuyler describes Crookman in this way:

> Dr. Crookman prided himself above all on being a great lover of his race. He had studied its history, read of its struggles and kept up with its achievements. He subscribed to six or seven Negro weekly newspapers and two of the magazines. He was so interested in the continued progress of the American Negroes that he wanted to remove all obstacles in their path by depriving them of their racial characteristics. His home and office were filled with African masks and paintings of Negroes by Negroes. He was what was known in Negro society as a Race Man.[21]

To add a further irony, one might level a similar accusation at Schuyler himself. Having published in "The Negro-Art Hokum" that "the Aframerican is merely a lampblacked Anglo-Saxon," it is entirely possible to see Schuyler as depriving African Americans of their racial characteristics as well.[22] However, although Crookman may be a crook, he is, at least, honest about and clear-sighted in his goals. Like Schuyler himself, he makes no apologies for his actions, which is far more than can be said for most of the other African American leaders in the novel. W. E. B. Du Bois, for instance, is represented as Dr. Shakespeare Agamemnon Beard, founder of the "*militant*

Negro organization, the National Social Equality League" (88, my emphasis). Schuyler goes on to lampoon this central figure of the era in this way:

> For a mere six thousand dollars a year, the learned doctor wrote scholarly and biting editorials in *The Dilemma*, denouncing the Caucasians whom he secretly admired and lauding the greatness of the Negroes whom he alternately pitied and despised. In limpid prose he told of the sufferings and privations of the downtrodden black workers with whose lives he was totally and thankfully unfamiliar. Like most Negro leaders, he deified black women but abstained from employing aught save octaroons. He talked at white banquets about "we of the black race" and admitted in books that he was part-French, part-Russian, part-Indian and part-Negro. He bitterly denounced the Nordics for debauching Negro women while taking care to hire comely yellow stenographers with weak resistance. In a real way, he loved his people.   (*Black*, 90)

If the idea of the New Negro is being promoted by such people, we are forced to ask via this satire, then what really lies at its heart? And although Du Bois may have less influence on Harlem Renaissance ideologies than someone like Alain Locke, he is still the godfather of African American intellectuals, and, as Schuyler and Thurman both knew, many ideas passed across his desk for approval and promotion.[23] By calling the very concept of the "New Negro" into question as a valid idea, by questioning what "new" could accomplish, Schuyler and Thurman bring to the fore the next logical, satirical step: the value of "race" as a concept in its own right.

"Race" as a social construct dominated lives of Americans in the writings of these authors. Thurman and Schuyler consistently and tirelessly attack the kinds of psychological, social, and economic damage done by American racialist ideology. One of their primary modes of attack, however, is to undermine the very "reality" of race as a concept. That is, they seek to dismantle racial identity as a stable and ultimately knowable set of categories. Jane Kuenz has described *Black No More* as valuable "not just for its comic and astute critique of the 'race hysteria' among white historians, anthropologists, and politicians, but for the way it links that hysteria with the parallel essentialist and primitivist rhetoric that emerged among Harlem Renaissance artists and intellectuals at the same time."[24] The belief in racial purity and knowability is undermined starting with the novel's dedication to "all Caucasians in the great republic who can trace their ancestry back ten generations and confidently assert that there are no Black leaves, twigs, limbs or branches on their family trees" (*Black*). It continues on to the end of the book where the leader of the Knights of Nordica, Schuyler's parody of the Ku Klux Klan, is forced to declare "I guess we're all niggers now" (193). As the plot of the novel reveals the depth of racial intermixing in American history, the characters end up having to do away with both black and white as useful descriptors. Schuyler concludes: "America was definitely, enthusiastically mulatto-minded" (222). The crisis of race is only averted by obliterating "race" as an essential or pure concept.

Even a novel like Thurman's *The Blacker the Berry*, which deals in a more realistic way with the color question, suggests that an insistence on racial essentialism, and a racialist hegemony that foregrounds color as a determining fact of life, can only lead to unreasonable social hierarchies. Thurman writes:

> Emma Lou had been born in a semi-white world, totally surrounded by an all-white one, and those few dark elements that had forced their way in had either been shooed away or else greeted with derisive laughter. It was the custom always of those with whom she came into most frequent contact to ridicule or revile any black person or object. (*Blacker* 6)

Emma Lou stands as the marker of the failure of blackness to ever be instilled with positive meanings. Emma Lou's continual quest to literally bleach and obliterate blackness from her body points not simply to some kind of psychological dysfunction on her part but rather toward the absolutely bankrupt future of race and color distinctions. The tragedy of this particular satire is not that Emma Lou is ashamed of her blackness, but that blackness is an always already shame-infused category while, at the same time, whiteness is illogically and disingenuously raised to a pinnacle of human perfection.

In *Infants of the Spring*, Thurman further elaborates on the delusional value of racialist categories by satirizing the notion of Harlem itself as a space fundamentally different from the rest of urban America. Raymond Taylor, the character in the novel who most closely represents Thurman himself, says to a white guest of his, "Harlem is New York. Please don't let the fact that it's black New York obscure your vision" (38). This is an instance where Thurman does not wish to *deny* that people see and experience racial categories, but he does wish to call into question the significance of those terms. When Ray's guest accuses him of being "cynical and silly," Ray responds that "if you had lived in Harlem as long as I have, you would realize that Negroes are much like any other human beings. They have the same social, physical and intellectual divisions. You're only being intrigued, as I have said before, by the newness of the thing" (39). Race distinctions are false distinctions, and the idea of being "much like" eventually transforms into being "precisely like." The age's obsession with newness simply clouds one's analytical abilities to see things for what they really are. The passage echoes Schuyler's denunciation of the category of "Negro art," but here Thurman confronts a white character with being the perpetuator of such fictions. Further he makes his critique specific to Harlem.

The "vogue" of Harlem in the 1920s and 1930s is a phenomenon that has received a great deal of attention. The geography of Harlem as an overly glorified and culturally overdetermined space, however, was not lost on Schuyler and Thurman in their own time. In fact, both writers go to some length to debunk the myth of Harlem as a special place and to satirize those who would insist upon it as the locus of a particular kind of racial difference. James Weldon Johnson, in his essay "Harlem: The Cultural Capital," names the space of Harlem in 1925 as "the great Mecca for the sight-seer, the pleasure seeker, the curious, the adventurous, the enterprising, the ambitious and the talented of the whole Negro world."[25] Mecca, of course, functions both as a real, sacred geography as well as a powerful *symbolic* space. Not all the work of Islam happens at Mecca, nor does all the work of renaissance happen in Harlem, yet these places anchor the imaginations of the faithful and the outsider alike. On another level they have come to be anti-modern, primitivist designations in some discourses. I would suggest that they are both resisted and fetishized in our contemporary language, and may be in need of some decentering. Thurman, too, uses similar language when he describes Emma Lou's state of mind; he writes:

> Now she wondered why she had been so painfully anxious to come to New York. She had given as a consoling reason to inquisitive friends and relatives, school. But she knew too well that she had no intentions of ever re-entering school. She had had enough of *that* school in Los Angeles, and her experiences there, more than anything else, had caused this foolhardy hegira to Harlem. She had been desperately driven to escape, and had she not escaped in this manner she might have done something else much more mad. (*Blacker* 66)

Thurman turns Harlem from an imagined site of redemption into a kind of sideshow. It is not, he insists, significantly different from any place touched by American racialist ideology, even if observers and pundits want to laud it as a locale of golden potential. Harlem is parodied not as the site of black potential and freedom, but as a space in which Euro-American moderns develop their own "new" subjectivities over and against the African American other. James Grossman points out, "Whites were mainly interested in something called 'The Negro,' an exotic neighbor who was not bound by the narrow conventions of social morality."[26] Schuyler describes one of the white characters visiting Harlem in *Black No More*: "Up here trying to get a thrill in the Black Belt but a thrill from observation instead of contact. Gee, but white folks were funny. They didn't want black folks' game and yet they were always frequenting Negro resorts" (23). Harlem actually enables distinctions between black and white, and it enhances intraracial distinctions for these two authors. Rather than healing racialist splits, it exacerbates them. It is the dichotomy between the self-consciously modern and the primitive labels that Schuyler and Thurman often seek to exploit and over-turn in their works. Even well-meaning liberals such as "social service work-ers, reformed socialistic ministers, foreign missionaries, caponized radicals, lady versifiers who gush all over the place, Y.M.C.A. secretaries and others of the same dogassed ilk" (*Infants* 14) only serve to further the racial divide. These satires leave, at best, a very limited possibility of a transracial under-standing because of the ways in which Harlem Renaissance modernity con-tinually reenforces the status quo.

It might be said that while Thurman concentrates on the domestic manners and politics of Harlem and the United States, Schuyler further ups the ante by looking outside national borders to a possible transnational racial politics. If, as George Hutchinson suggests, the *Messenger* columnist Eugene Gordon argued that, "the Negro masses should be taught *national* rather than *racial* consciousness," Schuyler wanted to look at how national conscious-ness had, in some ways, been always already achieved, and how it might also fail as a panacea for the race question.[27] Well aware of the Harlem Renaissance's relationship to the Nègritude Movement in Francophone Africa, the Caribbean, and Europe, and Marcus Garvey's Universal Negro Improvement Association which had major support in Harlem, Schuyler sought to examine how people desired to link the "New" Negro to peoples of African descent beyond the boundaries of nation and continent. In his serialized novellas "Black Internationale" and "Black Empire," Schuyler creates what one might call New Negro Tom Clancy tales. They are the stories of how an African American physician, Dr. Henry Belsidus, sur-rounded by aides gathered from the world's Black Talented Tenth, plots and succeeds in liberating the African continent from European colonial powers. Though the novel begins on the streets of Harlem, it quickly moves downtown, then across state lines, then across regional and national borders, and ultimately spans three continents. The victorious descendants of the African Diaspora are unapologetically ruthless when it comes to their attacks on white, European modernity and civilization.

The tales are told from the perspective of an African American journalist who stumbles upon an aspect of the plot and then is virtually enslaved into the service of the great schemer, Dr. Belsidus. Reluctant at first, the narrator quickly becomes a convert to the cause of African liberation at any price, sitting in rapt attention in front of Belsidus "as he spun out this strange, almost insane scheme, [while] a malevolent, satanic smirk played about his stern mouth and his deep-set eyes glowed like coals in a cavern."[28] Though much of the book is taken up with very serializable, cliff-hanging plot twists, Schuyler unceasingly returns to Belsidus's vision that "white world supremacy must be destroyed ... And it will be destroyed" (*Empire*, 10). Schuyler draws specifically on African American contexts of his day, such as Garveyism and its relation to some of Belsidus' political vision and W. D. Fard and the founding of the Nation of Islam in the Black Internationale's creation of a New Black religion. Yet the major theme to which Schuyler, via Belsidus, returns time and again is the turning of the modern against itself. It is the hijacking of the modern by peoples of color to be used as a weapon against the forces of Empire. Tellingly, Schuyler does not seem to think that the countermodern turn toward a Black Empire will be a panacea, but it seems to be a necessary step in the political evolution of the world. His satire is of those who see Black Empire as an end in itself, who see the merging of diasporic people in Africa as a way to "hide discontinuities and differences" and to invoke Pan-African consciousness as "metaphors for alienation, outsiderness, home and various binary relationships such as alien/native."[29]

Schuyler insists on representing the complexities and ambiguities of political power and its exercise, as well as the effects that these have on our notions of difference. Throughout the novellas the reader is constantly reminded of the Machiavellian trade-offs we might have to countenance in the name of racial liberation. Schuyler has Belsidus lay out a kind of manifesto to his narrator right at the outset, and much of the doctor's subsequent dialogue returns to reiterate or elaborate on these initial remarks. Belsidus says:

> [A]ll great schemes appear mad in the beginning. Christians, Communists, Fascists and Nazis were at first called scary. Success made them sane. With brains, courage and wealth even the most fantastic scheme can become a reality. I have dedicated my life ... to destroying white supremacy ... I plan to do this by every means within my power. I intend to stop at nothing ... whether right or wrong. Right is success. Wrong is failure. I will not fail because I am ruthless. Those who fail are men who get sentimental, who weaken, who balk at a little bloodshed. Such vermin deserve to fail. Every great movement the world has ever seen has collapsed because it grew weak.
>
> [White men] have [power] now, but they will not have it long. I and my comrades shall destroy them or make them destroy themselves. We have brains, the best brains in the Negro race. We have science of which the white man has not dreamed in our possession. We have courage. And we are absolutely ruthless.　　　　　　　　　　　　　　　　　　　　(*Empire* 10–11)

The "modern," "civilized" white underestimates the "atavistic," "primitive" black, and that, along with the willingness to rawly exercise power, is what will allow the Black Internationale to triumph. The Talented Tenth will turn the modern against itself. It will use the master's tools to unseat the master.

And if blacks are supposedly unbounded by moral convention in the same ways as Europeans, so much to their advantage when it comes to global, strategic politics. Of course, the result may be thrilling, but it is hardly flattering.

Schuyler brings transnational black politics further into focus with his second novel, *Slaves Today* (1931), which grew out of a journalistic expedition he made to Liberia. By and large it is not the biting satire that we find in other books like *Black No More* or *Black Empire*, but rather it is a revision of the African American slave narrative in which the enslaved person is an African sold into bondage by his diasporic brother. "The Negro's Americanness" is highlighted by the absolute corruption of Liberian government officials, who have learned their chicanery from sojourns in the United States and long to emulate – indeed have been fully inculcated into – modernist imperial practices. Schuyler describes his fictional Liberian president in this way:

> President Johnson was a Liberian aristocrat. He seemed to belong in rooms like this in which he could look down from the French windows upon the sprawling capital he rules. Three generations before, his ancestors, Philadelphia freedmen, had helped found the republic with the assistance of American philanthropists and perturbed slaveholders. They had fought off aboriginal inhabitants, battled white slave traders, and cut farms out of the virgin jungle. The tropical climate to which they were unused had not made life easy but they had persevered with the true pioneer spirit.[30]

The same Americanness he extols in other writings is only satirically embraced here. Because of people like President Johnson, Zo, the novel's protagonist, can never triumph over a social and political system which has Liberia mired in untenable debt to developed nations and the corrupt greed of the country's elite, "foreign" black rulers. Zo is whisked from his village into a diaspora internal to the African continent, but he cannot ever truly return to what has been usurped and corrupted. Even in the geographic locus of the "African primitive," we must begin to rethink the era's "common sense" invocations of black identity. The "liberated" space of Liberia becomes, not unlike the geography of Harlem, the space in which the trickster becomes not the liberator, but the corrupted itself.

In some sense, Schuyler's fantasy of international liberation and transnational diasporic solidarity targets the politics of cultural conformism which might be both the motivation and the result of New Negro ideologies. Belsidus declares that he has led people of African descent to make "a new philosophy for ourselves" (*Empire* 257), but is that philosophy, at best, a sinister recasting of other kinds of oppressive ideologies?

In Thurman's *Infants of the Spring*, "Raymond was pleased with the sarcastic jibes he had summoned to include in the review. He was tired of Negro writers who had nothing to say, and who only wrote because they were literate and felt they should apprise white humanity of the better classes among Negro humanity" (*Infants* 91). Again, these satirists share a vision. They want to insist that, as Thurman points out, "any writer preparing to write about Negroes in Harlem or anywhere else ... should take whatever phases of their life that seem the most interesting to him, and develop them as he pleases."[31] Thurman and Schuyler take up with all seriousness Alain Locke's dictum that "if it ever was warrantable to regard and treat the Negro *en masse* it is becoming less possible, more unjust and more ridiculous" to do so.[32] Yet they also point out what they find to be the very public aesthetic and political hypocrisies in such a New Negro intellectual tradition. When, in *Infants of the Spring*, Thurman creates the character of Dr. A. L. Parkes as a send-up of Locke himself, he satirizes the urge to write for racial "uplift." He exposes the problematic paradox at the heart of New Negro thinking: show the virtually uncategorizable diversity of African America on the one hand, but do not let go of racialist, indeed even essentialist, notions of race on the other. A logical impasse such as that can only be food for satirists.

When W. E. B. Du Bois declares in the first sentence of *The Souls of Black Folk*, "Herein lie buried many things which if read with patience may show the strange meaning of being black here at the dawning of the Twentieth Century," he unintentionally throws down a gauntlet for Wallace Thurman and George Schuyler.[33] For these satirists, the urge to explicate blackness is also the urge to reify it, to turn it into a limiting construct. "Race" is often useful material for the artist, but it can never become an end in itself.

NOTES

1. Bernard Bell, *The Afro-American Novel and Its Tradition* (Amherst: University of Massachusetts Press, 1987), p. 149.
2. Dexter B. Gordon, "Humor in African American Discourse: Speaking of Oppression," *Journal of Black Studies* 29.2 (November 1998), 258.
3. For a lengthier argument about the concept of the "folk" and its critical place within the Harlem Renaissance and African American literary criticism more generally, see J. Martin Favor, *Authentic Blackness* (Durham, NC: Duke University Press, 1999).
4. Sterling A. Brown, "The American Race Problem as Reflected in American Literature," *Journal of Negro Education* 8.3 (July 1939), 286.
5. Terrell Scott Herring, "The Negro Artist and the Racial Manor: *Infants of the Spring* and the Conundrum of Publicity," *African American Review* 35.4 (Winter 2004), 588.

6. Walter Lippman, quoted in Thomas Hobson, *Mencken: A Life* (Baltimore: Johns Hopkins University Press, 1994), p. xi.
7. Richard Wright, *Black Boy* (1945; New York: Harper and Row, 1966), p. 270.
8. Eleonore van Notten, "Harlem's Black Bohemia," *African American Review* 27.4 (Winter 1993), 693. For a far more expansive discussion of Thurman's life and work, see van Notten's book, *Wallace Thurman's Harlem Renaissance* (Amsterdam: Rodopi, 1994).
9. Wallace Thurman, *Infants of the Spring* (1932; Boston: Northeastern University Press, 1992), p. 142. Further citations to appear in text.
10. Hobson, *Mencken*, p. 247.
11. John C. Gruesser, "George S. Schuyler, Samuel I. Brooks, and Max Disher," *African American Review* 27.4 (Winter 1993), 679.
12. Hobson, *Mencken*, pp. 247–8, 455.
13. George Schuyler, *Black and Conservative* (New Rochelle, NY: Arlington House Press, 1966), p. 161.
14. George Hutchinson, "Mediating 'Race' and 'Nation': The Cultural Politics of *The Messenger*," *African American Review* 28.4 (Winter 1994), 531–2.
15. Herring, "The Negro Artist," p. 583.
16. Wallace Thurman, "Fire Burns," in *Fire!!* 1.1 (1927), ed. Wallace Thurman, 48.
17. George Schuyler, "The Negro-Art Hokum," in Angelym Mitchell, ed., *Within the Circle* (Durham, NC: Duke University Press, 1994), p. 54.
18. Wallace Thurman, *The Blacker the Berry* (1929; New York: Collier, 1970), p. 122. Further citations appear within the text.
19. In this way, Emma Lou *also* – along with Walter Truman – represents Thurman himself, as someone who has moved from the West to Harlem. It is particularly interesting to think about the significance of Thurman gendering himself female for the major portion of the novel. Such a move on the author's part adds another layer of complexity to questions of gender and sexuality in the Harlem Renaissance that is only now coming into serious scholarship.
20. Van Notten, "Harlem's Black Bohemia," p. 695.
21. George Schuyler, *Black No More* (1931; Boston: Northeastern University Press, 1989), p. 55. Subsequent references will appear in the text.
22. Schuyler, "Hokum," p. 52. Further, Crookman and Schuyler are both married to white women, deepening the self-parody at work here.
23. Anne Elizabeth Carroll's book *Word, Image and the New Negro* (Bloomington: Indiana University Press, 2004) has a great deal of interesting analysis on the Du Bois-edited *Crisis* magazine.
24. Jane Kuenz, "American Racial Discourse, 1900–1930: Schuyler's 'Black No More,'" *NOVEL: A Forum on Fiction* 30.2 (Winter 1997), 171.
25. In Alain Locke, ed., *The New Negro* (1925; New York: Athenaeum, 1968), p. 301.
26. James Grossman, "A Chance to Make Good," in Robin Kelley and Earl Lewis, eds., *To Make Our World Anew* (Oxford: Oxford University Press, 2000), p. 402.
27. Hutchinson, "Mediating 'Race' and 'Nation'," p. 536.
28. George Schuyler, *Black Empire* (1937–38; Boston: Northeastern University Press, 1991), p. 12.

29. Tiffany Patterson and Robin Kelley, "Unfinished Migrations: Reflections on the African Diaspora and the Making of the Modern World," *African Studies Review* 43.1 (April 2000), 20.

30. George Schuyler, *Slaves Today* (1931; New York: AMS Press, 1969), p. 11.

31. Thurman, "Fire Burns," p. 48.

32. Alain Locke, "The New Negro," in Loche, ed., *The New Negro*, p. 6.

33. W. E. B. Du Bois, *The Souls of Black Folk* (1903; New York: Bantam, 1989), p. xxxi.

15

CARLA KAPLAN

Zora Neale Hurston, folk performance, and the "Margarine Negro"

I'm going to sit here on this porch chair and prophesy that these are the last days of the know-nothing writers on Negro subjects.

> Zora Neale Hurston, "You Don't Know Us Negroes"[1]

We almost lost Zora to the choose-between games played with Black art.

> June Jordan, "Notes Toward a Balancing Act of Love and Hatred"[2]

"Magical Zora"

Magical Zora, our truth-telling fore-mother.

> Ruth Sheffey, founder, The Zora Neale Hurston Society[3]

When an author's work is taught in colleges, and produced for television (by Oprah Winfrey), and her face graces postage stamps, coffee mugs, calendars, notecards, and refrigerator magnets, it is a safe bet that her status, in popular culture at least, is secure. Because so many of my friends and colleagues have bought them for me, I happen to own a great many Zora Neale Hurston finger puppet refrigerator magnets – complete with floppy hat, purple dress, pearl necklace, and "Magnetic Personalities" data card.[4] Of the four dozen or so figures marketed in the magnet's celebrity series, Hurston is the only one identified by first name alone. This is not insignificant. Hurston has become a national celebrity and a folk heroine, as Sheffey's proclamation, quoted above, attests. Her intimacy with the shared heritage of folk traditions no doubt contributes to this sense that "Zora" is our familiar, someone we can approach on a first-name basis and imagine as our own. But, as I will suggest, there are myriad ironies involved in making Hurston into a folk heroine, not least of them being her own highly complex relation to the folk traditions she documented and referenced in almost everything that she wrote. This chapter, then, returns to some of Hurston's use of the folklore she collected to rethink the ways in which we have imagined her relationship to it.

My Zora magnets remind me that the work of critical recuperation and cultural revaluation – the very work to which Hurston dedicated her career – is often fraught with conflict. And, as it turns out, tensions between the popular and the scholarly have always dogged Hurston. She was quick to point out the inferior scholarship of other black writers she often called "know nothings," even as they, in turn, were most skeptical about her work whenever she was most popular. So although Hurston is now, as Henry Louis Gates, Jr., puts it, "a cardinal figure in the Afro-American canon, the feminist canon, and the canon of American fiction,"[5] some of the historic tensions between her popular and her scholarly tendencies recur in her reception. In particular, her status as folk icon raises certain questions. Does it mean that she has now become what she would have derided as a "Pet Negro,"[6] the special exception of white society who must always be misunderstood to be loved above her peers? *Is* she best described as a "folk novelist" and what is at stake in presuming that she is?

Hurston's relationship to the folklore she chronicled was always a source of controversy. Frequently compared to already established and highly regarded white folk novelists such as DuBose Heyward and Julia Peterkin, Hurston was often lauded as an "unspoiled,"[7] "homespun,"[8] naturally gifted medium for the stories and sayings of her people, a writer whose "artlessness"[9] came from being an "insider" with "double authority as a Negro and a student of folklore"[10] (a persona, it must be said, which Hurston herself helped to fashion, especially in her notoriously unreliable autobiography *Dust Tracks on a Road*). White reviewers were particularly taken with the idea that Hurston would escort them behind the veil black culture draws to protect itself from white racism: "a young Negro woman with a college education has invited the outside world to listen in while her own people are being as natural as they can never be when white folks are literally present," one reviewer wrote.[11] And this was precisely what rankled some of Hurston's Harlem contemporaries. While agreeing that her work might be "folklore fiction at its best," as friend and teacher Alain Locke put it, many expressed doubts that "folklore fiction" could ever "tell a story convincingly" or dive "deep either to inner psychology of characterization or to sharp analysis of the social background."[12]

Richard Wright was sure that it could not do so. He was even more convinced that Hurston would not be the folklore writer to achieve that goal. "Miss Hurston seems to have no desire whatever to move in the direction of serious fiction," his infamous review of *Their Eyes Were Watching God*, declared: "Miss Hurston can write," he conceded:

> but her prose is cloaked in that facile sensuality that has dogged Negro expression since the days of Phillis Wheatley. Her dialogue manages to catch the

psychological movements of the Negro folk-mind in their pure simplicity, but that's as far as it goes. Miss Hurston *voluntarily* continues in her novel the tradition which was *forced* upon the Negro in theater, that is, the minstrel technique that makes the "white folks" laugh. Her characters eat and laugh and cry and work and kill; they swing like a pendulum eternally in that safe and narrow orbit in which America likes to see the Negro live: between laughter and tears . . . The sensory sweep of her novel carries no theme, no message, no thought. In the main, her novel is not addressed to the Negro, but to the white audience whose chauvinistic tastes she knows how to satisfy. She exploits the phase of Negro life which is "quaint," the phase which evokes a piteous smile on the lips of the "superior" race.[13]

Wright's attack is partly fueled by his manifest indifference to feminism. Only by failing – or refusing – to recognize the sexual politics of Hurston's choice to make over the ancient quest romance into the story of a poor, young, black woman's search for fulfillment (and an orgasm!), can Wright conclude the novel lacks "message."[14] But it is Hurston's use of folklore, even more than her feminism, which truly has Wright's back up.

Although many black writers, from the Harlem Renaissance to the present, have regarded Hurston's use of such folklore elements as storytelling, proverbs, songs, jokes, sermons, games, riddles, sayings, signifying,[15] music, labor, and courtship rituals as, in Alice Walker's words, a "*devoted* appreciation of her own culture, which is an inspiration to us all,"[16] folklore is a risky resource for writers of color. Once a novel is classified as "folklore fiction," praise for it often smacks of patronization, and condemnation comes easily. For many it will always ring of "the annual minstrel show" presented for the "illiterate . . . yokel."[17] For others, including contemporary, black, feminist critics Hazel Carby and Ann duCille, it will seem an avoidance of politics, a "discursive displacement of contemporary social crises," in Carby's words. Hurston's portrayals of Eatonville, the all-black, rural, southern town where she grew up, if read as a "pre-lapsarian Eden, isolated from the racial politics associated with Jim Crow,"[18] will contribute to the idea that "the genuine, honest, authentic black experience is that of a unilaterally permissive rural peasantry."[19] In that case, Hurston's use of folklore will inevitably seem "nostalgic," "romantic," and "colonial": a "utopian . . . creation of a folk who are outside of history" and her "celebration of black life," a "representation of 'Negroness' as an unchanging, essential entity."[20]

Must we choose, however, between idolization and condemnation? Virtually every scholar writing on Hurston's use of folklore, in fact, takes it for granted that because she was a committed folklorist, a trained anthropologist who published both folklore and fiction, and because her fiction indeed incorporates folklore, her writing therefore adds up to "folklore fiction," and that all of her work did indeed promote "a genuine folk cultural essence in her writings."[21] To arrive at that conclusion, some critics fail to distinguish between her extensive folklore, anthropological, ethnographic, essayistic, and fictional work, merely concluding that it all serves as "reliable representations of African-American folk culture."[22] Others argue that in Hurston's writing the "folk and narrative registers are seamlessly woven together" and that *she* succeeds in "eroding the distinction between fiction and folklore."[23] Yet others provide a complex and nuanced analysis of Hurston's "innovative" bridging of "standard English and black dialect" (*Signifying*). But few have ever treated her fiction as performing a *critical* commentary upon the folklore which it uses and preserves. Given Hurston's characteristic boldness and attention grabbing and given that Hurston, as Gates points out, is "the first scholar to have defined the trope of Signifying . . . the first to represent the ritual itself" (*Signifying*), why *wouldn't* we look for her to demonstrate her mastery of black discursive traditions by signifying upon signifying?[24] In addition to helping to rescue folklore, I'd argue, Hurston's writing also signifies[25] upon the very folklore that it celebrates.

This is not to say that Hurston was careless about folklore. On the contrary. Folklore – "the life and color of my people," "the boiled-down juice of human living," "the greatest cultural wealth of the continent"[26] – was her first love. And when she set about collecting it, she gave it her all – determined "to do this tremendous thing with all the fire that genius can bring."[27] Without understanding what Hurston saw in African American folklore – a people's artistry and sensibility, their humor, their grievances, their worldview and, perhaps most importantly, their strategies of resistance – her writing loses some of its force. But at the same time, it is important not to romanticize Hurston as a folklorist, with her model T and her pistol, searching out the "Negro farthest down" and "woofing" in "Jooks" along the way. As a collector, Hurston worked hard in terrible conditions: traveling in blistering heat, sleeping in her car when "colored" hotel rooms couldn't be had (which was most of the time), risking her safety as a woman in the backwoods, conscript-staffed turpentine camps, sawmills, and phosphate mines she studied, and risking her life, as a black woman, by occasionally traveling with white, male, folklore colleagues. As a commentator on the folklore she collected, Hurston also took great risks. The Harlem literati offered valuable cultural belonging (and significant material reward) to those who depicted black folklore in certain ways, while mainstream, white society offered its rewards for those who depicted it in others. Stubbornly askew of both sets of demands, Hurston adopted a very unusual and iconoclastic folklore aesthetic which never quite gave either what it wanted. Most brilliantly, she disentangled two of the most privileged terms of the twenties: "originality" and "authenticity." This was one of the most visionary aesthetic ideologies to come out of the Harlem Renaissance, even if Hurston never realized it consistently or completely and even if it proved, in the end, too forward to seem other than backward to many of her friends. By rethinking the ways Hurston used folklore in some of her writings we can begin to uncover how this aesthetic worked to make folklore itself a vital creative resource for Hurston's other writings, offer her solutions to certain artistic and philosophical problems – such as the question of what race is – which were plaguing other members of the Harlem Renaissance.

The "Margarine Negro" and the folk

... that instant emotional release that is the great solace of the negro ... [he] dozes lightly under the terrific heat, as only a full-blooded negro can ... bodies that could give themselves utterly to a rhythm swayed and bent ... she had the negro's faculty of giving her whole being to an emotion.

DuBose Heyward, from *Porgy* and *Mamba's Daughters*

The decade just past was the oleomargarine era in Negro writing. Oleomargarine is the fictionalized form of butter ... it has everything butterish about it except butter. And so the writings that made out they were holding a looking-glass to the Negro had everything in them except Negroness.

Zora Neale Hurston, "You Don't Know Us Negroes"[28]

What is Africa to me:
Copper sun or scarlet sea,
Jungle star or jungle track,
Strong bronzed men or regal black
Women from whose loins I sprang
When the birds of Eden sang?
One three centuries removed
From the scenes his fathers loved
Spicy grove, cinnamon tree,
What is Africa to me?

Countee Cullen, "Heritage"

Foundational to much of the Harlem Renaissance was faith that art could serve as a – even *the* – principal means of social justice and race advancement. Folklore in particular could show the world the rich legacy of African American culture. As early as 1903, W. E. B. Du Bois argued that while "little of beauty has America given the world ... by fateful chance the Negro folk-song – the rhythmic cry of the slave – stands today not simply as the soul of American music, but as the most beautiful expression of human experience born this side of the seas ... It still remains as the singular spiritual heritage of the nation and the greatest gift of the Negro people."[29] By the twenties, this view had become a virtual Harlem Renaissance credo, as we can see in James Weldon Johnson's often-reprinted preface to his ground-breaking anthology, *The Book of American Negro Poetry*:

> A people may become great through many means, but there is only one measure by which its greatness is recognized and acknowledged. The final measure of the greatness of all peoples is the amount and standard of the literature and art they have produced. The world does not know that a people is great until that people produces great literature and art. No people that has produced great literature and art has ever been looked upon by the world as distinctly inferior ... nothing will do more to change that mental attitude and raise his status than a demonstration of intellectual parity by the Negro ... the Negro has already proved the possession of these powers by being the creator of the only things artistic that have yet sprung from American soil and been universally acknowledged as distinctive American products: folk stories, spirituals, the cakewalk, and ragtime ... this material is a "a vast mine of material that has been neglected almost absolutely" ... the Negro's folklore is "the touchstone, it is the magic thing, it is that by which the Negro can bridge all chasms."[30]

The possible value of black folklore was also given an important articulation in Alain Locke's influential preface to *The New Negro*, widely considered *the* Harlem Renaissance's manifesto. "Immediate hope," Locke wrote, "rests in the revaluation by white and black alike of the Negro in terms of his artistic endowments and cultural contributions ... the especially cultural recognition they win should in turn prove the key to that revaluation of the Negro which must precede or accompany any considerable further betterment of race relationships."[31]

The twenties were an opportune, but complicated, time for this agenda. Throughout the nation there was "almost a national obsession with American's folk heritage."[32] A largely "idealized" and "romanticized" pursuit, this folklore craze was initially centered on what Margaret Mead called the "search-and-rescue" mission to isolate and protect the original works hidden away by rural guardians of our pre-civilized heritage: in this case, British ballads located in the Appalachian mountains among a population understood as the direct descendants of the English peasantry.

The folklore craze was a double-edged phenomenon for black Americans. On the one hand, the search for a native heritage represented radical opportunities to supplant conventional, European models, and thus opened new ground. On the other hand, however, conservatives could invest the folklore search-and-rescue mission with deep-seated anti-immigrant and anti-black energy by using it to cast the nation as originally, and hence authentically, white. Even recognition could serve a racist cause. While attitudes toward folklore never fell out neatly along race lines,[33] it was true in some cases that "the idea of blacks as a 'folk' people was attractive to whites in part because it could be used to discredit their artistry while exalting their instincts."[34] If African Americans could successfully seize this terrain and demonstrate possession of this longed-for native heritage, without deflecting credit for their other forms of physical and intellectual labor, then the importance of their cultural contributions would become undeniable.[35]

But this would not prove easy terrain to seize. To many, for one thing, black folklore sounded too much like the many racist stereotypes already in circulation and resonated too strongly with both the modern cult of the primitive savage and the simplified, sentimentalized "Old Negro"[36] of plantation writers and minstrel shows: the sayings and antics of "aunties," "uncles," and "mammies," as Alain Locke put it.[37] For another thing, it seemed at least as pressing to counter racist portrayals of African American life with literary realism as to make a case for the value of a lot of old folklore. As even James Weldon Johnson, who argued for folklore, put it, "The Negro in the United States has achieved or been placed in a certain artistic niche. When he is thought of artistically, it is as a happy-go-lucky, singing, shuffling, banjo-picking being or as a more or less pathetic figure. The picture of him is in a log cabin amid fields of cotton or along the levees."[38] What Hurston dubbed the "Margarine Negro" was everywhere. It seemed that mainstream culture couldn't get enough of him. "Show some folks a genuine bit of Negroness," Hurston wrote in her unpublished essay "You Don't Know Us Negroes":

> and they rear and pitch like a mule in a tin stable. "But where is the misplaced preposition?," they wail. "Where is the Am it and I'se?" The rules and regulations of this Margarine Negro calls for two dumb Negroes who chew up dictionaries and spit out grammar. They will and *must* go into some sort of business and mess it all up. The big one always taking advantage of the little one. A fanatical religious scene, or a hoodoo dance (although there is no such thing in the popular Negro concept in America) is dragged in for no other reason than to prove that the author has gone deep into Negro life … Oh yes, and another thing. All Negro characters must have pop eyes. The only time when they are excused from popping is when they are rolling in fright … Special delivery rejection slips for those [writers] found unsound on this fright-and-eye business.

One of the problems with using folklore was this tendency to margarinize all portrayals of blacks – seeing tortured grammar and pop eyes (and, as Hurston pointed out in a later essay, razor fights), even when there were none. To some, a realist agenda and novels about northern, bourgeois blacks (doctors preferably) seemed the best curb on such misreadings.

To make matters even more vexing, many of the early – and most energetic – champions of black folklore, especially those with the most useful cultural connections and, hence, the greatest cultural authority, were white scholars. While not, perhaps, meaning to create "Margarine Negroes," these whites, it seemed, just couldn't help condescending as they collected and patronizing as they praised. Howard Odum, for example, well-known co-author of *The Negro and His Songs* (1925) and *Negro Workaday Songs* (1926), described the material he collected as "far from elegant," "[un]dignified," "a bit repulsive," "inelegant," and "trite."[39] Chandler Harris was notorious for sentimentalizing and infantilizing blacks in his "Uncle Remus" tales.[40] John Lomax, who did so much to generate the nation's regard for the "power and dignity" of black music, described it as having "a note of weird almost uncanny suggestion of turgid, slow-moving rivers in African jungles."[41] And even Rowena Jelliffee, who did so much to build a vernacular black theater, reverenced what she thought of as "the earthy quality of Negro folk life."[42]

"Let the Negro speak for himself"

> Whoever wishes to see the Negro in his essential traits, in the full perspective of his achievement and possibilities, must seek the enlightenment of that self-portraiture which the present developments of the Negro are offering ... So far as he is culturally articulate, we shall let the Negro speak for himself.
>
> Alain Locke, foreword to *The New Negro*

It should not be surprising, then, that many black writers saw the solution as self-representation. After decades of seeing themselves lampooned and demeaned, romanticized and caricatured, the time had finally come to "let the Negro speak for himself"[43] so that the record could finally be set straight. "There is an opportunity now for Negroes themselves to replace their outworn representations in fiction faithfully and incidentally to make themselves better understood," declared sociologist, editor, and university president Charles S. Johnson in *Opportunity*, the periodical of the National Urban League.[44]

Although she was in a difficult position because so many of her sponsors, mentors, teachers, patrons, and friends were white,[45] Hurston was particularly fervent about putting representations of black culture into black hands. During her years collecting folklore in the South (1927 and 1928 especially), she even determined to keep some of her best sources and materials secret so that whites could not exploit them. "Found another one of the original Africans," she wrote Langston Hughes, "older than Cudjoe about 200 miles up state on the Tombighee river. She is most delightful, but no one will ever know about her but us" (ZNH to Langston Hughes, *LIL*, p. 121). And when she could do so without offending her patrons, she expressed unqualified loathing for white representations of blacks. "White people could not be trusted to collect the lore of others," she wrote to Alain

Locke. They "take all the life and soul out of everything," she told Charlotte Osgood Mason, her wealthy white patron (ZNH to Charlotte Osgood Mason, *LIL*, p. 223). "It makes me sick to see how these cheap white folks are grabbing our stuff and ruining it," she told Langston Hughes (ZNH to Hughes, *LIL*, p. 126).[46] Hurston felt that "the negro is [having his] ... Negroness ... rubbed off" (ZNH to Franz Boas, *LIL*, p. 97) by whites and she wanted to present authentic African American folklore, not something doctored to suit either dominant aesthetics or stereotyped notions of black culture.

But if keeping black folklore out of white hands was difficult, it was actually the easiest part of Hurston's – and her contemporaries' – bid for cultural authenticity. The hardest part of speaking for themselves, as it turned out, would be deciding what to put forward in place of the "Margarine Negroes."

For the young wing of the Harlem Renaissance, the opportunity to speak for themselves offered a chance to revalue that which had been denigrated and demeaned and to accurately represent those aspects of black life which had been lampooned, romanticized, or caricatured. For others, this opportunity for authentic self-representation meant putting one's best foot forward to depict those aspects of African American life which most resembled white (and thus were often normalized as "universal") society and which, to date, had received scant treatment: the lives of the middle class, the everyday ordinariness of black families, and so on. Advocates of both agendas laid claim to "authenticity." And black folklore could be called in to boost either.

The dialect debate, still ongoing in the twenties, took its shape, in large part, from these opposing tendencies. Most black writers had despaired of creating any form of written black English which would seem authentic. James Weldon Johnson, who had promoted the preservation and presentation of black folklore to the American public, finally conceded that dialect was simply unrecuperable:

> Negro dialect is at present a medium that is not capable of giving expression to the varied conditions of Negro life in America, and much less is it capable of giving the fullest interpretation of Negro character and psychology. This is no indictment against the dialect as dialect, but against the mould of convention in which Negro dialect in the United States has been set. In time these conventions may become lost, and the colored poet in the United States may sit down to write in dialect without feeling that his first line will put the general reader in a frame of mind which demands that the poem be humorous or pathetic.[47]

Hurston neither used nor avoided dialect but, instead, developed a form of free indirect discourse which was somewhere between the two,[48] thereby making herself the only arbiter of the "authenticity" of the black speech she created. This move was not the norm.

To wrest authority over black folklore from white folklorists and establish its authenticity, many Harlem intellectuals turned, instead, toward African origins, which seemed to ground black folklore and the folklorist in something original and sure. "The Negro intellectuals were attempting to build a race and define a culture," Nathan Huggins writes:

> If there was validity in the notion of distinctive racial cultural contribution, it must be in the special experience of the race itself. So the whole people and the whole Afro-American experience had to be searched and exploited for clues to heritage. Folk materials and the expression of the common man had to be the essence of such a tradition ... when the promoters of the New Negro looked back to find his [sic] origins, or when they tried to discuss racial culture, they were always thrown back upon Africa.[49]

But images of Africa did not prove easily recuperable either and the turn to African origins could be as destabilizing, ultimately, as stabilizing.

Countee Cullen's "Heritage," one of the most well-known poems of the Harlem Renaissance, voices some of the skepticism that Hurston's Harlem Renaissance contemporaries began to feel about grounding African American identity in African origins. Rather than take for granted that Africa will help to fix the narrator's woes or ground his floundering identity, the poem *asks*, over and over, "What is Africa to me?" Clearly, the answer is that it is an idea, a fantasy, a desire, a dream, a racial memory, a wish, a song, a heritage (perhaps), but – most importantly – an invention, a literary myth which serves (or fails to serve) a pressing need:

> Quaint, outlandish heathen gods
> Black men fashion out of rods,
> Clay, and brittle bits of stone,
> In a likeness like their own.

The poem refuses to answer the question of what race is or how African heritage can help determine it. It refuses to adjudicate the then-current Harlem Renaissance debate over whether race is an essence or a social construction. And it refuses the position, central to much Harlem Renaissance writing, that race incurs moral or ethical obligations.[50] Unable to decide, finally, whether his remote African heritage endows him with tangible difference or is instead a mere idea, "a book one thumbs/Listlessly, till slumber comes," the speaker struggles for "peace" and wonders if consciously playing "a double part" might answer to his "need" to resolve his identity. Hence, the poem winks at its own proposition. Finding origins, it points out, means inventing them.[51] The poem's rhetorical question about

origins was very much a part of the Harlem Renaissance search for authenticity in which many participated but by which most felt stymied. If there
were no originals, just inventions, then what would ground the authority of
the African American to "speak for himself"? Why would his (or her) inventions carry more weight or be more authentic than a Howard Odum's, a Julia
Peterkin's, a DuBose Heyward's?

Hurston was not unaware of this question. She was simply unbothered by
it. Given her background (in Eatonville and amongst storytellers), her training (in anthropology at Barnard and Columbia), her different milieus (rural
Florida, the Harlem Renaissance, national folklore communities, and aca-
demia), and her personality (naturally "bodacious"), folklore was a kind of
perfect storm for her. She knew everyone, could call on anyone for assis-
tance, and was herself sought out by an array of famous writers and thinkers
(from Fannie Hurst to Melville Herskovits) to bridge conflicting schools of
thought as a resident expert in the meaning of race. This gave her the
confidence to assert her own original answer to the authenticity question.

"The life and color of my people"

The Negro's outstanding characteristic is drama. That is why he appears so
imitative. Drama is mimicry. note gesture is [in] place of words.
                    Zora Neale Hurston to Langston Hughes, April 12, 1928

The Negro's universal mimicry is not so much a thing in itself as an evidence of
something that permeates his entire self. And that thing is drama.
                    Zora Neale Hurston, "Characteristics of Negro Expression"

Hurston did not take recourse to a theory of African origins to ground the
authenticity of the folklore she collected. Throughout her life, what interested her was principally American, southern, rural and working class: the
writing of "his majesty the man in the gutter" (ZNH to Hughes, *LIL*, p. 126).
She repeatedly asserted that authenticity was not a matter of origins but
instead inhered in self-expression and faithful transcription.[52] What was
self-expressed and transcribed, in her view, could be complete invention, as
long as these two conditions were met.

For Hurston, folklore's great strength was that it was "still in the making"
and so could be remade, as necessary, until it got across. "Negro folklore is
not a thing of the past," she wrote. "It is still in the making. Its great variety
shows the adaptability of the black man."[53] Folklore was not something for
scholars to dig up (although she did put in her time as an academic, doing
more than her share of digging), but, rather, was what the "people create."
The original version of a tale might not be the best one, but rather its

newest rendering. "It is obvious," Hurston wrote, "that to get back to original sources is much too difficult for any group to claim very much as a certainty."[54] When she called something "authentic," she meant that mostly in the sense that we might call something a "true fiction." "What we really mean by originality is the modification of ideas ... the exchange and re-exchange of ideas."[55]

Because her folklore aesthetic was fluid and alive, Hurston had less ambivalence about either popularity or appealing to mass audiences than did many others, either in the academy or in the Harlem Renaissance, who worried that popularity signaled inauthenticity. To Hurston, it made sense to combine authenticity and popularity, especially since the value of folklore did not inhere for her so much in getting originals right as it did in how that folklore was received. The most natural place for this synthesis for her was the theater, with its potential to reach large audiences and present visual and oral cultures more extensively than print, radio, or cinema could offer at this time. Some have misread Hurston as turning away from folklore in her later career. "With the publication of *Mules [and Men]*," one scholar writes, "Hurston abandoned folklore."[56] Nothing, however, could be farther from the truth. Hurston turned to drama as the ideal arena to realize a folklore that would be authentic without being original in the usual sense.

Hurston's work with folk theater in the thirties was extensive.[57] And while I do not think Hurston ever "hyperidealized" folklore or fostered an "indulgent celebration of folk culture as the only undiluted voice of black America,"[58] her folklore theater was far and away the most affirmative presentation of folklore materials we can find, outside of her anthropological writings. Among the folk productions on which she worked were: *Fast and Furious*, *Batouala*, *Mules and Men*, *The Great Day*, *From Sun to Sun*, and *Singing Steel*. For these latter productions especially, Hurston hauled a troupe numbering as many as sixty people from New York to Washington, DC, St. Louis, Chicago, Nashville, and Florida. She taught folk theater at a number of colleges (though never with much success), worked for the Federal Theater Project, and accompanied folklorists John and Alan Lomax on music-collecting trips to the South. In an effort to realize her ambitions for the theater she put aside other work, went deep into debt, made enemies, and attempted a number of famously stressful and ill-fated collaborations. What merited such sacrifice? What made her theater plans "Glorious!" (ZNH to Hughes, *LIL*, p. 117)?

The ambitions Hurston considered "a really new departure in the drama" (ZNH to Hughes, *LIL*, p. 117) date back to the 1920s when she first described her plans for a "*real* Negro theater" where she could "act out the folk tales, however short, with the abrupt angularity and naivete of the primitive 'bama nigger'" (ZNH to Hughes, *LIL*, p. 116). Her idea was to create a thoroughly vernacular theater, drawing on vast stores of black folklore for both its themes and its forms. Ideally, it would look nothing like traditional – or avante garde – European or American theater. Instead, the best black theater would come from "some humble Negro boy or girl who has never heard of Ibsen."[59] Her theater would most certainly not be the product of any black intellectual who "goes to Whiteland to learn his trade! Ha!" (ZNH to Hughes, *LIL*, p. 116). And unlike the inauthentic but profitable shows on Broadway, *Shuffle Along*, *Porgy and Bess*, and *The Green Pastures*, for example, it would not have "squeezed all Negro-ness out of every thing" (ZNH to Mason, *LIL*, p. 226).

What would make Hurston's theater more authentic, clearly, is that it would be under her control. As she quickly learned, however, the finances of the theater world made such control virtually impossible. Hurston's greatest theater success was *The Great Day*, which she did write, produce, direct, and act in herself, and which she performed under various titles and in many different cities, including New York, Florida, North Carolina, and Tennessee. Featuring a day in the life of a railroad camp, the dramatic review included worksongs, a sermon, lullabies, spirituals, children's games, jook scenes, a fire dance, signifying contests, Bahamian dances, and a conjure ritual (which was cut out of the New York production at the last moment) and, in later performances, a short one act play about slavery entitled *The Fiery Chariot*. Hurston aggressively marketed the production as authentic. Alain Locke wrote program notes to capitalize on the idea that black authenticity meant dropping the veil for whites:

> The folkways and folk-arts of the American Negro have been presented in tinctured and adulterated approximations. That they have seemed characteristic and have been so movingly effective is, in view of this fact, all the greater testimony to their power and originality in the pure undiluted folk-forms that for generations have been in the shrewd and disarming custody of the common people. These folk have always had two arts, – one for themselves and one for the amusement and beguilement of their masters. And seldom, if ever, can the white man or even the sophisticated Negro break through to that inner circle so well-guarded by the instinctive make-believe and 'possum-play of the Negro peasant.
>
> *Great Day* is a stage arrangement of part of a cycle of Negro folk-song, dance and pantomime collected and recorded by Miss Zora Hurston over three years of intimate living among the common folk in the primitive privacy of their own Negro way of life. It is thus a rare sample of the pure and unvarnished materials from which the stage and concert tradition has been derived; and ought to show how much more unique and powerful and spirit-compelling the genuine Negro folk-things really are. That this legacy has not been irrevocably lost or completely overlaid is good news of the highest spiritual and practical importance for all who wish to know and understand the true elements of the Negro heart and soul.

Ironically, Locke's preface references the one aspect of African American folklore which, evidently, Hurston did *not* include in this drama, although it was one she revered: the tradition of dissembling, double speak, and masking which she called "feather-bed resistance":

> The Negro, in spite of his open-faced laughter, his seeming acquiescence, is particularly evasive. You see we are a a polite people and we do not say to our questioner, "Get out of here!" We smile and tell him or her something that satisfies the white person because, knowing so little about us, he doesn't now what he is missing. The Indian resists curiosity by a stony silence. The Negro offers a feather-bed resistance. That is, we let the probe enter, but it never comes out. It gets smothered under a lot of laughter and pleasantries.
>
> The theory behind our tactics: "The white man is always trying to know into somebody else's business. All right, I'll set something outside the door of my mind for him to play with and handle. He can read my writing but he sho' can't read my mind. I'll put this play toy in his hand and he will seize it and go away. Then I'll say my say and sing my song.[60]

Hurston loved documenting examples of feather-bed resistance, the array of practices and strategies of subtle rebellion African Americans use to avoid, precisely, the kind of invitation to outsiders which Locke's preface promises. When Hurston restaged *The Great Day* at Rollins College, under the title of *Sun to Sun*, Locke's preface was removed from the theater program.

While Hurston used many kinds of folklore in her fiction, to the consternation of some of her critics, the folklore form she most prized and used most often was "feather-bed resistance." Because "feather-bed resistance" is a strategy of double-speak, masking, avoidance, evasion, and silence, it has often gone undiscerned or unexplained by critics of her work. It has allowed Hurston to put one folklore "play toy" in the hands of her readers while, in fact, saying even more complex things about folklore just outside of their conscious hearing.

"Folklore fiction at its best"?

> And now, Zora Neale Hurston and her magical title: *Their Eyes Were Watching God* . . . But as always thus far with this talented writer, setting and surprising flashes of contemporary folklore are the main point. Her gift for poetic phrase, for rare dialect, and folk humor keep her flashing on the surface of her community and her characters . . . It is folklore fiction at its best, which we gratefully accept as an overdue replacement for so much faulty local color fiction about Negroes . . . Having gotten rid of condescension, let us now get over oversimplification!
>
> Alain Locke, review of *Their Eyes Were Watching God*

There is not a folk tale in the entire book.   Zora Neale Hurston[61]

Hurston's most well-known fictional work is *Their Eyes Were Watching God*. There is no question that the novel incorporates forms of folklore – sermons, Signifying, courtship, humor, animal tales, and storytelling – though not, Hurston rightly protested, much in the way of actual folktales. Critics have dubbed it a "folklore novel" and, by and large, have read the novel's use of folklore in one particular way. But being mindful of "feather-bed resistance," which saturates the novel from beginning to end, we might consider a greater multiplicity of views of the folk and their world at play in this novel.

Their Eyes Were Watching God tells the story of Janie Crawford and her search for fulfillment. Its form – a frame narrative where Janie tells her story to her best friend, Pheoby – stresses the key role that storytelling plays in that search. The novel also provides a rich background in the everyday life of a folk community, homing in on storytelling sessions on the town's store porch. Janie is not a part of these rituals. And critics have read her exclusion as the primary obstacle which she must overcome. Hurston actively celebrates the folk community, the argument goes, by having Janie first shut out of the folk traditions of her community and then restored to them. Hence, in the criticism of this novel we find a nearly universal claim that Hurston signals Janie's development by having her acquire a voice, one that resonates with the communal, authoritative voice of folklore traditions. "Janie's development is above all a function of her meaningful participation in black folk traditions . . . She tells her story," for example.[62] "A major feature of Janie's plight," Michael Awkward argues, "is the fact that she is denied access to the expressive rituals and traditions of the Eatonville community . . . Janie's is a struggle . . . for the ability to display her grasp of the sophisticated tropes of black vernacular expressivity in order to be able to participate in the story-telling sessions that took place in Eatonville and that helped to determine one's status within the community."[63]

As I have argued elsewhere,[64] it is remarkable how many critics – including such shrewd Hurstonians as Robert Hemenway,[65] Houston Baker,[66] Barbara Johnson,[67] Karla Holloway,[68] Susan S. Lanser,[69] and Henry Louis Gates, Jr.[70] – argue that Janie *gains* her voice in the novel. It is made plain, however, that she is a "born orator,"[71] always has a voice, and either finds it impossible or *chooses* not to use it with a community she derides as "Mouth Almighty" (17): a waste of time and breath. "Ah don't mean to bother wid tellin' 'em nothing," Janie declares to Pheoby, "'tain't worth de trouble" (17). Hurston figures human desire, our "oldest human longing," as the desire to participate in storytelling or "self-revelation" and then depicts, throughout the novel, how rare it is to find – or be able to create – the conditions under which this "longing" might be satisfied. Janie, the novel's main character, waits twenty years to find the one "hungry" listener, her best friend Pheoby, with whom, at last (and with whom *only*), this "longing" can be met.

Is it possible that critics read a non-existent reconciliation between Janie and her community into the novel[72] because *they* romanticize storytelling? Does Hurston idealize storytelling as an "active interchange between responsive storytellers and participatory listeners"[73] or do we? Imagining that "Hurston empowers Janie Crawford to liberate herself and her friend Pheoby through storytelling,"[74] we can romanticize Eatonville as the nurturing, pastoral community where such exchange occurs. Or, we can more easily insist that this is what Hurston does.

While Hurston's portrayal of Eatonville in *Their Eyes Were Watching God* contains many delightful scenes of animated storytelling and "lies," the overall portrait here and elsewhere is anything but idealized.[75] Even *Dust Tracks*, her most sentimentalized portrait of home, relates that "the Village seemed dull to me most of the time. If the Village was singing a chorus, I must have missed the tune" and she confesses a feeling of "terrible aloneness . . . a world of vanished communion with my kind."[76] It is not so much that the Village excludes her from talking rituals she longs for, but rather that their talk, as we see it in *Their Eyes Were Watching* God, is filled with petty, and not so petty, cruelties. Janie's folk sit in "judgment" like "lords of sounds and lesser things," "made burning statements with questions and killing tools out of laughs," "gnaw on" all the unkind thoughts they can, and they are simply awful listeners, the kind of folks who miss all the nuance and cannot take a hint (a particular sin given that African American discursive contexts so often depend on double meanings). Even worse, they are particularly unkind to women. The women in Janie's family history have been not only raped and abused, but denied a chance to speak up and speak for themselves. "Ah wanted to preach a great sermon about colored women," Janie's grandmother tells her, "but they wasn't no pulpit for me" (31). Only a woman whose pride and spirit were totally broken, one like poor Annie Tyler, with her "hanging bosom and stomach and buttocks and legs that draped down to her ankles," would even give them a try.

To miss the critical dimension of Hurston's portrayal of the folk world, in other words, is to overlook her feminist critique of it. As she points out here and in writings such as "My People, My People!," the joyous discursive rituals of African American folk speech are historically gendered territory. Women are not only often excluded from these rituals, but are often their targets. "I found the Negro and always the blackest Negro, being made the butt of all jokes – particularly black women."[77] Hurston's gendered critique of the folk world she loved makes *Their Eyes Were Watching God* a much more complex work of art than folklore novels such as George Wylie

Henderson's *Ollie Miss* (1935), Arna Bontemps' remarkably sexist *God Sends Sunday* (1931), Julia Peterkin's *Scarlet Sister Mary* (1929), or Heyward's *Porgy*, 1925.

Hurston used her deep knowledge of and respect for folk traditions to analyze how they get romanticized, rather than to romanticize them herself. To do this she took a page straight out of folklore itself, which may account, in part, for why it has drawn so little critical attention. Because it uses folklore, her questioning of folklore ends up looking a bit like one of those camouflage insects that mimics a leaf or a twig, but of course is something else entirely (although it may live off the thing that it mimics). Earlier I suggested that the best way to think of Hurston's interrogation is not as critique, which tends to work from outside that which it analyzes, but as Signifying, which works from the inside out, staying within the terms of what it questions but giving those terms a twist. And unlike critique, which is all too often a humorless enterprise, Signifying depends heavily on humor. Signifying does not tear down what it signifies upon; it *plays* with it. And for Hurston, to *play* with folklore is a special form of Signifying, since the way that so much folklore plays is to make up stories *about* women, not to invite them into the game.

Play is especially important in *Their Eyes Were Watching God* and, as Gates points out, "figures of play are the dominant repeated figures in the second half of *Their Eyes*" (*Signifying*). Janie learns to play when she falls in love with Tea Cake, and she is delighted: "Somebody wanted her to play. Somebody thought it natural for her to play." Play carries multiple meanings. It is, as Gates points out, "the text's word for . . . Signifyin(g) rituals." "Play" carries the meaning of drama, of discourse as performance: "They know it's not courtship. It's acting out courtship and everybody is in the play," Janie says of the Signifying the men in the novel revere. Effective Signifying is both performance and what we now call "performative": speech which is also an action, which names into being that to which it seems merely to refer, a speech act which signifies upon (or cites) prior speech acts to repeat them but to do so with a subversive difference.[78] Hurston's playful performativity, like her Signifying on folklore, has drawn too little attention. But it points to even larger aesthetic and philosophical issues.

In "Characteristics of Negro Expression" Hurston wrote that "it is obvious that to get back to original sources is much too difficult." She was specifically referring to folklore sources, but her skilled use of Signifying and performatives, combined with her disentangling of originality and authenticity, suggests that something larger is at stake. By aligning authenticity with cultural authority, not original sources, and treating folklore as a performance rather than as a static storehouse of timeless sayings and acts, Hurston did not so much folklorize her fiction as underscore the fictionality – and the performativity – of folklore. "What we really mean by originality," Hurston continued, "is the modification of ideas." In other words, we need not see Hurston's use of folklore as a way, always, to shore up a "representation of 'Negroness' as an unchanging, essential entity." Instead, a fluid and alive folklore aesthetic can open onto a non-essential idea of race, a view that race itself is an endlessly modified idea without a source original, and which, therefore, remains open to endless reinvention and even play. Folklore, in other words, didn't so much bolster an essential and transcendent Negroness for Hurston. It was what allowed her to *play* with blackness and with our ideas of what black folk are like.

NOTES

1. Unpublished essay, originally intended for *The American Mercury* and cancelled after typesetting. Lawrence Spivak Papers, Manuscript Division, Library of Congress.
2. June Jordan, "Notes Toward a Balancing Act of Love and Hatred," *Black World*, 23 (August 1974), p. 5.
3. Cited in http://www.cas.usf.edu/anthropology/women/hurston/Zora.html.
4. Hurston is one of two black women in the "Magnetic Personality" line up which includes: Dickens, Einstein, Foucault, Roosevelt (Eleanor), Freud, Diego Rivera, Frida Kahlo, Shakespeare, Geronimo, Harriet Tubman, Hegel, Jane Austen, Joyce, Jung, Kafka, Lincoln, Buddha, Che, Virginia Woolf, Ghandi, Van Gogh, Kant, Machievelli, Mozart, Frederick Douglass, Nietzsche, Poe, Plato, Tolstoy, Trotsky, Dali, Dorothy Parker, Newton, Karl Marx, Ben Franklin, Darwin, G. W. Carver, Teddy Roosevelt, Marie Curie, Washington, Napoleon, Joan of Arc, and Edison.
5. Henry Louis Gates, Jr., *The Signifying Monkey: A Theory of African-American Literary Criticism* (New York: Oxford University Press, 1988), p. 180. Future references are to this edition and will be cited parenthetically.
6. Zora Neale Hurston, "The 'Pet Negro' System," *American Mercury* 56 (May 1943), 593–600. Condensed in *Negro Digest* 1 (June 1943), 47–9.
7. H. I. Brock, review of *Mules and Men* (1935), *New York Times Book Review*, November 10, 1935.
8. Percy Hutchison, review of *Moses, Man of the Mountain* (1939), *New York Times Book Review*, November 19, 1939.
9. Margaret Wallace, review of *Jonah's Gourd Vine* (1934), *New York Times Book Review*, May 6, 1934.
10. Martha Gruening, review of *Jonah's Gourd Vine* (1934), *New Republic*, July 11, 1934.
11. Brock, review of *Mules and Men*.
12. Alain Locke, review of *Their Eyes Were Watching God* (1937), *Opportunity*, June 1, 1938.
13. Richard Wright, "Between Laughter and Tears," review of *Their Eyes Were Watching God* (1937), *New Masses*, October 5, 1937.

14. For a more extensive discussion of the feminist politics of *Their Eyes Were Watching God*, see Carla Kaplan, "'That Oldest Human Longing': The Erotics of Talk in *Their Eyes Were Watching God*," in *The Erotics of Talk: Women's Writing and Feminist Paradigms* (New York: Oxford University Press, 1996), pp. 99–122.

15. Geneva Smitherman defines "signifyin" as: "The verbal art of ritualized insult, in which the speaker puts down, needles, talks about (*signifies on*) someone, to make a point or sometimes just for fun. Signifyin depends on double meaning and irony, exploits the unexpected, and uses quick verbal surprises and humor. When used as social critique, it is characterized by nonmalicious and principled criticism. Malcolm X once began a speech with this bit of *signifyin*: 'Ladies and gentlemen, friends and enemies.'" *Black Talk: Words and Phrases from the Hood to the Amen Corner*, revised edition (Boston: Houghton Mifflin Company, 2000), p. 260.

16. Alice Walker, "On Refusing To Be Humbled by Second Place in a Contest You Did Not Design: A Tradition by Now," in *I Love Myself When I Am Laughing ... And Then Again When I Am Looking Mean and Impressive: A Zora Neale Hurston Reader*, ed. Alice Walker (New York: The Feminist Press, 1979), p. 2.

17. Harold Preece, "The Negro Folk Cult," first published in *Crisis* 43 (1936); reprinted in Alan Dundes, ed., *Mother Wit from the Laughing Barrel: Readings in the Interpretation of Afro-American Folklore* (Jackson: University of Mississippi Press, 1990), p. 35.

18. Anthony R. Hale, "Framing the Folk: Zora Neale Hurston, John Millington Synge, and the Politics of Aesthetic Ethnography," *Comparatist* 20 (1996), fn. 1, p. 59.

19. Ann duCille, *The Coupling Convention: Sex, Text, and Traditions in Black Women's Fiction* (New York: Oxford University Press, 1993), p. 71.

20. Hazel Carby, "The Politics of Fiction, Anthropology and the Folk: Zora Neale Hurston," in Geneviève Fabre and Robert O'Meally, eds., *History and Memory in African-American Culture* (New York: Oxford University Press, 1994), pp. 32, 34, 32. Originally published in 1990 in Michael Awkward, ed., *New Essays on Their Eyes Were Watching God* (Cambridge: Cambridge University Press), this essay has been widely reprinted and excerpted. Future references are to this edition and will be cited parenthetically.

21. Hale, "Framing the Folk," p. 53.

22. David Todd Lawrence, "Folkloric Representation and Extended Context in the Experimental Ethnography of Zora Neale Hurston," *Southern Folklore* 57.2 (2000), 120.

23. Eric J. Sundquist, *The Hammers of Creation: Folk Culture in Modern African-American Fiction* (Athens: University of Georgia Press, 1992), pp. 53, 85.

24. "A feminist does not simplify signify, she signifies on signifying itself," Catherine Gunther Kodat writes. While I disagree with key points in Kodat's reading of voice in *Their Eyes Were Watching God*, this statement applies well to Hurston's larger folklore aesthetic. See Catherine Gunther Kodat, "Bite the Hand that Writes You: Southern African-American Folk Narrative and the Place of Women in *Their Eyes Were Watching God*," in Anne Goodwyn Jones and Susan Donaldson, eds., *Haunted Bodies: Gender and Southern Texts* (Charlottesville: University Press of Virginia, 1997), p. 331.

25. As Claudia Mitchell-Kernan points out, there are broader senses of signifying which "also refers to a way of encoding messages or meanings which involves, in most cases, an element of indirection. This kind of *signifying* might be best viewed as an

alternative message form … and may occur embedded in a variety of discourse." "Signifying," in Dundes, ed., *Mother Wit from the Laughing Barrel*, p. 311.

26. Zora Neale Hurston to Langston Hughes, April 30, 1929, in *Zora Neale Hurston: A Life in Letters*, collected and ed. Carla Kaplan (New York: Doubleday, 2002), p. 132; Zora Neale Hurston, "Folklore and Music," in Cheryl Wall, ed., *Zora Neale Hurston: Folklore, Memoirs, and Other Writings* (New York: Library of America, 1995), p. 875 (a slightly different version of "Folklore and Music" can be found in *Go Gator and Muddy the Water: Writings by Zora Neale Hurston from the Federal Writers Project*, ed. Pamela Bordelon (New York: Norton, 1999); Zora Neale Hurston to Thomas E. Jones, October 12, 1934, in *Zora Neale Hurston: A Life in Letters*, p. 315. All future letters are from this edition and will be cited parenthetically with the abbreviation *LIL*.

27. Zora Neale Hurston to Langston Hughes, March 8, 1928, in *LIL*, p. 113. On Hurston's goals, experiences, and travels collecting folklore and studying anthropology, see *LIL* and the Introduction to *Every Tongue Got To Confess: Negro Folk-Tales from the Gulf States*, ed. Carla Kaplan (New York: HarperPerennial, 2002). Robert Hemenway agrees: "Folklore was the passion of her life and informs all of her work," he writes. "She made incredible sacrifices and took extraordinary risks to collect it, record it, and broadcast it to a wide audience." See his Foreword to *LIL*, p. 4.

28. Unpublished essay, Lawrence Spivak Papers, Manuscript Division, Library of Congress.

29. W. E. B. Du Bois, *The Souls of Black Folk* (1903; New York: The Library of America, 1986), p. 536.

30. James Weldon Johnson, "Preface," in *The Book of American Negro Poetry* (New York: Harcourt Brace, 1922). Embodying this notion, Johnson's *Autobiography of an Ex-Colored Man* depicts a narrator who aspires to a bring black music to the white public, but cannot do so because he has passed for white, tragically selling out his "birthright for a mess of pottage" and letting the salvaged genius of his people degenerate and decay: "yellow manuscripts" consigned to a locked "little box" that no one would ever see.

31. Alain Locke, "The New Negro," in Locke, ed., *The New Negro* (New York: Atheneum, 1992), p. 15 (first published New York: Albert and Charles Boni, 1925).

32. Benjamin Filene, *Romancing the Folk: Public Memory and American Roots Music* (Chapel Hill: University of North Carolina Press, 2000), p. 9.

33. For an excellent discussion of this, see George Hutchinson, *The Harlem Renaissance in Black and White* (Cambridge, MA: Harvard University Press, 1995). Hutchinson points out that among whites, "the interest in black folklore … was not restricted to its assimilation to the romantic and pastoral, let alone the exotic" (181). Nor was it the case, he writes, that all blacks collapsed white folklore under such rubrics. Sophisticated black critics, writing in venues such as *Opportunity*, he points out, "drew a distinction between respecting black folklore as a basis of American art and extolling the exotically 'primitive,'" (182).

34. Ann Douglas, *Terrible Honesty: Mongrel Manhattan in the 1920's* (New York: Farrar, Straus, Giroux, 1995), p. 559.

35. "The Negro's importance to American culture, it was argued, was that he provided its only genuine folk tradition. From the Afro-Americans had come a rich and complex folklore and music which was the most distinctively American

contribution to world culture." Nathan Huggins, *Harlem Renaissance* (New York: Oxford University Press, 1971), p. 72.

36. Locke, "The New Negro."

37. Ibid.

38. "Preface," in *The Book of American Negro Poetry*.

39. Howard Odum, "Religious Folk-Songs of the Southern Negroes" (1909), as quoted by Filene, *Romancing the Folk*, p. 31. In her correspondence, Hurston made frequent reference to Odum's mischaracterizations. About *The Negro and His Songs*, she wrote that "it is not so stupendous as the critics make out. It is inaccurate in a dozen places ... Perfectly honest, no doubt, but misinformed." Zora Neale Hurston to Alain Locke, May 1, 1928, in *LIL*, p. 118. To Franz Boas she reiterated her view that Odum and Johnson were "in error constantly" and could "hardly be less exact." Zora Neale Hurston to Franz Boas, December 27, 1928, in *LIL*, p. 135, and October 20, 1929, in *LIL*, p. 151.

40. In *The New Negro* Arthur Huff Fauset described Harris' work as "misrepresentation." See "American Negro Folk Literature," in *The New Negro*, pp. 238–44.

41. From John Lomax, Sr. to Ruby T. Terrill in the Lomax Family Papers, University of Texas, Austin, as cited by Filene, *Romancing the Folk*, p. 53.

42. Cited in Hutchinson, *The Harlem Renaissance*, p. 197.

43. Alain Locke, "Foreword," in *The New Negro*.

44. Charles S. Johnson, "An Opportunity for Negro Writers," *Opportunity* 2 (1924), p. 258.

45. For discussion of Hurston's complex relations with white patrons and teachers, including her private correspondence about the complexities of these relationships, see *LIL*.

46. Fortunately, in her view, their folklore and fictions were so far off the mark that she could hardly believe anyone would take them seriously. "My one consolation," the same letter continued, "being that they never do it right and so there is still a chance for us."

47. Johnson, "Preface," in *The Book of American Negro Poetry*. For an excellent discussion of black dialect see Sundquist, *The Hammers of Creation*, pp. 55ff.

48. See Gates, *The Signifying Monkey*. Sundquist argues that "in a signifying reversal of the denigration of black dialect ... Hurston ... sought to value and preserve the sounds of slave culture." Sundquist, *The Hammers of Creation*, p. 61. But as Gates' analysis of Hurston's free indirect discourse demonstrates, Hurston was inventing more than she was preserving any pre-existing form of black speech.

49. Huggins, *Harlem Renaissance*, p. 78.

50. For more on this ethics of race, see Carla Kaplan, Introduction to The *Norton Critical Edition of Nella Larsen's Passing* (New York: W. W. Norton, 2007), "Nella Larsen's Erotics of Race."

51. Filene makes the case that such invention is endemic to the folkloric "rescue" mission. "From the start," he writes, "'discovering' folk cultures involved reimagining them." *Romancing the Folk*, p. 12.

52. The original manuscript of *Mules and Men* establishes the extent to which Hurston wanted the folklore she collected to be published exactly as she transcribed it. "I have tried to be as exact as possible. Keep to the exact dialect as I could," she wrote Franz Boas. "The dirty words must be toned down," she told Langston Hughes. "Of course I knew that. But first I wanted to collect them as

they are." "I am leaving the story material untouched," she wrote in another letter to Hughes. We know, from Hurston's correspondence, that the various other narrative devices joined to the folklore when *Negro Folk-Tales from the Gulf States* became *Mules and Men* were added at the urging both of Hurston's publisher and, ironically, of Franz Boas (who wanted Hurston to create "the intimate setting in the social life of the Negro" for the uninitiated) – the mentor whose theories of exact transcription Hurston had tried to duplicate. See *Every Tongue Got To Confess: Negro Folk-Tales from the Gulf States* and *Zora Neale Hurston: A Life in Letters*.

53. Zora Neale Hurston, "Characteristics of Negro Expression," in Nancy Cunard, ed., *Negro: An Anthology*, first published 1934, abridged edition ed. Hugh Ford (New York: Ungar, 1970), p. 27. She repeated this phrase, "still in the making," in a footnote to a letter to Hughes. "Discovery 7," she wrote: "Negro folk-lore is still in the making a new kind is crowding out the old." Zora Neale Hurston to Langston Hughes, April 12, 1928, in *LIL*, p. 116. She also repeated the phrase in "Folklore and Music" where she wrote that "Folklore in Florida is still in the making." "Folklore and Music," Library of America, p. 875. Even for someone as prone to repeating and recycling her own work as Hurston was – a method she learned, in part, from folklore – the repetition of this phrase is significant and indicates both how important this idea was to her and how much she felt it lacked wide acceptance.

54. "Characteristics of Negro Expression," p. 28.

55. "Characteristics of Negro Expression."

56. Miriam DeCosta Willis, "Folklore and the Creative Artist: Lydia Cabrera and Zora Neale Hurston," *College Language Association Journal*, 27 (1983), 81–90.

57. This section draws on various discussions of Hurston and theater in *LIL*.

58. Sundquist, *The Hammers of Creation*, pp. 50–1, 54.

59. Zora Neale Hurston, "Race Cannot Become Great Until It Recognizes Its Talent," *Washington Tribune*, December 29, 1934.

60. Zora Neale Hurston, *Mules and Men* (Bloomington: Indiana University Press, 1978), pp. 4–5. Hurston repeats the "feather-bed resistance" passage, almost verbatim, in her unpublished "You Don't Know Us Negroes."

61. "The Chick with One Hen," unpublished manuscript, response to Locke's review. James Weldon Johnson Collection, Beinecke Library, Yale University.

62. Klaus Benesch, "Oral Narrative and Literary Text: Afro-American Folklore in *Their Eyes Were Watching God*," *Callaloo* 36 (Summer 1988), 634.

63. Michael Awkward, "Introduction," in *New Essays on Their Eyes Were Watching God* (Cambridge: Cambridge University Press, 1990), p. 18.

64. See Carla Kaplan "The Erotics of Talk in *Their Eyes Were Watching God*." The following discussion draws on this chapter.

65. "The Personal Dimension in *Their Eyes Were Watching God*," in Awkward, *New Essays*, pp. 29–49. "Janie is eventually able to tell her story because she reclaims her communal narrative endowment," Hemenway writes, p. 43.

66. Houston A. Baker, Jr., *Blues, Ideology and Afro-American Literature: A Vernacular Theory* (Chicago: University of Chicago Press, 1984), pp. 58–9.

67. Barbara Johnson, "Metaphor, Metonymy and Voice in *Their Eyes Were Watching God*," in Henry Louis Gates, Jr., ed., *Black Literature and Literary Theory* (New York: Methuen, 1984), p. 212.

68. Karla F. C. Holloway, *The Character of the Word: The Texts of Zora Neale Hurston* (New York: Greenwood Press, 1987), p. 40.

69. Susan Lanser, *Fictions of Authority: Women Writers and Narrative Voice* (Ithaca, NY: Cornell University Press, 1992), pp. 201–2.

70. See *The Signifying Monkey*, where Gates claims that Janie "gains her voice" by speaking aloud and Signifying.

71. Zora Neale Hurston, *Their Eyes Were Watching God* (Urbana: University of Illinois Press, 1978), p. 92. All future references to the novel are to this edition and will be cited parenthetically.

72. Perhaps the oddest instance of this misreading of Janie's storytelling is Hazel Carby's. Carby points out, quite rightly, that there is an "antagonistic relation" between Janie and the town, that "Janie refuses to tell her story directly to the community," and that this refusal dramatizes that antagonism. But she then goes on to misread Janie as having "the desire to 'sit down and tell [the folk] things'" and to claim, on that basis, that "reconciliation, then, between the position of intellectual and the folk as community takes place through acts of narration." See Carby, "The Politics of Fiction," pp. 37–8.

73. Awkward, "Introduction," p. 2.

74. Bernard W. Bell, *The Afro-American Novel and Its Tradition* (Amherst: University of Massachusetts Press, 1987), p. 25.

75. Günter Lenz insists that Hurston "discovers and 'celebrates' the folk community" of Eatonville, but also notes that "she does *not* describe an idyllic, harmonious scene of people telling folk tales and jokes." "Southern Exposures: The Urban Experience and the Re-construction of Black Folk Culture and Community in the Works of Richard Wright and Zora Neale Hurston," *New York Folklore* 7 (1981), 31. Similarly, Juniper Ellis writes that "the communities she conveys are rural, but they are not idealized." "Enacting Culture: Zora Neale Hurston, Joel Chandler Harris, and Literary Anthropology," in C. James Trotman, ed., *Multiculturalism: Roots and Realities* (Bloomington: Indiana University Press, 2002), p. 160. Catherine Kodat writes that "she does construct a voice through Southern African-American oral traditions, but her relation to those traditions remains a critical one." "Biting the Hand that Writes You," p. 321.

76. Zora Neale Hurston, *Dust Tracks on a Road* (1942; Urbana: University of Illinois Press, 1984) pp. 46, 49.

77. Ibid. p. 225. In *Authentic Blackness: The Folk in the New Negro Renaissance*, J. Martin Favor notes that "the form of folk expression is gendered by exclusion, meaning that when we speak of folk culture, we generally speak of *male* folk culture" (Durham, NC: Duke University Press, 1999), p. 18. Similarly, Cheryl Wall has written that "women were, of course, historically denied participation in many of these traditions; for instance, speechifying, whether in the pulpit or on the block, has been a mainly male prerogative." "Response" to Kimberly W. Benston, in Houston A. Baker, Jr. and Patricia Redmond, eds., *Afro-American Literary Study in the 1990's* (Chicago: University of Chicago Press, 1989), p. 188.

78. For more on performativity, see Judith Butler, *Gender Trouble: Feminism and the Subversion of Identity* (New York: Routledge, 1990) and my discussion of performativity in *The Erotics of Talk*.

PART III

The post-renaissance

16

LAWRENCE JACKSON

"The Aftermath": the reputation of the Harlem Renaissance twenty years later

In 1945 the editors of the Atlanta University journal *Phylon* wrote to a sixty-five-year-old Carl Van Vechten and asked for his comments on a Hugh Gloster essay they were publishing. Gloster's "The Van Vechten Vogue" sketched out the influence of the best-known white American – half architect, half voyeur – connected to the explosion of black writing in the 1920s. *Phylon*'s editors, the sharp-minded young sociologist Ira de a Reid and the illustrious W. E. B. Du Bois, printed Van Vechten's brief comment. According to the man who had been the leading light of the "Negrotarians," the white cultivators and supporters committed to the exploration of black life in Manhattan in the 1920s, Gloster was so "eminently fair" in his essay that nothing was left to say. The novelist, photographer, and spirited collector of African American letters could not avoid the fact that he was seeing something that he had predicted would end certain varieties of discrimination. "Negroes are kept down because they lack NERVE and initiative," Van Vechten had written to his friend Langston Hughes in 1942.[1] Gloster showed both qualities, hallmarks of a new generation of writers and critics, a cadre that would rely considerably less on the support of individual patrons like Van Vechten. He was a man whose era had passed and whose most deeply held convictions about racial equality led the way to the vastly reduced scope of his own role.

In his essay, Gloster targeted not even so much Van Vechten singly as the entire movement during which Van Vechten's most famous relationships with Langston Hughes, James Weldon Johnson, Zora Neal Hurston, and Nella Larsen, among many others, had flourished. In an unusually ironic twist of fate, the movement for black artistic development in the United States, always hand-in-glove with the larger movement for racial justice, and the even broader shift for modernist artistic expression, seemed deliberately employing segregationist logic in its historical self-representation. A literary movement of blacks partly engineered by a bi-sexual playboy, one that left little evidence of confrontation or belligerent protest, seemed humiliating. For Gloster and his generation, Van Vechten, at least by the way of his 1926 book *Nigger Heaven*, "dramatized the alleged animalism and exoticism of Harlem folk" and "influenced the writings of Negro Renascence authors."[2] Thus the subsequent Van Vechten School of black novelists (Claude McKay, Wallace Thurman, Arna Bontemps) stressed "jazz, sex, atavism and primitivism." Gloster, though not completely dismissive of Van Vechten's iconoclast import as the first novelist to capture the Harlem scene of the 1920s and to develop an audience, articulated all of the touchstones that would come to haunt the period. The Renaissance was "primarily a fad" and Van Vechten and his friends' "fatal mistake" was to "make a fetish of sex and the cabaret rather than to give a faithful, realistic presentation and interpretation of Harlem life" (314).

The Hampton Institute professor Hugh Gloster was, perhaps, pointing out the ambivalent effects of Van Vechten's leadership during the 1920s in order to symbolize a particularly acute problem that black progressives faced during the 1940s from their famously "liberal" white peers in the South and North. But he did not make up his critique from scratch. By the middle 1940s, there was a substantial tradition of reproach surrounding the outburst in art and letters that had had its epicenter in Harlem roughly between 1924 and 1929, known then as the Alain Locke-named "New Negro" Movement, but remembered better by posterity when combined with the geographic sobriquet that symbolized all of black America, the "Harlem Renaissance."

This phenomenon, the repudiation of a group of socially marginalized black creative writers by a subsequent and similarly marginalized generation of black critics, is doubly curious because the critics of the 1930s, 1940s, and 1950s were fairly conspicuous in their devotion to and appreciation of vernacular black culture. But for more than a score of years following the 1920s, these writers and critics expressed mainly the utmost impatience with the achievement of African American writers during the 1920s. It was an impatience and disregard that would not really be reversed until the success of the modern Civil Rights Movement and the creation of Black Studies academic programs in the late 1960s and early 1970s.

A particularly stinging and early reprimand of black literary talent from the late 1920s came internally from the man reported to be the group's undeniable genius, the editor (of the Renaissance journals *Fire!!* and *Harlem*) and writer Wallace Thurman. The energetic but dilettante novelist Walter White (the most regularly published black writer by large New York houses during the 1920s), the sonneteer Countee Cullen, and the reliably genteel Jessie Fauset, embodied the narrow literary abilities, and Zora Neal Hurston and Richard Bruce Nugent the outrageous personalities, that Thurman had in mind when he wrote in 1927 that white critics thought of then contemporary black writers as "a highly trained trick dog doing dances in the public square."[3] Five years later Thurman went further with his critique of the movement in an engaging roman à clef, *Infants of the Spring*. In the book Thurman complained of the multiple paradoxes that haunted the new generation of black writers: blacks who excelled at proving white stereotypes of blacks; prejudiced whites leading the liberal vanguard for racial justice; untalented blacks promoted as virtuosos; black artists personally disdainful of folk culture; make-believe black artists scaling the dramatic heights of bohemian burlesque to escape the label of race; and the failure of the black writer to find an audience.

Despite the slight orbit of Thurman's own career, his objections were received as more than petty caviling. Two of his contemporaries both called into question the organic connection to black folk and the aesthetic value of the writing after 1925. (Consider as well that the best-known works of the 1920s – Claude McKay's "If We Must Die" (1919), James Weldon Johnson's "The Creation" (1920), Langston Hughes' "The Negro Speaks of Rivers" (1921) and "Mother to Son" (1922), and Jean Toomer's *Cane* (1923) – were always and remain to this day recognized as nearly constituting a tradition within a tradition.) One of the two was Howard University philosophy professor Alain Locke. In yearly book reviews for the Urban League's *Opportunity* journal, beginning in 1929 and ending in 1942 (and excepting 1930), the moneyless patron of the Renaissance fired on the group of writers whom he had helped to launch, many of whom he thought petulant, bohemian, and ungrateful. As black writers began to shift away from sentimentalized "beauty" into the field of realistic "truth," Locke admitted that the group had been guilty of "spiritual bondage" and that "much exploitation has had to be admitted."[4] That was in 1929. Two years later, Locke decided that the entire movement had suffered from "inflation and overproduction."[5] Langston Hughes, no special admirer of Locke's, concurred in some respects to the estimate, if for different reasons. In the early 1930s he was, like Du Bois, appreciative of a strenuous form of Marxism, and when in 1940 he published his memoir *The Big Sea*, he contributed the most frequently cited passages that proposed a truncated chronology for the artistic movement as well as the chief source of its demise. According to Hughes, at the end of "the generous 1920s," black artists were "no longer in vogue," at least in the minds of white customers of black culture.[6]

The emerging critique from the 1930s emphasized the political and sociological, not the artistic, an understandable tendency during the financial collapse of the American economy. It praised naturalist realism in literature and the wielding of liberal progressive social science in the public sphere. James Weldon Johnson, who had believed that "nothing will do more to change that mental attitude [white American racial prejudice] and raise his status than a demonstration of intellectual parity by the Negro through the production of literature and art," was laid to rest not merely in body in 1938, but principally in spirit, in so far as black writers continued to subscribe to his belief in the power of art as a proof of civilization.[7] Armed with widely accepted scientific advances regarding racial parity in biology and anthropology and insight into sociology and political economy by way of the analytical techniques of Marxism, Hugh Gloster's generation withheld patience for less than full racial equality. The ground was shifting from a celebration of black life to the exposure of the pathology behind the black condition. Increasingly, black writers who had developed their craft in an integrated environment produced the fiction and poetry that supported, extended, and sometimes initiated these analyses. Their voices of dissent and rounding criticism emerged after the deaths of Thurman and Rudolph Fisher in 1934, and were especially engaged following the development of the Federal Writers Project between 1935 and 1939, the National Negro Congress between 1937 and 1945, and the League of American Writers, which held writers' congresses beginning in 1935 and into the early 1940s. While Locke and Hughes both limited the scope and heft of the movement, it fell to the writers who became known in the 1930s and 1940s to trim sharply the value of 1920s renaissance.

The same year as the deaths of Thurman and Fisher, fitting epitaphs to the renaissance in David Levering Lewis's commanding account *When Harlem Was in Vogue*, Malcolm Cowley offered a portrait of the decadent and "lost" generation of American writers called *Exile's Return*. Although he ignored the black writers in his midst in Manhattan, he had at least noticed the changing environment of the modern world by taking note of educated upper-class blacks in Paris. Cowley proposed that the American writers who had fled the commercialism and shallow traditions of America for Europe now had been exiled, uprooted from regional tradition, and confusedly embittered by the breakdown of traditional values that accompanied the slaughter of World War I. If these factors had caused the exile, his advice to the returning artist was straightforward and prescriptive. Cowley believed that white artists must in the 1930s choose the side of the "worker" in the class struggle, and, more or less, he charged the new generation to eradicate boundaries of social class as well as race and ethnicity. The pampered writers who had left the United States to work in the ambulance corps during World War I must now suture themselves to "people without manners or distinction, Negroes, hill billies, poor whites, Jews, Wops and Hunkies."[8] The radical nature of Cowley's invitation emerges when considering that, by the end of the 1920s, major public liberal intellectuals like John Dewey,

Horace Kallen, and Robert Park were effectively abandoning the struggle against racial discrimination and the messy field of cultural politics in favor of working to ameliorate economic differences.[9] It took a long time for more typical members of the literary establishment, like Harold Rosenberg, to admit to black Americans having a cultural tradition. They believed that "lowercase Americans have been and remain 'aliens,'" and held that for this group "culture exists in the future not in the past."[10] Black writers attributed their racial erasure to the sad fact that there was no single author of unequivocal genius to emerge from the 1920s, one too noteworthy to be ignored by the "Lost Generation." Where was the black writer with blockbuster appeal and whose magnificence trod over the crass borders of racial prejudice?

The absence of this kind of successful writer could be understood by agreeing with J. Saunders Redding who said that "Negro mothers, too, bore children into the 'lost generation.'"[11] Even if their flight to Europe had not taken place under precisely the same conditions, even if the Sacco-Vanzetti case had not been the brook of fire for their political radicalism, it made sense to connect those of the Harlem Renaissance to their white peers. Black writers had experienced exile too – in their own native land. They had been estranged from the rural past and moved into the swift urban and black international current that was Harlem. Many had traveled to Europe, but they had also traveled back to the rural South, to the Caribbean, and, for that matter, to Chicago. They could trace their political radicalism, not just to personal slights, but to the riots in 1919. They had wrestled with and been a bit disfigured by expectations of their "primitive" vitality. Their position in the art-for-art's-sake struggle was compounded by their political liability; they were a visible ethnic minority in a vigorously chauvinist white country. The overriding pressures of racial integrity often tempered the art-for-art's-sake creed.

One writer who verged on fulfilling dramatically that role of broadly appealing Negro writer was the gifted vernacular poet Sterling Brown. While Brown might be counted as an "official" member of the Harlem Renaissance – he won an *Opportunity* prize in 1925 and published "When De Saint's Go Marching Home" in Countee Cullen's *Caroling Dusk* in 1927 – during those years he had been teaching at Virginia Seminary in Lynchburg, Virginia, at Lincoln in Jefferson City, Missouri, and at Fisk in Nashville, Tennessee. The experiences he soaked up in these diverse and earthy teaching posts caused Brown always to assert that though the bell cow may have been in Harlem, the renaissance had "spatial roots elsewhere in America."[12] Brown started teaching at Howard in 1929, but for the rest of his life always possessed an animus toward the idea of black writing as an urban and northern phenomenon. In an influential essay called "The Negro Character as Seen by White Authors" published in 1933, Brown identified seven "stereotypes" or leitmotifs that governed the creation of African American characters in American literature and culture. The essay captured not only the new defiance of black intellectuals and their rejection of patronage, but also showed the immense libraries now open to the intellectual avant-garde who had earned advanced degrees at exclusive American universities. Brown had also taken seriously Walter Lippman's warning that "stereotypes," a printing term referring to metal plates made from type, would create permanent and narrow mental images. In the essay Brown rejected an entire geological strata of American literature as being completely false to black life. He dismissed as especially harmful writers who ground the accuracy of their depictions of black Americans in their early lives on plantations worked by slaves and their being nursed and potty-trained by black mammies. Speaking of the popular writer Roark Bradford, Brown was succinct. "All this, he believes, gives him license to step forth as their interpreter and to repeat stereotypes in the time-hallowed South. It doesn't."[13] This was a tone of learned defiance, even anger.

The young Howard professor went on to identify seven recurring stereotypes: contented slave, wretched freeman, comedian or buffoon, brute, tragic mulatto, "local color" negro, and "exotic primitive." Unafraid to offend whites or burn bridges, Brown also evinced shades of dialectical materialism. Slavery expanded in the nineteenth century owing to the cotton gin and the profit margin, and the result in relation to the development of American fiction was a stereotype of black contentedness under bondage. But Brown showed his real ire toward the conclusion of the essay and the final example, the falsely championed "exotic primitive." For this violation he pointed to Carl Van Vechten, easily recognized as a visible supporter of African American writing and culture, especially during the 1920s, as among the culprits. Instead of an original exploration of the vitality of black life and the spirited and modern embrace of sexuality and rejection of Victorian gentility, Brown saw "cabarets supplanting cabins, and Harlemized 'blues,' instead of the spirituals and slave reels" (176). Van Vechten, author of *Nigger Heaven*, was certainly not sacrosanct, in spite of the devotion he received from Langston Hughes, Zora Neal Hurston, and James Weldon Johnson was not incidental (which Van Vechten did not let go unrepaid). In the name of advancing American black literary images, Brown's readiness to reject Van Vechten (whom, forty years later, he called a "rascal," a "voyeur" who had "corrupted the Harlem Renaissance and was a terrible influence") and, by extension, whites of "good will," staked a claim of independence and fitness that was a shocking break.[14] A year-and-a-half later, it was unsurprising to see Brown in print sparring over the film *Imitation of Life* with another popular white liberal "friend" of the Negro, Miss Fannie Hurst.

The legendary environment on the Howard campus in the 1930s and 1940s nourished sharp critiques of society. Alongside Abram Harris in economics, Ralph Bunche in political science, Rayford Logan in history, librarian Dorothy Porter, and E. Franklin Frazier in sociology, Brown expressed an artistic vision decidedly in concert with the political left wing. By the second half of the 1930s, Brown was working as the head of Negro Affairs for the Federal Writers Project, and employing as his research assistant Eugene Clay Holmes, a young instructor in the philosophy department. Holmes was actively involved in the Communist Party, that small, vocal, beleaguered, paranoid, and tightly disciplined group that recognized the cachet of providing a forum for black writers to discuss their views on their literary tradition and their relationship to the white mainstream. The two men vigorously participated in the League of American Writers, a "Popular Front" organization created by the communists to unite writers and artists across the political spectrum in order to resist the growing fascist menace. Not everyone supported these institutions. The most influential groups to emerge from the 1930s, the so-called New York Intellectuals massed around the journal *Partisan Review*, had gravitated toward Trotsky's brand of Marxism and strove to expose any of the communist-organized efforts as evidence of Stalinist brutality. However, the specter of communist insincerity or exploitation was greatly balanced by a fair degree of racially exclusive elitism practiced by the New York Intellectuals, the southern Agrarian and New Critics, and the Ivy League literary academics. In the comparatively discrimination-free communist milieu appeared some of the steadiest condemnations of the Harlem Renaissance writers, who were seen as lacking a political agenda, acquiescent to prejudiced whites, unconcerned with urban black masses struggling for economic survival, and unable to write literature aesthetically competitive with elite writers of the modern art movement.

Speaking before the League of American Writers conference in 1935 as Eugene Clay, Professor Holmes maligned the inevitable result of poor cultural stewardship that was the "Harlem tradition" of "amusements and new thrills" for the white American bourgeoisie.[15] Seeking to dismantle the celebrated détente between black writers and white publishers in favor of the interracial comity of the communists, whose American party had in 1932 run a black candidate for vice president, Clay described the Renaissance as ersatz, the "pseudo-rapprochement of Negro and white in their artistic relations" (152). In the essay Clay went on to herald the work of Sterling Brown, Langston Hughes, and Richard Wright, all writers whose work then and for the next several years emphasized politics and the working class.

Even further indicative of the effect of the left-wing line of the 1930s was the spreading of the "nation-within-a nation thesis." Howard University philosophy instructor Eugene Gordon presented portions of the thesis on the same panel with Clay. Though the idea had at least some of its origins with black nationalists and black socialists from the 1910s, by 1928 when the communists began using their organizational apparatus to promote the idea of "self-determination" in the "black belt" of the USA, they would remarkably reshape black critical appraisals of the 1920s. Instead of pointing to the interracial character of the Harlem Renaissance as the final recognition of the dawn ahead (which, it seems by all accounts, was perhaps the key feature of the movement), the communist critics avowed that blacks had weakened their cultural stewardship by excessive racial compromise. The movement had been wrongly seeking assimilation. The result of this striving had been fawning writers "with their ears, however, attuned to the voice of bourgeois authority."[16] No longer content to shock the bourgeois, newer black writers challenged the idea of a middle class at all.

> These works reflect the sentiment of that section of the Negro upper class which, having hoped to be accepted, with its cultivation and polish, open-armed in to the white upper class, shows its anger and despair in acrimonious condemnation of all whites . . .
>
> Having been rebuffed by the white ruling class continually . . . The Negro upper class thereupon turned in upon themselves, resolved to cultivate a polite middle-class racial chauvinism within the protective folds of the capitalist system. The works of George S. Schuyler, James Weldon Johnson, Du Bois, Nella Larsen, and Jessie Fauset reflect this resolve. (Gordon, "Problems" 144)

Gordon split the Renaissance in half. Because they sought ways of conforming to the American socio-economic model of success and to diminish the more extreme elements of ethnic difference, the educated upper class of blacks had done nothing beyond assimilation. If their counterparts, the bohemians, had exploited (and been exploited by) ethnic primitivism, the bourgeois strove to become, in Schuyler's memorable argot, "lampblacked anglo-saxons." Neither tradition held the esteem of the left, which was vigorously promoting black nationalism.

Elements of the "nation-within-a-nation" thesis were promoted by communists before and after (but not during) the Second World War, as well as used by black nationalists like Hubert Harrison, Marcus Garvey, Carlos Cook, Sufi Abdul Hamid, conveners of the "Negro Youth" movement of the 1940s, and Elijah Muhammad. The popularity of the credo need not be overstated. For the active African American literati during the middle thirties, Gordon's rationale may have been even a bit suspect. Langston Hughes, a faithful Marxist at least during the 1930s and early 1940s, claimed, when under questioning of Senator McCarthy's committee in 1953, that he had been unable to join the Communist Party precisely because he thought the "nation-within-a-nation" thesis flawed.[17]

Of course, the confident certainty of the communists, combined with prime examples of racial unrest – from the Scottsboro and Angelo Herndon trials to the Harlem Riot of 1935 – impressed a devoted core of young literary strivers. Eighteen months after the LAW congress, Richard Wright published the now famous essay "Blueprint for Negro Writing" in an obscure little magazine called *New Challenge* that he was co-editing alongside Dorothy West and Marian Minus. The magazine had changed its name from *Challenge*, which had operated for five years. Between the two titles, the West-headed group introduced the writers who would take the place of Harlem Renaissance heads: Frank Yerby, Margaret Walker, Wright, William Attaway, and Ralph Ellison. The Wright essay's most frequently quoted line was nearly a copy of Wallace Thurman's ten years earlier. Wright thought the Harlem Renaissance had produced nothing but manicured poodles "dressed in the knee pants of servility curtsying to show that the Negro was not inferior, that he was human."[18] Since he was a communist at the time, Wright, like Gordon, believed that the greatest defect of the literary movement had been its inability to focus on the travail of working-class black life, and that the writers either emphasized the cozy lives of the few black elites or gave themselves up to recording the sensuality of a Harlem Saturday night. These two diverse groups of Negroes were not seen in contact with one another, and young pundits like Wright prescribed to reconcile them through black nationalism, symbolized by the popular National Negro Congress of the late 1930s and early 1940s. Later, the political formation itself could be transcended.

After Wright's blockbuster *Native Son*, his left-wing colleague and friend Ralph Ellison continued to express a condescending attitude toward the writing of the 1920s. For a young person who had few ties himself to the movement, Ellison's near contempt toward established writers seems indicative of more than the growing pains of a new literary tribe. Although his talent had been "discovered" by Langston Hughes, Ellison felt little allegiance to the scattered group who had made their names in the 1920s. Ellison's entire career was conspicuously racially integrated and he started publishing reviews in the left-wing journals and those that had been created for members of the WPA. But another source of his strident criticisms came about partly because the conditions of his writing in the early 1940s were fundamentally different than even a decade earlier. Katherine Anne Porter, Wallace Stevens, William Carlos Williams, and Lionel Trilling all registered a growth in the "serious" reading audience between 1929 and 1939, but the change in literary audience was most startlingly true for black Americans.[19] The expanding US economy and the beginnings of an exodus of black Americans away from the rural South after the First World War helped to create, between 1936 and 1942, some 24,000 black college graduates, more black Americans with a college education than had been graduated from colleges in the United States, ever.[20] By 1942, 46,000 blacks would be enrolled in college, and 2,500 black teachers were their instructors, and among them more than 200 holders of the doctorate in philosophy. Spasmodically and unintentionally perhaps, segregated America was turning out a genuine black intelligentsia.

Ellison, a college freshman in 1933, ranked highly among this new group who had received extensive college training. He also took leadership positions in the League of American Writers and at the left-wing radical magazines like *New Masses*. At the publication of *Native Son*, Ellison had the opportunity to become a regular interpreter of black American life. Ellison received further literary exposure from literary critic and philosopher Kenneth Burke (Malcolm Cowley's best friend), and throughout his life he remained sharply suspicious of the work of the "lost generation," black and white. Burke also schooled Ellison in a version of the "New Criticism," the formalist method of literary interpretation linked to T. S. Eliot that was flourishing in the academy. Combining his growing interests in the symbolist criticism with his Cowley-style passion for social justice, Ellison considered much of the 1920s decadent and flabby aestheticism, with the exceptions of Hemingway and Faulkner. However, even when he examined those writers, he found their portraits of black Americans shabby enough as to challenge the entire moral and ethical enterprise of their novels. In Ellison's version of literary history, the black writers of the 1920s were politically and aesthetically unsophisticated. They had been taken advantage of in the 1920s. He heralded the dawn of naturalism and the work of Wright because, "[U]nlike the fiction growing out of the New Negro Movement, it has avoided exoticism and evolved out of an inner compulsion rather than a shallow imitativeness; it has been more full of the stuff of America."[21] Ellison then launched into the fullest and most vivid assessment of the Harlem Renaissance that he ever wrote.

> The fiction which appeared during the post-war period was timid and narrow of theme, except in few instances. Here appeared such writers as Countee Cullen, Claude McKay, Rudolph Fisher, Zora Neil [*sic*] Hurston, Wallace Thurman and Jessie Fauset; all expressing certain general ideas and tendencies which grew out of the post-war prosperity and the rise of a conscious Negro middle class. Usually the work was apologetic and an expression of middle class ideology rather than the point of view of Negro workers and farmers. Except for the work of Langston Hughes, it ignored the existence of Negro folklore and perceived no connection between its efforts and the symbols and images of Negro folk forms; it avoided psychology; was unconscious of politics;

and most of the deeper problems arising out of the relationship of the Negro group to the American whole, were avoided. Not that it contained no protest, it did. But its protest was racial and narrowly nationalistic. (Ellison, "Wright" 12)

The twenty-eight-year-old critic was green enough to forget Nella Larsen, and, probably because Hurston had dismissed Wright's *Uncle Tom's Children*, he eliminated her folk novels. Ellison still traveled in communist circles and his scoffing at the "narrowly nationalistic" element of the Renaissance anticipated the Party's four-year repudiation of black nationalism.

But more valuable than applying hindsight to Ellison's sense of literary history is the simpler observation of palpable embarrassment that young, soon-to-be-famous black writers of the late 1930s and early 1940s held toward writing of the 1920s. A year later, when Ellison was editing the important black magazine of art and politics *Negro Quarterly*, he introduced Chicago critic Edward Bland, who more openly sneered at the 1920s writers. Bland, who died in combat in Europe in 1945, began his most important piece of work, "Social Forces Shaping the Negro Novel," with what was by then a ritual spilling of Harlem's blood: "One of the outstanding features of the Negro novels that appeared during the twenties was their literary incompetence."[22]

The second half of the 1940s scored the Harlem or New Negro Renaissance over and again, and it is not difficult to understand the reason why. Of the five black literary giants of the 1940s – Richard Wright, Frank Yerby, Ann Petry, Willard Motley, and Gwendolyn Brooks – Wright, Yerby and Motley wrote best-sellers and Petry and Brooks won major prizes. Financial success and widespread artistic recognition were accolades unknown to blacks during the 1920s and 1930s. And since Yerby and Motley wrote books without black protagonists, the Renaissance crew fell in for yet another critical flaw. The problem was no longer that the movement had failed to find its true racial spirit and to resist white control. The black writers of the 1920s were now – in the era of Motley (who withheld information regarding his race so that he wouldn't receive literary favoritism), Yerby's post-bellum romans, Petry's *The Country Place*, and William Gardner Smith's *Anger at Innocence* – too racial, overly obsessed with race.[23] Waters Turpin, a novelist, dramatist, critic, and English professor at Lincoln and Morgan State College, called the movement an "exotic on American culture" that did mainly the work of allowing the next generation of black writers "to emerge as literary craftsmen unshackled by race or nationality."[24]

And always the Renaissance writers were blamed and blamed themselves for failing to erect permanent institutions. Arna Bontemps, a key Harlem Renaissance figure who became librarian of Fisk University, believed that the limitations of the Renaissance had everything to do with the flaws of its human descendants. He contrasted the Harlem of the 1940s with what he'd recalled from two decades earlier and decided that "The children born during the beautiful years of the middle 'twenties had grown up to be muggers and cultist."[25] Devastated by riots in 1935 and 1943, the Harlem dream of a racial mecca had turned into "a black ghetto and a slum, a clot in the American bloodstream." The body of writing associated with the place seemed quite frail when compared to the human tragedy of two decades.

The Harlem lava had cooled into a bedrock symbol of black literature. But black writers publishing in the 1940s saw mainly a plate on which to crack, with violence, their identity. The Hampton College professor and *Afro-American* newspaper reviewer J. Saunders Redding was that rare black to have published in 1930 a story of dissolute cabaret life called "Delaware Coon" in the Paris magazine *transition* – bona fide renaissance and "lost generation" credentials. But the Brown University-educated Redding, whose literary estimates were well regarded by both blacks and whites, sounded the steady note of discontent that by then marred the period. The renaissance was too greatly overvalued. "Almost every writer or would be writer who so much as lived in or around New York in the middle or late Twenties, or who had any contact with the literary figures and enterprises of that period, have gotten some sort of critical attention or another, and some of those who got attention simply were not worth it."[26] The orthodoxy of disparagement was intense enough that by 1951, when Richard Gibson was attending a Kenyon College dominated by the New Criticism of John Crowe Ransom, Gibson felt compelled to free himself from the entire tradition of black writing. At bottom, he could hold only "disgust for all ... the incompetence, the sentimentality, the hypocrisy, the intellectual irresponsibility, in sum the entire minstrel psychology."[27] "[T]here is not as yet a single work by an American Negro which, when judged without bias, stands out as a masterpiece" (255). Gibson believed that the liberal press in his day was ruining the black writer, and Redding too blamed the conjunction of publishers and patrons for misshaping black writing. When he recorded an obituary for Countee Cullen in 1946, he recounted the period with no small dose of bitters. The black artists constituted an "indominitable band," but they were plagued by "some white observers" "saying that primitivism was the essential attribute of colored writers and artists." The most sensitive of the artists, Cullen had been psychologically "bothered" by the fact that the requests for him to produce work showing the pure black racial essence barely hid the cruel assumption "that the colored man was not quite civilized."[28] Twenty years later, with few exceptions, the concentration was on the tragedy and not the triumph of the movement.

It took close to fifty years for major reconsiderations of the Harlem Renaissance to catch hold. The black social and political consciousness movement in the 1960s and 1970s stimulated scholarship in all periods of African American literature and history, and the writing that took place during the 1920s benefited enormously. The judgments in totality tended to remain harsh, partly because of the optimism of scholars in the 1970s concerning the potential for full black integration into American society. In the book that began the sweeping reconsideration of the black writers of the 1920s called *Harlem Renaissance*, Nathan Huggins proffered an explanation of the phenomenon that had punished Cullen and the rest. He held that white voyeurs pursued black life to find an "alter ego," and "blacks – sensing this psychic dependency – have been all too willing to join in the charade, hiding behind the minstrel mask, appearing to be what white men wanted them to be, and finding pleasure in the deception which all too often was a trick on themselves."[29] But Huggins implicitly forecast an era when "deception" was impossible. This was also the broad view held by the writers who followed the 1920s. The next generation of black writers decided that even the elegant sonnets, the cultivated learning, the joyful exploration of ordinary black pleasures, and even the seats on platforms in halls of radicalism had become merely another version of a minstrel mask, ultimately painful and distorting. However, they were unable to predict the kind of resolution that would address the American dilemma of racial injustice, of slavery and segregation, a resolution incomplete and still engaging formidable problems after the chief legal barriers had fallen.

Meanwhile, the mounting succession of political setbacks to the Civil Rights Movement during the 1980s and 1990s and the resulting reconstitution of de facto racial segregation had an ironically beneficial effect for studies of the Renaissance. The writers' movement no longer suffered the crippling criticism of being an inadequate mover of social historical change. In addition, the emergence of feminist, post-structuralist, and historicist analytical techniques displaced the formalist literary hierarchies that had been more generally embraced by American and British elites. Harlem Renaissance textual contributions now receive credit for their transgressive, fragmentary, referential, occlusive capacities and are no longer dismissed for lacking density, high seriousness, complexity, or even widespread popularity, necessary features for critical attention during the 1940s, 1950s, and 1960s.

NOTES

1. Carl Van Vechten to Langston Hughes, October 8, 1942. *Remember Me to Harlem*, ed. Emily Bernard (New York: Random House, 2001).
2. Hugh Gloster, "The Van Vechten Vogue," *Phylon* 6.4 (1945), 310.

LAWRENCE JACKSON

3. Wallace Thurman, "Nephews of Uncle Remus," *Independent* September 24, 1927, 298; quoted in Charles Scruggs, "All Dressed Up but No Place to Go: The Black Writer and His Audience during the Harlem Renaissance," *American Literature* 48.4 (1977), 543–63.

4. Alain Locke, "1928: A Retrospective Review," *Opportunity* 7 (January 1929), 8.

5. Alain Locke, "This Year of Grace," *Opportunity* 9 (February 1931), 48; quoted in Abby Arthur Johnson and Ronald Mayberry Johnson, *Propaganda and Aesthetics: The Literary Politics of Twentieth Century African American Magazines* (Amherst: University of Massachusetts, Press 1991), p. 103.

6. Langston Hughes, *The Big Sea* (1940; New York: Hill and Wang, 1963), p. 334.

7. James Weldon Johnson, "Preface" to *The Book of American Negro Poetry*; reprinted in *Norton Anthology of African American Literature*, ed. Henry Louis Gates, Jr. and Nellie McKay (New York: Norton, 1997), p. 861.

8. Malcolm Cowley, *Exile's Return: A Narrative of Ideas* (New York: Norton, 1934), p. 301.

9. Gary Gerstle, "The Protean Character of American Liberalism," *American Historical Review* 99.4 (1994), 1055–6, 1065–9.

10. Harold Rosenberg, "The Situation in American Writing: Seven Questions," *Partisan Review* (Summer 1939), 48.

11. J. Saunders Redding, *To Make a Poet Black* (1939; Ithaca, NY: Cornell University Press, 1988), p. 120.

12. Sterling A. Brown, "The Negro in Literature (1925–1955)," in Rayford Logan, Eugene C. Holmes and G. Franklin Edwards, eds., *The New Negro Thirty Years Afterward: Papers Contributed to the Sixteenth Annual Spring Conference of the Division of Social Sciences, Howard University* 9.1 (1955), 58.

13. Sterling A. Brown, "Negro Character as Seen by White Authors;" reprinted in Brown, *A Son's Return*, ed. Mark Sanders (Boston: Northeastern University Press, 1996), p. 150.

14. Joanne Gabbin, *Sterling A. Brown: Building a Black Aesthetic Tradition* (Westport, CT: Greenwood, 1985), p. 199.

15. Eugene Clay, "The Negro in Recent American Literature," in *American Writers' Congress*, ed. Henry Hart (New York: International Publishers, 1935), p. 147.

16. Eugene Gordon, "Problems of the Negro Writer," in *American Writers' Congress*, p. 145.

17. Langston Hughes, "Resumé of Information Offered the Senate Permanent Sub-Committee on Investigations by Langston Hughes 24–26 March 1953," Yaddo Papers, Box 255 folder 29, New York Public Library, Manuscripts and Archives Division.

18. Richard Wright, "Blueprint for Negro Writing," *New Challenge* 1.1 (1937), 53.

19. "The Situation in American Writing" Parts I and II, *Partisan Review* (Summer and Fall 1939).

20. Edwin R. Embree, *Brown America: The Story of a Tenth of the Nation* (New York: Viking, 1943), pp. 107–8.

21. Ralph Ellison, "Richard Wright and Recent Negro Fiction," *Direction* (Summer 1941), 12.

22. Edward Bland, "Social Forces Shaping the Negro Novel," *Negro Quarterly* 1.3 (1942), 241.

23. Willard Motley, letter to Horace Cayton, n.d., in Horace R. Cayton, "Literary Expansion: Another Best Seller by a Negro Is Not of the Negro or His Environs," *Pittsburgh Courier* May 24, 1947, p. 7. "Had the reading public known I was colored some people would have bought the book and praised it because I am a Negro. I wanted to know if the book was good or bad on its merits alone."
24. Waters Turpin, "Major Problems of the Negro Writer," *Morgan State College Bulletin* (March 1949), 6.
25. Arna Bontemps, "The Two Harlems," *American Scholar* 14.2 (1945), 171.
26. J. Saunders Redding, Review of *We Have Tomorrow*, by Arna Bontemps, *Afro-American Newspaper*, August 10, 1946, p. 4.
27. Richard Gibson, "A No to Nothing," *Kenyon Review* 13.2 (1951), 254.
28. J. Saunders Redding, "Countee Cullen Is Dead," *Afro-American Newspaper* January 19, 1946, p. 4.
29. Nathan I. Huggins, *Harlem Renaissance* (New York: Oxford University Press, 1971), p. 84.

This list includes works cited and further reading provided by the contributors.

Primary works

Bontemps, Arna. *Black Thunder*. New York: Macmillan, 1936.
  God Sends Sunday. New York: Harcourt Brace, 1931.
Boyd, Valerie. *Wrapped in Rainbows: The Life of Zora Neale Hurston*. New York: Scribner, 2003.
Brown, Sterling A. *The Collected Poems of Sterling A. Brown*, ed. Michael S. Harper. Evanston, IL: TriQuarterly Books, 1996.
Brown, Sterling A., Arthur P. Davis, and Ulysses Lee, eds. *The Negro Caravan: Writings by American Negroes*. 1941; Salem, NH: Ayer, 1991.
Cowley, Malcolm. *Exile's Return: A Narrative of Ideas*. New York: Norton, 1934.
Cullen, Countee. *The Ballad of the Brown Girl*. New York: Harper and Brothers, 1927.
  The Black Christ and Other Poems. New York: Harper and Brothers, 1929.
  ed. *Caroling Dusk: An Anthology of Verse by Negro Poets*. New York: Harper and Brothers, 1927.
  Color. 1925; Salem, NH: Ayer, 1993.
  Copper Sun. New York: Harper and Brothers, 1927.
  My Soul's High Song: The Collected Writings of Countee Cullen, ed. Gerald Early. New York: Anchor Books, 1991.
Du Bois, W. E. B. *Book Reviews*, ed. Herbert Aptheker. Millwood, NY: Kraus-Thompson Organization, 1985.
  Creative Writings by W. E. B. Du Bois: A Pageant, Poems, Short Stories, and Playlets, ed. Herbert Aptheker. Millwood, NY: Kraus-Thompson Organization, 1985.
  Dark Princess: A Romance. New York: Harcourt, Brace & Co., 1928.
  Darkwater: Voices from Within the Veil. New York: Harcourt, Brace & Co., 1920.
  The Quest of the Silver Fleece: A Novel. New York: Harcourt, Brace & Co., 1911.
  Selections from The Crisis, ed. Herbert Aptheker. Millwood, NY: Kraus-Thompson Organization, 1983.
  The Souls of Black Folk: Essays and Sketches. Chicago: A. C. McClurg, 1903.
Fauset, Jessie Redmon. *The Chinaberry Tree: A Novel of American Life*. 1931; College Park: McGrath Publishing Co., 1969.
  Comedy, American Style. 1933; New York: G. K. Hall, 1995.
  Plum Bun: A Novel without a Moral. 1929; Boston: Beacon Press, 1999.

There Is Confusion. 1924; Boston: Northeastern University Press, 1989.

Fire!! 1 (November 1926).

Fisher, Rudolph. "The Caucasian Storms Harlem." *American Mercury* 11 (August 1927), 393–8.

The City of Refuge: The Collected Stories of Rudolph Fisher, ed. John McCluskey. Columbia: University of Missouri Press, 1991.

The Conjure Man Dies: A Mystery Tale of Dark Harlem. 1932; Ann Arbor: University of Michigan Press, 1992.

The Walls of Jericho. 1929; New York: Arno Press, 1969.

Frank, Waldo. *Our America*. New York: Boni and Liveright, 1919.

Gable, Craig, ed. *Ebony Rising: Short Fiction of the Greater Harlem Renaissance Era*. Bloomington: Indiana University Press, 2004.

Garvey, Marcus. *Philosophy and Opinions of Marcus Garvey*. 2 vols. Comp. Amy Jacques Garvey. Paterson, NJ: Frank Cass, 1923, 1925.

Grimké, Angelina Weld. *Rachel*. 1916; reprinted in *The Prentice Hall Anthology of African American Literature*, ed. Rochelle Smith and Sharon Jones. Upper Saddle River, NJ: Prentice Hall, 2000.

Selected Works of Angelina Weld Grimké, ed. Carolivia Herron. New York: Oxford University Press, 1991.

Harrison, Hubert. *A Hubert Harrison Reader*, ed. Jeffrey B. Perry. Middletown, CT: Wesleyan University Press, 2001.

Hatch, James V., and Leo Hamalian, eds. *Lost Plays of the Harlem Renaissance: 1920–1940*. Detroit: Wayne State University Press, 1996.

Hemenway, Robert E. *Zora Neale Hurston: A Literary Biography*. Urbana: University of Illinois Press, 1977.

Henderson, George Wylie. *Ollie Miss: A Novel*. New York: Frederick A. Stokes, 1935.

Hughes, Langston. *The Big Sea: An Autobiography*. New York: A. A. Knopf, 1940.

The Collected Poems of Langston Hughes, ed. Arnold Rampersad. New York: Vintage, 1995.

Fine Clothes to the Jew. New York: A. A. Knopf, 1927.

Five Plays by Langston Hughes, ed. Webster Smalley. Bloomington: Indiana University Press, 1968.

"Harlem Literati of the Twenties," *Saturday Review of Literature* 22 (22 June 1940), 13–14.

"The Negro Artist and the Racial Mountain." 1926; reprinted in *The Norton Anthology of African American Literature*, ed. Henry Louis Gates Jr. and Nellie Y. McKay. New York: Norton, 1997. 1267–71.

Not Without Laughter. New York: A. A. Knopf, 1930.

The Weary Blues. New York: A. A. Knopf, 1926.

Hurston, Zora Neale. *The Complete Stories*. New York: HarperPerennial, 1996.

Dust Tracks on a Road. 1942; New York: HarperPerennial, 1996.

"How It Feels To Be Colored Me." 1928; reprinted in *The Norton Anthology of African American Literature*, ed. Henry Louis Gates Jr. and Nellie Y. McKay. New York: Norton, 2004. 1030–3.

Jonah's Gourd Vine. 1934; New York: Perennial Library, 1990.

Moses, Man of the Mountain. 1939; New York: HarperPerennial, 1991.

Mules and Men. 1935; New York: Perennial Library, 1990.

Tell My Horse: Voodoo and Life in Haiti and Jamaica. 1938; New York: Perennial Library, 1990.

Their Eyes Were Watching God. 1937; New York: HarperPerennial, 1998.

Zora Neale Hurston: A Life in Letters, ed. Carla Kaplan. New York: Doubleday, 2002.

Johnson, Charles S. *Ebony and Ivory: A Collectanea.* 1931; Freeport, NY: Books for Libraries, 1971.

"The Negro Renaissance and Its Significance," in *The Portable Harlem Renaissance Reader.* New York: Viking, 1994. 206–18.

Johnson, Georgia Douglas. *The Selected Works of Georgia Douglas Johnson*, ed. Claudia Tate. New York: G. K. Hall, 1997.

Johnson, Helene. *This Waiting for Love: Helene Johnson, Poet of the Harlem Renaissance*, ed. Verner D. Mitchell. Amherst: University of Massachusetts, 2000.

Johnson, James Weldon. *Along This Way: The Autobiography of James Weldon Johnson.* New York: Viking Press, 1933.

The Autobiography of an Ex-Coloured Man. Boston: Sherman, French & Co., 1912.

Black Manhattan. New York: Knopf, 1930.

"The Dilemma of the Negro Author," *American Mercury* 15 (December 1928), 477–81.

God's Trombones: Seven Negro Sermons in Verse. 1927; New York: Penguin Classics, 1990.

"Preface" from *The Book of American Negro Poetry.* 1921; reprinted in *The Norton Anthology of African American Literature*, ed. Henry Louis Gates Jr. and Nellie Y. McKay. New York: Norton, 1997. 861–84.

Larsen, Nella. *"Quicksand" and "Passing."* 1928, 1929; ed. Deborah E. McDowell, New Brunswick, NJ: Rutgers University Press, 1986.

"Sanctuary," in *An Intimation of Things Distant: The Collected Fiction of Nella Larsen*, ed. Charles R. Larson. New York: Doubleday, 1992. 19–27.

Liscomb, Harry F. *The Prince of Washington Square.* New York: Frederick A. Stokes, 1925.

Locke, Alain. *The Critical Temper of Alain Locke: A Selection of His Essays on Art and Culture*, ed. Jeffrey C. Stewart. New York: Garland, 1983.

ed. *The New Negro: An Interpretation.* New York: A. and C. Boni 1925. New York: Touchstone, 1997.

Locke, Alain, and Montgomery Gregory, eds. *Plays of Negro Life: A Source-Book of Native American Drama.* New York: Harper and Brothers, 1927.

Maran, René. *Batouala: véritable roman nègre.* Paris: A. Michel, 1921. Trans. as *Batouala* by Adele Szold Seltzer, New York: Thomas Seltzer, 1922.

Martin, Tony. *Literary Garveyism: Garvey, Black Arts, and the Harlem Renaissance.* Dover, MA: Majority, 1983.

McKay, Claude. *Banana Bottom.* 1933; Chatham, NJ: Chatham Bookseller, 1970.

Banjo. 1929; New York: Harcourt Brace Jovanovich, 1970.

Complete Poems, ed. William J. Maxwell. Urbana: University of Illinois Press, 2004.

Gingertown. New York: Harper, 1932.

Harlem: Negro Metropolis. 1940; New York: Harcourt Brace Jovanovich, 1968.

Home to Harlem. 1928; Boston: Northeastern University Press, 1987.

A Long Way from Home. 1937; New York: Harcourt Brace and World, 1970.

Selected Poems. New York: Bookman Associates, 1953.

Nugent, Richard Bruce. *Gay Rebel of the Harlem Renaissance: Selections from the Work of Richard Bruce Nugent*, ed. Thomas H. Wirth. Durham, NC: Duke University Press, 2002.

O'Neill, Eugene. *The Emperor Jones and All God's Chillun Got Wings*. In *Eugene O'Neill: Complete Plays (1920–1931)*. New York: Library of America, 1988.

Patton, Venetria K., and Maureen Honey. *Double-Take: A Revisionist Harlem Renaissance Anthology*. New Brunswick, NJ and London: Rutgers University Press, 2001.

Perkins, Kathy A., ed. *Black Female Playwrights: An Anthology of Plays before 1950*. Bloomington: Indiana University Press, 1989.

Perkins, Kathy A., and Judith L. Stephens, eds. *Strange Fruit: Plays on Lynching by American Women*. Bloomington: Indiana University Press, 1998.

Richardson, Willis. "The Hope of Negro Drama," *Crisis* 19.1 (November 1919), 338–9.

Richardson, Willis, and May Miller. *Plays and Pageants from the Life of the Negro*. 1930; Jackson: University of Mississippi Press, 1993.

Roses, Lorraine E., and Ruth E. Randolph, eds. *Harlem's Glory: Black Women Writing, 1900–1950*. Cambridge, MA: Harvard University Press, 1996.

Schuyler, George. *Black Empire*, ed. Robert A. Hill and R. Kent Rasmussen. Boston: Northeastern University Press, 1991.

Black No More: Being an Account of the Strange and Wonderful Workings of Science in the Land of the Free, A.D. 1933–1940. 1931; New York: Modern Library, 1999.

"The Negro-Art Hokum." 1926; reprinted in *The Norton Anthology of African American Literature*, ed. Henry Louis Gates Jr. and Nellie Y. McKay. New York: Norton, 2004. 1221–3.

Survey Graphic 6.6 (March 1925) [Special Issue entitled "Harlem: Mecca of the New Negro"].

Thurman, Wallace. *The Blacker the Berry . . .* 1929; New York: Scribner, 1996.

Collected Writings of Wallace Thurman: A Harlem Renaissance Reader, ed. Amritjit Singh and Daniel M. Scott III. New Brunswick, NJ: Rutgers University Press, 2003.

ed. *Fire!!: A Quarterly Devoted to the Younger Negro Artists*. Facsimile edition. Metuchen, NJ: Fire!! Press, 1982.

Infants of the Spring. 1932; Boston: Northeastern University Press, 1992.

Toomer, Jean. *Cane*. 1923; ed. Darwin T. Turner, New York: Norton, 1988.

Jean Toomer: Selected Essays and Literary Criticism, ed. Robert B. Jones. Knoxville: University of Tennessee Press, 1996.

A Jean Toomer Reader: Selected Unpublished Writings, ed. Frederik L. Rusch. New York: Oxford University Press, 1993.

The Letters of Jean Toomer, 1919–1924, ed. Mark Whalan. Knoxville: University of Tennessee Press, 2006.

The Wayward and the Seeking: A Collection of Writings by Jean Toomer, ed. Darwin T. Turner. Washington, DC: Howard University Press, 1982.

Van Vechten, Carl. *"Keep A-Inchin' Along": Selected Writings of Carl Van Vechten about Black Art and Letters*, ed. Bruce Kellner. Westport, CT: Greenwood Press, 1979.

Nigger Heaven. New York: Knopf, 1926.

Remember Me to Harlem: The Letters of Langston Hughes and Carl Van Vechten, 1925–1964, ed. Emily Bernard. New York: Random House, 2001.

Walrond, Eric. *Tropic Death*. New York: Boni and Liveright, 1926.

"Winds Can Wake Up the Dead": An Eric Walrond Reader, ed. Louis J. Parascandola. Detroit: Wayne State University Press, 1998.

White, Walter. *The Fire in the Flint*. New York: Knopf, 1924.

Flight. New York: Knopf, 1926.

Williams, Edward Christopher. *When Washington Was in Vogue*, ed. Adam McKible. New York: Amistad, 2003. (Originally *The Letters of Davy Carr*, serialized in the *Pittsburgh Courier*.)

Wright, Richard. "Blueprint for Negro Writing." *New Challenge* 1.1 (1937), 53–65.

Secondary works

Abramson, Doris E. *Negro Playwrights in the American Theatre, 1925–1959*. New York: Columbia University Press, 1967.

Anderson, Jervis. *This Was Harlem: A Cultural Portrait, 1900–1950*. New York: Farrar Straus Giroux, 1982.

Anderson, Paul Allen. *Deep River: Music and Memory in Harlem Renaissance Thought*. Durham, NC: Duke University Press, 2001.

Andrews, William L. *Classic Fiction of the Harlem Renaissance*. New York: Oxford University Press, 1994.

Archer-Straw, Petrine. *Negrophilia: Avant-Garde Paris and Black Culture in the 1920s*. New York: Thames and Hudson, 2000.

Bailey, Frankie Y. *Out of the Woodpile: Black Characters in Crime and Detective Fiction*. New York: Greenwood Press, 1991.

Baker, Houston A., Jr. *Afro-American Poetics: Revisions of Harlem and the Black Aesthetic*. Madison: University of Wisconsin Press, 1996.

Blues, Ideology, and Afro-American Literature: A Vernacular Theory. Chicago: University of Chicago Press, 1984.

A Many-Colored Coat of Dreams: The Poetry of Countee Cullen. Detroit: Broadside Press, 1974.

Modernism and the Harlem Renaissance. Chicago: University of Chicago Press, 1987.

Baldwin, James. "Everybody's Protest Novel." 1949; reprinted in *Notes of A Native Son*. London: Penguin, 1995. 19–28.

Bassett, John E. *Harlem in Review: Critical Reactions to Black American Writers, 1917–1939*. Selinsgrove, PA: Susquehanna University Press, 1992.

Bean, Annemarie. "Playwrights and Plays of the Harlem Renaissance," in *The Companion to Twentieth-Century American Drama*, ed. David Krasner. Malden: Blackwell, 2005. 91–105.

Bell, Bernard W. *The Folk Roots of Contemporary Afro-American Poetry*. Detroit: Broadside Press, 1974.

Bone, Robert A. *Down Home: A History of Afro-American Short Fiction from Its Beginnings to the End of the Harlem Renaissance*. New York: Putnam, 1975.

Bontemps, Arna, ed. *The Harlem Renaissance Remembered: Essays*. New York: Dodd, Mead, 1972.

"The Negro Renaissance: Jean Toomer and the Harlem Renaissance of the 1920s," in *Anger, and Beyond: The Negro Writer in the United States*, ed. Herbert Hill. New York: Harper and Row, 1966. 20–36.

"The Two Harlems." *American Scholar* 14.2 (1945), 167–73.

Brown, Sterling. "Negro Character as Seen by White Authors." 1930; reprinted in *A Son's Return: Selected Essays of Sterling Brown*, ed. Mark Sanders. Boston: Northeastern University Press, 1996. 149–203.

Negro Poetry and Drama, and The Negro in American Fiction. 1937; New York: Atheneum, 1969.

Butler, Judith. "Passing, Queering: Nella Larsen's Psychoanalytic Challenge," in *Bodies That Matter: On the Discursive Limits of "Sex"*. New York: Routledge, 1993. 167–86.

Byrd, Rudolph P. *Jean Toomer's Years with Gurdjieff: Portrait of an Artist, 1923–1936*. Athens: University of Georgia Press, 1990.

Campbell, Mary S., ed. *Harlem Renaissance: Art of Black America*. New York: Abrams, 1987.

Carby, Hazel. *Reconstructing Womanhood: The Emergence of the Afro-American Woman Novelist*. New York: Oxford University Press, 1987.

Carroll, Anne Elizabeth. *Word, Image, and the New Negro: Representation and Identity in the Harlem Renaissance*. Bloomington: Indiana University Press, 2005.

Chauncey, George, Jr. *Gay New York: Gender, Urban Culture and the Making of the Gay Male World, 1890–1940*. New York: Basic, 1994.

Christian, Barbara. *Black Women Novelists: The Development of a Tradition, 1892–1976*. Westport, CT: Greenwood Press, 1980.

Clay, Eugene. "The Negro in Recent American Literature," in *American Writers Congress*, ed. Henry Hart. New York: International Publishers, 1935. 145–53.

Cooper, Wayne F. *Claude McKay: Rebel Sojourner in the Harlem Renaissance. A Biography*. New York: Schocken, 1990.

Cruse, Harold. *The Crisis of the Negro Intellectual*. New York: William Morrow, 1967.

Dash, Michael J. *Haiti and the United States*. New York: St. Martin's Press, 1988.

Dawahare, Anthony. *Nationalism, Marxism, and African American Literature between Wars: A New Pandora's Box*. Jackson: University of Mississippi Press, 2003.

De Jongh, James. *Vicious Modernism: Black Harlem and the Literary Imagination*. New York: Cambridge University Press, 1990.

Donnell, Alison, and Sarah Lawson Welsh. *The Routledge Reader in Caribbean Literature*. London: Routledge, 1996.

Douglas, Ann. *Terrible Honesty: Mongrel Manhattan in the 1920s*. New York: Farrar, Straus and Giroux, 1995.

Dray, Philip. *At the Hands of Persons Unknown: The Lynching of Black America*. New York: Modern Library, 2003.

duCille, Ann. *The Coupling Convention: Sex, Text, and Tradition in Black Women's Fiction*. New York: Oxford University Press, 1993.

Dunn, Allen, and George Hutchinson, eds. *The Future of the Harlem Renaissance.* Special issue of *Soundings: An Interdiscplinary Journal* 80.4 (Winter 1997).

Edwards, Brent Hayes. *The Practice of Diaspora: Literature, Translation, and the Rise of Black Internationalism.* Cambridge, MA: Harvard University Press, 2003.

Embree, Edwin R. *Brown America: The Story of a Tenth of the Nation.* New York: Viking, 1943.

English, Daylanne K. *Unnatural Selections: Eugenics in American Modernism and the Harlem Renaissance.* Chapel Hill: University of North Carolina Press, 2004.

Fabre, Geneviève, and Michel Fleiss, eds. *Temples for Tomorrow: Looking Back at the Harlem Renaissance.* Bloomington: Indiana University Press, 2001.

Fabre, Michel. *From Harlem to Paris: Black American Writers in France, 1840–1980.* Urbana: University of Illinois Press, 1991.

Favor, J. Martin. *Authentic Blackness: The Folk in the New Negro Renaissance.* Durham, NC: Duke University Press, 1999.

Ferguson, Blanche. *Countee Cullen and the Harlem Renaissance.* New York: Dodd, Mead, 1966.

Ferguson, Jeffrey. *The Sage of Sugar Hill: George S. Schuyler and the Harlem Renaissance.* New Haven, CT: Yale University Press, 2005.

Floyd, Samuel A., ed. *Black Music in the Harlem Renaissance: A Collection of Essays.* New York: Greenwood Press, 1990.

Foley, Barbara. "Jean Toomer's Washington and the Politics of Class: From 'Blue Veins' to Seventh-Street Rebels." *Modern Fiction Studies* 42 (1996), 289–321.

  Spectres of 1919: Class and Nation in the Making of the New Negro. Urbana Champaign: University of Illinois Press, 2003.

Franklin, V.P. *Living Our Stories, Telling Our Truths: Autobiography and the Making of the African-American Intellectual Tradition.* New York: Oxford University Press, 1995.

Gabbin, Joanne V. *Sterling A. Brown: Building a Black Aesthetic Tradition.* Westport, CT: Greenwood, 1985.

Garber, Eric. "A Spectacle in Color: The Lesbian and Gay Subculture of Jazz Age Harlem," in Martin Bauml Duberman, Martha Vicinus, and George Chauncey Jr., eds., *Hidden from History: Reclaiming the Gay and Lesbian Past.* Harmondsworth: Penguin, 1991. 318–31.

Gates, Henry Louis, Jr., ed. *Langston Hughes: Critical Perspectives Past and Present.* New York: Amistad Press, 1993.

  "The Trope of a New Negro and the Reconstruction of the Image of the Black." *Representations* 24 (Fall 1988), 129–55.

Gilroy, Paul. *The Black Atlantic: Modernity and Double Consciousness.* Cambridge, MA: Harvard University Press, 1994.

Gloster, Hugh. "The Van Vechten Vogue." *Phylon* 6.4 (1945), 310–14.

Gray, Christine Rauchfuss. "Discovering and Recovering African American Women Playwrights before 1930," in Brenda Murphy, ed., *American Women Playwrights.* Cambridge: Cambridge University Press, 1999. 244–53.

  Willis Richardson, Forgotten Pioneer of African-American Drama. Westport, CT: Greenwood, 1999.

Greenberg, Cheryl. *"Or Does It Explode?": Black Harlem in the Great Depression.* New York: Oxford University Press, 1991.

Hamalian, Leo, and James V. Hatch. *The Roots of African American Drama: An Anthology of Early Plays, 1858–1938*. Detroit: Wayne State University Press, 1991.

Harris, Leonard. *The Philosophy of Alain Locke: Harlem Renaissance and Beyond*. Philadelphia: Temple University Press, 1989.

Harris, Trudier. *Afro-American Writers from the Harlem Renaissance to 1940*. *Dictionary of Literary Biography*, vol. 51. Detroit: Gale, 1986.

Harrison, Daphne Duval. *Black Pearls: Blues Queens of the 1920s*. New Brunswick, NJ: Rutgers University Press, 1998.

Hatch, James, and Errol Hill. *A History of African American Theatre*. Cambridge: Cambridge University Press, 2003.

Hay, Samuel A. *African American Theatre: An Historical and Critical Analysis*. New York: Cambridge University Press, 1994.

Helbling, Mark. *The Harlem Renaissance: The One and the Many*. Westport, CT: Greenwood Press, 1999.

Honey, Maureen, ed. *Shadowed Dreams: Women's Poetry of the Harlem Renaissance*. New Brunswick, NJ and London: Rutgers University Press, 1989.

Huggins, Nathan I. *Harlem Renaissance*. New York: Oxford University Press, 1971.
  ed. *Voices from the Harlem Renaissance*. New York: Oxford University Press, 1976.

Hull, Gloria T. *Color, Sex and Poetry: Three Women Writers of the Harlem Renaissance*. Bloomington: Indiana University Press, 1987.

Hutchinson, George. *The Harlem Renaissance in Black and White*. Cambridge, MA: Belknap/Harvard University Press, 1995.
  In Search of Nella Larsen: A Biography of the Color Line. Cambridge, MA: Belknap/Harvard University Press, 2006.
  "Jean Toomer and American Racial Discourse," in Werner Sollors, ed., *Interracialism: Black–White Intermarriage in American History, Literature, and Law*. New York: Oxford University Press, 2000.
  "The Whitman Legacy and the Harlem Renaissance," in Ed Folsom, ed., *Walt Whitman: The Centennial Essays*. Iowa City: University of Iowa Press, 2002.

James, Winston. *A Fierce Hatred of Injustice: Claude McKay's Jamaica and His Poetry of Rebellion*. London: Verso, 2000.
  Holding Aloft the Banner of Ethiopia: Caribbean Radicalism in Early Twentieth-Century America. London: Verso, 1998.

Janken, Kenneth Robert. *White: The Biography of Walter White, Mr. NAACP*. New York: New Press, 2003.

Johnson, Abby A., and Ronald M. Johnson. *Propaganda and Aesthetics: The Literary Politics of African-American Magazines in the Twentieth Century*. Amherst: University of Massachusetts Press, 1991.

Johnson, Eloise E. *Rediscovering the Harlem Renaissance: The Politics of Exclusion*. New York: Garland, 1997.

Kellner, Bruce. *The Harlem Renaissance: A Historical Dictionary for the Era*. Westport, CT: Greenwood Press, 1984.

Kerman, Cynthia, and Richard Eldridge. *The Lives of Jean Toomer: A Hunger for Wholeness*. Baton Rouge: Louisiana State University Press, 1987.

Knopf, Marcy, ed. *The Sleeper Wakes: Harlem Renaissance Stories by Women*. New Brunswick, NJ: Rutgers University Press, 1993.

Kornweibel, Theodore. *No Crystal Stair: Black Life and the Messenger, 1917–1928*. Westport, CT: Greenwood Press, 1975.

Kramer, Victor A., ed. *The Harlem Renaissance Re-examined*. New York: AMS Press, 1987.

Krasner, David. *A Beautiful Pageant: African American Theatre, Drama, and Performance in the Harlem Renaissance, 1910–1927*. New York: Palgrave Macmillan, 2002.

Lemke, Sieglinde. *Primitivist Modernism: Black Culture and the Origins of Transatlantic Modernism*. New York: Oxford University Press, 1998.

Levine, Lawrence W. *Black Culture and Black Consciousness: Afro-American Folk Thought from Slavery to Freedom*. New York: Oxford University Press, 1977.

Lewis, David Levering. *W. E. B. Du Bois: Biography of a Race, 1868–1919*. New York: Henry Holt, 1993.

   W. E. B. Du Bois: The Fight for Equality and the American Century, 1919–1963. New York: Henry Holt, 2000.

   When Harlem Was in Vogue. 1981; New York: Oxford University Press, 1989.

Maxwell, William J. *New Negro / Old Left: African-American Writing and Communism between the Wars*. New York: Columbia University Press, 1999.

Mishkin, Tracy. *The Harlem and Irish Renaissances: Language, Identity, and Representation*. Gainesville: University of Florida Press, 1998.

Mitchell, Angelyn, ed. *Within the Circle: An Anthology of African American Literary Criticism from the Harlem Renaissance to the Present*. Durham, NC: Duke University Press, 1994.

Mitchell, Verner D., ed. *This Waiting for Love: Helene Johnson, Poet of the Harlem Renaissance*. Amherst: University of Massachusetts Press, 2000.

Moses, Wilson. "The Lost World of the Negro, 1895–1919: Black Literary and Intellectual Life before the 'Renaissance,'" *Black American Literature Forum* 21 (Spring–Summer 1987), 61–84.

Munson, Gorham. *The Awakening Twenties: A Memoir-History of a Literary Period*. Baton Rouge: Louisiana University Press, 1985.

Nadell, Martha Jane. *Enter the New Negroes: Images of Race in American Culture*. Cambridge, MA: Harvard University Press, 2004.

Nelson, Cary. *Repression and Recovery: Modern American Poetry and the Politics of Cultural Memory, 1910–1945*. Madison: University of Wisconsin Press, 1989.

Nicholls, David G. *Conjuring the Folk: Forms of Modernity in African America*. Ann Arbor: University of Michigan Press, 2000.

North, Michael. *The Dialect of Modernism: Race, Language, and Twentieth-Century Literature*. New York: Oxford University Press, 1994.

Notten, Eleonore van. *Wallace Thurman's Harlem Renaissance*. Costerius New Series 93. Amsterdam: Rodopi, 1994.

Osofsky, Gilbert. *Harlem: The Making of a Ghetto*. New York: Harper and Row, 1966.

Perry, Margaret. "A Fisher of Black Life: Short Stories by Rudolph Fisher," in Victor A. Kramer, ed., *The Harlem Renaissance Re-Examined*. New York: AMS Press, 1987. 253–63.

   The Harlem Renaissance: An Annotated Bibliography and Commentary. New York: Garland, 1982.

Silence to the Drums: A Survey of the Literature of the Harlem Renaissance. Westport, CT: Greenwood Press, 1976.

Posnock, Ross. *Color and Culture: Black Writers and the Making of the Modern Intellectual.* Cambridge, MA: Harvard University Press, 1998.

Rampersad, Arnold. *The Life of Langston Hughes.* 2 vols. New York: Oxford University Press, 1986–88.

"Racial Doubt and Racial Shame in the Harlem Renaissance," in Genevieve Fabre and Michel Feith, eds., *Temples for Tomorrow: Looking Back at the Harlem Renaissance.* Bloomington: Indiana University Press, 2001. 31–44.

Redding, J. Saunders. *To Make a Poet Black.* 1939; Ithaca, NY: Cornell University Press, 1988.

Sanders, Mark A. *Afro-Modernist Aesthetics and the Poetry of Sterling A. Brown.* Athens: The University of Georgia Press, 1999.

"American Modernism and the New Negro Movement," in Walter Kalaidjian, ed., *The Cambridge Companion to American Modernism.* Cambridge: Cambridge University Press, 2005. 129–56.

Schwarz, A. B. Christa. *Gay Voices of the Harlem Renaissance.* Bloomington: Indiana University Press, 2003.

Scruggs, Charles. *The Sage in Harlem: H. L. Mencken and the Black Writers of the 1920s.* Baltimore: Johns Hopkins University Press, 1984.

Scruggs, Charles, and Lee VanDemarr. *Jean Toomer and the Terrors of American History.* Philadelphia: Pennsylvania UP, 1998.

Shucard, R. Alan. *Countee Cullen.* Boston: Twayne, 1984.

Singh, Amritjit. *The Novels of the Harlem Renaissance: Twelve Black Writers, 1923–1933.* University Park: Pennsylvania State University Press, 1976.

Singh, Amritjit, et al., eds. *The Harlem Renaissance: Revaluations.* NY: Garland, 1989.

Smethurst, James. *The New Red Negro: The Literary Left and African American Poetry, 1930–1946.* New York: Oxford University Press, 1999.

Soitos, Stephen. *The Blues Detective: A Study of African-American Detective Fiction.* Amherst: University of Massachusetts Press, 1996.

Somerville, Siobhan. *Queering the Color Line: Race and the Invention of Homosexuality in American Culture.* Durham, NC: Duke University Press, 2000.

Spencer, Jon Michael. *The New Negroes and Their Music: The Success of the Harlem Renaissance.* Knoxville: University of Tennessee Press, 1997.

Stephens, Judith L. "The Harlem Renaissance and the New Negro Movement," in Brenda Murphy, ed., *American Women Playwrights.* Cambridge: Cambridge University Press, 1999. 98–117.

Stephens, Michelle A. *Black Empire: The Masculine Global Imaginary of Caribbean Intellectuals in the United States, 1914–1962.* Durham, NC: Duke University Press, 2005.

Stewart, Jeffrey C. "Alain Locke and Georgia Douglas Johnson, Washington Patrons of Afro-American Modernism," *George Washington University Washington Studies* 12 (1986): 37.

Tillery, Tyrone. *Claude McKay: A Black Poet's Struggle for Identity.* Amherst: University of Massachusetts Press, 1992.

Tracy, Steven C., ed. *A Historical Guide to Langston Hughes.* New York: Oxford University Press, 2004.

Langston Hughes and the Blues. Urbana: University of Illinois Press, 1988.

Tyler, Bruce M. *From Harlem to Hollywood: The Struggle for Racial and Cultural Democracy, 1920–1943*. New York: Garland, 1992.

Waldron, Edward E. *Walter White and the Harlem Renaissance*. Port Washington, NY: Kennikat Press, 1978.

Wall, Cheryl A. "Histories and Heresies: Engendering the Harlem Renaissance." *Meridians* 2.1 (2001), 59–76.

Women of the Harlem Renaissance. Bloomington: Indiana University Press, 1995.

Watson, Steven. *The Harlem Renaissance: Hub of African-American Culture, 1920–1930*. New York: Pantheon Books, 1995.

Werner, Craig. *A Change Is Gonna Come: Music, Race & the Soul of America*. New York: Penguin, 1999.

Wintz, Cary D., ed. *Encyclopedia of the Harlem Renaissance*. 2 vols. New York: Routledge, 2004.

INDEX

Cambridge Companions to ...

AUTHORS

TOPICS